CHICAGO DREAMING

CHICAGO DREAMING

MIDWESTERNERS AND THE CITY, 1871–1919

TIMOTHY B. SPEARS

THE UNIVERSITY OF CHICAGO PRESS
CHICAGO & LONDON

TIMOTHY B. SPEARS is professor in the Department of American Civilization and Literature at Middlebury College. He is the author of *100 Years on the Road: The Traveling Salesman in American Culture,* and his articles have appeared in *American Quarterly, Chicago History, American Studies,* and the *Journal of Urban History.*

The University of Chicago Press, Chicago 60637
The University of Chicago Press, Ltd., London
© 2005 by The University of Chicago
All rights reserved. Published 2005
Printed in the United States of America

14 13 12 11 10 09 08 07 06 05   1 2 3 4 5

ISBN: 0-226-76873-2 (cloth)
ISBN: 0-226-76874-0 (paper)

Library of Congress Cataloging-in-Publication Data
Spears, Timothy B., 1957–
    Chicago dreaming : Midwesterners and the city, 1871–1919 / Timothy B. Spears.
        p. cm.
    Includes bibliographical references and index.
    ISBN 0-226-76873-2 (hardcover : alk. paper) — ISBN 0-226-76874-0 (pbk : alk. paper)
    1. Chicago (Ill.)—History—1875–   2. Chicago (Ill.)—Social conditions.
3. Rural-urban migration—Illinois—Chicago—History.   4. Rural-urban migration—Middle West—History.   5. Whites—Middle West—Migrations—History.   6. Chicago (Ill.)—Intellectual life.   7. American literature—Illinois—Chicago—History and criticism.   8. American literature—19th century—History and criticism.   9. American literature—20th century—History and criticism.   I. Title.
    F548.5.S74 2005
    977.3′1104—dc22

                                                                    2004016544

FOR LIZA AND BAIRD

CONTENTS

ILLUSTRATIONS

ACKNOWLEDGMENTS

I began work on this book in Chicago, where I spent the 1994–95 academic year conducting research. I would like to thank the National Endowment for the Humanities for awarding me a fellowship to conduct that research, and Middlebury College for supporting this project since its inception. I am especially grateful to the Newberry Library for hosting me during my year in Chicago. The Newberry is a special place, and Fred Hoxie and Jim Grossman went out of their way to foster a collegial environment for visiting scholars like myself. A large portion of this book was written in Vancouver, British Columbia, where I spent a second sabbatical in 2003–4 as a visiting faculty member in the English Department at the University of British Columbia. My thanks to department heads Sherrill Grace and Gernot Wieland for arranging this appointment, and to Margaret Tom-Wing for her logistical support throughout that year.

In the decade it has taken me to complete this project, I have benefited from the insights of various friends and scholars. Conversations with Dan Aaron, Young-soo Bae, Robin Bachin, Josef Barton, Henry Binford, Jim Campbell, Tim Gilfoyle, Jim Grossman, Daniel Horowitz, Pam Laird, Janice Reiff, Nancy Schnog, Susan Schulten, John Stilgoe, Steve Szaraz, and Tom Underwood helped me formulate research questions. The late Alan Heimert was an important sounding board at the outset, and I wish I could show him this book. Carl Smith generously shared his extensive understanding of Chicago literature and history. My colleagues at Middlebury College—Holly Allen, Bob Buckeye, Stephen Donadio, Deb Evans, Leger Grindon, Karl Lindholm, John McWilliams, Brett Millier, Will Nash, Pete Nelson, Michael Newbury, and Jim Ralph—gave good commentary along the way. Josh Howe was an excellent research assistant, Paul Amsbary helped prepare the illustrations, and Ron Liebowitz provided administrative support when I needed it most. For help in locating research materials, I want to thank Linda Evans at the Chicago Historical Society; Julia Hendry in University Library's Special Collections at the University of Illinois at Chicago; and Corina Carusi at the Glessner House Library. Thanks also to Michael Ebner and Andrew Sandoval-Strausz for giving me the chance to present my research and test ideas at the Chicago Urban History Seminar and the University of Chicago Social History Workshop.

In addition to talking with me about this project, several friends read portions of the manuscript and made valuable comments. Victoria Brown reviewed the chapter on Jane Addams and steered me to key sources. Julia Stern read selected chapters and sharpened my literary analyses. Elliott Gorn read the first half of the book in draft and offered expert editorial advice. I am indebted to all three of them for helping me write a better book.

At the University of Chicago Press, Alan Thomas provided encouragement early on, and Robert Devens has been an exemplary editor. I am also grateful to the Press's readers, whose thoughtful suggestions enhanced the manuscript.

Finally, I'd like to thank Pete and Christina Fawcett, Tim Gilfoyle, Elliott Gorn, and Julia Stern for their hospitality during my return visits to Chicago. Without their support, this book would have been much harder to write.

Chicago Dreaming is dedicated to Liza and Baird, who have come to understand (for better or worse) that writing a book is a family affair. No one knows this better than Nancy Spears, who read every word in this book more than once and improved each one.

INTRODUCTION

—————

"There is a Chicago that lives in the minds of young people all through the Middle West," novelist Floyd Dell wrote in 1913, "a Chicago that exists by virtue of their aspiration and their need, and that begins to die with their first sight of the town."[1] As Dell noted, such dreams that led provincial migrants to the gates of Chicago—and beyond—lie at the heart of Theodore Dreiser's novel *Sister Carrie* (1900). They are also the subject of this book.

"Chicago Dreaming" refers to the expectations and desires that prompted thousands of small-town and rural midwesterners to leave their homes and make a new start in Chicago in the years between 1871 and 1919. Yet the dreaming that made Chicago an object of desire for migrants also figured prominently in the city's general character. In this respect, what E. B. White once said of New York City applies equally to the Chicago of the late nineteenth and early twentieth centuries: the "greatest" city is that of "the person who was born somewhere else and came to [that city] in quest of something." Arguing that the newcomer is the source of the city's "incomparable achievement," its "poetical deportment," and its "passion," White offers a compelling vision of how metropolitan culture gains form and energy from migrants who treat the city as the "final destination" for realizing their ambitions. As contemporary critic Jonathan Raban puts it, "For every immigrant, the city is a different dream." For Raban, the greenhorn's daily confrontations with perspectives different from his own and his ongoing reassessment of his own vision epitomize the dynamic pluralism of urban life. Though the city engenders conflict, the conflict is creative and relatively uncoerced, since the city is, finally, a place of great freedom: "a society which is in essence unfixed, plastic, and amenable—a society on which you are called to impose your choice, rather than a society which imposes its historical and customary order upon you."[2] In this view, the migrant's efforts to recreate himself and the world around him become the means by which provincialism gives way to cosmopolitan culture—a transition that is often depicted, in literature and the arts, as being synonymous with social progress and modernity.

One of the most famous representations of Chicago's status as a magnet for hinterland migrants is Carl Sandburg's image of "painted women under gas lamps luring the farm boys" in his poem "Chicago" (1914).[3] Evoking more than a century's worth of anxiety about the role of cities in American society, his portrayal of a Chicago street at night highlights the desires and temptations that preoccupied critics of nineteenth-century urban life. Yet in the context of the poem as a whole, the passions that animate this scene not only attract migrants, they also serve as the life force for the entire city.

Even today, the lure of the city remains a potent theme in American popular culture. The packed suitcase at the bus terminal, the tearful wave from the train, the bright lights of the skyline—these images, no matter how clichéd, still have currency, and their persistence in a number of media highlights the exclusive, magnetic preserve of metropolitan culture in contemporary society. Part of a familiar narrative about leaving home and starting over, they also underscore the culture's abiding faith in the relationship between physical and social mobility, a belief powered, and sometimes challenged, by a variety of desires and longings.

In the most romantic version of this story, the prospect of leaving home inspires a rhapsody of feelings, beginning with the longing for urban excitement and ultimately leading to a wistful reconsideration of the home that was left behind. So country-rock singer Steve Earle's song "Telephone Road" (1997), which tells the story of a young blue-collar worker who leaves his home in Louisiana for an oil job in Houston, earns its driving beat by juxtaposing the narrator's anticipation of big-city pleasures with his retrospective longing for home and his guilt for leaving it and his "mama." On the other hand, the heartbreak that infuses Bessie Smith's "Chicago Bound Blues," written in 1923 in response to the Great Migration, is so powerful that the abandoned lover can barely communicate the feelings that implicitly follow her "daddy" to Chicago.[4] Smith's blues dramatize what Floyd Dell suggested ten years earlier: the mystery trains which have captured the imaginations of would-be migrants and fellow travelers have led just as often to feelings of ambivalence and dissatisfaction as to a new and better life in the big city.

Although neither Steve Earle nor Bessie Smith figure in the pages to come, the emotional landscape described in their songs would have been familiar to the migrants who followed the metropolitan corridor to Chicago during the late nineteenth and early twentieth centuries.[5] Railroad maps of the period announced Chicago's importance in no uncertain terms: all roads led to the city by the lake. At once awe-inspiring and brutally raw, Chicago grew rapidly from its founding in the 1830s and by the 1870s was known internationally as the "shock city" of the Western world. Like London, New York, and Paris, it was a city whose great expectations more than matched the sense of anticipation that newcomers brought to it. Like modern-day California, it was a place where almost everyone seemed to come from somewhere else. This demographic reality and the resultant mix of feelings— restlessness, displacement, excitement, and dread—spurred the boosting ethos that distinguished Chicago since its settlement and flamed anew when civic leaders sought to rebuild the city after the fire of 1871. Both an economic and a cultural proposition, the vision of the rising metropolis that guided Chicago's growth throughout the nineteenth and early twentieth centuries was aimed at lifting the city up from its provincial roots and establishing it as the cosmopolitan center not just of the Midwest but also of the nation. While the effort to improve Chicago's cultural standing was carried out by the city's upper- and middle-class elites, the general vision of uplift not only appealed to many potential migrants, whose hopes of self-making paralleled the larger civic plan, but its successful completion depended on the contributions of talented newcomers. In this way and others, midwesterners from across the region were critically linked to Chicago's destiny.

By current definitions, the Midwest includes Ohio, Indiana, Michigan, Illinois, Iowa, Minnesota, Wisconsin, North Dakota, South Dakota, Nebraska, Missouri, and Kansas. For the purposes of this study, when I refer to the Midwest (or the Middle West, as it was called in the early twentieth century), I usually mean Ohio, Illinois, Indiana, Michigan, Wisconsin, and Iowa—that is, the states that constituted Chicago's immediate hinterland.[6] Throughout the latter half of the nineteenth century, Chicago's economic and cultural fortunes were crucially linked to this general geographic area. As William Cronon has shown in *Nature's Metropolis* (1991), the city's ascendancy in the region took place by virtue of the economic relationships that its manufacturers and merchants established in the hinterland, which served as both the source for raw materials and a market for finished goods. Cronon's analysis of the flow of capital that bound the small-town merchants and rural producers to Chicago and, in turn, joined the city to the hinterland underscores a truth about urban culture that Raymond Williams and T. J. Clark, among others, have made in writing of London and Paris—that "city" and "rural" typically develop not as separate, exclusive entities, but rather as mutually dependent cultures.[7]

In pursuing this insight, I do not mean to deconstruct the differences between urban and rural or small-town life, but rather to highlight the cultural and emotional terms by which Chicago's migrants measured their progress and interpreted a city that, despite its rapid and remorseless modernization, looked and felt like a metropolis still in the making. At the same time, I mean to be alert to the possibility that, for some migrants, the difference between city and country was slight, and that the movement from one to the other represented a natural, matter-of-fact extension of interests that were first developed in the hinterland.

Nonetheless, as Cronon shows in his wonderful description of how wheat becomes grain and grain then becomes an abstract commodity, the differences between rural and urban are real and significant enough to support the notion that urban industrial capitalism is the great leveler in American life. But commodities cannot talk back as people do. Hence, the benefit of studying literary and cultural texts rather than the economic processes that structured urban-hinterland relations is the potentially more nuanced view of how migrants made sense of their transition from country to city and of whether—if at all—they retained any of their provincial origins.

For the migrants considered here, Chicago's significance rested most of all on its opportunities for *self-making*, a term I use to emphasize the economic forces that brought the hinterland into Chicago's orbit and to underscore the connection of those forces to the culture of middle-class professionalism, whose scope expanded along with Chicago's importance as a business center. Yet there are risks to focusing on the connection between social and spatial mobility. Examining only "successful" migrants can produce an overly positive picture of the economic conditions in the city. Such a focus also ignores migrants who "failed" in Chicago and returned home. By attending carefully to how migrants presented themselves and their experience in a variety of texts and venues, however, I hope to illuminate the significance of the migration experience and Chicago's powers to attract instead of further mythologizing the city's lure.

It is only fair to point out that this is not the study of "men in motion" that Stephan Thernstrom and Peter R. Knights had in mind more than thirty years ago when they underscored the need to know more about the internal migrations that shaped nineteenth-century American cities.[8] It has little to say about household persistence and out-migration and provides little in the way of quantitative analysis. It also leaves out those urban migrants who became part of the city's working classes, and it deals only indirectly with the city's large immigrant population. Furthermore, while I draw selectively from the large body of social scientific writing on migration, I do not offer any comprehensive review of the literature. Essentially, this is a study of literary and cultural representation, driven by questions about how Chicago was imagined by migrants and those who claimed an interest in its evolving identity as a provincial metropolis.

For instance, how did Chicago emerge as the "center" of the region, and even the nation, while still harboring the status of provincial city? Or, more pointedly, what difference does it make for our understanding of nineteenth-century Chicago culture that its chief writers approached their work with a strong sense of dual citizenship—as hinterland natives and spokespeople for both the powerful urban hub they had adopted as their home and the provincial communities they left? By virtue of powerful historical currents, not unlike the forces at work in today's globalizing economies, Chicago's literary migrants were products of a diasporic movement aimed at discovering a cosmopolitan center beyond their seemingly small native worlds. Although they were not constrained by political forces and while their migration to Chicago advanced their professional development and contributed to the cultural uplift of the city, they still approached their work with a strong, even defensive, sense of their status as hinterland natives and, in some instances, keenly felt the loss of their rural and small-town cultures.

These emotions and attitudes were somewhat familiar, since Chicago's hinterland migrants came from places where pulling up stakes and leaving home was an acknowledged, even celebrated part of community life. "Migration created the Old Northwest," the opening line of one Midwest history bluntly states. The transience that distinguished the region throughout the first half of the nineteenth century stemmed largely from settlers pursuing economic opportunities through migration. Bearing the ideological imprint of migrants from New England and New York, the market-oriented

"Yankee West" was literally and figuratively "behind" any migrant who came to Chicago in the late nineteenth century.[9]

The psychic and imaginative energies that flowed into Chicago during the late nineteenth century were thus inseparable from the Midwest as a whole. But the rise of Chicago and the dreaming that informed the development of its literature constituted an important transition in midwestern cultural history, a moment when Chicago came to represent a set of opportunities and perspectives distinct from those available in any other city or town in the region. The writers who came to Chicago from the city's hinterland were fully conscious of this difference and wrote about it in their fiction.

Representing both the colonies of Chicago's commercial empire and the Emerald City they had chosen as their new home, Chicago's migrant writers were thus "in the city but not of it," as journalist George Ade once put it. At once liberating and alienating, the position in which they found themselves was based on the union "between the cultural idea of *self*-development and the real social movement toward *economic* development." As Marshall Berman notes, this joining of individual ambition and economic transformation was at the heart of the modern experience and served as a primary theme for nineteenth-century artists and critics such as Karl Marx and Johann Goethe, who recognized that the romance of change held the possibility of human advancement and catastrophe. Goethe's *Faust*, Berman points out, was the century's great tragic poem on the human desire for world-altering transformation.[10] Not incidentally, Faust is a migration narrative; so are Balzac's *Lost Illusions* (1837–43) and Hardy's *Jude the Obscure* (1895). In all three tales, the heroes' journeys from country to city serve as the vehicle for their overweening ambitions, while the consequences of their move—nostalgia, regret, and worse—figure as the emotional costs of dramatic personal and social change.

By these terms, Chicago was the most modern and the most romantic city in nineteenth-century America. Although the movement from country to city is richly detailed in such works as Benjamin Franklin's *Autobiography* (1791), Charles Brockden Brown's *Arthur Mervyn* (1799), and Herman Melville's *Pierre* (1852), these texts necessarily treat the migrant as a cultural exception. This is in contrast with realistic novels of the late nineteenth century—William Dean Howells's first two important novels, *A Modern Instance* (1882) and *The Rise of Silas Lapham* (1885), are good examples—which not only assume that urbanization and urban migration had become key indicators of the American condition, but also link the protagonist's desires (and moral dilemmas) to the migration experience. Realism Chicago style underscores Eric Sundquist's observation that the substance of American literary realism "lies in the journey between rural and urban" by showcasing, in an unusually dramatic fashion, the emotional dimensions that constituted this transition and the genre.[11] In this respect, it is not surprising that the text that most vividly exemplifies the longings at issue in much realistic fiction, Theodore Dreiser's *Sister Carrie* (1900), is a migration novel set in Chicago.

The desires that sustained migrants in their search for a better life in Chicago and compelled migrating writers to write the story of the city through the eyes of ambitious or homesick newcomers distinguished Chicago from almost all other American cities during this time. However, these desires cannot be easily summarized. They circulated discursively, as Michel Foucault notes in his history of sexuality, and often in the service of power; however, they were not only erotic.[12] To be sure, the language that migrants and practicing writers used was often sexually charged, and the unconscious energies that structure economic relations and nostalgic attachments may, in the end, be essentially sexual in nature. Still, I have taken a broader tack, preferring instead to focus on the historical and geographic context in which desire or longing intersected with, and shaped, the culture of hinterland migration.

From the 1880s onward, Chicago writers portrayed America's "shock city" in famously realistic detail, frankly and sometimes critically revealing the excesses of urbanization. As Carl Smith has noted, a distinctive urban literature developed in Chicago when late nineteenth- and early twentieth-century writers tried "to encompass a city which strained their aesthetic vocabulary, a vocabulary which included inherited forms and conventions that were based on assumptions about literary art and social reality that were perhaps no longer relevant. The challenge which Chicago raised to the literary imagination was to find modes of artistic control that would make it possible to write about the city in a way that revealed its essential nature."[13] I want to shift the focus both inward and outward to consider the perspective that Chicago writers and migrants brought to their narratives: inward, toward the emotional energies that drew migrants to the city from their hinterland homes; and outward, toward the historical forces that located Chicago as the center of the nation's inland empire and created the conditions for a regional literature of cosmopolitan reach.

While this study is primarily concerned with how Chicago's literary migrants addressed questions of urban and regional identity, it also examines how these questions were linked to concerns about class, gender, and ethnicity. Written mostly by white, native-born men from the Midwest, the literary history of Chicago's evolving relationship with the hinterland frequently dramatizes the rising city's importance for self-making male migrants and the cultural hegemony enjoyed by middle- and upper-class elites. On the other hand, the migration narrative provided a framework and discourse that writers adapted to challenge dominant cultural assumptions—for instance, in Jane Addams's case, to revise notions of American citizenship; and in Willa Cather's, to provide a vision of female artistry. In this regard, the figurative territory forged of the connection between Chicago and the provinces formed the basis for progressive change.

Organized into four sections or parts, *Chicago Dreaming* covers roughly seventy years of the city's literary and cultural history in a necessarily selective fashion. Although the book is primarily concerned with literary texts and literary tradition, a significant portion of it deals with what might be called traditional historical issues. These two realms exist in close proximity throughout the book—close enough, I hope, that the theoretical question of what is literary and what is historical seems moot. The first chapter of each section is organized biographically and focuses on individual migrants to Chicago, while the second chapter examines the literary expression of the cultural ideas and themes suggested by the case study. I deviate from this structure in part 1, which includes three chapters, by beginning with a historical overview of Chicago's identity as a destination for hinterland migrants.

Chapter 1 examines the ethos of self-making and boosterism that has defined the city since its settlement in the 1830s, and argues that these energies formed the context for hinterland migration during the nineteenth century and beyond. The second chapter (and the representative portrait for part 1) focuses on businessman John Glessner and his wife, Frances, who moved to Chicago from Springfield, Ohio, in 1870, and whose H. H. Richardson–designed home on Prairie Avenue became a focal point for the city's emergent cosmopolitan culture. While the Glessners' accomplishments are an important part of Chicago history—and coincided with middle- and upper-class efforts to "uplift" the city's cultural institutions—their Ohio-formed desires were part of the bourgeois culture that shaped the midwestern hinterland during the midcentury. The third chapter looks at how the desire for self-making propelled migration from the hinterland during the 1880s and '90s and served as the conceptual core for fiction by Joseph Kirkland, Hamlin Garland, and Henry Blake Fuller. Throughout the book, I argue that the formative history of Chicago literary culture—by which I mean the connections that writers established with one another and the aesthetic concerns that governed their work—cannot be fully understood outside the context of hinterland migration.

Part 2 highlights the emotional and cultural forces that continued to tie many migrants to the hinterland even after their arrival in Chicago. As I show in chapter 4, which is about George Ade and John McCutcheon, the Hoosier journalist and cartoonist who moved to Chicago in the late 1880s and whose carefully drawn reports on small-town and rural transplants brought the migrant into public discourse as a recognizable urban type, many hinterland migrants underwent a process of "ethnicization" that paralleled the assimilation process that immigrants experienced. The galvanizing force in this process was the migrants' nostalgia, a desire for their provincial hinterland that shaped their lives in Chicago and helped to underwrite the city's "provincial" identity. As Ade and McCutcheon's involvement in the Indiana Society of Chicago demonstrates, the nostalgia that led hinterland migrants to celebrate and reconstruct their provincial homes was an important aspect of the identity they fashioned for themselves as middle-class Chicagoans. Chapter 5 argues that nostalgia consequently was both a critical element in turn-of-the-century Chicago fiction, particularly but not exclusively in Dreiser's *Sister Carrie,* and a primary sentiment in this city of romance, whose search for a better future was ironically but unavoidably linked to the midwestern origins of its inhabitants. In reading Carrie's anti-nostalgic demeanor against the hinterland culture that forms the basis of her migratory longing, and by comparing Dreiser's novel to the work of two lesser-known contemporaneous novelists, Brand Whitlock and George Barr McCutcheon, I examine the spectrum of desires—from aggressive self-making to paralyzing nostalgia—that formed the context in which migrating writers represented Chicago and constructed a vision of the midwestern hinterland. As the theoretical centerpiece of the book, this chapter surveys the internal landscape on which Chicago's writers established an urban and regional literature.

Part 3 looks at Chicago's ethnic communities through the eyes of hinterland migrants, underscoring the cultural authority of these native-born newcomers in mediating the assimilation of foreign immigrants. Chapter 6 focuses on the work of Jane Addams, who pragmatically developed a model of community and citizenship at Hull-House based on her small-town upbringing near Rockford, Illinois. Addams's pragmatism, I argue, was critically informed by her status as a hinterland migrant. Chapter 7 considers how

Chicago's multiethnic community is portrayed in Edith Wyatt's and Elia Peattie's fiction, and in Carl Sandburg's poetry. Throughout this section, I am most of all interested in how the midwestern hinterland—what commentators now call America's heartland—served as a political touchstone for native-born elites who longed to shape the city's character in the face of its increasingly "foreign" population.

In part 4, I examine the role of provincial migrants in the burgeoning of aesthetic innovation and clustering of talent in the 1900s and 1910s, the second phase of what has been called the Chicago Renaissance. Following Raymond Williams's claim that the experiments of modernism derived from the physical and cultural "border crossing" experienced by provincial writers and artists, I show how the linguistic and cultural stylings of Chicago's literary migrants took shape within a bohemian culture highly conscious of the midwestern roots it longed to transcend through art.[14] Chapter 8 focuses especially on Floyd Dell, Sherwood Anderson, and Tennessee Mitchell—who became Anderson's second wife—tracing their movements into Chicago's literary and artistic circles. Chapter 9 addresses literary and aesthetic structure, particularly the evolving notions of migratory desire that accompanied changes in the migration narrative itself. So, for instance, Willa Cather's *Song of the Lark* (1915) and Sherwood Anderson's *Winesburg, Ohio* (1919) feature artists as protagonists and self-consciously highlight the emergence of a universal artistic consciousness that is both shaped by desire and capable of representing all human emotions. Marking the transition from more realistic modes of regionalism to that of modernism, these texts also qualify Chicago's importance as a destination for migrating writers.

Finally, the coda juxtaposes the theories of urban migration developed by Chicago school sociologists with Richard Wright's fictional treatment of the Great Migration in *Native Son* (1940). Although *Native Son* is principally concerned with Chicago's Black Belt, the surreal images of desire and longing that lace the novel are consistent with earlier representations of the migrant's role in the city—only Wright turns these images inside out to underscore the emptiness of the city as a signifier of promise and hope. In emphasizing the ramifications of this nightmarish vision for Bigger Thomas, Wright's representative migrant and his version of Chicago's native son, I treat the novel as a portrait of thwarted desire that turns autoerotic and violent in a city that appears decidedly *un*romantic. Published as it was at the end of the Great Depression and in the context of Chicago's waning dream of becoming the nation's first city, Wright's portrayal of desire gone "to smash" was well timed.

For Wright, as for so many literary migrants, Chicago remained a city haunted by desire and dreams of future success. The dreams they left behind, in stories based on their own journeys to Chicago, are one measure of the decisive influence the city's migratory culture had on its literary traditions. Another, perhaps less positive, is that nearly every hinterland writer whose career was launched in Chicago ultimately left the city for another metropolis, usually New York. The desires and expectations that initially led these writers to forsake their small-town homes for Chicago may thus be seen as a pattern of movement—and insatiability—that, when carried to its logical conclusion, eventually compelled them to leave their now small-seeming city for the brighter lights and increased opportunities of a bigger place.

PART ONE

FRONTIERS OF DESIRE

They tell me you are wicked and I believe them, for I have seen your
painted women under the gas lamps luring the farm boys.

CARL SANDBURG, "CHICAGO" (1914)

The Anglo-Saxon portion of mankind is a home-making, home-loving race. I think
the desire is in us all to receive the family home from the past generation and hand it
on to the next with possibly some good mark of our own upon it. Rarely can this be
accomplished in this land of rapid changes. Families had have not held and cannot
hold even to the same localities for their homes generation after generation,
but we can at least preserve some memory of the old.

JOHN J. GLESSNER,
"THE STORY OF A HOUSE" (1923)

1

SHOCK CITY

In a nation distinguished by its apparently unprecedented mobility—both physical and social—turn-of-the-century Chicago loomed as a city for restless dreamers and doers. It was, as the protagonist of Floyd Dell's 1920 autobiographical novel *Moon-Calf* remembers in a lyrical gloss on the city's capacity to move people and capital, a "dark blotch" on a railroad map that seemed to spread outward toward the rest of continent. Throughout the nineteenth and into the twentieth century, Chicago was populated chiefly by people who came from somewhere else. What exactly fueled this migratory city is a question that has preoccupied novelists, commentators, and scholars since the city's founding in the 1830s. While their answers vary along economic, political, ethnic, and social lines, they tend to agree on at least one thing: Chicago was a city where anything seemed possible.

As Chicago's population surpassed 1 million people during the 1890s, this tenet became a leading feature in the city's identity and a subject of discussion among visitors and citizens alike. German sociologist Max Weber noted during a 1904 visit to Chicago that the freedom to act appeared literally part of the landscape. Although Weber was a seasoned traveler, he was unprepared for what he saw when he paused for a tourist's view of Halsted Street.

As far as one can see from the clock tower of the firm of Armour and Son—nothing but cattle lowing, bleating endless filth—in all directions—for the town goes on for miles and miles until it loses itself in the vastness of the suburbs—churches and chapels, storage elevators, smoking chimneys (every large hotel has its own elevator run on a steam engine) and houses of every kind. This is why the town is so extraordinarily far-flung; the areas of the city are distinguished from each other in degrees of cleanliness in accordance with the nationality of the residents. The devil has broken loose in the stockyards: a lost strike with great numbers of Italians and Negroes brought in as strike-breakers; shootings daily with dozens dead at both sides; a trolley car was pitched over and a dozen women were crushed because a "non-union man" was sitting in it. There were threats of the use of dynamite against the "elevated-railway" on which a car was derailed and fell into the river. Close to our hotel, a cigar dealer was killed in broad daylight, a few streets away at dusk, three Negroes robbed a trolley car—all in all, a unique flowering of culture! There is a swarming interaction of all the peoples of the human race on every street. Greeks are polishing the shoes of Yankees for 5 cents, the Germans are their waiters, the Italians do the dirtiest heavy labor. The whole powerful city, more extensive than London—resembles, except for the better residential areas, a human being with his skin removed, and in which all the physiological process can be seen going on.[1]

In this chaotic mix of buildings, labor, crime, violence, racial/ethnic tensions, and mundane human habits, Weber saw the traditional veneer of civility break apart in a dramatization of individual desire and social transgression that in other cities takes place more covertly—under the skin. Illustrative of French sociologist Henri Lefebvre's proposition that space "unleashes desire" and "encourages it to surge forth," this vision underscores the city's expansive physical development, industrial economy, and brutish character as well as its utter lack of pretense and self-consciousness.[2] Chicago with its skin peeled away is a dreamscape where the relationship between intention and behavior is transparent and the mechanisms of human agency have yielded wholly to human spontaneity and desire. According to Weber's anatomical cross section, desire is the lifeblood of the city that circulates throughout the urban body, animating its component parts even without its inhabitants' knowledge.

Other visitors to Chicago characterized this desire more specifically. Writing in the mid-1890s, Frenchman Paul Bourget, for example, noted a "business fever which here throbs at will, with an unbridled violence like that of an uncontrollable element. It rushes along these streets, as once before the devouring flame of a fire; it quivers; it makes itself visible with an intensity which lends something tragical to this city, and makes it seems like a poem to me."[3] In his tract *If Christ Came To Chicago* (1894), the British journalist and reformer William T. Stead likewise remarks on the "intense feverish restlessness" that pervaded the city and claims that Chicagoans know only "one common bond": to make money. Around this primary, all consuming desire, the city's various illicit markets—in liquor, political favors, and sex—were arrayed.[4]

As the "shock city" of the Western world, Chicago epitomized the fantastic growth and violent contrasts that increasingly came to characterize nineteenth-century cities. In fact, these contrasts were precisely what drew visitors like Stead to Chicago in the first place: to examine, at the epicenter, the unfolding, and as yet unknown, meaning of modernity.[5] As historians have noted, the sights that most compelled the attention of tourists—for instance, the "killing beds" of the slaughterhouses, the trading pits at the Board of Trade, and the imperial designs of the 1893 Columbian Exposition—dramatized the technological, economic, and cultural developments that reshaped urban landscapes across the United States and Europe.

Although Stead, Bourget, and Weber were struck, as so many others were, by the material changes taking place in turn-of-the-century Chicago, their comments reveal a fascination with the intangible forces—one might call them emotional or psychic energies—at work beneath the surface of things. Bourget and Stead maintained that an intensely felt desire to make money and do business was the operating force in Chicago. Weber, too, acknowledged the motivating force of the city's internal economy, but suggested that a wide range of desires besides the specific drive to make money accounted for the city's distinctive character. All three implied that the human interactions, cultural exchanges, and daily goings-on that constituted the city should be understood as a palpable manifestation of Chicagoans' individual and collective aspirations.

On this score, Weber was the most pointed. Vitally connected to the collective dream life of the city, the urban landscape (he seems to say) can be read inside out as a direct reflection of the desires and ambitions that Chicagoans bring to the city. Restlessness and motion—whether as pulsing feeling, the movement of people, or economic mobility (metaphorically speaking)—emerge from his description as being the city's signature features, underscoring the extent to which late-nineteenth Chicago was literally a culture in transition—a city, as Weber indicates, of migrants.

Behind these efforts to encapsulate Chicago's distinctive character lies what may well be the central drama in the city's rise during the late nineteenth and early twentieth centuries: the ongoing movement of human capital into the city and the attendant effort, on economic, cultural, and aesthetic grounds, to establish Chicago as a homegrown, cosmopolitan center. Understanding Chicago in these terms is to think about the city's centrality, and its modernity, from outside the city limits, in light of the cultural and historical factors that have made *diaspora* and *imperialism* key terms at the turn of our own century. More specifically, it means considering the ways in which Chicago figured as both the object and site of desire for hinterland migrants, an investigation that focuses most of all on the imaginative lives of incoming Chicagoans and the writers who represented the migration experience in print.

A line from Carl Sandburg's famous poem "Chicago" (1914) helps to define the terms of this discussion. "They tell me you are wicked," Sandburg writes about the city, "and I believe them, for I have seen your painted women under the gas lamps luring the farm boys."[6] Acknowledging and dismissing the traditional notion that cities are "evil," Sandburg suggests that the "lure" of Chicago is an erotic energy that spreads out into the prairie, where restless farm boys internalize it and bring it to town. In contrast with Stead's and Bourget's depictions of restlessness, this image places Chicago's desire-filled streets in close proximity to the hinterland that supplies the emotion. It positions Chicago as a city of migrants who have been drawn to pursue their dreams in the metropolis.

This idea—that Chicago's status as a modern urban center has something to do with its provincial roots—dominates the literature written about Chicago between 1890 and 1940. Indeed, when one considers the fiction that designates the Chicago "school" of literature—Hamlin Garland's *Rose of Dutcher's Coolly* (1895), Theodore Dreiser's *Sister Carrie* (1900), the work of Henry Blake Fuller, and later, novels by Floyd Dell, Sherwood Anderson, Willa Cather, and Richard Wright—it seems clear that the migration narrative proved the definitive text for representing the personalities and emotions that went into the creation of modern Chicago. At first glance, the stories told by these writers mirror the plot conventions developed in Horatio Alger novels as well as the nineteenth-century formula for masculine character building implicit in those tales. Frequently, though, they depart from this familiar trajectory to provide a local and critical view of self-making. Most important, they present desire as a catalyst for both female and male protagonists, raising questions about the gender of Chicago's identity and whether—to return to Sandburg's infamous image—the women under the gas lamps might also be migrants, drawn to the city by their own desires.

Max Weber offers an apt starting point for considering these hinterland relations if only because his name conjures the emotional dynamic that lies at the heart of Chicago's economic rise: the translation of passion and desire into the process of becoming middle class. Presumably, Weber would have agreed that the spirit of Chicago, like the spirit of capitalism, was an engrained disposition—common to bourgeois society but not peculiar to any one place. It also seems likely that Weber would have found in Chicago evidence of rigid modern bureaucracies. Yet, as the passage quoted above suggests, Weber waxed poetic over Chicago. In fact, he admired the city. Compared to the social constraints of German society, American culture—and Chicago especially—appeared to present great opportunities for economic advancement and community building.[7] Weber and his wife were as impressed by the outpouring of religious spirit in Chicago and the work of Jane Addams there as they were by the atomized pursuits of desiring individuals on Halsted Street. Propelling all these movements was an energy that Weber associated with the migratory spirit of the frontier. Once back in Germany, as John Patrick Diggins has noted, Weber celebrated the "magic of freedom" that he witnessed in America and, reversing the conditions established by historian Frederick Jackson Turner, located the impetus for upward mobility and democratic culture in the passionate movement *away* from the soil and toward a new frontier.[8]

Though Weber's own reading suggests that the urban frontier was hardly a Turnerian democracy, there was no question in the 1890s but that Chicago represented an important shift in the reformation of American culture. Even so skeptical an observer as Henry Adams paused at the 1893 Columbian Exposition to wonder whether the White City was a "rupture in historical sequence" in which case a "new American world could take [a] sharp and conscious twist toward ideals."[9] Ultimately, Adams doubted this idealistic turn was real, but the desire to believe that it might be so was a desire that Chicago, more than other American cities, could inspire.

"Go To Chicago Now"

Adams's observation, no matter how ambivalent, deviated from the mainly negative judgments made by eastern elites and intellectuals, who believed

Chicago to be uncivilized and corrupt.[10] What Adams sensed, and Weber clearly understood, was that Chicago's future would be determined largely by people who were not from the city itself. Between 1860 and 1890, Chicago grew at an explosive rate—from 100,000 residents to 1 million, with much of this increase coming from foreign immigration. By 1890, more than three-quarters of the residents claimed foreign-born parents.[11] However, in political and cultural terms, native-born Americans—of the middle and upper classes—maintained a strong upper hand. Within the ranks of the native born, the proportion of Chicago residents born in the Old Northwestern states, including Illinois, gradually increased over the course of the nineteenth century. This shift is consistent with the developments that William Cronon has so powerfully demonstrated: Chicago's rise as a commercial-transportation hub was predicated on its economic relationship with the hinterland.[12] With so much hinterland close at hand and an extensive railroad network to bring it even closer, it is not surprising that provincial migrants—like the capital that Cronon examines—flowed into the city. Nor is it surprising that these migrants were in an ideal position to occupy the increasing number of white-collar, middle-class jobs that Chicago's business expansion afforded.

These geographic terms were arguably as important to Chicago's emerging cultural and literary identity as the economic transformations that marked the city's rise. Self-making Chicago style was a story of migration, told from the provincial point of view. This perspective came naturally to Chicago's first-generation writers, most of whom were migrants themselves, trying to build literary careers in the city. The migration narrative was a good fit structurally, since its trajectory of movement paralleled the writers' own striving, describing a trail from home to city that could be blazed with any number of emotional landmarks. Although writers took pains to describe the dramatic, even unsettling, physical environment of the city, they were just as concerned to represent the interior lives of their protagonists: small-town and rural dreamers determined to find in Chicago a suitable match for their ambitions and desires. Of course, the lure of Chicago has been a defining component of the city's identity since the town was settled—and boomed—in the 1830s by eastern businessmen. This boosting ethos came to the fore after the Great Chicago Fire of 1871, when William Bross, one of the city's chief propagandists, traveled to New York City and encouraged young men to "Go To Chicago now. . . . You will never again have such a chance to make money."[13]

This is a curious thing, for a city's character to depend so much on what it might be, as opposed to what it actually is. While boosterism is a time-honored American tradition, perhaps no city—with the exception of Los Angeles (New York being another case altogether)—has been so much the object of prospective fantasy. Journalists Lloyd Lewis and Henry Justin Smith alluded to this fact in the title of their chronicle of the city's first one hundred years: *Chicago: The History of Its Reputation* (1929). The city's best-known nicknames also illustrate the point. In the 1880s, people began to call Chicago the Windy City not because of the city's weather conditions but because boosters never tired of bragging about the place.[14] Similarly, Chicago came to be known as America's Second City—second, that it is, to New York—because it appeared so intent on becoming number one. Subsequent characterizations of the city carried this future-oriented identity well into the twentieth century. Theodore Dreiser's ruminations on Chicago as a "giant magnet," Richard Wright's "fantasies" that the city would free his literary aspirations from Southern racism, Bessie Smith's "Chicago Bound Blues" and other blues numbers that imagine a promised land at the northern terminus of the Illinois Central Railroad—these and other expressive forms join the desire of would-be Chicagoans to create the city's always developing identity, what Frank Sinatra sings of as "that toddling town."

Although this vision of urban promise was not the sole property of migrants, the idea that Chicago is chiefly a destination for future growth is crucial to the city's identity. Indeed, it is impossible to understand the shape of present-day Chicago, and its many ethnic and racial communities, without considering the city's hold on the imaginations of newcomers. The arrival of various immigrant groups from the nineteenth century onward hinged on Chicago's positive image, which spread abroad through the various communication channels that linked American ethnic communities to their original homes. So, too, the Great Migration was fueled by the hopes that Chicago inspired in southern African Americans.

Chicago's raw, unfinished quality—so aptly captured at the outset of Dreiser's *Sister Carrie* through the image of sidewalks extending out into the prairie—announced its potential as a metropolis and destination for would-be migrants. Despite its extensive buildup in the years immediately following the fire, late-nineteenth-century Chicago resembled a work in progress. In 1870, "Chicago was truly the Garden City," remembered Ohio-born businessman John Glessner, "with no apartment houses, few double houses, and only occasional blocks of houses. Even the lowly homes were detached cottages, usually of wood and behind wooden sidewalks, but each with a small plot of ground."[15] Descriptions like this—and they abound in accounts of early Chicago—reveal a semi-urban city, struggling, like an adolescent bound for adulthood, to become a metropolis.

By the mid-1890s, Chicago sprawled more than 180 square miles, much of it still rural in appearance. According to one estimate, half the city was "farm and garden land, open prairie untouched by scythe or plow, or timber country which has been allowed to remain unaltered."[16] Chicago's country spaces allowed people to keep cows, cultivate vegetable gardens, and harvest crops of dandelion greens; the far-flung landscape also yielded a population that was relatively low in density, especially in comparison with established eastern cites.[17] This patchwork landscape persisted into the twentieth century, a world of factories, skyscrapers, trolley cars, crowded streets—and open fields (fig. 1). For instance, in a 1926 interview conducted by one of Ernest Burgess's sociology students at the University of Chicago, a South Side resident noted,

I lived on 87th place, near Cottage Grove Avenue, until 1919. A farmer's field is the northern boundary of this section of the neighborhood, while beyond was Chatham Fields, then a real woods. Up to very recently there has been plenty of prairie space, with few homes, almost entirely single residences, scattered along different streets.[18]

William Cronon and other scholars who have written about the development of Chicago have shown how important this organic imagery was to the city's first generation of boosters. In their minds, or at least in their rhetoric, there was no question that Chicago would "naturally" bypass competitors like St. Louis and Cincinnati and become the preeminent city in the region. This assumption, that Providence and nature had already assured a city's future greatness, was a common rhetorical device among nineteenth-century civic boosters, and in Chicago's case it became a self-fulfilling prophecy.[19] Implicit in the appeal to would-be investors and residents, however, was the promise that individuals would profit by the city's rise. In this respect, the making of Chicago was inseparable from the self-making that the city's economic growth enabled.

This equation is particularly evident in the writings of John S. Wright, who was Chicago's most fervid booster during the 1850s, '60s, and '70s. Having arrived in the city in 1832 at the age of seventeen, Wright carried the

FIGURE 1 Even in 1917 there was open agricultural space in Chicago. Note the smokestacks in the background. (Chicago Historical Society DN-0068001; *Chicago Daily News* photograph)

ambitions of the "old settlers" well beyond these early years through incessant appeals to outside investors and migrants. During the late 1840s he frequently traveled to the East Coast, boosting the advantages of the West to prospective migrants and describing the prominent role that Chicago would soon play in the nation's economy.[20] While Wright sketched a future built on railroads, manufacturing, and agriculture, he spoke directly to the personal ambitions of his audience. In 1867, noting that the city's "unexampled growth" was the result of "non-residents from every section of the country, rushing to Chicago for its commerce and manufactures," he urged the "busy men of New England" to consider investing in the inland metropolis.[21] Wright underscored the importance of population growth, yet he typically avoided the question of who would actually fill up the city. "The future of Chicago is sure as the rising sun to the meridian," he wrote in another pre-fire "proposition" to potential railroad investors, "and you are offered Stock in a Company arranged to suit yourself, with the certainty of purchase of the very choicest suburban property of that City."[22] Although Wright assumed that people would want to live in Chicago, he did not necessarily encourage investors to migrate. Rather, he assumed that migration would take place as matter of course, and that absentee owners would profit accordingly as land values rose.

FIGURE 2 After the Chicago Fire of 1871—an empty city seen from Cook County Court House and City Hall, looking north on Clark Street. (Chicago Historical Society ICHi-02795; photographer unknown)

William Bross, who was just as evangelical about Chicago's future as Wright, likewise appealed to individual ambitions and desires for self-improvement as he worked to repopulate the scarred city in the aftermath of the fire (fig. 2).[23] More so than Wright, though, he stressed the opportunities there for all men, not just investors, provided, of course, they were willing to move to Chicago. In Bross's democratically pitched formulation, migration and upward mobility are one and the same. "Thousands anxious to locate in this focus of Western commerce have been deterred from doing so for the reason that the business in each department had become concentrated in comparatively few hands," he told the New York Chamber of Commerce in the spring of 1872. "There has not been for the last twenty years so good a time for men of capital to start business in Chicago as now. With few exceptions all can now start even in the race for fame and fortune. The fire has leveled all distinctions. . . . Now, therefore, is the time to strike."[24]

In propositions such as these, boosters fluctuated between an abstract understanding of migration and a more concrete vision of people choosing to live in Chicago. The abstract view hewed to laws of political economy, and looked at migration as a natural occurrence that seemed curiously removed from individual motivation. This perspective was in step with the approach taken by European intellectuals such as Malthus or E. G. Ravenstein, whose monograph "The Laws of Migration," published in 1889 in the *Journal of the Royal Statistical Society,* treats the study of population movement as a science. While aware that the "laws" of population movement are "continually being interfered with by human agency," Ravenstein nonetheless attributed the "drift" of migrants from one region to another or from rural areas to cities to changing labor markets. In particular, he observed that the growth in U.S. and European urban populations was due chiefly to short-distance migrations that drew rural migrants to cities. This "accounts for the fact that even the largest of cities in Europe partake of provincial characteristics." [25]

Closer to home and just one decade later, Adna Weber, a political economist at Columbia University, also addressed the provincial sources of American city populations. Weber, too, noted that in the United States, internal migrants were clearly drawn to urban areas for economic reasons. However, he was also aware that wages alone could not explain why rural and small-town boys dreamed of leaving home for the big city. And, in tortured syntax that likely reflected his own efforts to explain why he left his boyhood home in Salamanca, New York, he postulated that the "magnet is the superior field for ambition, which modern industrial organization has rendered the city." [26]

Like other commentators, Weber struggled to find an image or concept that explained the movement to cities as a natural force that carried migrants from village to city. He also struggled to acknowledge the complex web of motives behind each decision to migrate — the individual will implicit in the word *ambition*. In selling Chicago, William Bross catered shamelessly to these ambitions, but the effect of his rhetoric was to subordinate the will of the individual to the future of the city. Behind such talk lay an ideological commitment to progress that joined the rise of Chicago — the "gateway to the West"— to the broader dictates of manifest destiny and allied notions of character building. [27] The lure of the city and, more to the point, migration to Chicago itself were hard to separate from the economic forces that placed the town on the map in the first place. In this sense, the rise of the city and the path of the migrant were one and the same.

A City for Self-Makers

Historians who labored in Weber's wake have confirmed and elaborated upon the importance of these economic motives, but had little success in quantifying them. The problem, as Arthur Schlesinger suggests in *The Rise of the City* (1933), was that while economic factors—better employment opportunities and a higher standard of living—may have given hinterland migrants the motivation to leave home, they were also means to various positive ends, all of which could imply a desire to escape the limitations of rural and small-town existence: larger and more diverse communities, greater social freedom, increased educational opportunities, an enlarged scope of leisure and amusements, and so forth. More recently, economic geographer Carville Earle concludes that in 1860, wages in Chicago were sufficiently high to attract young men and women from the hinterland, but he notes, too, that country boys "regarded the dynamics of city life with a certain wonder, and that a decision to go there involved more than a rational accounting of comparative net incomes." [28]

Certainly, conditions in early Chicago favored the rapid accumulation of wealth. By midcentury, more than 80 percent of the residents who were worth at least $25,000 had arrived before 1840. The majority of these settlers were eastern migrants, men like Bross and Wright, or the merchant Potter Palmer, who came with enough capital to take advantage of the city's fluid, surging economy.[29] Chicago's antebellum elite made its money in commerce, agriculture-related enterprises, and sometimes real estate speculation, which flourished in the 1840s as landowners bought and sold parcels, often charging extravagant interest rates to buyers.[30]

Although many of them began with a considerable head start, this first generation of business leaders helped establish Chicago's reputation as a city of self-made men and distinguished its social landscape from established urban centers such as Boston and New York, where the inequalities in wealth seemed mediated by history and tradition. In 1860, Chicago appeared to be a frontier outpost, at least to the eastern eye; still, the claims its boosters made were generally true. As historian Frederic Jaher has noted, the example of nineteenth-century Chicago "supports the widely held notion that newer settlements have higher rates of upward mobility than do older communities." Nothing marked Chicago's difference more dramatically than the fact that aggressive entrepreneurs who were born somewhere else dominated its upper class. By the 1890s, the list of millionaires was still commanded by men born in New England and the Middle Atlantic. However, this elite was now joined by a considerable number of men born in the Old Northwest, states like Indiana, Michigan, and Ohio. This shift was consistent with general demographic trends, which even more clearly reflected Chicago's strong grip on its hinterland, though the percentages themselves were not at all representative of the population at large. Of the 1 million people residing in Chicago in 1890, nearly half were born in the Old Northwest (with 40 percent coming from Illinois), one-third were foreign born, and the rest came from other regions, with the New England and the Mid-Atlantic natives comprising about 8 percent of the total population.[31]

During the final decades of the century, Chicago's middle classes expanded as a wide array of white-collar professions developed around the city's corporate industrial economy. One dramatic sign of this growing economy was the looming presence of skyscrapers in downtown Chicago and the corresponding rise in the price of downtown real estate, which by 1910 constituted 40 percent of the entire city's value, as opposed to 13 percent in the early 1870s.[32] Chicago's many storied office buildings were designed to house the growing ranks of white-collar workers, and though the foreign born and their children were well represented in this group, native-born whites and their offspring dominated the city's professional class.[33] Indeed, many of the city's lawyers and physicians were the sons of native-born farmers of modest means. Their rise was but one indication of Chicago's capacity to bring ambitious young countrymen into its midst.[34]

In his history, *The Tale of Chicago* (1933), the lawyer and poet Edgar Lee Masters suggests that the upward mobility of these hinterland migrants was synonymous with the city's rise. Like Sandburg, Masters came to Chicago from Galesburg, Illinois, and though his portrayal of city-country relations is less erotic than that of his fellow poet (and rival), it also provides a vision of the city's empty spaces being filled by the energies and ambitions of migrating young men.

During the War and during the 'seventies, and to a greater extent in the 'nineties the young men of Missouri, Indiana, Wisconsin, Michigan and from all parts of Illinois and all about the Middle West came out of the small colleges where they had earned their way, and from the farms and small shops and stores of the villages and poured themselves into Chicago. Its population mounted by these accessions; but also it added to its citizenry industrious and earnest spirits who had profited by hard discipline in youth. They became well known lawyers, judges, merchants, and business men of all kinds; and many of them made fortunes, though scarcely any of them became magnates as important as Field, Pullman, Armour, and a few others. These young men were the hall-bedroom youths of that period. They lived on little and worked hard. They lost and profited by the Fire; they saw a return of the cholera in the late 'sixties and buried their mates, and returned to their rooms undisturbed in their life's ambitions. They saw the city rebuilding and rebuilt.

Forty pages later, Masters returns to this theme.

In the early 'nineties, and especially before the World's Fair, the youth of all the surrounding country came to Chicago by the tens of thousands. . . . Thousands of middle-aged people, and even people growing old, likewise rushed to the great city, there to open boarding houses, or to resume lives as clerks. Students out of college, young doctors and lawyers, civil and electrical engineers, youths who had learned stenography by themselves in the country, men who had clerked in the stores of the villages and had read of the power and glory of Field and Armour, and wanted to breathe a larger air arrived daily at the Union Station, and the other stations of Chicago. Others dreaming of the theaters and the amusements of the city, of the notables who contributed to a life of such exciting richness, wanted to become a part of the scene.[35]

While here Chicago attracts migrants of all ages who "pour" and "rush" into the city, it is primarily a destination for the young men, who yearn to lead existences—"to breathe a larger air"—that are possible only in the big city. In the first passage, Masters treats these youthful lives as self-willed biographies, created by young men who aspire to the success of well-known giants like Philip Armour. In the second, individual accomplishment blends with the desires and dream life evoked by the city. Either way, Masters's Chicago is a place of youthful beginnings, where older people (the "middle-aged") play mostly supportive roles, and more junior migrants take the lead as disciplined fortune seekers concerned primarily with their own self-making.

Masters's impressions of young men on the make are supported by more quantitative studies of living arrangements in late nineteenth-century Chicago. For instance, one recent study estimates that in 1890, 44 percent of the male population over the age of fifteen was unmarried. The great majority of this group was between the ages of fifteen and thirty-four, and most of these bachelors were native-born whites of native parents. Outnumbering the population of same-aged, single women living in Chicago by more than

2 to 1, these young men comprised a bachelor subculture, the development of which added considerably to American city life between 1880 and 1920. The concrete, visible features of this culture—boardinghouses, barbershops, saloons, pawnshops, and YMCA branches—served to accommodate the social and economic needs of a floating male population as they established lives in the city. The occupational data also confirm what Masters sensed: these bachelors tended to be employed in higher-level white-collar jobs.[36]

At the same time, the number of women living alone, or "adrift," in Chicago during this time was also quite high. Depending on the year, between 40 percent and 50 percent of these women were single and under the age of thirty; in this group as well, the native-born offspring of native-born parents were more heavily represented than they were relative to the general female population. Here, too, women born in midwestern states other than Illinois, most likely migrants who came to Chicago in search of work, increasingly dominated this group. While in 1880 these sojourners equaled roughly 40 percent of all white, native-born single women, by 1910 that number had risen to nearly two thirds. During these years, and up until the 1930s, the number of clerical and sales jobs available to women in the commercial and retail sectors burgeoned, while relatively fewer women found work as domestic servants.[37] For young women as well as men, Chicago proved a beacon of opportunity and an object of desire (fig. 3).

The business of celebrating the self-makers of Chicago began as early as 1868, with the publication of *Biographical Sketches of the Leading Men of Chicago*, written "By the Best Talent of the Northwest." In this, the city's first promotional history, commercial writers and publishers developed a genre—basically a "who's who" for the rising city—that illuminated the careers of great men within a broader, almost mythological civic history.[38] Subsequent volumes gave equal attention to the "pioneer" efforts of leading citizens while acknowledging the increasing diversity of the city. In *Chicago and Its Distinguished Citizens, or the Progress of Forty Years* (1881), David Wood and his collaborators note that "the same enterprise that first led the white man to step his foot upon this territory, and to build here in his imagination first a village and then a city" was responsible for attracting eastern businessmen to the city. Consequently, the "cities of the old world have awakened to realize that they have met with irreparable loss in the emigration of representative citizenship, and Chicago has awakened to find that the loss has been her gain."[39]

Given their epic reach, these self-congratulatory histories not surprisingly trumpeted the accomplishments of many Chicagoans, native and foreign

FIGURE 3 State Street north from Madison Street during the early 1900s. (Chicago Historical Society ICHi-19294; Barnes-Crosby photograph)

born alike. The minibiographies that packed the multivolume sets likewise noted the various migrations that contributed to Chicago's economic and cultural vitality. By comparison, Masters's narrower focus on the contributions of hinterland migrants is misleading. Still, despite his self-referential view of Chicago's growth, and perhaps because of it, his account has authority.

In stressing the importance of ambitious hinterland newcomers, Masters aligned himself with his fellow literary migrants, whose stories about Chicago, written decades before the publication of his book, similarly assumed the centrality of the provincial perspective and, by implication, the enduring significance of white, native-born Americans. The ideological implications of this assumption are clear: inasmuch as white, native-born Chicagoans struggled to impose order on what they deemed a socially and politically volatile landscape, hinterland writers joined the fray in print.

Containing the Migrant's Desire

A significant portion of the scholarship on nineteenth-century Chicago has focused on middle- and upper-class efforts to contain the city's apparent disorder. Echoing other studies of the middle class's emergence in nineteenth-century America, historians of Chicago have underscored the efforts of native-born elites to curb the political and social unrest that accompanied the city's rapid growth. The two most serious episodes of class conflict in Chicago during this period—the 1886 Haymarket tragedy and the Pullman strike of 1894—demonstrate the middle and upper class's unwillingness to tolerate political and social dissent among the immigrant and working-class communities.[40] Prime examples of the unrest that generally distinguished American economic and industrial expansion, these incidents underscore Chicago's extraordinary capacity to reflect the cultural tensions of the time.

Yet as Max Weber correctly intuited, the city's social and economic fluidity also created conditions for positive, cultural work. Among many middle- and upper-class Chicagoans it generated the belief that urban culture could actually be rebuilt, an opportunity that elites grasped by establishing an astonishing number of institutions of culture and higher learning during the 1880s and '90s. By such efforts, philanthropists "sought to redirect their city's values and preoccupations, to lift Chicago from materialism to the realm of spirit."[41] In his examination of Chicago's pioneering elites, James Gilbert has argued that these attempts to create and shape the culture stemmed from a utopian impulse that was instilled in them during their highly moral, antebellum upbringings in New England and New York's "burned-over" district. "Evangelicalism and millennialism," Gilbert writes, "were thus a crucial background for capitalist, Utopian thinking of antebellum period and beyond, into the 1890s."[42] As he notes, middle- and upper-class Chicagoans participated in the same cultural revolutions that they sought to control, an irony that pertained especially to the consumer and entertainment attractions that characterized the urban landscape, whose democratic appeal cut across the social spectrum. This irony was manifest in the 1893 World's Fair, whose White City and Midway symbolized the two sides of the equation: classic order and polyglot commercial culture. And it surrounded the development of department stores like Marshall Field's, whose luxurious interiors defined the new empire of the consumer by arousing desires that threatened the values—sobriety, restraint, prudence—upon which the nineteenth-century culture of character and production was based. From the traditional viewpoint, these attractions added to the temptations, like the saloon and the brothel, which moral arbiters and reformers had long identified with the city's moral failings. However, as urban America increasingly became a "land of desire," to use William Leach's apt phrase, the imperatives governing the older culture were transformed and accommodated within modern consumer society.[43]

These complicated transitions also figured in the emotional energies that drew migrants to Chicago. The "lure" of city, as it evolved in nineteenth-century popular thought and received wisdom, exemplified desires that fit uneasily with middle-class mores and standards. In the starkest of terms, the taboo pleasures of urban culture were opposed to the virtues of rural life. This dichotomy was most commonly and powerfully expressed in religious language, as in the ongoing characterization of the city as a repository of evil or the frequent retelling of the prodigal son parable. While these views were especially pronounced during the first half of the nineteenth century, they persisted into the twentieth, as evidenced by a pamphlet called *That Boy "The Modern Prodigal" in Chicago. Or, From a Farm to the Snares of a Great City* (1903). Such tracts warned against the sins that youths encountered in the city—from prostitution to drink—and counseled migrants to return home or to "cling to the cross" if they did not.[44] In offering this second piece of advice, reformers assumed the fact of migration and looked to internal mechanisms to regulate the desires excited by the city.

On the other hand, much of the reform work, and later professional social service, that took place in American cities focused on providing institutional support for urban migrants. The most famous of these institutions, the Young Men's Christian Association, or YMCA, was established in 1844 in London and then adapted in the early 1850s by American Protestant groups concerned about the moral status of rural youths who had migrated to Boston and

New York City. By the late nineteenth century, the YMCA was no longer connected to any church and had become an autonomous urban institution, though still vitally concerned with providing support for migrating youths.[45] In Chicago, as in other cities, the YMCA led from a distinctly middle-class perspective, establishing reading rooms and exercise rooms that provided outlets for desires which otherwise might be directed toward immoral activities. Organized in 1858, the Chicago association was particularly keyed to the city's exponential growth and "the increase in the numbers of young men who come to Chicago as strangers for temporary or permanent residence."[46] This "massing of population," the Chicago YMCA's General Secretary wrote in 1899, "makes the city not only a nerve center but a danger center." Having come from small towns and rural areas, the young men "are surrounded with the worst forms of temptation" and "at the formative period of life . . . are inclined to take liberties with conscience and to modify principles supposedly fixed."[47] Time and again, leaders of the Chicago YMCA echoed the warnings luridly sketched in the organization's constitution, that the city's migrants were "far from the hallowed influences of home, and the salutary restraints of parental counsels" and therefore prone to following the "paths of sin."[48]

The compensatory home life that the YMCA provided was, according to one spokesman, "preventive rather than charitable," and meant to keep "respectable" young men from the provinces from descending into the "lower classes."[49] In this sense, the "metropolitan plan" that YMCA leaders developed for Chicago in the 1890s—a network of departments and social services spread throughout the city—was a "system of supervision" aimed at bolstering the middle class and preserving a regimen of values that appeared threatened by the disorder of the city.[50] Significantly, the YMCA acknowledged this disorder and, instead of striving to eradicate the city's urban ills, established a social infrastructure around them. By the end of the century, Chicago's YMCA's encompassed an impressive array of services, including a large, multipurpose facility, which opened in 1894 with a dramatic show of support from the city's carriage-driving elite.[51]

To be sure, the YMCA was not the only organization or place to which newcomers could turn for support in late nineteenth-century Chicago. The Chicago Home for the Friendless, for instance, ministered to the needs of migrants, especially women and children, and beginning in mid 1870s, the YWCA (Young Women's Christian Association) offered parallel services in the form of almost thirty branch offices and more than a dozen boardinghouses, which it helped run.[52]

However, the YMCA deserves mention for reasons beyond its expansive, highly visible services. Not only did it seek to guide the emotional and physical energies of young men toward middle-class forms of self-making, but its originating mission derived from the recognition that the source for potentially misguided desires lay outside the city. It made perfect sense, then, that grocery merchant John V. Farwell and evangelist Dwight Moody were early leaders in the Chicago YMCA. Both came to Chicago from the Northeast; both believed that young male migrants were especially susceptible to the temptations of the city. Both probably understood, moreover, that the YMCA's broader goals coincided perfectly with the general objectives of Chicago elite: the economic and cultural uplift of the city. To the extent that this vision of individual and civic growth was based on the moral imperatives that shaped *That Boy "The Modern Prodigal" in Chicago,* it differed significantly from that parable in at least one important respect: Chicago could not survive by imagining itself as a city of prodigal sons whose salvation depended on going back home. The challenge was to create new homes and identities while preserving some sense of the old.

Underscoring the powerful role played by domestic ideology in these reform efforts, Frances Willard—a leader in the temperance movement and herself a migrant to Chicago—observed in the 1880s that "[i]f I were asked the mission of the ideal woman, I would reply: it is to make the whole world homelike."[53] But if ideal women, that is to say white, Protestant, middle-class mothers and wives, understood their duties in these evangelical terms, they assumed that men and women differed in their ability to withstand the depredations of city life. As Joanne Meyerowitz has pointed out, the YWCA assumed that women "adrift" in the city were potential victims of unscrupulous men or prostitution schemes and therefore needed the protection of reform agencies, while the YMCA treated men as agents capable of managing their own salvation.[54] Implicit in these formulations was a worry that reflected conventional readings of scripture: once "fallen," a woman was beyond saving, but a "prodigal son" could be reclaimed. More to the point, the conclusion that underlay much of the nineteenth-century rhetoric about urban migration was that migrating men, more than women, were self-making creatures. That many midwestern women also had the initiative to move to Chicago was a contradiction seized upon by some of the city's more acute observers, particularly novelists who put women at the center of migration narratives and struggled to represent the meaning of their movement from their original home to a new one.

Yet alongside the efforts of middle-class institutions to control the emotional lives of migrating youths, a larger vision of the city remained. Spurred by the idea that a better life was just a train ride away, small-town and rural midwesterners left their homes for Chicago, where their dreaming became an indelible part of the city and region's identity. Even in their homes, the heart of bourgeois culture, Chicago's middle-class migrants found a place for desire.

2

JOHN AND FRANCES GLESSNER

At two o'clock on the afternoon of December 7, 1870, John Jacob Glessner and Frances Macbeth were married at the home of James R. Macbeth in Springfield, Ohio. Roughly thirty guests — family, friends, and business acquaintances — crowded into the Macbeth's modest house at 176 Limestone Street to witness the ceremony, performed by the Reverend Philip H. Mowry of the Second Presbyterian Church. At five o'clock, accompanied by members of the extended Glessner family, the newlyweds left in the rain for Zanesville, John's birthplace and parents' home one hundred miles east of Springfield. Poor rail connections slowed their travel, and the party did not arrive until three in the morning. The couple remained in Zanesville for a week, visiting with family and friends, attending a reception given for them by John's parents, and preparing to move to Chicago, where John would open a branch office for Warder, Mitchell, & Co., one of nation's largest manufacturers of agricultural machinery.[1] Glessner began working for the Springfield-based company in 1863 as a bookkeeper; now, as a partner, he would be directing its distribution network.

Throughout the fall of 1870, news of John Glessner's promotion and impending departure spread fast among his Ohio relatives, provoking speculation and stirring ambitions. Though Glessner himself said little about this move, in October he received at least two inquiries about it from his brother George, who worked at their uncles' drug wholesaling business in Wheeling,

West Virginia. In a letter written on the twelfth, George attributed his curiosity to one of his uncles, who "enquired of me if I had learned any thing further in regard to your going to Chicago" and "takes it for granted if you go to Chicago, I will leave them and go with you or to Springfield." Later in the letter, George explicitly addressed his own prospects, telling his brother that he had often hoped that "we may be connected in the same business together some day, and I still hope such may be the case, and I have thought if I could get in with W. M. & Co. in some kind of moderate salary it might be a stepping-stone towards this long-looked-for object." On the twenty-third, not having received an answer, he pressed the question: "Hope soon to hear something definite about your going to Chicago, and would like it if I could be pressed into the service along with you in Chicago."[2]

In November, John's sister, Mary Glessner Kimball, wrote her brother from Zanesville to say that her husband, Tom, "had heard a rumor that you were going to Chicago to live." Seeming to restrain her own irritation for having to explain a move that she apparently knew nothing about, Mary reported that "I told him that I guessed nothing of that kind was settled or I would have heard of it. He seemed a little sore that you did not tell him you were going to be married." Still, Mary continued her letter as if the rumors were true, adding, almost apologetically, that she "just thought that if you & Fannie go to Chicago from here without arrangements made for a house etc. that it would be pleasant for you to go & board with Dan & his wife until you get settled at housekeeping." Staying with the Fasts—family friends who had moved to Chicago in 1866—"would be much less expensive than being at a hotel. I merely suggest this. It may not be practicable and it may be worthy of a thought."[3]

Given the twenty-eight-year-old Glessner's character and reputation, these queries were to be expected. The eldest of four children, John occupied a position of authority in the family that was enhanced by his business talents. For instance, in the fall of 1870 he persuaded his siblings to supplement their father's annual income by $150 a year. Though Jacob Glessner, a one-time newspaper publisher and Democratic state congressman who now ran a paper manufacturing business, was a man of some standing in Zanesville, he had recently suffered some financial setbacks. A year and a half later, John again stepped in to manage the family's economic affairs when his father asked him to give his younger brother, William, career advice.[4] As Glessner's career developed, his influence within the family grew, as his father and brothers regularly turned to him for business advice and investment suggestions.

Glessner's reputation as a man destined for success was not limited to his immediate family. Just months before the Glessners left for Chicago, Fannie's brother, Charles Macbeth, asked John to go into business with him. John turned him down for reasons that would have been clear to anyone familiar with the Springfield business community: he was thriving at Warder, Mitchell, & Co. On December 2, when the *Springfield Republic* reported his promotion and move to Chicago, it noted that the firm had just been "re-enforced" by "a young gentleman who has been keeping the books of the concern" and "who, by his affability and efficiency has gained many personal and business friends." As a result of this "new arrangement," the firm was opening an office in Chicago "which is to be in Mr. Glessner's charge, and which will the headquarters for the great North-west of the famous and unapproachable Champion Reapers and Mowers."[5] Five years after the Glessners' move to Chicago, R. G. Dun and Co. confirmed this estimate with a sterling endorsement of John Glessner's creditworthiness: "A man of good char + habits stands well with some of our best people + is held good for any contract he would make."[6]

By the 1880s, there was little doubt of John Glessner's business abilities or the success of his firm, now called Warder, Bushnell, & Glessner Co. One of several affiliated companies that manufactured the Champion line of agricultural machinery, the firm had expanded from its factory and headquarters in Springfield, Ohio, to become one of the nation's leading manufacturers of agricultural machinery and a primary competitor of Cyrus McCormick's Chicago-based reaper empire. With factories and shops that encompassed more than thirteen acres of floor space and employing more than two thousand workers, the Champion interests claimed in the mid-1870s to oversee the most extensive agricultural machine shops in the world (fig. 4). This fact was not lost on Springfield boosters, who dubbed their home the "Champion City" and, assuming its continued growth, also called it "Little Chicago."[7] The latter reference was apt, but not for the reasons that town fathers might have hoped, since Springfield's prospects as an expansive metropolitan hub dimmed in the late nineteenth century. Still, the city's importance as a manufacturer of agricultural machinery persisted into the twentieth century, and Warder, Bushnell, & Glessner Co. continued to thrive, though its role changed in 1902 when, after twenty years of fierce competition within the industry, it joined a new combination capitalized at $120 million. The corporation was called International Harvester Company, and while representatives from the McCormick enterprise dominated the board,

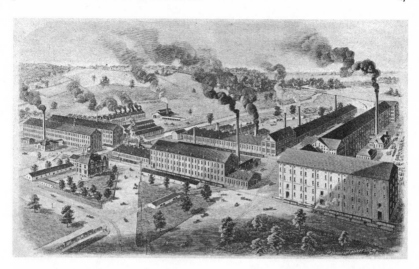

FIGURE 4 The Warder, Bushnell, & Glessner Co. in Springfield, Ohio. (Clark County Historical Society)

Glessner—the sole active partner remaining from the Warder firm—was named a vice-president and director of the company.[8]

Although the Glessners were hardly Chicago's typical migrants, the ambition and desire that brought them from Ohio symbolize the emotional energies that reshaped the Midwest and established Chicago as the nation's Second City. An exemplar of nineteenth-century business acumen who helped shape the dimensions of the modern corporation, John Glessner was passionate yet controlled, and visionary without being reckless. For him, as for his wife, Frances, moving to Chicago was a signal transition in an unceasing effort to build a life modeled on the highest aspirations.

Did John Glessner dream about success when he considered his future life in Chicago? The record does not say. Although he was obviously aware that relocating to the city was a momentous event, he remained tight-lipped about his impending departure. Indeed, the surviving correspondence does not show whether Glessner ever discussed with his family his move to Chicago before it was announced publicly. Perhaps he was reluctant to acknowledge a business decision that had not yet been officially confirmed. Or he may have wanted to hold off his family's entreaties until he was settled in his new position. Regardless of his silence, Glessner was planning his move to Chicago. On October 29, shortly after brother George sent his most pressing inquiry, the Thayer & Tobey Furniture Co. of Chicago sent

John Glessner a reply to his request for information about merchandise. A company representative explained that they did not send out catalogs or price lists and urged Glessner to visit the store when he arrived in the city.[9]

It is not clear how much Fannie Glessner knew of these arrangements. The couple was never engaged to be married, nor, apparently, did they speak publicly about that possibility. Instead, they proceeded from a shared, though seldom spoken, assumption that their futures were linked.[10] A formal betrothal might have dispelled some of the speculation about John Glessner's move to Chicago; in its absence, the future of their relationship and his career became an occasion of intrigue. However, there was nothing mysterious about the manner in which Glessner apparently organized their exit from Springfield—at least not for Fannie. For years she had lived in the atmosphere of her beloved's ambitions and was familiar with his caution and need of control; these qualities had both enabled and stymied their passionate, sometimes troubled courtship. She may not have known about his efforts to purchase furniture in advance of their establishing a household in Chicago. But her confidence in his judgment and the prospect of escaping the narrow confines that defined their relationship in Springfield were probably cause enough for her to yield control of these details to him.

Out of Springfield

Many years later, John Glessner left a great deal unsaid when he wrote in a family history that he was fortunate to have "inspired" the love of the Macbeths' youngest daughter. Aptly titled "Migrations, Emigrations, and Transmigrations of the Glessner Family," Glessner's genealogical essay captured the movements of his family's pioneering past, but barely touched on his cosmopolitan success story, a journey that formed the occasion of its writing. As Glessner told it, this story began very prosaically with the "necessity to start to work early in the morning." Upon arriving in Springfield in 1863, he lived with Elisha Vose, the factory manager whose home was close by the "Works." However, when the Voses announced that they were expecting a child and would no longer have room for their boarder, Glessner began his search for new lodging that was within walking distance of the factory offices. "[F]inally," Glessner notes, "the Macbeth family, pitying me, found a place for me in their home on corner of Limestone and Pleasant Streets. This was a very fortunate move for me, for not only was I made very comfortable, but I inspired the love of Frances, the youngest daughter of the household, and I married her December 7, 1870."[11] It would have been unseemly for him to note the support he gave the Macbeths during his years of residence with them, and dramatically out of character to have used any forum to promote his role as benefactor. Nonetheless, shortly after John and Frances's wedding and their departure for Chicago, his mother-in-law, Nancy Bayard Macbeth, wrote to thank him for all his past kindnesses to her family and to emphasize that she could not imagine allowing her "baby" to marry anyone else.[12]

About these kindnesses, Nancy Macbeth did not have to be specific. Since Glessner began boarding with the Macbeths in the mid-1860s, he had given the family whatever assistance he could, including financial advice and perhaps money as well. The 1870 census report lists over thirteen people living in the Macbeth household: James and Nancy Macbeth, their five children, four boarders, and two Irish-born servants, though it is not clear whether either domestic worked in the Macbeth house. The father, James Reed Macbeth, was a failed storekeeper who in the 1860s worked as a railroad agent, and struggled to support his family. During the late fall and winter of 1866, he was living in New York City to work for Erie Transportation and making only $25 a month, which barely paid his expenses. The two sons, James, twenty-six, and George, twenty-three, worked as a machinist and drug agent (perhaps a sales clerk) and together owned $9,000 of property, but were still living at home. Helen, the oldest child, was a teacher. The Macbeth family thus drew on three incomes, but had eight mouths to feed and a large house to maintain. Like many nineteenth-century families who owned homes but struggled meet their daily expenses, they took in boarders.[13]

For John Glessner, the Macbeth home was ideally located. Just blocks away from the Lagonda Agricultural Works, the home of the Warder, Mitchell, & Co. offices, Glessner could easily walk to work. Interlaced by factories, machine shops, and residential structures, Springfield was an industrial city with the feel of a small town. When Glessner walked to work in the morning he headed north on Limestone Street, passed three blocks of houses, crossed over the railroad tracks, skirted the depot, and then, crossing the tracks again, turned left into the machine works. Across the street from the factory was a coffee and spice mill. A block north, spreading to the east and west, were additional homes, as well as the Lagonda House hotel, the city jail, the high school, and several churches serving a variety of faiths: Episcopal, Congregational, Universalist, Lutheran, Methodist, Baptist, and

Catholic. If Glessner turned east just before the tracks and followed the railroad's path, he would have quickly reached another large block of his company's machine works, which also fronted a row of houses. With the Lagonda Creek meandering through the agricultural works, the railroad yard, and the nearby residential sections, the setting reflected the town's origins as a rural mill village.[14]

When John Glessner was growing up in Zanesville in the 1840s, Springfield was still primarily a country town, surrounded by the rich farmland of southwest Ohio. As the seat of Clark County and a principal stop on the National Road, antebellum Springfield boasted a distinguished brick courthouse, several famous inns, and a vigorous Main Street economy. In 1850, its population was about 5,000, a number which, had it held steady over the succeeding decades, would have made Springfield something more like the "middle border" towns whose Main Street cultures typified the nineteenth-century Midwest. But it did not. During the years leading up to the Civil War, Springfield grew at a rapid pace, becoming the commercially progressive industrial hub that small towns throughout the region aspired to be. In the late 1840s, a railroad and telegraph line came to Springfield, and visionary industrialists such William N. Whitely began manufacturing farm machinery, an industry that transformed the town into a city. In 1846, it founded a college—Wittenberg. By the mid-1850s, Springfield was incorporated as a city; on the eve of the Civil War and its increased demand for farm machinery, the population exceeded 7,000. In 1870, when Glessner left for Chicago, more than 12,000 people lived in Springfield, and the industrial and technological innovations that spurred its growth continued after Glessner's departure. In 1880, Springfield established telephone service, and three years later the city installed electric lights—at roughly the same time Chicago was pursuing the same improvements.[15]

In contrast with Chicago, Springfield was a small town, so much smaller, in fact, that well after the couple arrived in Chicago, John and Fannie's family joked—without envy or animus—about the big-city ways now separating the couple from their former home. On the other hand, Springfield, too, was an industrial city committed to modernization, and a good deal more like Chicago than many of the other small towns and rural villages which midwestern migrants left for the city. Compared with Chicago, it was a second- or even third-tier city; however, its economy and culture were not critically linked to Chicago. Rather, urbanization in Springfield seemed to parallel Chicago's development in some interesting ways.

Springfield's progressive agenda would also have been evident to the Glessners in less visible, but equally important details of culture and society. For instance, Benjamin Warder and Asa Bushnell, the senior members in Glessner's new partnership, were broad-thinking civic leaders, similar in certain ways to the generation of businessmen who established Chicago. Warder's family had been in Springfield since the early nineteenth century — they were Quakers from Philadelphia — and contributed significantly to the town's economic and cultural development. Warder himself lobbied the state legislature in 1870 to bring the new Ohio State University to Springfield, and later supported the building of a new town library, which was named for the family. Asa Bushnell, the president of Warder, Bushnell, & Glessner Co. in the late 1880s, was also the principal leader of other economic institutions in Springfield. A force in the state's Republican Party, he was elected governor of Ohio in 1895.[16]

What lessons in self-making Glessner learned from these men were perhaps more easily grasped in Springfield than in Chicago, since the social landscape was smaller and more easily navigated. Since the 1830s, ambitious men from small places had worked hard to promote Chicago's furious growth. The accomplishments of such men as Marshall Field, Potter Palmer, and John Farwell, while not always visionary, suggest that what cosmopolitan identity Chicago could claim was in part based on the provincial backgrounds of its founding business leaders. Similarly, John Glessner's — and his wife's — rise to civic prominence and world citizenship would be hard to imagine without the developmental influence of central Ohio. Although the Glessners followed the path from "province" to "metropolis" in apparently classic migratory fashion, their social and artistic education was well under way before they left Springfield.

Just exactly how Glessner developed a larger sense of purpose is hard to say. Raised in a respectable Zanesville family (his father was active in politics and ran the town newspaper), Glessner was ambitious and unusually conscientious. Though Warder, Child, & Co. — as the firm was called in the mid-1860s — originally hired him as a bookkeeper, he proved as skilled in grasping complex business problems as in handling the details of accounting. The surviving correspondence clearly demonstrates the confidence that Glessner's partners placed in his ability to handle a wide range of issues. Benjamin Warder in particular developed an affectionate, paternal regard for his younger colleague, and in the letters that went back and forth between Chicago and Springfield asked regularly about the Glessner family and informed him about personal developments in his own life. Like many companies that emerged in the precorporate era, Warder, Bushnell, & Glessner functioned as a family business and took a familial interest in the many things it touched, building the foundations for the corporate paternalism of the twentieth century and Glessner's own development as a modern businessman.

In Springfield, Glessner's responsibilities also included the Macbeth family, especially Fannie, who featured prominently, if rather uneasily, in John Glessner's thoughts about future. Fannie seems to have become important to Glessner as early as the 1860s, but her age and, perhaps more significant, his still developing career prospects, kept him from making a stronger commitment to her. Glessner's caution on this front led to friction between the two, tensions that were complicated by the supportive role that Glessner was already playing in the Macbeth household. In November of 1866, these tensions came to a head when Helen Macbeth wrote her sister Fannie, who was away at school in Brookfield, Indiana, to apprise her of the family's straitened financial situation and tell her that she might not be able to return to school after Christmas. At age twenty-four, Helen was the oldest of the Macbeth children, while Fannie, aged fifteen, was the youngest; this reminder of familial duty grew naturally from her nearly maternal role. Helen also informed her sister that John Glessner was now her "best friend"—his only shortcoming being that he did not care about religion—and that they have been staying up late at night reading together, a development which, Helen noted, concerned her mother. This second point was also a reminder, and perhaps even a warning, about another obligation Fannie had incurred at home: her relationship with Glessner. In December Helen urged Fannie not to break with John and take up with a young man she had met in Indiana. "How have you changed so much in so short a time?" she asked her sister. "Where is that constancy I thought you possessed? Did you not once like John just as much as this present beau?"[17] What, she wondered, would they do when John left their home to board somewhere else? When would they see him?

For Helen, the answers hung on issues of character that were more important than the romance itself. In her eyes, Glessner was a "model of a young man," while Fannie had not yet settled down.[18] Two days after questioning Fannie's resilience, she wrote again and advised her sister not to invite her new beau home to Springfield for a visit. But by the end of the holiday season, the visit had already taken place, and Helen wrote with the understanding that Fannie was engaged to another man.

You know nothing could have pleased me better than for you and J. to have agreed—but now that you are engaged to Will—I would not for *anything* you would forget or prove unfaithful to him—much as I like J. Now he's rooming with George and of course is here every evening—and being with him could not be avoided—and I must say, you made a *bad beginning* when you were here last week. Not with the talk you had with him, but the general intercourse. Sitting in the corner together—Joking, smiling—exchanging glances—assisting each other in various little ways etc. etc. etc. *Little things* they seem—but after all—they are what make us happy or unhappy—and soon we lose our independence—and are dependent entirely upon those around us.[19]

Helen was willing to accept her sister's shift in affections but not at the expense of John's feelings or, most important, to the detriment of Fannie's moral development. In looking to Fannie's social conduct, Helen taught by example and tried to steer her sixteen-year-old sister away from selfish, fickle behavior. Despite her sister's youth and the apparent gaiety of this affair, Helen took her flirtations very seriously, if only for how they reflected on Fannie's, and by implication the family's, autonomy. Here, Helen admonished her sister that indulging in the emotions of the moment and leading on Will might undermine her self-respect and threaten the family's fragile independence. Given the Macbeth family's finances and Helen's earlier efforts to make Fannie appreciate the difficulty of their situation, independence or dependence was a freighted term.

Helen tried to convince her sister—and herself—that Glessner's personal feelings were beside the point. He "gives no expression to them," Helen explained after the holiday event, "and of course they are not to be considered—(as long as we know nothing of them)." What mattered in terms of principle was that he be treated consistently and with the respect to which a well-meaning, spurned suitor was entitled. But even as she embraced this idealistic perspective, personal feelings crept in. In debating as she wrote her January 5 letter whether Fannie should stay away from home in order to avoid uncomfortable encounters, she doubled back on her suggestion when she realized that "the *idea* of our taking John in—and driving you away is *preposterous*. But that is *almost* what it is. He asked me what you went for—I half believe he suspects we are thinking of *him* in our arrangements."[20]

And they were. The underlying subject of the sisters' discussion, and perhaps the motivation for Fannie's developing romance, was Glessner's long-range intentions. Fannie had evidently acknowledged her true feelings to her school friend, Lizzie Fisher, who wrote to her in early January and expressed her hope that her New Year was happy and that "you had that 'naughty, naughty man,' Mr. Glessner to cheer you." Leaving "jesting aside," she wished that "you would never be deprived of his society a day if by having him always with you no black clouds would darken your horizon." Reminding Fannie that "this is Leap Year Dearie," she asked: "why not avail yourself of the privilege it gives you and & propose to him?"[21]

Back in Springfield, in one of their late-night discussions, Helen and John also talked about John's apparent reluctance to commit to marriage. After much back-and-forth about how Fannie's new love interest had strained conversation in the Macbeth house, Glessner conceded that his ability to commit himself to a woman depended on the progress of his career. On January 9, 1867, Helen reported to her sister that John had acknowledged that "he had very peculiar notions & ideas about engagement & matrimony—and they *might* be *wrong*. He does not believe in long *engagements*," Helen continued. "No man has a *right* to propose marriage to a lady till he sees the time for consummating it not far distant. He must be *well settled*—and be able to *set the time* almost—when the first proposition is made. No man has a *right* to ask a lady to *wait* for him—the very *best years* of *her life*. I mentioned Will's circumstances—and he said—'he is a fortunate man—as *unfortunate* as the other.' And so our talk ended."[22]

As in many romances, the hothouse atmosphere that evolved around John Glessner and Fannie Macbeth had much to do with the uncertainty of the relationship and the vulnerabilities limiting each participant's capacity to express their feelings. The third-party interlocutor and her efforts to ferret out and communicate what he "really" feels, amid circumstances that, in Helen's rendering, tilt toward the melodramatic—all this may seem very familiar and perhaps even a bit comic, especially since we know that this story has a happy ending. Yet it is precisely the conventionality of this situation, and its resolution three years later in happier, but equally urgent circumstances, that deserves attention. Through the two yoked events, first their marriage and then their departure for Chicago, the Glessners satisfied both John's anxieties about his career prospects and financial security, and Fannie's concerns about their future together. Although their marriage took place according to the terms John had spelled out in his 1867 conversation with Helen, it would be a mistake to see this consummation of romance and career as only an exercise of power and control on his part. That it was, but in a manner characteristic of nineteenth-century mores, his prudence and sobriety as a man of business found their natural expression in the establishment of marriage and under the moral tutelage of true womanhood.[23] In fact, John's emotions or desires, no matter how restrained and calculated they may have in been business and courtship, were just as focused on domestic concerns as Fannie's.

While it may seem ironic that this passion for self-making and homemaking found its expression in migration, the Glessners' movements were consistent with the pattern of settlement that had helped create midwestern middle-class society. During the 1840s and, '50s, ambitious men and women established themselves as elites and developed a bourgeois regional culture by seeking out economic opportunities through migration and then cultivating in their homes and communities the hallmarks of genteel society. As historian Timothy Mahoney has argued, this settlement pattern depended on a fine balance of domestic and public concerns, as the ambitions of these genteel migrants "drew them centripetally home while pushing them centrifugally out into a broader regional and national system."[24] For the Glessners, then, leaving home to make a home was a familiar step in a society accustomed to settling frontiers. But it was also something new, since their energies were now so intently trained on the rise of a metropolis and so clearly enabled by the growth of an expanding transregional business.

Metropolitan Ambitions

In July of 1879, Fannie Macbeth Glessner charted the flow of these energies in a family journal she was to maintain for more than fifty years. In addition to the time and place of their wedding, she included the names of the guests as well as a list of the gifts they received: a check for $100 (from the senior Mr. Glessner), a Bible (from Mrs. Glessner), silver forks, a butter dish, a knife and bell, teaspoons, a caster, a cake basket, and so forth. Then she enumerated the highlights of their first year in Chicago.

Our first guest was Mrs. A. S. Bushnell. We heard Nielson during the winter and Brignoli in Crosby's Opera house. Our first servant was Kate—whose name changed to Keely during the first year. In the spring we bought a Decker bros. piano. Warder, Mitchell & Co.'s business was first located at 65 S. Canal st. We attended the third Pres. church on the corner of Washington and Carpenter sts. We had frequent visits from our friends, one from Mrs. Macbeth and one from Mrs. Bushnell in March—one from Mrs. Kimball in Feb.—and during the summer of 1871 a visit from Helen, Mrs. Glessner, Mrs. Kimball and Jessie. Kate married a Policeman and Ellen, who came in her place, was married in six weeks after she came—but remained with us until Oct.

Oct. 2nd John George Macbeth Glessner was born—Monday afternoon at three o'clock, with Dr. E. M. P. Ludlane in attendance and Mrs. Hatfield. Oct. 3rd Mrs. Macbeth arrived.[25]

In this catalog of firsts, Fannie Glessner moves quickly from the threshold of their arrival to sketch a vivid picture of bourgeois success. Clearly proud of her husband's professional accomplishments, she takes satisfaction in being able to greet the wife of his business partner—Mrs. Asa S. Bushnell—as an equal. While her father had struggled to support his family, on Glessner's salary they were able to avoid boardinghouse life (which they knew all too well) and could afford a home, servants—and more. By July of 1879, when she began the journal, those wedding gifts must have seemed like good-luck tokens and her financial struggles in Springfield a matter of history. She had given birth to three children (one of whom died in infancy), John's business was prospering, and in 1874 the young family was able to move out of the two-story frame house they rented near Union Park and purchase a larger brick home on West Washington Street, west of the Loop. As if to validate the claims of Chicago's boosters, the Glessners' fortunes were on the rise.

The deliberate, self-conscious steps that John, and especially Fannie, took to beautify their new home became a hallmark of their lives together in Chicago. Soon after moving into the house, they began furnishing it with craftsman-style furniture designed by Isaac E. Scott, a Pennsylvania-born carver and artist and one of Chicago's earliest and most significant followers of William Morris. Over time, Scott would become the Glessners' "old and valued friend," and a touchstone for their increasingly sophisticated tastes in decorative arts. Scott's first design for the Glessners was for a bookcase, which, as the couples' financial condition improved, was followed by others—a library table, a desk, mantelpieces, pottery, and assorted picture frames. These pieces, which, like much Arts and Crafts design, featured natural imagery reminiscent of medieval art, were important enough to the Glessners that they took them to the new home they had built in 1887 on Prairie Avenue.[26] Designed by Henry Hobson Richardson (who was likewise a proponent of Morris's art) and located in a neighborhood that included some of Chicago's wealthiest families, the house's mere exis-

tence underscored their prominent status in Chicago society.[27] Inside the
building's granite massing, an expanse of public and private rooms offered plenty of space for Scott's furnishings, as well as a rich array of furniture, wallpaper, textiles, tiles, and bric-a-brac designed by William Morris
himself.[28]

Nor were the Glessners' aesthetic tastes confined to their home. When in
1883 Warder, Bushnell, & Glessner Co. constructed a new office on West
Adams Street to house the Champion Reaper Company, Scott designed the
interior, which *The Inland Architect and Builder* judged to be "the finest appointed mercantile offices west of New York." Indeed, the expansive rooms,
frescoed ceilings, stained-glass windows, red-oak finishings, and Turkish
rugs prompted the reviewer to observe, "one is apt to forget that this is an
office devoted to the demands of trade, and not a costly private apartment."
Still evident one hundred years later, many of these finer details were enhanced when the five-story building was renovated—and renamed the
Glessner Center—in 1986.[29]

In a genealogy he later wrote for his children, John Glessner gives special
attention to the homes the family occupied during their formative years in
Chicago. With a mixture of pride and sadness, he remembers the first home
they purchased as a "very substantially built" house with a "beautiful large
lawn." "I remodeled the house, and we lived there comfortably. Here the
little baby brother died. Here my daughter Frances was born." Then, seeming to push these bittersweet emotions aside, he underscores a signal
achievement: "We lived here until the fall of 1886, when I built the home on
the Southwest corner of Prairie Avenue and Eighteenth Street, from designs
by Henry H. Richardson, America's greatest architect."[30]

In the fullest sense of that well-worn phrase, Richardson helped to create
the Glessners' "dream house." Certainly the house expressed the couple's
passionate interest in the decorative arts; more important, it gave them the
space and a venue for fostering the development of artistic/intellectual culture in late nineteenth-century Chicago. While in Springfield, John Glessner and Frances Macbeth's passions for literature and music were, like their
feelings for one another, constrained by circumstances and time; in Chicago, they burgeoned with the growth of the new metropolis and their
home. On Prairie Avenue, the Glessners brought to fruition a vision of social intercourse that began on Limestone Avenue and was further developed
on West Washington Boulevard. As members of Chicago's elite, they aggressively cultivated a cosmopolitan point of view, which is to say, in very

literal terms, that the furnishings that graced their home and the people who entered it belonged to "all parts of the world."[31]

Glessner's rise is surely a Chicago story, but his success, and that of Warder, Bushnell, & Glessner Co., hinged on large-scale economic transformations that stretched well beyond his adopted city. Like other business enterprises that expanded in post–Civil War America, the agricultural implement industry spanned regions, and its growth depended on economic relations that developed among cities, small towns, and rural areas. Chicago was literally at the center of this marketplace, emerging over the course of the late 1800s as the transportation and industrial hub of the Midwest. As what historian William Cronon has called "the gateway" to the West, the city shaped the economic development of the hinterland when Chicago businesses and financial institutions lent money, processed raw materials, and then sold new and modern commodities back to consumers.[32]

In overseeing the distribution of Champion agricultural machinery in the company's Northwest territory, Glessner helped secure Chicago's centrality in the region's rapidly developing market. At the same time, the functions of his office — a branch of Warder, Mitchell, & Co. — suggest a slightly different view of Chicago's importance. After all, the company had its headquarters in Springfield, the Champion Reaper was manufactured there, and the company was financed by Ohio economic interests. More important, the company's business was national, even international, in scope. During the first six months of 1875, the firm sold roughly 8,500 units, with more than half the sales coming in Glessner's own district: Chicago and the Old Northwest. The remaining sales were to customers in other midwestern states, New York, Pennsylvania, Oregon, California, and — somewhat surprisingly — Europe, where the company sold 1,850 machines.[33] As the demand for agricultural machinery grew, the Champion line cut an increasingly wide swath in the market, and by 1890 the company had warehouses in Chicago, Baltimore, and Jackson, Michigan, as well as Springfield.[34]

The letters and telegrams that joined Glessner to his home office track this commercial traffic in relentless detail. Mixing personal news with business suggestions, directives, and queries about market conditions, Glessner and his partners matched their expansive production and marketing capacities to farmers' growing dependence on agricultural machinery. In one revealing letter written during the spring of 1872, Benjamin Warder complains to Glessner that ineffective management had required Asa Bushnell to spend extra time in the shops attending closely to operations. The result, Warder notes, was that Bushnell then did not have time to visit customers, supervise their traveling salesmen, and therefore develop the business. "I do not consider that we have followed our men near as closely as you have yours. While we have made no glaring mistakes we can see many places in our territory where we could have done much better if a better man with full knowledge of the bearings had personally made the contracts." Warder notes the company's intention to build 5,000 machines in 1873, but holds off on speculating how many machines might be destined for California, since he lacked full sales information from that region, and, he reminds Glessner, "you do not say in any of your letters what prospect of crops is in the West nor breadth of land sowed." From production to sales to management to general strategic planning, the partners exchanged information from their offices in Springfield and Chicago in developing a multinational business.[35]

Glessner's specific responsibilities within this far-flung business were reflected in the layout of his offices at the corner of West Adams and Jefferson Streets, west of the Loop. On the first floor, next to the elegantly appointed administrative rooms that the *Inland Architect* so admired, were facilities for shipping and receiving machinery. Since the building backed up to a railroad spur, equipment could pass in and out of the building by railcar or horse-drawn team. The second floor consisted of three rooms: an advertising room, from which the office sent out promotional material; a sample room, where customers could view the Champion line of machinery; and a repair room, where farmers could order replacement parts for their machinery. "The system in this department," *The Farm Implement News* noted of the repair work in 1890, "is so perfect and exact that orders are filled and delivered on board the express train within fifteen minutes." Yet even as the reporter praised the efficiency with which Glessner attended to business, he also underscored his role as civic leader, noting that "Mr. Glessner takes a prominent and active part in all public affairs of his adopted city and is ever ready to aid in any movement to promote her interests and the welfare of her people."[36]

Needless to say, the Glessners would not have been able to build a house designed by Henry Hobson Richardson without John Glessner's extraordinary success in business. In 1874, Glessner confided to Fannie that his yearly share of the company's profits was $39,600; in February 1877, R. G. Dun and Co. valued Glessner's assets at $180,637; by 1883, according to a Zanesville newspaper, Glessner was worth more than $1 million.[37] This wealth and the attending social capital formed the foundation of the Glessners' new home.

On Prairie Avenue, the Glessners joined a neighborhood that included the Marshall Fields, the George Pullmans, the Potter Palmers, and other members of Chicago's elite. Having paid $50,000 for the property alone, Glessner was seen by the *Tribune* as one of those men "who have the disposition and the means to gratify their taste for an elegant home." Moreover, Glessner had to be pleased by the newspaper's estimate—at least he included the clipping in the family journal—that the price he had paid, "about $675 per square foot," was "not considered an extravagant one for this choice corner."[38]

Yet if after leaving the compact landscape of industrial Springfield fifteen years earlier the Glessners had now arrived at what one journalist sarcastically called "that holy of holies where only the elect do dwell," their choice of building design was, for some, an act of apostasy.[39] Although today the Glessner house is regarded as a landmark in residential architecture, in 1887 it sparked a good deal of controversy. A thickly massed building of roughly hewn granite, limestone, and brick, the house faced the street with severe, punched windows, and seemed to some onlookers more like a fortress or a bunker than a residence. Acutely aware of how their neighbors, random onlookers, and indeed, one suspects, history itself, regarded their house, the Glessners documented the public's response in their journal, including in one section more than fifteen pages of comments. Although the journal is primarily a unreflective record of daily events interspersed with public notices and newspaper clippings, the section devoted to the house appears to have been carefully constructed to reveal the Glessners' ironic and sometimes humorous opinions of the debate that was taking place around them. The following sampling of comments, recorded by Frances Glessner, captures the flavor of that debate:

Pullman, Henderson, Wheeler, etc. wrote a letter to John protesting against his house being set out further than theirs and the general character of the building— basing all their objections upon hearsay—before they sent the letter Mr. Bartlett, and Mr. Birch advised them not to send it, both of these men and Otho Sprague told John about it.

Mrs. Dexter wrote me a letter giving her views and objections.

These and many remarks besides were all done before our house was commenced. . . .

Prof. Swing encouraged me and said it would come out all right and be beautiful.

Frederick Law Olmstead said it was the most beautiful house that had ever been put upon paper.

When we were looking at the house the first time after we came home we heard one lady say to another in passing, "there is not a single pretty thing about it."

"There are no windows in the first floor of the house" has been said and printed many times.

"The most singular house," Mrs. Kelley. "A singular structure, is it a private residence?" an old man wandering through one day without permission.

"How do you get in it?" many people.

"Have you light enough?"

"How do you see in the street?"

"A *very* large house!"

"I presume your house will be *very* elaborate on the inside?" No. "Where is the expense then, every one says it is the most costly house every built here."—Mrs. Hale. . . .

"The best house in that street." An Englishman — everyone almost.

"I don't like it." Many.

"It expresses an idea." Mr. Boyeson.

"I don't like the idea." Mr. Page.

"The most interesting house I ever saw." Many. . . .

"I don't like it and wish it was not there." George M. Pullman. . . .

"That house is coming out all right. I have kept still and now can have the laugh on them." Marshall Field. . . .

"It looks like a fort." Many.

"What church is this?" A passer-by.

"The apartment house on corner of 18th and Prairie Ave." Newspaper.

"It is very imposing." Miss Monroe.

"The Glessner house is full of egregious blunders — they would ask or take no advice and had never seen any good houses anyway." Mrs. Warder.

"Is this an apartment house?" A visitor.

"It is in no respect what I should want." Mr. Warder.

"Mr. Richardson planned this house I believe." "Yes," Mr. Cameron replied to a woman who with two gentlemen was going through the house. "He died I believe." "Yes." "Well this was enough to kill him."

"I would just as soon criticize Shakespeare," a man said later the same day.[40]

FIGURE 5 The Glessner house, designed by Henry Hobson Richardson and completed in 1887. (The Glessner House Museum, courtesy of Glessner House Museum, Chicago, IL)

Ranging from personal opinion to high-minded criticism, these remarks illustrate the various ways in which the Glessners' new house challenged prevailing concepts of residential architecture. The house was too big and seemed out of scale, it failed to maintain a proper distance from the street, it lacked windows and a sense of openness — these and other features alarmed some observers and charmed others. Architectural historians have since confirmed the innovative nature of Richardson's design, with more than one critic stressing the "urbane" manner in which this monumental, ruggedly built home met the demands of modern city life.[41] The Glessners' contemporaries also seemed to recognize that something new was being created on Prairie Avenue. While neighbors Marshall Field and George Pullman differed in their assessment of the house (with the department store magnate seeming to delight in the railroad baron's discomfiture), both took for granted that the house was a significant departure from past practice. This assumption was confirmed by Frederick Law Olmsted, whose endorsement — the most beautiful house ever put on paper — gave the design the imprimatur of a nationally known designer and lifted discussion beyond the local level (fig. 5).

The Story of a House

For the Glessners, the house on 1800 Prairie Avenue was both the culmination of their journey out of Springfield and the basis of their future success
in Chicago. As Glessner would later suggest in the account from which this
part 1's epigraph was taken, "The Story of a House" (that is, their house)
was also the history of their family. In Glessner's formulation, the house represented a deep and human desire to promote generational continuity and
"preserve some memory of the old." [42] In the 1920s, after the Prairie Avenue
neighborhood lost its social cachet and the mansion once inhabited by the
Pullmans became a rooming house, Glessner sought to redirect this history
and, in effect, preserve the identity of the house and the family. Writing from
the fourth floor of the Harvester Building in downtown Chicago, he laments
to his son George that he and Fannie would stay in the house as long as they
could but that they realized that the children could not live there. "The
house has always been associated with us," Glessner continues, "& your
mother & I are not willing to have it occupied by persons of much lower
grade after we are gone." [43]

Given how the Glessners met and fell in love on Limestone Avenue in
Springfield, Ohio, this next chapter in their domestic history must at some
level have seemed bitterly ironic to the couple. Yet nothing that can truly be
called bitter crept into the several retrospective accounts that the elderly John
Glessner prepared for his children. Even the letter he wrote to his son George,
with its stated bias against people of a "lower grade," is marked by an even-
handed if wistful acceptance of the "state of transition" that Prairie Avenue
was undergoing. In the view of Arthur Meeker, whose best-selling novel
Prairie Avenue (1949) later dramatized these transitions, the rise and fall of
the neighborhood symbolized the city's aggressive, forward-looking character. As one of Meeker's characters maintains, while arguing with his neighbors—in the 1890s—that they may soon need to leave Prairie Avenue, "now
ain't forever. If we've learned anything from the past, it's that nothing stays the
same very long in Chicago. That's why we chose to come here in the first
place, I guess. All of us were born somewhere else, but we came this way because we saw it was the land of opportunity and we were looking for a chance
to spread ourselves a bit. It's plain mulish obstinacy to try to buck the tide!" [44]

Glessner's own experiences suggest that he, too, understood that the
story of Prairie Avenue, and of Chicago itself, extended beyond the city
limits to include those places "somewhere else" that people left to pursue

opportunities in the emerging metropolis. In fact, as the chief executive of a firm whose business was defined by the deepening connections between city and hinterland, and the increasingly complex marketing system that yoked the agricultural Midwest to its industrial counterpart, Glessner had a more nuanced understanding of this larger story than most people.[45] His frequent correspondence with the company's home office in Springfield as well as his regular trips back to Ohio—business travel, mirrored by his Springfield colleagues' trips to Chicago—belied the notion that he was now simply pursuing a career *in* Chicago.

The rhythm of the Glessners' home life was similarly paced by the family's enduring connection to Springfield. From the moment they arrived in Chicago and long after they settled on Prairie Avenue, the Glessners maintained close ties with their friends and family in Ohio. More than a commemorative occasion, Mrs. Bushnell's housewarming visit in the fall of 1871 was one of many social visits that brought the Bushnells, the Warders, and other Springfield friends to Chicago—and the Glessners back to Springfield. Both John and Fannie's extended family were frequent visitors on Prairie Avenue, and they likewise spent time at "The Rocks," the New Hampshire summer home that the Glessners purchased in the 1880s.

Despite the strength of these connections, the Ohio relatives remained very conscious of Chicago's difference from Zanesville and Springfield, and of John and Fannie's increasingly elevated social status. For instance, three months after the Glessners arrived in Chicago, Anna Macbeth wrote to her brother-in-law and sister that "I don't know if Springfield has changed either for better or worse—since you took your departure—if being missed constantly—being enquired for by one's friends—and envied by the balance—constitutes a part of one's happiness—then you & Fanny ought to be happy in the superlative degree—I never make a call but that the first question is 'well did you hear' etc." Yet the importance of being loved and missed was not inconsistent with another truth that Anna goes on to convey in the same letter: that "[i]t must be nice to live in a City—and do as one pleases—and have some variety added to every day life." Familial love and urban enticements mixed less easily in a letter Anna wrote to her sister and mother, who were in Chicago visiting John and Fannie. "[J]ust you dare put on a long face when you come home—and sigh for Chicago," Anna admonishes her mother in mock indignation, "you must bear in mind that we are all *common* folks and can't afford to live like those rich folks in Chicago."[46]

However affectionate, these jibes at big-city ways were based on a deeply held sense of inferiority, the suspicion that Chicago was qualitatively different from or better than Springfield. Despite pride in John and Fannie's accomplishments, these attitudes persisted in a low-grade fashion, even after the Glessners' presence in Chicago was a familiar fact. When Fannie and John invited his parents to join them at the opening of the Columbian Exposition in 1893, Mary Glessner declined, noting that they would like to visit the fair later but that on this occasion "your house will be full of guests from every section, all of whom will claim your attention and it would be a great addition to your care were we added to their number. This would be particularly the case as we are so very ignorant of the ways and usages [of] city life and would consequently be more troublesome to you." [47] So age and province gave way to the apparent sophistication and intensity of the Glessners' metropolitan world.

Some of these concerns about social status and regional identity are evident in the Glessners' journal description of what their friends and neighbors thought of the house. Here, as in Meeker's novel, few of the voices were native Chicagoans. Like many of the city's first-generation settlers, George Pullman and Marshall Field were from New York and New England, respectively. David Swing, one of the city's best-known clergymen and a close friend of the Glessners', grew up on a farm near Cincinnati, attended Miami University of Ohio and Lane Seminary, and served as the principal of the preparatory school that Fannie had attended as a girl—this before coming to Chicago in 1866 as the pastor of Westminster Presbyterian Church in 1866.[48] Closer to John Glessner's Zanesville roots were Will and George Glessner, who, not surprisingly, spoke in unison on the house's merits and their brother and sister-in-law's good "taste." The extent to which these aesthetic judgments were also comments on the Glessners' emergent social status is perhaps best exemplified by the criticism offered by Glessner's business partner, Benjamin Warder, and his wife, who implicitly classed herself above the Glessners when she noted that the couple lacked the social background and sophistication (never seen any "good houses") to make informed design decisions. In this near-textbook example of status anxiety, Mrs. Warder apparently wished to remind people that no amount of social or regional mobility—not even a Prairie Avenue address—could, or should, obscure the Glessners' more limited upbringing.

What makes this last bit of jousting over social status so interesting is that the Warders and the Bushnells themselves were building homes designed by

H. H. Richardson or his followers. Early in 1887, the Glessner journal reveals, the Bushnells spent an evening at the Glessners' West Washington Boulevard residence talking about the drawings for the house they were planning to build in Springfield. Then, in September of 1887, the *Springfield Sunday News* reported—in an article that made its way into the journal—that Benjamin Warder was completing a $400,000 home in Washington, D.C. "Wages at Lagonda are being reduced 10 to 20 per cent this season," the newspaper goes on to report. "The contrast in 'result' is so marked and unavoidable that the workingman, the 'greasy, dirty, common-place clay called the working man,' sees and feels that injustice is done him and that he is not given his share of the profits of his toil. It may be legal but he knows it is not right."[49]

The *News* article is worth remarking upon for a couple of reasons. For one, it suggests that advocates of Lagonda Agricultural Works' labor force recognized that economic growth had altered the management or ownership's relationship to the company, and to Springfield itself. Once a resident entrepreneur and civic leader, Warder was now able—in semiretirement—to establish residency in Washington, D.C., and still realize his share of the company's profits. Although in the 1880s the concept of the transregional or multinational corporation was only just emerging, the article assumes that the firm of Warder, Bushnell, & Glessner had a financial and cultural life that extended well beyond Springfield. Second, by including the article in their journal (without commentary), the Glessners indicated that they, too, recognized the economic interests upon which their cosmopolitan ambitions rested.

Inasmuch as all three senior partners at Warder, Bushnell, & Glessner were drawn to H. H. Richardson's design aesthetic, each man aspired to own and live in a house that fittingly represented his accomplishments and ambitions. Renowned for his artistic idiosyncrasies and brilliance as well as his ability to satisfy commercial and private clients, Richardson was a good choice for any cosmopolitan-minded businessman. Richardson's Harvard background and eastern connections also must have appealed to the three Ohioans. Glessner, however, was the first of the three partners to hire Richardson, choosing him after first meeting with New York architects Stanford White and Willie Potter, who had designed residences for wealthy clients. According to Glessner, Benjamin Warder engaged Richardson's services after Glessner wrote to Warder and described his dealings with the architect.[50] Asa Bushnell was too late to hire Richardson, since the architect died before the Warder and Glessner houses had been built. Nonetheless, the soon-to-be governor of Ohio went ahead and built a residence in Springfield that drew heavily on Richardson's idiom, and was probably designed by a member of Richardson's firm.[51]

Yet it was the Glessner house—and the Glessners themselves—that benefited most from Richardson's artistic talents. Characterized by one critic as a "garden in the machine" that was "in but not necessarily part of the public urban environment," the house wrapped around a courtyard and spacious interior, which was the heart of the Glessners' family life and their busy social life.[52] Inside the house, Richardson followed a scheme he had used in his own house in Brookline, Massachusetts, and in other homes he had designed: off the Prairie Street entrance he placed a large hall, which gave way to the library and the living room. Visitors entering the living room passed by a large staircase that led upstairs to the parlor and music room, which could also be used for social occasions. Beyond the living room was the dining room, and beyond that the kitchen and then the stable. All these public spaces backed onto the courtyard, which created a sense of openness in a building that otherwise appeared closed to the city. Richardson also placed the Glessners' master bedroom on the first floor, separating it from the more public spaces but also giving the Glessners easy access to the workaday, social world that lay outside their private quarters.

In linking these private and public spaces and by clearly separating the house from the outside world, Richardson adapted a long-standing New England design practice to urban use.[53] Like the "ell" that links the domestic space of the New England farmhouse to the barn and various agricultural tasks, these connections integrated the work of the household, revealing, in functional and symbolic terms, the Glessners' commitment to fostering a cosmopolitan milieu within the rapidly growing city. This commitment was evident throughout the house—in the Morris-designed wallpaper, draperies, and furniture; in the industrial and handmade ceramic tile that appeared in the kitchen and around the fireplaces, underscoring the Glessners' passion for the Arts and Crafts movement; in their extensive book collection, which Fannie took pains to catalog and which reflected the couple's abiding interest in classic and contemporary American literature.[54] Through the integration of these spaces, each conceived in a highly aesthetic but functional manner, the house yoked the artistic and the social, bringing to fruition the Glessners' longing for a complete home.[55]

While on the one hand, the artistic ambience that the Glessners cultivated in their home seems like an antidote to Chicago's brutal industrial culture, on the other, their interests in art and culture were intimately connected to the economic and industrial forces that enabled their lives together.[56] It was not simply that the couple was familiar with industrial capitalism or had happened to witness the blurring of lines between rural and urban culture. Rather, the forces of modernization that transformed American society in the nineteenth century were the very ground of their relationship and the source of John Glessner's livelihood. Despite the dislocating effect these forces had on many Americans, they liberated John Glessner and Fannie Macbeth from their existences in industrial Springfield, enabling them to pursue deeply held ambitions and desires. In this sense, the world they created on Prairie Avenue—whether a center for cosmopolitan self-making, a fortified refuge from urban disorder, or both—was the culmination of their migration to Chicago.

For their part, however, the Glessners stressed their connection to the world they had apparently left behind. More than collectors or connoisseurs of art and literature, they believed—as John Glessner suggested in a talk he gave in 1927—they were marking the history that came before them, and their place in it, both for themselves and for others. As Glessner noted of one item he mentioned in his catalog of the house's contents—an 1862 Springfield newspaper article about the fall of Fort Donelson in the Civil War—it is "of no intrinsic value whatever." However, the Glessners saved the article because it was representative of a time "that tried men's souls," a time that "you could not know, for you were not."[57] Years after their house was completed, Glessner continued to see in it the times, places, and passions that brought them to Chicago.

Most of all, the Glessners' ambitions were reflected in the extraordinary procession of friends and acquaintances who were regular guests in their home. Throughout the 1880s and '90s, they hosted a wide range of nationally and internationally known figures: Frederick Law Olmsted, Daniel Burnham, Henry Ward Beecher, Theodore Thomas, Enrico Caruso, Charles Dudley Warner, Ignacy Paderewski, Charles W. Eliot, Isabella Stewart Gardner, and others.[58] Some of these guests were good friends of the Glessners'; many were closely linked to various cultural and philanthropic initiatives the Glessners helped promote. As trustees of the Art Institute of Chicago and the Chicago Symphony Orchestral Association, the couple literally brought the arts into their house, holding chamber music performances in their front hall and annually serving full-course dinners for all the members of Theodore Thomas's Chicago Symphony Orchestra. On the occasion of the Glessners' twenty-fifth wedding anniversary, the full orchestra slipped into the Eighteenth Street entrance of the house, set up their instruments, and gave a surprise concert.[59]

While there is little, if any, substantive discussion in the family journal of their interests in literature, the Glessners were clearly aware of the cultural forces and trends that were making Chicago the literary mecca of the Midwest. John Glessner was a principal benefactor of *Poetry,* the groundbreaking magazine edited by Harriet Monroe, and provided important support to Iowa-born Hamlin Garland in his efforts to develop the Cliff Dwellers' Club, an organization committed to promoting the literary arts in Chicago.[60] When regional writers and humorists James Whitcomb Riley and Bill Nye read from their work at the Central Music Hall in the winter of 1889, the Glessners attended. When Henry Blake Fuller was beginning to make a name for himself in the early 1890s as a writer of Chicago fiction, they invited him to dinner.[61] Joseph Kirkland, whose writings about frontier Illinois helped establish the standards for American realism, was a family friend and regular visitor to the house. When he died in the spring of 1894, his daughter, Caroline—who spent a summer vacation with the Glessners—wrote Fannie to thank them for their kindnesses and tell her how "very attached" her father had been to Mrs. Glessner.[62] Although Major Kirkland, a Civil War veteran and attorney who wrote literature as an avocation, lacked the wealth and social status that many of the Glessners' friends enjoyed, he shared with the couple a vital connection to an older Midwest.

In all these endeavors, the nature and scope of the Glessners' cosmopolitan vision bore the imprint of their status as elite Chicagoans. Thus while they proved remarkably supportive of the city's cultural life, and opened their home to artists, musicians, and intellectuals of all political persuasions, they remained conservative philanthropists who seldom questioned the legitimacy of the political economy that upheld their social positions.[63] On the other hand, though their success in Chicago took them well beyond their Springfield antecedents, they never lost sight of the provincial culture they left back home in Ohio.

In February 1898, nearly thirty years after the Glessners arrived in Chicago, their daughter Frances was married in the parlor of their house on Prairie Avenue. Officiating was Philip Mowry, the same minister who had presided at the couple's wedding celebration on Limestone Avenue in

Springfield, Ohio. In Chicago as in Springfield, the marriage brought family and friends together in a ceremony that was both public and private and, by virtue of Mowry's participation, symbolically connected to the good fortunes that launched John and Fannie's life together. Beyond the personal links forged by this occasion, had the Glessners allowed themselves a backward glance—as surely they must have—they might have seen in their own extraordinary journey a story that was representative of Chicago's equally remarkable rise. It is to this larger story that I now turn.

3

STORIES OF THE RISING CITY

Fiction writers who engaged Chicago's migratory nature highlighted the challenge of making a new home in the city, but like other late-nineteenth-century writers, they were also generally concerned with the nation's transition from a rural to an urban culture. As Eric Sundquist has explained, American realists were chiefly concerned with "the journey between rural and urban," which is to suggest first that urban migration as a social fact and problem formed the basis for literary realism, and second that the geography and culture of migration supplied these writers with a vocabulary and set of images for representing a variety of cultural issues and tensions.[1] Realists did not simply take urban migration as their subject, but rather explored worlds held together by the sinewy connections that joined urban centers to small towns and rural areas—the beginnings of American mass culture. Many of them wrote out of a complicated awareness of the economic and political forces that were reshaping the cultural map, not only by changing particular places—city or village—but also by altering the relations between those places. Most important, they were alert to structures of feeling that developed around these new geographic and cultural differences. Economically and demographically, urban migration obviously promoted the growth of cities and the decline of crossroad towns; literarily and culturally, it created the notion of the "boondocks." Yet it also gave rise to a metropolitan sensibility that reoriented the consciousnesses of rural and small-town inhabitants, generated new desires and expectations among them, and threatened established values and attitudes about home.

That this cultural shift especially preoccupied American writers is hardly surprising, since their own careers were critically implicated in the rise of the city and its attendant literary institutions — for instance, publishing houses and nationally syndicated periodicals. Many, in fact, were migrants themselves and therefore felt "responsible" — in ways their writing often self-consciously signals — for the growing gap between metropolis and province. As Richard Brodhead has shown, the emergence of regionalism as a niche in the American literary marketplace was predicated on the rise of an urban middle-class readership that had become accustomed, through tourist travel and general economic development, to think of remote locations in the South or New England as exotic places worth reading about.[2]

Thus urban sensibilities helped establish the "provinces" or the "hinterland" as an identifiable cultural taste. Still, that does not mean that for migrating realists the gap between provincial and urban life was wholly constructed. While many developing writers longed for the artistic and professional resources available only in cities, they also felt urban life to be dramatically and sometimes unsettlingly different from what they left behind. This sense of difference is especially evident in the work of William Dean Howells, whose protagonists — from Lemuel Hopkins to Bartley Hubbard to Silas Lapham to Royal Langbrith — are typically caught up in the cultural, economic, moral, and psychological forces that govern urban migration and town-country relations. For Howells, as for other realist writers, the territory between city and country served as a primary context for examining the new ways in which men and women now "made" themselves.

This territory is palpably manifest in the literary work identified with Chicago's rise. Indeed, the story of Chicago was the story of American realism writ locally. Again and again, Chicago writers treated the city as a regional magnet and, in certain instances, suggested that the city was itself the product of provincial ambitions — an urban landscape "unleashed" (to use Lefebvre's term) by hinterland desires. As migrants themselves, Chicago writers thus claimed these desires and the city as their own.

Chicago's preeminent place in the region's geographic and emotional history was apparent even to Chicago writers who chose not to focus on the city itself. For instance, although Chicago's first realist writer, attorney-novelist Joseph Kirkland, never wrote a word of fiction about his adopted hometown, his novel *Zury: the Meanest Man in Spring County* (1887), suggests a strong Chicago subtext. A migration narrative that begins with the settling of the Illinois prairie in the 1830s and ends about the time of the Civil War, Kirkland's novel takes an urban turn when an ambitious member of the featured family's second generation migrates once again—to Chicago. More important, the novel's protagonist, Usury Prouder, is, according to his name and behavior, a tight-fisted, self-interested farmer-businessman whose relentless disciplining (and sublimation) of desire appears representative of the emotional economies that enabled the growth of Chicago business elite. As Kirkland notes of Zury's contribution to the family's "sordid economy," soon after he and his parents have arrived from the East,

He was without associates, ambitions, or objects in life, except, in the first place, "subduing" that farm; in the next place, clearing it of the mortgages; in the third place, increasing its money-making possibilities; and thenceforth and forever adding dollar to dollar, mortgage to mortgage (on other people's farms), note to note, and gain to gain, with all the force of a strong intellect pent into a narrow channel.[3]

Kirkland's childhood migration to the Michigan frontier—an experience that his mother, Caroline Kirkland, depicted in her novel *New Home—Who'll Follow?* (1839)—as well as several business jobs he held in central Illinois, enabled him to create this authoritative portrait of rural life. Moreover, as a young man he worked as a clerk for *Putnam's Monthly Magazine* in New York City. As a strong proponent of manifest destiny, *Putnam's* editor, Charles F. Briggs, filled the magazine with articles about the West. He also was the author of *The Adventures of Harry Franco: A Tale of the Great Panic* (1839), a novel of migration that deals explicitly with the economic benefits (and moral temptations) that drew young country boys to Manhattan. Whether Kirkland read Briggs's novel is unknown, but there is little doubt that his apprenticeship at *Putnam's* confirmed his interest in literature of the West and kindled his interest in returning to the region, which he did in 1858 to take a position with a coal mining company based in Chicago.[4]

By the time Kirkland wrote *Zury*, he had been practicing law in Chicago for more than a decade, was a leading figure in its genteel literary circles, and had friends like the Glessners who also had prospered in their chosen home. His "realism," then, was not unrelated to the Chicago scene. In fact, Zury's economic practices—his single-minded pursuit of money and his systematic, horizontal integration of farm mortgages—seems to apply as much to the first generation of Chicago businessmen (many of whom were eastern migrants who made fortunes in real estate speculation) as to self-making farmers. To it put another way, Zury's sordid channeling of economic desire was an earlier manifestation of the erotic energy that, in Sandburg's view, lures farm boys to the big city.

Although *Zury* was not the first novel written in or about Chicago (*Wau-Bun* [1856], a tale of how real estate speculators purchased the city from Native Americans, claims that distinction), literary historians often regard it—and Kirkland's writerly ambitions—as the beginning of serious writing in Chicago. Yet if *Zury* does mark the start, it does so in distinctly geographic and emotional terms—with a regional history that anticipates and assumes Chicago's status as Emerald City of the Midwest. (What is *The Wizard of Oz* [1900], after all, but a migration narrative written by a Chicago window trimmer—L. Frank Baum—who knew very well the city's capacity to arouse desire?) For at least one of his contemporaries, Kirkland's handling of these issues marked him as a likely chronicler of urban life. After reviewing *Zury*, Hamlin Garland wrote to him and encouraged him to write a novel about Chicago. "I do not dare to try Chicago," Kirkland wrote in return, "or very modern times."[5]

"Rock it to 'em"—Hamlin Garland's Chicago

Kirkland's sense that Chicago was complicated in a too modern way begs the question of how an urban novel might be written from a provincial point of view. Ironically, Garland was pressed to consider the very same question several years later, when Henry Blake Fuller sent *him* a letter, urging him to write about Chicago. And, just as ironically, the novel that Fuller had in mind had as much to do with the hinterland as with urban life. After all, he explains, "'Chicago' means more than Chicago merely; it means Chicago and the outlying 'provinces'—Iowa, Wisconsin, and the rest." Since Fuller had, in his words, already "corralled the *town*" in writing his novel *The Cliff-Dwellers* (1893), it was now time for Garland "to hitch the town and country together."

Plant yourself on both legs and rock it to 'em—one foot in Chicago, the other in LaCrosse or Cedar Rapids or Rock River. Bring your small-town people to the big city; do the battledore-and-shuttlecock act. . . . Bring your clean, honest, ambitious countryfolk to town, and make $40-flat Westsiders of them, and let them see (and perhaps judge) the metropolis from that point of view. Ain't that your real "lay"? 6

The "real" story of the city, Fuller implies in this and other salvos delivered during the 1890s and early 1900s, ought to be told by a migrant who had himself undergone the experience of becoming a Chicagoan.

Fuller wrote yet another letter, roughly two years later, to journalist George Ade (Ade had arrived in Chicago in 1890, nearly fresh out of Purdue), encouraging *him* to write the definitive Chicago novel and likewise suggesting that he take into account the provincial point of view. In this instance, Fuller was responding to a sketch that Ade had written for the *Chicago Daily News* in May 1895 in which a street-smart office boy named Artie urges Walter, a recent country migrant, not to be overwhelmed by the crowds in Chicago or the tough-seeming characters he might meet. Artie says that "when you first get in [to the city] you kind o' feel that your up against a lot o' wise city mugs and that they must be purty fly because they live right here in town," but reassures him that "there's just as many pinheads on State street as you'll find anywhere out in the woods" and that eventually he will overcome his discomfort and realize that the city is "as common as plowed ground."

Then, as now, *pinhead* referred to a dull or stupid person. However, in the 1890s, it was more obviously a pejorative term for rural folk—like *hayseed*. Literally—and this definition gives depth to Artie's observation that the city is as common as plowed ground—a pinhead is the end point on one of the needled prongs on a rake or plow, the positions of which regulate the depth of the furrow. Figuratively speaking—and this is what caught Fuller's attention—Artie is telling Walter to ignore the wise city mugs, since many of them were country migrants themselves (pinheads) who were trying to pass for urban tough guys. In other words, the streets of Chicago were filled with country migrants, even though their rural origins may not have been immediately evident.

Fuller was impressed by Ade's handling of this truth and told him so.

The urban "pinhead" who passes for a 'wise city mug' is one of the most obvious and perennial of types, but you are the first man to capture him: I don't know why the thing that lies right in the way should be the thing that everybody passes by.— I have often wondered to what extent the newcomer was impressed by the 'horrible

front' of the native-born, and now I kind of seem to know.—If, in the fullness of
time, you come to find a disposition to write the 'Chicago novel' that people are
beginning to expect from you, I don't know anybody who wouldn't be glad to pull
off to one side and give you all the room you need![7]

Here Fuller returns Ade's wit in full, and compliments him first for identifying the relocated pinhead who struggles to "pass" for a wise city mug, and
second for highlighting an urban type that most observers of the urban
scene "pass" by. Fuller's verbal play, replete with the language of ethnic and
racial assimilation, concludes with a third twist on the term *pass* in which he
encourages Ade to write the Chicago novel that everyone expects of him. He
reassures Ade, just as Artie reassures Walter, that his fellow writers will step
aside and let him pass so he can accomplish the work.

Fuller's role as encourager of young writers and spokesperson for
Chicago literary culture is remarkable for a couple of reasons. For one, he
presents himself as a kind of recruiter of literary talent, determined to construct a literary tradition for the city. Second, Fuller suggests that "the
Chicago novel" must take into account the hinterland migration that was
transforming the city. Given Fuller's status as an upper-class, native-born
Chicagoan as well as his identification with cosmopolitan, European standards of culture, this emphasis may be surprising. On the other hand, as a gay
man who struggled to find a comfortable place in society—and felt isolated
for much of his adult life—Fuller understood that many hinterland migrants
came to the city to realize long-held desires and reinvent themselves. And he
knew how difficult a journey this figurative migration could be. (Fuller continued to play the role of avuncular mentor to newly arrived writers and
artists, offering encouragement to Glenway Wescott when he came to Chicago in the 1910s.)[8] Indeed, in both the letters cited, Fuller's ventriloquized
country voice and strategic use of slang suggest that the provincial writer was
the consummate "insider" to the drama of self-making for which Chicago was
becoming known. To be such an insider was to experience migration as a
physically alienating process that continuously placed the migrant's identity
in two places at the same time. However, to write about this experience and
"rock it to 'em" was also a potentially regenerative (and erotic) act of imagining that could place the provincial migrant's restless ambitions—his desire—
at the center of Chicago culture. So Fuller suggested that the migrating
writer's career and identity were yoked to the class aspirations of other ambitious migrants—by their shared journey from country to town.

Garland took Fuller's advice and in 1895 published *Rose of Dutcher's Coolly,* a naturalistic novel whose migrant-heroine is pulled by artistic ambition and instinctual desires to Chicago. The decision to write an urban novel presumably came at some sacrifice for the Iowa-born regionalist, since in *Crumbling Idols* (1894) he had argued for a national literature based on provincialism. True literary art ("veritism"), Garland claims in this manifesto, must be made of homegrown materials and based on local knowledge. "The real utterance of a city or a locality can only come when a writer is born out of its intimate heart," he explains. "The novel of the slums must be written by one who has played there as a child. . . . It cannot be done from above nor from the outside."[9] Fuller disagreed, and his tactful challenge to Garland—to write about his own experience as a literary migrant to Chicago—insinuated that any theory of literary realism that failed to account for the movement between city and country was limited and provincial.

Garland had already begun to explore the nebulous territory between town and country in the short stories collected in *Main Travelled Roads* (1891). For instance, "Under the Lion's Paw," his famous diatribe against the evils of absentee landownership, gestures vaguely at the economic power emanating from urban centers. Perhaps an even better example of the urban turn that Garland's fiction would take is "Up the Coulé," the story of Howard McLane, a successful actor who returns home to Wisconsin after years of living in Boston, only to find his mother and brother living a grim rural existence. In reworking the prodigal son parable, Garland stages several domestic confrontations that lead Howard to concede his mistake in leaving the family to pursue his ambitions in the city. However, Garland is concerned less with moral accountability than with the psychological and aesthetic conflicts that define Howard's attempted recovery of "home." Turning the domestic drama inward, he presents Howard as a victim of nostalgia: determined to find pastoral beauty in a world of hard labor or, when confronted with harsh economies of farm life, committed to romantic notions of urban-rural conflict. Howard's inclination to see the countryside in highly aestheticized terms emerges here as a taste he has developed as a middle-class urbanite—at one point he compares farmland to a painting of rural scenery he keeps in his Boston apartment—as well as the product of his long-evolving nostalgia.

In undermining these genteel perceptions, Garland emphasizes the differences between his western veritism and the sentimentalized local-color writing that had become so popular in late nineteenth-century periodicals.

As a local-turned-urban tourist, Howard seems part of the middle-class culture whose interests in country vacations and exotic rural environs helped underwrite a literary market for regional writing. Yet because Howard also understands what rural life is really like and feels guilty for leaving his home and family, he is not a simple part of the urban culture whose tastes he now shares. As a returning migrant, he sees the region from inside and out. To the extent that Howard—an ambitious farm boy who follows his artistic interests to Boston—resembles Garland, his dual vision reflects the cultural conditions that helped construct Garland's literary perspective. To have the opportunity to write about conditions out West and to develop the vision necessary to see the region, the would-be writer had to leave home for the city. Only that perspective allowed the metaphoric return home that went toward the creation of regional life. To stay at home, as Howard's brother does, means giving up professional success and literary vision; inevitably, the artist must migrate. At the same time, the nostalgia that overcomes Howard and the anxiety that Garland felt in leaving the middle border for urban literary centers like Boston and Chicago stem from the possibility of deracination—the fear that in leaving home in order to represent it, he might lose all ties to his provincial roots.

Although he postulated in *Crumbling Idols* that only a city native should write an urban novel, stories like "Up the Coulé" suggest just how close Garland, the practicing writer, was to abandoning his still-developing theory of realism. Indeed, the idea that a novelist could (and perhaps should) realistically account for an urban migrant's experience occurred to Garland as early as 1890, when he reviewed *The Minister's Charge* (1887), William Dean Howells's story of Lemuel Barker, a young man from rural New England who migrates to Boston in order to launch a literary career. Garland noted that Barker's story is "representative, in great measure, of those of thousands of young fortune seekers, students of music, painting, sculpture, journalism, who come and go in Boston and who make up a large and distinctive class. They do not all come with poems to sell, or with the avowed intention of succeeding Mr. Lowell, but they do have a vague, inarticulate desire for a more intellectual life, a broader and more public activity." [10]

For Garland, Howells's novel must have seemed particularly compelling, since Barker's intellectual and artistic longings were so much like his own. Growing up in Osage, Iowa, Garland had escaped the tedium of rural life by reading the wide variety of literature—newspapers, dime novels, romantic fiction, Shakespeare—available through the community's informal borrowing network. As an ambitious young writer, he had had little hesitation in leaving Wisconsin for Boston. The promise of studying literature in "the land of Emerson, Longfellow, and Hawthorne," he explains in *Son of the Middle Border* (1917), was far more appealing than staying at home and farming with his father. It was also more appealing than heading west to California or Colorado, as many of his peers were doing. In choosing to go east, Garland believed he was "reversing all the laws of development, breasting the current of progress, stemming the tide of emigration." On the other hand, his belief that migration held the key to his ambitions and desires was obviously consistent with these laws. Several pages later in his autobiography, Garland seems to acknowledge this fact in the self-consciously conventional account of the journey he made by train in 1884 from Wisconsin to Boston, where he finally collapsed in a chair at a cheap boardinghouse "with such relief as only the poor homeless country boy knows when at the end of a long tramp from the station."[11] Here, Garland's journey, like Lemuel Barker's, derives its significance from its typicality.

More than the product of authorial anxiety, however, the weariness evoked in this passage derives also from the sense of homelessness that pervades the entire autobiography. A westerner adrift from his home and parents, Garland describes both his search for a literary community and his experience of the same pangs of guilt ascribed to Howard McLane in "Up the Coulé." Though Garland never fully resolved this remorse, his move from Boston to Chicago in 1893 brought him back West and closer to the home he had left. Most important, this return to "the heart of America" dovetailed with the formation of his own literary perspective and career. "I belonged here," Garland later noted of his new home in Chicago. "My writing was of the Middle Border, and must continue to be so. Its spirit was mine. All of my immediate relations were dwellers in the west, and . . . it was inevitable that I should ultimately bring my workshop to Chicago, which was my natural pivot, the hinge on which my varied activities would revolve."[12]

Though living in Wisconsin appeared impossibly provincial to Garland, in Chicago he hoped to construct his career anew as an indigenous literary voice of the West. In quickly becoming part of the city's emergent literary culture, he found himself splitting time between two distinct, sometimes overlapping social circles. One was an "'artistic gang'" that included Henry Blake Fuller, painter Charles Francis Browne, sculptor Lorado Taft (whose sister, Zulime, eventually married Garland), and supporters of the arts from the business community, such as Franklin Head and Melville Stone. The other circle was a "'journalistic gang'" made up of newspapermen like Eugene Field, Opie Read, George Ade, and cartoonist John McCutcheon. While Garland took what he called an "elder brother interest" in Ade's and McCutcheon's work—Hoosier migrants who likewise identified with the middle border—he felt "more at ease" with the more socially refined artistic crowd.[13] Generally speaking, the two groups exemplified contrasting tendencies in his social and literary perspective, and even seemed to offer choices as he made his way in Chicago. The tensions are evident in *Rose of Dutcher's Coolly,* which Garland began writing in Chicago.

In many ways, the book was a fitting reply to Fuller's call for fiction about Chicago written from the provincial perspective.[14] The first novel to capture the migratory spirit of Chicago, *Rose of Dutcher's Coolly* may likewise be read as a commentary on Garland's own movement into bourgeois urban society. The heroine is Rose Dutcher, a beautiful, artistically sensitive girl who leaves her Wisconsin farm to attend the state university in Madison. Eventually, Rose's ambitions take her to Chicago, where she meets Warren Mason, an older newspaper writer whose world-weary skepticism prove a perfect complement to her youth and natural poetic power. The novel ends with their agreement to marry and live in the city, an existence, Warren tells her, that invites "pain and sorrow and care" but will allow them the freedom to pursue their artistic ambitions.[15]

Yet in the overall scheme of the narrative, this conclusion seems less like a decision than a preordained outcome. Migration is expressly embodied here as biological-cultural destiny, as Garland repeatedly underscores Rose's "fine animal nature" and her "organic magnificent inheritance of moral purity" that is too big for the small towns of Wisconsin (114, 127). Beginning with her birth, the novel follows Rose's coming-of-age in geographic terms, linking her physical, intellectual, and emotional development to her movement away from the provinces. Like Balzac's famous chronicles of rural–urban movement—for instance, *Lost Illusions* (1837–43)—but without the irony, *Rose of Dutcher's Coolly* is a bildungsroman and a migration narrative. Though Rose feels uprooted when she leaves home, she is drawn by a "deep, pure emotion" to Chicago: "a shining atom of steel [she is now the train, carrying her to the city] obeying the magnet, a clear rivulet from the hills hurrying to the sea. On every train at that same hour, from every direction, others, like her, were entering on the same search to the same end" (181). Apart from social or economic forces, Garland's evolutionary narrative makes Chicago the target of Rose's inchoate desires, ambitions over which she has little control. Although Rose feels remorse for leaving her goodhearted father, the natural forces that sweep her toward the city absolve her of much of the guilt that Howard McLane feels in the "Up the Coulé," or that Garland himself felt when developing his own literary career.

While Rose's perspective is central to the novel, Garland contrasts it with other viewpoints, the sum total of which presents a rather conflicted picture of urban migration. Rose's father is an honest, successful farmer and the closest Garland gets to representing the solid power of the earth that has spawned Rose. Warren—a migrant himself from a small Illinois town and ultimately Rose's suitor—criticizes Chicago but counsels her to make the most of its potential. In one of Rose's first ventures into drawing-room society, he asks her if she feels part of a "predestinated movement" of "fortune-seekers setting always to the city," and then goes on to characterize Chicago as a city of "colossal vices and colossal virtues. It is now devouring, one day it will begin to send back its best arterial blood into the nation. . . . Its future is appalling to think of. In 1920 it will be the mightiest center of the English speaking race . . . I envy you young people who have come now when the worst of the fight against material greed is nearly over." He urges her to "sit above the city's tumult" and not "mix in the grind" (234, 233, 234).

Warren's metaphor extends to the language that Garland uses to describe the city's changing population. Sitting in a Chicago park, lost in reverie, Rose gazes at "streamed floods of the city's newly acquired residents, clerks, bookkeepers, typewriters, shop-girls, butcher's boys, salesmen, all fresh from the small towns and from the farms of the West." Many of them she recognizes as "familiar types"—all "bright restless spirits of the country towns and wide-awake school districts come to try their fortunes in the great city like herself" and all determined to assume "blasé airs as old residents" in order to pass as authentic Chicagoans. In describing other urban types less familiar to Rose, Garland dramatizes the friction caused by polyglot Chicago: snobbish New Englanders, sharp-witted Jews, "swart Italian girls" whose voices "sounded like the chattered colloquies of monkeys in the circus." When she first arrives in the city, Rose has difficulty seeing anything but "contrasts." In language typical of urban novels of this period, Garland notes that the city is an "illimitable jungle filled with unrecognizable forms." All this threatens confusion, Garland suggests, because the "home-life of the city had not yet revealed itself to her" (225, 205, 182, 206).

The development of this home feeling marks the beginning of Rose's assimilation. Or, as Garland puts it, "the home feeling began to make itself felt, and the city grew less appalling, though hardly less oppressive" (333). Once again, his use of passive construction makes Rose both the object and agent of her emotional state—a state of desire, which Garland figures in wholly "domestic" terms. For though his Chicago is clearly a city of newcomers, the newcomers who matter most to the city's future are the American-born hinterland migrants. To be sure, his portrayal of "streamed floods" resembles Max Weber's description of Halsted Street—both track the movement of desiring migrants into and within the city. But where Weber sees far-flung movement and swarming interaction, Garland pays special attention to American-born migrants—the provincials. To him, it is the hinterland migration channel that really counts. It is this manifestation of desire—of upwardly mobile "native-born" migrants—that will build the city. In other words, it is Rose's dreaming of what Chicago may become—her reverie— that sets the standard for the city.

At the same time, Rose's dreams are limited by the city's determinative power; by what Chicago will become. Garland comments on this power when Rose and Warren, standing by the city's lakefront, watch two schooners break up in tumultuous waters. Though a black sailor struggles heroically to save his comrades, he drowns and the men onboard go down. Witnessing this event, Rose admits she has "drifted" through life and vows hereafter to "*sail*" (349). Here she maintains that she now hopes to master the natural forces that up to this point have carried her along from one phase of life to another. More to the point, she implies that she wants to become a self-conscious agent in her own migration: no longer just obeying the magnet, she plans to direct her own desires. However, the limits to this plan are fully evident in the black sailor's noble yet unsuccessful efforts to master the currents and save his crew. His death suggests the difficulties of one person meaningfully affecting the environment around her. Given Rose's powerful, nativistic identity, this scene also assumes an unintended irony, since Rose shows neither the inclination nor the capacity to identify with the nonwhite Chicagoans around her. She is not familiar with the African American's life, and does not attempt to know the swarthy Italian girls she sees on the street.

Garland's story thus proves curiously at odds with the transformative process that Fuller placed at the center of the migration experience—curiously because Garland seems to acknowledge the city's pluralism and its capacity to effect change in migrants such as Rose. However, he sidesteps the complications implicit in such a novel of assimilation, and instead leaves Rose remarkably unchanged. Though in marrying Warren she becomes part of Chicago's drawing-room culture, there is no doubt but that her powers as a woman and poet derive from her rural home. Given the social landscape described by Garland, the hinterland is felt in this novel as an imperial force, not just of rural virtue, but also of purebred American stock.

In this sense, Garland's representation of how Chicago becomes the object of Rose's ambition and how Rose becomes part of middle-class Chicago culture bends the story of migration toward nativist fantasy. Nor does this outcome seem much different when one gives full credence to Rose's status as a New Woman. Despite her emergent powers and departure from the traditional womanly roles—differences that Garland emphasizes throughout the novel—Rose resolves her potential by marrying Warren Mason and settling down in Chicago, thereby annexing her talents to urban knowledge and economic power. Although Garland struggles to show how Chicago is constructed from the interplay of transregional forces, by the end of the novel the difference between the city and the country boils down to an unresolved either/or proposition.

Thus Garland tried to "rock it" to readers, finding a channel for desires that in Weber's depiction of the city appear chaotic. In this sense, the home feeling that finally comes to Rose domesticates her strong artistic impulses and keeps them in check, so that she and her husband embrace a vaguely bohemian, but unthreatening, middle-class way of life. This social position in turn parallels the moderate perspective that Garland adopted as a migrating writer, one that first promises a fresh view of the city and a break from literary convention, but which finally gives in to a predetermined status quo.

Henry Blake Fuller Rejoins

This characterization—or criticism—is the conclusion that Henry Blake Fuller reaches in "The Downfall of Abner Joyce" (1901), a novella that he published several years after the appearance of *Rose of Dutcher's Coolly*. "Downfall" is a migration narrative that deflates both the myth of migration and the image of the rising new writer as artistic genius or political reformer. Clearly modeled on Garland, Joyce is a son of the middle border and a resolute Populist who has come to Chicago with the hope of righting the wrongs that have been done to the nation's farmers. "This was a simple enough task," Fuller explains of his intentions, "were it but approached with courage, zeal, determination." The sardonic irony with which Fuller treats Joyce's ambitions sets the tone for the story. In the first paragraph Fuller hints at the fall that lies ahead when, in describing the impact of Joyce's first book, *The*

Weary World, he explains, "readers felt the world of fiction to be the richer by one very vital and authentic personality." Although Joyce earnestly underscores the need for collective political action and thinks of his writing as "sweaty, panting, begrimed" labor, his progress in the world appears to lie along the path of individual accomplishment and literary celebrity.[16]

Abner is as commanding and desiring a figure as Rose, but Fuller treats his gendered powers satirically, noting his "robust masculinity" that "march[ed] in firm phalanxes over solid ground toward the mastery of the great Problem." By the end of the novella, however, the greenhorn has lost his pretensions and his passions. He succeeds in his work. He falls in love. He makes his peace with bourgeois society. And he capitulates to the city. At the close of the story, when he sits down for dinner at the home of a wealthy plutocrat, he is wearing evening clothes, not the old-fashioned swallowtail suit he had clung to throughout the story. "Yes," Fuller concludes, "Abner had made his compromise with the world. He had conformed. He had reached an understanding with the children of Mammon. He—a great, original genius—had become just like other people. His downfall was complete" (23, 139).

While Joyce's capitulation to a more "decorous Bohemia" may be read as a critique of bourgeois culture and its paradoxical tendency to showcase and then neutralize adversarial politics and art, it also serves to deflate the myth of migration and the image of the rising new writer as charismatic pilgrim. When Joyce arrives in Chicago, he is a naive greenhorn who speaks "massively"—and naively—of his "fatalistic belief in the efficacy of mere legislation such as dominates the rural townships of the West." Still, despite his simplistic attitudes and countrified manner of dress, he has a passion and idealism that affects everyone he meets. By the end of the story, though, he has lost this energy and his originality, having adopted the more "sophisticated" perspectives of his elite patrons, who, Fuller suggests, are shallow and provincial in their own way (13, 22, 23).

As a writer, Joyce is taken to task for not having what *Rose of Dutcher's Coolly* lacks: a nuanced sense of irony and detail. However, Fuller's overwrought characterization of robust masculinity marching toward the great Problems offers more than a critique of Hamlin Garland's heavy-handed style. It also suggests a more complicated understanding of urban migration. Joyce wants to see the city as a social problem in need of a conquering hero, and is surprised to discover, amid his sentimental celebrations of rural values, that a fair number of Chicago's elite also came to the city from the country. Joyce's real problem, as Fuller comically unfolds it, is that he fails to see himself in the city. More to the point, he fails to understand that Chicago is not a "maw" or monolith but a complicated mix of newcomers—including hinterland migrants—whose interactions constitute the city's culture. Abner Joyce should not be simply mistaken for Hamlin Garland, but Fuller's treatment of him suggests that he believed Garland had missed an opportunity in *Rose of Dutcher's Coolly* to capture Chicago's true provincial character.

Fuller's "criticism" of Garland warrants qualification in a couple of ways. For one, although *Rose of Dutcher's Coolly* was the first Chicago novel to approach the city's rise from the hinterland perspective, it was hardly the last. Subsequent migration novels, published in the late 1890s and early twentieth century, likewise addressed the issues underscored by Fuller and failed in similar ways to envision a cultural order beyond the bourgeois maw that absorbs Rose and Abner. Although the protagonists in these novels dream of making lives in the city—a new cultural order—the existences awaiting them after their migration fall short of their hopes and expectations. For instance, at the outset of Bert Leston Taylor's pointedly titled novel, *The Charlatans* (1906), the small-town heroine, an aspiring musician named Hope, is "dreaming of the world beyond her valley; of men and women who mattered in the scheme of things, who lived to some purpose and did things, because the opportunity to live and do was theirs. Ah, that the opportunity might also be hers!" [17] Eventually it is (and the novel ends in her marriage to a well-to-do Chicagoan), but along the way, Hope comes to see the city from a more realistic, disillusioning perspective while preserving her dreams of realizing her musical talents there.

Understood in these terms, Fuller's novella expresses his increasing disappointment in Chicago's unrealized promise and its inability to move beyond its initial commitment to cosmopolitan greatness. This second qualification goes to the heart of Fuller's motive for encouraging Garland's and Ade's literary ambitions: to build a literary tradition based on indigenous materials and develop an intellectual and artistic climate that was as robust as Chicago's rough, provincial nature. In the early 1890s, when he urged Garland and Ade to write their migration novels, and throughout the decade, Fuller proved a strong believer in the city's future. In 1897 he gave full voice to this optimism in an *Atlantic Monthly* article, "The Upward Movement in Chicago," which described the city's investment in cultural institutions and looked ahead to even brighter prospects. [18] Yet by the early twentieth century, Fuller's boosting flagged, and as "The Downfall of Abner Joyce" indicates, he became preoccupied with Chicago's declining fortunes.

Fuller expressed his growing pessimism explicitly (and ironically) in an anonymous editorial for the *Chicago Evening Post* in 1901. In it he blames Chicago's lack of metropolitan sophistication on the very group whose assimilation and cultural development he had once championed as a subject worthy of the great Chicago novel. Whether the provincial migrant characterized in the *Post* still merited extended literary treatment, Fuller does not say. But he leaves no doubt of his belief that the migrant, as a general social type, had failed to assimilate to urban ways and therefore enhance the city's development.

The countryman, whether American or European, is the dominant element in Chicago, which in many of its social and material aspects is but the country town grown big. Abundant evidences of our origin still cling to us. The freedom with which we make our gutters do service as livery stables relates us at once to the thousands of "Main Streets" all over the West. Numberless open porches and barless windows recall the day when we were too young and too small to have a criminal class strong enough to fight with honesty and decency on even terms, and our use of these porches on summer evenings bears witness to a social guilelessness that still perseveres in its heroic determination to know no evil.

Seven-eighths of our people are totally without the urban tradition. Of the native half, the great bulk, drawn from the Mississippi Valley, have never seen a city in their lives — there are none west of the Alleghanies — and do not know what a city is, or ought to be, nor what restraints and concessions are necessary for successful living under civic conditions. The foreign half, very largely from the rural districts of the continent, are nearly as guiltless of metropolitan knowledge as the native; and the few who have lived in cities are glad to escape the taut rein held over them by officials occupied in keeping municipal life up to the level exacted by a dominant gentry. The great mass of our new citizens do not, cannot, criticise a city. Our streets may indeed be filthy, but what are they compared with the roads in Jo Daviess County or in Galicia during a rainy spring?

Chicago is not yet . . . a city. True, we have had [a] . . . metropolitan moment . . . but we had to strain on tiptoe to do it.[19]

Whereas in the early 1890s, Fuller assumed that hinterland migrants aspired to urban and perhaps even cosmopolitan standards of behavior and culture, a decade later their provincialism—unreconstructed and unconscious—stands in the way of Chicago becoming a true city. Main Street social energies continue to play a key role in the city's rise, only now the "mass" of small-town migrants has taken on the stereotypical traits of foreign immigrants. Despite their robust middle-class presence (single-family homes and open porches), they appear ignorant, too familiar, a bit slovenly, and a lot like the country "jays" or "jakes" who were frequently the object of ridicule in nineteenth-century urban newspapers.[20] With an acuity reminiscent of his contemporary Henry James, Fuller longs for a metropolitan moment worthy of Paris or Florence while conceding that Chicago's one concerted effort to achieve cosmopolitan greatness, namely the 1893 Columbian Exhibition, has receded in history.

In the most general sense, Fuller's lament that Chicago was just a country town grown big touches on a question that concerned all Chicagoans, regardless of their ethnic origins and class identity: what kind of home would the city become? In complaining about dirty street gutters, Fuller suggests that country migrants were perhaps *too* much at home in the city, too comfortable in their ignorance of metropolitan culture to criticize and improve their own practices. But there may be another reason for his complaints. Kenneth Scambray has suggested that Fuller—who kept his homosexuality a secret from friends and family—sought companionship in European and Canadian cities that offered more social opportunities for gay men.[21] Lonely in his native city but nonetheless unwilling to leave, Fuller was perhaps unusually sensitive to Chicago's shortcomings. Although readers of the *Post* would not necessarily have shared Fuller's longing for cosmopolitan community, they certainly would have understood his concern about Chicago as home. In questioning how or what aspects of the migrant's native culture would be carried over, abandoned, or transformed in turn-of-the-century Chicago, he expressed the primary anxieties—and hopes—of this rapidly changing city.

This is also the question behind John Glessner's remark at the start of this section, that Anglo-Saxons are a "home-making, home-loving race." And it is the problem Garland, Taylor, Fuller, and others sought to resolve in their stories of migration and assimilation. That both the questions and the answers were laden with ideological, economic, and ethnic tensions seems obvious now, though it did not appear quite so clear then. In this respect, Fuller was perhaps all too prescient in his observation that Chicago's migrants— and its migrating writers as well—were strangely innocent (and guileless) of their desires to feel at home in the city. For as Fuller shrewdly suggested, to feel at home in a place is to be comfortably unconscious of the motivations and limitations that govern one's behavior.

The notion that Chicago's "provincial" character was closely linked to its citizens' longing for what Hamlin Garland called "home feeling" suggests that the proper end of all self-making was, literally, the bourgeois home. From this perspective, the most powerful expression of the Glessners' migratory ambitions was the construction of their Richardson-designed home on Prairie Avenue. Similarly, it makes sense that the migration narratives written during the 1890s and 1900s end in marriage and/or the establishment of a home in the city, and that the central protagonists in these novels were often women whose migratory desires could—in fictional terms—be more easily domesticated. The logic at work in this conception of urban migration is obviously repressive, since it suggests a limited number of options for the ambitious newcomers. Indeed, this is precisely what Henry Blake Fuller seems to have objected to in Garland's prosaic representation of hinterland migration. And it is what Robert Herrick implicitly notes in his novel *Memoirs of an American Citizen* (1905), which depicts the journey from hinterland to city as a deterministic process that inevitably casts the migrant as a seeker after money, power, and an attractive wife.

Like "The Downfall of Abner Joyce," *Memoirs* is something of neomigration novel that comments critically on an already established narrative. Herrick and Fuller knew (or hoped) that there were other ways of imagining hinterland migration, other possible of ways of inventing a life, making a home, and writing literature. But both men were also aware of the intense drive in Chicago, and in America for that matter, to subordinate desire to bourgeois success. Hence in Herrick's fictitious life story—which begins in the 1880s, at the moment of Chicago's rise—Chicagoan and American are one and the same.

Sweet Home Chicago

Yet the ideological significance of home was by no means limited to the middle class, or, for that matter, to domestic space, strictly defined. To be sure, as scholars of nineteenth-century America have repeatedly noted, the domestic sphere was the "cradle" of middle-class values broadly defined, and so served as an incubator for developing responsible market behavior among young men.[22] However, domestic values played a critical role across economic lines and ethnic/racial differences, and the term *home* was capable of generating meanings that extended well beyond the family values at the hearth to pertain to regional and place affiliations as well. For instance, by the second decade of the twentieth century, Americans had begun to refer to the city, town, or village where they had been raised as their "hometown"— a change in usage that suggests the increasing mobility of American society and, perhaps more to the point, the impact of migration on the concept of domesticity.[23]

The multifaceted importance of home is testified to by the extraordinary popularity of a still well-known song. As music historian Charles Hamm has shown, "Home, Sweet Home" (1823)—an Englishman wrote the music; an American, the lyrics—was the most popular song of the nineteenth century. And its widespread popularity, he notes, had mostly to do with the its sentimental appeal to people who had been separated or exiled from their primary homes.[24] "Home, Sweet Home" was the nostalgic set piece for a nation of migrants and immigrants.

In Chicago, "Home, Sweet Home" gained a privileged audience on December 9, 1889, when opera singer Adelina Patti performed it at the opening ceremony of the Auditorium Building. Designed by Louis Sullivan and now recognized as a masterwork of modern architecture, the Auditorium was conceived as a monument to, and showcase for, Chicago's emerging cosmopolitan status. News of the building's opening was the lead story in the *Chicago Tribune* and no wonder, as both President Benjamin Harrison and Vice President Levi Morton attended the ceremony, which the *Tribune*, not surprisingly, treated as a major American event. "The cheers, the music, the waving of flags—who that were present can forget the occasion when a chapter in our national history was written?"[25]

Although we cannot listen to Patti's rendition of "Home, Sweet Home," we can reasonably speculate that this much beloved song was presented as high art—a formal, dramatic performance that brought the emotional landscape of home into monumental public space (fig. 6). And while it is impossible to know whether it was more popular in Chicago than in other American cities, we might reasonably conclude that the song's heavy nostalgia—its heart-tugging evocations of "home"—appealed especially to Chicagoans, many of whom had been separated from their original homes. The lyrics, which are mundane and sentimental, suggestively highlight the place of "home feeling" in Chicago's civic culture: "Mid pleasures and palaces though we may roam, / Be it ever so humble, there's no place like home! / A charm from the skies seems to hallow us there, / Which, seek through the world, is

FIGURE 6 The *Chicago Tribune*'s portrayal of Adelina Patti singing "Home, Sweet Home" (Author's collection)

ne'er met with elsewhere. / Home! Home! Sweet, sweet Home! / There's no place like Home! / There's no place like Home!"[26]

Needless to say, these lyrics verge on universal truth and sentiment. Yet the power of Patti's performance surely had something to do with the questions that lay beneath the melody's soothing surface and the audience's widely shared commitment to family and home. What sort of home would this young city become? Would the sum of its disparate parts—people and resources drawn from throughout the region, and across the continent and globe—yield the cosmopolitan culture that boosters like Fuller and Glessner longed for? The very presence of the Auditorium argued that there would indeed be a place in Chicago for artistic culture to thrive and grow. However, the song's earnest celebration of a home beyond urban pleasures and palaces, as well as the inescapable fact that many Chicagoans came from rural and small-town backgrounds, confused the relationship between "home feeling" and the place that hinterland migrants now called their home. What could their backgrounds have to do with Chicago's development? In acknowledging the debt that all people had to some humble home, distant in time as well as geography, "Home, Sweet Home" brought into high relief the city's antecedents and its future. For while Chicago's elite listened to Patti sing feelingly of domestic origins, many of them must have dreamed of a cosmopolitan Chicago, a city "belonging to all parts of the world."[27]

Patti's performance and the civic splendor in which it took place epitomize the state of metropolitan development in turn-of-the-century Chicago. Though they appeared startlingly different in expression, the restless urge to self-making and the nostalgic celebration of home were complementary desires. At least in Chicago, they existed in close proximity to one another.

Make no mistake: the migratory impulse that infused the still growing city during the 1890s and 1900s was oriented primarily toward the boosting of self and city. Still, as forward seeming as this drive for success was, the youth of the city as well as the provincial backgrounds of the citizens highlighted not just the gap between hinterland and city, migrant and cosmopolite, that needed to be covered but also the ambition and energy required to succeed. To prosper in Chicago, it seemed, one had to dream. However, dreaming itself was no guarantee that this gap would be filled.

Given this distance between longing and success, it was inevitable that the dreams that brought some migrants to the city went unfulfilled. So journalist and politician Brand Whitlock, a migrant to Chicago in the 1880s, wrote to a friend from his home in Toledo in 1898, wondering if he had somehow missed his chance by leaving the city.

Sometimes I close my eyes and see the big tall buildings whose roofs and chimneys form a high and jagged skyline along Michigan Avenue and sweep with a mighty swing around the graceful curve of the cold lake. I can feel the sharp lake breeze coming in at my window, or if I choose to go out into the street I can feel the brush of the crowds, who seem to be burdened with the whole woe of humanity, and hear the roar, that typical city roar, which is the outcry of mankind and brutekind under the stress and strain of modern commercial life, and is louder and more insistent in Chicago than in any of the cities that I know about. And I can catch the odors—never faint—from the restaurants under the sidewalks, and now and then the smell of printer's ink and the press rooms comes to me, with all its fascination, and I conclude that I am exiled and away from my own and my own kind. But somehow, with a perversity that is so ironical as to be amusing the gates of Chicago, once so hospitable, have been closed against me.[28]

These images, of careers half-begun, of a city partially built, of desires barely satisfied, and of dreams still lingering, would be a signature of Chicago in years to come.

PART TWO

EXILES IN SUCKERLAND

MAMIE

Mamie beat her head against the bars of a little Indiana town and
        dreamed of romance and big things off somewhere the way
        the railroad trains ran.
She could see the smoke of the engines get lost down where the
        streaks of steel flashed in the sun and when the newspapers
        came in on the morning mail she knew there was a big
        Chicago far off, where all the trains ran.
She got tired of the barber shop boys and the post office chatter and
        church gossip and the old pieces the band played on the
        Fourth of July and Decoration Day.
And sobbed at her fate and beat her head against the bars and was
        going to kill herself.
When the thought came to her that if she was going to die she
        might as well die struggling for a clutch of romance among
        the streets of Chicago.
She has a job now at six dollars a week in the basement of the
        Boston Store.
And even now she beats her head against the bars in the same old
        way and wonders if there is a bigger place the railroads run to
        from Chicago where maybe there is
                romance
                and big things
                and real dreams
                that never go smash.

CARL SANDBURG, CHICAGO POEMS (1916)

4

GEORGE ADE AND
JOHN T. MCCUTCHEON

In the spring of 1911, the Indiana Society of Chicago invited members to the "annual summer outing to take place at Indianapolis, Indiana, where you will be the guest of the Fatted Calf Society." Founded in 1905 by a group of transplanted Hoosiers, the Indiana Society of Chicago was organized around a nostalgic attachment to being, thinking, and staying Hoosier. The invitation, with its tongue-in-cheek invocation of the prodigal son parable, foregrounds these common ties, suggesting that all will be forgiven if the migrants give up their profligate urban existence and return to Indiana soil.[1]

The souvenir booklet commemorating this homecoming—written by the Come On Home Society of Indianapolis and copyrighted by Those Who Stayed at Home—addresses these divided loyalties explicitly. "Dear Exiles in Suckerland," one of the enclosed letters begins, "I am greatly pleased to join the 'Native Bunch' in a most cordial invitation to you to come back home for a brief spell in the merry month of June." It goes on to wonder "why it should be necessary to send an invitation to a native Hoosier who has lived in exile even for a day in Chicago, to come back to good old Indiana."[2] The plaint of the uprooted Hoosier echoes throughout the literature of the Indiana Society and can be heard in some of the more popular expressive forms of the period, such as the song by Paul Dresser, "On the

Banks of the Wabash Far Away," and James Whitcomb Riley's poem "The Hoosier in Exile," which pictures an Indiana migrant making his way through "the thronging maze/Of alien city streets" with his thoughts "set in grassy ways/And woodlands' cool retreats," where "he hears the dove/And is at peace within." Like Thomas Hovenden's painting, *Breaking Home Ties,* one of the most popular exhibitions at the 1893 World's Columbian Exposition in Chicago, Riley's poem and Dresser's song both underscore the emotional ties that linked urban migrants to their former homes.[3]

In the restless atmosphere of late nineteenth-century Chicago, Adelina Patti's rendition of "Home, Sweet Home" undoubtedly called to mind a variety of homes and emotions. However, for many provincial migrants, the only home worth remembering—and longing for—was the rural or small-town place they left behind. "On the Banks of the Wabash" and "The Hoosier in Exile" serve their nostalgia straight, providing a full measure of longing for Home. The Indiana Society invitations, on the other hand, treat such sentiment with self-conscious humor, acknowledging its members' nostalgia for a home that is no longer accessible. The society's membership roster helps explain this detachment: with jobs ranging from modest white-collar work to corporate directorship, these enterprising rubes-turned-Chicagoans seem to have done quite well in the big city.[4]

The example of the Indiana Society invites a deliberately ironic view of nostalgia, suggesting that for some hinterland migrants such expressions of loyalty played an important role in the construction of middle-class urban identity. Here the paradoxical nature of Chicago's modernity seems especially acute: to become Chicagoans, these migrants also had to become Hoosiers. And yet this is not especially surprising, given the demographics of late nineteenth-century Chicago. In a city numerically dominated by the foreign born and their children, small-town and rural newcomers stood out as native-born Americans, their claims to an indigenous birthright reinforced simply by linguistic and religious differences. While these claims were seldom explicit, they gathered power discursively as journalists, writers, and organizations underscored the successful assimilation of provincial migrants into Chicago's ethnically diverse society. As historian Jon Gjerde has shown, the midwestern hinterland also included a rich weave of immigrant population; however, in the public rhetoric that evolved around Chicago's hinterland migrants, Main Street seemed primarily the home of the native born.[5] Small-town migrants might have felt like outsiders in metropolitan society, but to the degree that American-born Chicagoans controlled the city's chief economic and

cultural institutions, they were potential insiders and a vital part of its burgeoning middle class.

Literally, *nostalgia* means "homesickness," and it was this sentimental attachment to home that distinguished groups such as the Indiana Society and
shaped the collective identity of provincial migrants. Like the ethnic identities associated with immigrant groups, this one derived from the cross-
hatching of shared experiences and cultural perceptions that were imposed
upon the group from the outside. Like foreign immigrants, hinterland migrants sought to construct an identity based on terms they recognized as
their own: their perceived differences from other social groups in Chicago,
their interactions with one another, and the attitudes, values, and historical
memories that they associated with their provincial homes. Known in theoretical literature as "ethnicization," the process by which provincial newcomers recognized, named, and acted upon their differences from other residents was part of the experience of home-leaving and self-making that made
the city, in some fashion, the product of the hinterland.[6]

One marker of provincial migrants' identity in Chicago, nostalgia was a
socially constructed emotion that referred primarily to geographic disloca-
tion and the longing for home that followed. Of course, nostalgia did not affect all migrants equally. Some people remained indifferent to the homes
they left behind and approached their change in station prosaically—as the
natural extension of lives begun on Main Street. Still, given the many dis-
cernible ties between Chicago and its hinterland, not to mention the ongoing movement of small-town and rural migrants into the city, many migrants
could not help but feel their provincial roots. For them, nostalgia was anything but a static recollection of past circumstances that developed in opposition to city life; rather, it was a pressing cultural and emotional matter,
alive and constantly evolving. In principle, then, hinterland allegiances
could possibly conflict with the migrant's developing identity as a Chicagoan. However, because he was by choice already committed to life in the
city, being a Chicagoan typically presupposed and guided the development
of a "complementary" provincial identity.[7] In this respect, nostalgia served
as a potentially creative force in urban culture, guiding the drive to "make
it" that compelled many migrants to leave home in the first place.

No one better knew the cultural and emotional dynamics that joined
country to city than George Ade and John McCutcheon, the cofounders of
the Indiana Society. Perhaps the best-known Hoosiers in turn-of-the-
century Chicago, the two arrived in the city in 1889 and 1890 respectively,
and went to work for the *Chicago Daily News*'s early edition, *The Morning*

News (later renamed the *Record*), McCutcheon as an illustrator and cartoonist, and Ade as a reporter. During the 1890s, they collaborated on hundreds of stories that helped make the *News* a leading paper in the Midwest,
with both urban and rural readers. By the end of the century, both men had
left the newspaper: Ade for a lucrative career as a syndicated journalist, humorist, and playwright; McCutcheon for a prominent spot on the *Chicago
Tribune*. These career paths made McCutcheon a Chicago institution and
enabled Ade to purchase an Indiana farm, which served as his home base
when he became a part-time Chicago resident and frequent traveler. As Purdue alumni and fraternity brothers, the men were close friends before they
arrived in Chicago, and they remained so — socially and professionally. After their work on the *News* ended, McCutcheon continued to illustrate Ade's
writings. Both men, even when they did not collaborate, remained intent on
their connection to the hinterland, especially Indiana, and the meaning this
connection had for their lives.

Growing Up Hoosier

Ade's and McCutcheon's careers were closely linked. Both men grew up in
genteel, middle-class families in small towns in northwest Indiana, where
the bourgeois values characteristic of Main Street culture predominated.[8]
Like many midwesterners who left small towns for urban opportunities,
they remembered their childhood homes as peaceful, upstanding communities. In their autobiographical writings they wistfully described the pleasures of going barefoot in the summer and exploring the nooks and crannies
of their communities, which for Ade was the small village of Kentland and
for McCutcheon, Lafayette.[9]

Despite retrospections approaching the idyllic, the men also noted the
ambitions that drew them away from home and the social forces that put them
in the orbit of Chicago's developing power. As Ade once reportedly joked
(and spent much of his public life denying), "A lot of smart men come from
Indiana, and the smarter they are the quicker they come."[10] Yet Ade's "revolt
from the village," as the intellectual migration to the cities would later be described, was less a rebellion than an example of midwestern self-making.
More than "jes folks," small-town Indiana in general adhered to socially
conservative, commercially progressive values, an agenda that made the
northern part of the state home to an emerging industrial economy. For

instance, Studebaker got its start in Kokomo and began manufacturing automobiles in 1902. This emphasis on economic innovation was consistent with the qualities that characterized many Indiana small towns and informed the Republican Party's influence in state and national politics. Northern Indianans took particular pride in the region's New England heritage, which placed a high premium on education and a genteel culture of letters. And by the turn of the century, state boosters could claim an "Indiana school of literature" and a thriving publisher as well: Bobbs-Merrill, based in Indianapolis.[11]

Settled in the early nineteenth century by Virginians who crossed over from Kentucky and by New Englanders and New Yorkers who, shortly afterward, moved into the northern half of the state, Indiana developed around two migratory streams, which are evident today in town names like Martinsburg and Middlebury and in the murky history of the state nickname, "Hoosier." On the one hand, the word resembles the English Cumberland dialect word *hoozer,* meaning "hill," which southern mountain pioneers brought to Indiana and which, in turn, was used to identify them; on the other, as early as the 1820s, *Hoosier* was a synonym for *Yankee,* thus marking the northern antecedents of a state that otherwise seemed to belong south of the Mason-Dixon line.[12] Yet by the late nineteenth century, *Hoosier* was widely accepted as the state nickname, a consensus encouraged by Indiana's increasing homogeneity. In 1880, just over 7 percent of the population was foreign born, compared with 14 percent in Ohio, 23 percent in Illinois, 24 percent in Michigan, and 44 percent in Wisconsin. By 1920, Indiana had the nation's lowest percentage of foreign-born residents, mostly of German and Irish descent. Throughout this forty-year period, the number of African Americans living the state was also quite low, hovering between 2 percent and 3 percent of the total population.[13]

In this respect, *Hoosier* stood for 100 percent native-born, white identity. During the 1880s and '90s, as Chicago and much of the nation underwent dramatic demographic transformations, the moniker signified Indiana's difference, and its connection to an older America. The immense popularity of James Whitcomb Riley (whose first book appeared in 1883) and the widespread currency of Kin Hubbard's folk sayings rested in large part on native-born sentiments. Although Riley's dialect poetry may have represented a way of life that was gradually slipping away, for many nineteenth-century Americans it seemed an authentic and true register of rural emotions and folkways.

But being, thinking, and staying Hoosier was no simple thing. Later in life, Ade alluded to the complications in noting the public's misconception of his own background: "Because I was born in a little Indiana town framed with corn-fields and showed a criminal preference for the mid-west vernacular and the homely types blooming in outer townships," people "assumed that I came from the most abandoned and uninformed Hoosier stock."[14] In fact, Ade's father, emigrated from England at the age of twelve, trained as a blacksmith in Cincinnati, married an Ohioan, Adaline Bush, and then moved gradually into white-collar occupations, first as a store owner and subsequently as a banker in Kentland, where George Ade was born.

McCutcheon's father had an even more varied career. After service in the Civil War, he returned to Lafayette, Indiana, to manage the two farms his father-in-law had given his wife, Clara, as a wedding present. During the years that followed, Captain "Barr" McCutcheon drove cattle, managed the dining hall at Purdue University, and served as sheriff of Tippecanoe County. When John McCutcheon was a boy, the family lived in Elston, just outside Lafayette. Although the McCutcheons moved back to town in 1885 when Barr was elected county sheriff, John spent his adolescence roaming the crossroads of a rural village that consisted of a general store, saloon, blacksmiths, and a grain elevator. As the county seat, commercial hub, and railroad junction, Lafayette served as town to Elston's countryside, and the young McCutcheon's view of the world expanded as he moved between the two. Once, as a teenager, he rode horseback from a Lafayette bank to the Elston grain elevator to deliver $1,500, imagining robbers in hot pursuit as he fulfilled this adult responsibility.[15]

The outside world that loomed over George Ade's childhood was likewise tinged with fantasies. Located eighty miles south of Chicago, Kentland had a population of several hundred in the 1870s and, Ade recalled, was "linked to the outer world by a railroad," but "isolated just the same." One of Ade's first memories was watching "a blur of illumination in the northern sky" when Chicago burned in the fall of 1871. While Ade's infrequent trips to Chicago piqued his interest in this outer world, it was reading—Charles Dickens, Mark Twain, and Beadle and Adams adventure books—that truly inflamed his imagination, encouraging him to dream "of distant cities and faraway lands."[16]

McCutcheon gravitated toward stories of pirates and detectives. He worked his way through Horatio Alger's novels and, at the age of fifteen, discovered *Tom Sawyer*. "This type of reading," he remembered, "quickened my imagination and stirred an intense desire to do things." So he planned adventures, joined a gang of boys, attended traveling theatrical performances, staged his own plays, began drawing pictures in the loft of his barn, and later, as a high school student, wrote, illustrated, and published his version of the *Elston News*.[17]

Through the fantasy worlds of literature and drama, both boys devised new ways of exploring the world around them. In their pastoral village homes, they were free to create what historians have called "boy culture," a realm of imaginary role-playing and real-life action, which reinforced the development of middle-class, masculine values.[18]

The turning point in Ade and McCutcheon's lives came when they entered Purdue University. At that moment, Ade claimed, his dreams of "distant cities and faraway lands" began to come true.[19]

Purdue

In 1883, when George Ade made the trip down to Lafayette from Newton County, Purdue University was still a fledgling institution. The first state-funded agricultural and technical school in Indiana to be established under the federal Morrill Land Grant Act of 1862, Purdue differed from other land-grant universities (whose curriculum tended to revolve around agriculture) in its emphasis on engineering. Emerson E. White, who became president of Purdue shortly after its founding in 1873, set the curricular priorities for the rest of the century by resisting "the stale mummeries" of classical education and promoting the industrial sciences, which he believed should be the centerpiece of a modern, practical education. His successor, James H. Smart (president when Ade and McCutcheon attended) was similarly iconoclastic in his belief that moral and spiritual values could be part of a technical education.[20]

Whether a majority of Purdue students shared White's and Smart's enthusiasm for integrating humanitarian ideals and applied sciences is unclear. However, there is no question that the university's raw-bone modernity and practical curriculum appealed to small-town midwesterners who were eager to get ahead. Of the forty-three students who entered with George Ade, all except one were from Indiana, and most — there were eight from Lafayette — came from small towns, including Millville, Wea, Otterbein, and Benham's Store. Two years later, when John McCutcheon matriculated, the pattern remained much the same. His freshman class was nearly twice the size of Ade's, with only six students entering from out of state.[21] The attrition rate for these classes was high, but those who did graduate typically left Indiana behind, embarking on careers that led them to metropolitan areas or took them to engineering projects elsewhere.[22]

By Purdue's curricular standards, Ade and McCutcheon were hardly model students. At a college that offered only a bachelor of science degree, neither had the aptitude nor the desire to succeed as engineers. Ade pursued a degree in the School of Science because it allowed him to take fewer courses in mathematics, a subject that he loathed, and McCutcheon switched from mechanical engineering to the School of Industrial Art during his freshman year to concentrate on his drawing skills and also to avoid math.[23]

Why, then, did Ade and McCutcheon choose Purdue? For McCutcheon, it was a logical choice because he was familiar with the university and had attended its preparatory program as a high school student. To Ade, it must have seemed like a long shot. In the 1880s, college was a rarity for middle-class youths. Even in the Northeast, where Ivy League institutions prepared the sons of elite families for careers in the ministry or some profession, most youths followed other paths into the workplace.[24] Although one of Ade's older brothers had considered going to seminary, there was no precedent for college attendance in the family. Yet as John Ade came to realize, with encouragement from the county superintendent of schools, his son was a talented student who might profit from college. Furthermore, George had shown little interest in farming and had proved an unenthusiastic worker. Attracted by the practical benefits of the state's new agricultural and mechanical arts school, John Ade applied on his son's behalf for a local scholarship. When George won the scholarship and left for Lafayette, he was the sole resident from his county to be attending Purdue and only one of three to be enrolled in college at all.[25]

Despite their struggles with Purdue's curriculum, Ade and McCutcheon enjoyed what today we would call a broad, liberal arts education. Learning from experiences that took place in and out of the classroom, they deepened their interests in the expressive arts and quickened their desire to explore the world—enterprises that for both young men were crucially linked. Gradually, and without knowing exactly where they were headed, they gravitated toward vocations based on the longing for adventure that they both developed as children. Although Ade was already feeling homesick when he arrived by train in Lafayette, these sentiments began to fade when he learned from his hack driver that the Grand Opera House in town featured a busy schedule of theatrical productions, owing to its proximity to Chicago, Indianapolis, and Cincinnati.[26] From this point on, Ade recalled, he became "an abject slave to the theater and the world of make-believe," never missing a show "no matter how low [his] finances."[27] He also discovered that other Purdue students shared his passion for drama and literature. Moreover, they recognized his talent as a writer and humorist by electing him president of the Irving Literary Society.

Although in the 1880s extracurricular life on American campuses was still in its nascent stages, Ade and McCutcheon belonged to Purdue's chapter of the Sigma Chi fraternity, which served as a base for their social foray into the town of Lafayette.[28] One such excursion, which became something of a ritual after Ade graduated in 1887 and was working for a local newspaper while McCutcheon continued at Purdue, involved the middle-class practice of calling on friends—which in this case meant spending their afternoons visiting eligible young women. Yet instead of engaging in polite conversation, Ade and McCutcheon preferred to sing. Asking their hostesses to pick from a list of 165 song titles they carried on their visits—show tunes, college songs, and hymns—the two men would then belt out the selection.[29] While this was a social trick worthy of two clever college men, it also reveals Ade's and McCutcheon's knowledge and love of popular culture. By singing tunes that residents of Cedar Rapids as well as New York City could recognize, they participated in a steadily developing mass culture that was shaping the tastes and customs of Americans in all regions and locales. Through their performance, they connected with the faraway lands of make-believe that had inflamed their boyhood imaginations and became, like the theatrical troupes that traveled from town to town, citizens of the wider world.

Charismatic and creative, Ade was the trailblazer in these explorations of new territory. To McCutcheon, Ade seemed "an exceptional person"; upon first seeing him at Purdue's obligatory chapel services, he developed something of a crush on the older, more sophisticated student. Years afterward, McCutcheon described the encounter.

An unusual face down among the sophomores—a refined, clean-cut delicately aquiline face—stood out among the surrounding run of rugged, freckled, corn-fed features. Several months later I learned that the possessor of this cameo-like profile was a youth named George Ade. The name appealed to me as much as the face.

He was thin and tall, and wore a sedate blue suit with tight spring bottomed trousers. And he had three outstanding characteristics that made him an inviting subject for caricature—an unusual expanse of head behind the ears, a sweep of strongly marked eyebrows and a striking lack abdominal fullness, described by realists as Slab Belly.[30]

Shaped by his years of experience as a cartoonist, McCutcheon's portrait plays on the difference between boyish college man and the journalist who would eventually stand out among the corn rows of the Midwest. Resisting the invitation to caricature, McCutcheon instead captures Ade's sense of potential and his own attraction to him—an appeal mediated, in retrospect, by the destiny the two men shared.

In his autobiography, *Drawn From Memory,* McCutcheon explains that from the time that he and Ade met at Purdue, "our paths lay intimately together. We were inseparable and people began to associate our names in a Damon and Pythias relationship."[31] Although this legendary story of enduring friendship between two Greek youths has, in recent years, been read as an account of gay love, there is nothing to suggest that McCutcheon, or any of his contemporaries, thought of their relationship in homoerotic terms. Within the conventions of nineteenth-century male friendship, Ade and McCutcheon's friendship could allow for a high degree of affection and intimacy without being deemed "unnatural" by moral arbiters.[32] Indeed, in after-dinner speeches given long after their days at Purdue, both men enjoyed telling audiences that they were so poor when they arrived in Chicago that they had to share a bed in the cheap boardinghouse room that they rented.

Had Ade and McCutcheon been born a generation later, their high jinks together—from the singing of popular tunes to their work as journalists and migrating Hoosiers—might be interpreted as coded performances indicating their participation in gay subculture.[33] But given their increasingly self-conscious adoption of metropolitan ways during the 1890s and 1900s, these collaborations suggest a different kind of drama, oriented around their mutual longing to move beyond Main Street and become part of something bigger than their native homes. That "something" was Chicago, and though Ade and McCutcheon's eventual decision to leave Indiana may be chalked up to ambition and career opportunities, their migration unfolded as a series of performances, in which they anticipated and tested out the new selves they might become once they reached the city.

Yet if Ade and McCutcheon were on their way to fulfilling their personal ambitions and fantasies, they did not necessarily realize it at the time. Despite Ade's avid interests in literature and drama, he had difficulty settling on a line of work. After graduating Purdue, he remained in Lafayette, where he held four jobs over a period of three years. His shortest stint, in a law office, lasted seven weeks. Then he worked at two town newspapers. Though he enjoyed the work, he had difficulty living on the wages ($6 a week) and left for a better offer ($12 a week)—to write advertising copy for a patent medicine company.[34] Ade's sustained exposure to Lafayette clearly influenced the view of the hinterland that he later developed as a reporter for the Chicago *Record;* it broadened his perspective on small-town life and sharpened his attention to human-scaled dramas. But whether this apprenticeship would ever be applied to big-city reporting was another question, since, two years after finishing at Purdue, George Ade gave little indication that he was headed for Chicago.

The impetus for such a move was John McCutcheon's own departure for Chicago. Unlike Ade, McCutcheon seems to have planned to go to Chicago soon after his commencement. Like Ade, McCutcheon addressed his graduating class. While the title of Ade's oration had been "The Future of Letters in the West" (with a special emphasis on Indiana literature), McCutcheon's was "Caricature in Art." Claiming that the spirit of the times was "imminently utilitarian and practical," McCutcheon argued for the newspaper's increased cultural importance (relative to the book) and declaimed the consequent influence of the illustrator. Looking back on this argument years later, McCutcheon doubted whether by then he was considering art as a profession. His actions speak otherwise, however, for he spent the summer studying the Chicago newspapers and preparing a dossier of his work that he could show prospective employers. Late in the summer he left for Chicago.[35]

Starting Out in Chicago

McCutcheon came to Chicago "with $17 in my pocket and not a friend in the city. Up to that time, I had been outside of Indiana only twice in my life. Both were hasty trips to Chicago with Purdue pals."[36] This time his stay was longer, but not as long as he had planned. After checking into a hotel near Dearborn and Madison, not far from the *Chicago Tribune* offices, he called on Horace Taylor, who was an illustrator at the *Chicago Herald.* Taylor, a college graduate and member of Sigma Chi, was a friend of Bob Jacques, a bookseller in Lafayette who had also been a fraternity brother of McCutcheon and Ade's at Purdue. Taylor looked at McCutcheon's work, told him to keep practicing, and suggested he find less expensive lodging. So McCutcheon moved to a boardinghouse on South Wabash—meals and lodging for $6 a week—and worked on his drawing until one day a fellow boarder was shot and the police raided the place. McCutcheon went back to Indiana.[37]

Exactly why McCutcheon went home at this point is unclear. Without a job and given his limited resources, though, he could not have lasted very long in the city—even in a cheap boardinghouse. In his autobiography, he admits that he was "young and green" and that he spent his free time wandering "up and down Michigan Avenue looking at the long, converging rows of gas lamps, and was very lonesome and homesick." Against this picture of the isolated urban migrant, a couple of details stand out. One is the connection McCutcheon established with Horace Taylor. Another is that, despite being friendless, McCutcheon did know people in Chicago. During that first short stay, he spent time in the home of a Lafayette woman who had moved to the city; moreover, a fellow boarder (also a woman) recognized his loneliness and inexperience and treated him kindly.[38]

These incipient feelings of being at home in the city are more evident in a letter McCutcheon wrote to his "Folks" soon after his return to Chicago in October, reassuring them that he was comfortably settled with the Langs, friends who were now living there (Mrs. Lang was a former Lafayette schoolteacher). Although he seems to have felt some guilt about leaving home, he was comfortable enough about his decision to poke fun at his newfound autonomy by humorously noting that he had "enough money to buy ink and paper" and that the Langs had "six children besides myself that are under care." That the Langs lived so far south on Michigan Avenue (the 3000 block) made it difficult for McCutcheon to wander too far from his surrogate family. Still, he could take the streetcar when he wanted to go downtown, and he made good use of his other Indiana connections. Not only was he exploring the city with the brother of a Lafayette friend, but he had seen the "great" hit play "Hoolahgoolah, the Oolah" at the Grand Theater; attended a Halloween party given by Purdue friends on the North Side; and was planning to visit the Hutchisons'—again, family friends—after having lunch at the Grand Pacific Hotel and going to a football game.[39]

McCutcheon also reports on his search for a job. He mentions his Purdue friend Samuel Saltmarsh, who had a "tough time getting work" but "struck it in the Auditor's office of the Santa Fe RR." He referrs to "several other LaF and Purdue folks here, all enjoying good jobs." Then, saving the best for last, and with a coy sense of timing, he announces,

I succeeded in getting on the "News" and commenced work Wednesday. I will stay a couple of weeks before I am put down as permanently settled for they want to see how I work. I am going to do my best. At present they are paying me $20 per week, with a possible raise if I stay. Saturday is the only day that I get off for they do not publish a Sunday paper.[40]

McCutcheon had again taken his samples to Horace Taylor, and apparently his work had improved enough for the illustrator to walk him across the street to the *Daily News* building and introduce him to the director of the art department, William Schmedgten. McCutcheon was offered and accepted a provisional job.[41] In December, when McCutcheon wrote his mother to say he would not be home for Christmas, he did so on stationery supplied by the *Daily News*—"Publisher, Victor F. Lawson"—and with news that assured this position.

I am very sorry that I will not be down, for it is my first Xmas away from home. The big cut I made for the News is bringing me glory. Mr. Lawson has it printed on large heavy cardboard and a copy given to each man on the News—about four hundred. I can think of no way in which his appreciation of my work can be shown. I wish you could see it. It looks a great deal nicer than it did in the common newspaper.[42]

As he notes in his autobiography, this "glory"—the enthusiastic response to a political cartoon depicting Chicago's successful bid to host the 1893 Columbian Exhibition which he had drawn when Schmedgten was out of town—was "a piece of luck which was the outgrowth of conditions I had no part in forming."[43] McCutcheon's triumph was fortuitous, but the circumstances that led to his success were the product of family support, hometown ties, and carefully cultivated Purdue contacts. Amid news of continued success at the *News,* sickness at the Lang's, and assurances that he would help his brother George get a job in the city, McCutcheon informs his family that he and fourteen friends had "effected the organization of the Chicago branch of the Purdue Alumni. We will perhaps have a membership of twenty and expect that it will prove a valuable and beneficial thing for ourselves and our friends who come to Chicago." By February, the organization was in place, and McCutcheon now wrote his mother on stationery bearing the logo of the Chicago Branch of the Purdue Alumni Association.[44]

Like other migrants or immigrants who follow a "chain" of family and friends to a new place, George Ade benefited from the connections that his friend had established in Chicago.[45] Drawn by McCutcheon's "glamorous letters about life in the big city" (as McCutcheon put it), desirous of more substantial writing opportunities, and now without a job, Ade came to Chicago in June. McCutcheon justifiably claimed partial credit for recruiting Ade, since — as Horace Taylor did for him — he introduced his friend to the editorial staff on the *News*. Like McCutcheon, Ade was given a provisional job. And like McCutcheon, he turned it into glory by writing a first-rate story about a steamer that exploded in the Chicago River, an event that none of the other reporters were able to cover. "From that moment," McCutcheon wrote, "he became not *a* but *the* star reporter."[46]

Despite this success, Ade was not completely happy with his prospects. Shortly after his arrival, he wrote to his friend in Lafayette and fellow journalist, Josh Hilderbrand, that he was having a "pleasant time," that he was "anxious to locate here," that he had "one chance to go to work already," and that he was "working on one or two others."[47] Two months later, writing again to Hilderbrand, Ade reports that he liked his now permanent position "first-rate" and that "I am getting some good hard newspaper experience that will be of advantage to me, no matter what business I should ever go into." This hedged endorsement, while evidence of Ade's restless temperament, also reflects a more skeptical view of the city than the reports McCutcheon had sent home. To be sure, Ade enjoyed the theater and took pleasure in reporting on the exploits of mutual friends in Chicago — Harry Kramer selling "bushels of his anti-knockup syringes" — but not in the enthusiastic terms that McCutcheon used with his family. As he suggested to Hilderbrand, he had some reservations about the relentless, perhaps senseless, pace of city life.

So LaFayette is quiet? Well, I don't know but that I would enjoy a little Tippecanoe County quietude and rest after the daily hustle and rustle of Chicago life. This "boom" business, that LaFayette is after, has been overdone here, for the streets are so full of cable-cars, hansoms, drays, express wagons, chippies, policemen, and other public nuisances that a man don't know when he starts down town in the morning, whether he will get back all right or land up in the morgue.[48]

Note that the same factors that (negatively) distinguish Chicago from Tippecanoe County account for the city's similarity to Lafayette. Relatively speaking, Chicago's hustle and bustle exceed the chaos of the small town, yet the disorder of both landscapes stems from a shared spirit of economic boosterism. As we shall see, Ade regularly pointed to this rural-urban continuum in his journalistic writing. But even as he ironically measured urban life along this sliding scale, he left no doubt that Chicago differed significantly from small-town Indiana.

Still, Ade remained in the city, teaming up with McCutcheon to continue the collaborative work they had begun in Lafayette. Soon after Ade's arrival, the two rented a back-hallway bedroom on the third floor in the annex of Bucklen Flats, an apartment building located at the corner of Michigan Avenue and Peck Court, on the south end of the Loop. The tiny apartment lacked a bathroom and a closet, and its sleeping facilities included a double bed that Ade and McCutcheon shared, as well as a pull-out sofa that was frequently occupied by Sigma Chi brothers in town for a visit. Later, as their income improved, they moved to the Near North Side, an area dominated by boardinghouses and hotels. Home to upwardly mobile bachelors, the area was at this time a respectable, middle-class neighborhood wedged between the prosperous Gold Coast to the north, business interests to the south, and an emerging immigrant population to the west. However, this neighborhood was also in transition, and during the time Ade and McCutcheon lived there, the gradual accumulation of inexpensive restaurants, cabarets, and affordable housing made it increasingly attractive to artists and writers, so that by 1900 it had become something of a bohemia. Though the two bachelors stayed in Bucklen Flats for just over a year, they lived together for most of the 1890s in various establishments on the Near North Side.[49]

Known to their fellow journalists as the "Hall Bedroom Twins," Ade and McCutcheon used their small apartment as the base camp for their explorations of the city.[50] Every Saturday, they pawned either McCutcheon's ring or Ade's watch and used the $5 loan to help pay the rent, fund an end-of-the-week meal at a "select" restaurant, or make payments on the suits both men were now buying on time. Redeeming the pawned item for $5.50 on Tuesday (after being paid), they were then free to repeat the transaction the following Saturday.[51] By this survival tactic, they were able to maintain their positions as "men-about-town" and see "everything and every place in Chicago." Without much money—or as McCutcheon humorously put it, "in consequence of a contracted currency system that lacked elasticity"—the pair "lived upon a high moral plane." But all the while, they took comfort thinking "of the ones at home, the envious ones who thought of our gay life in the great city." When they periodically returned to Lafayette for visits, they dressed "conspicuously" in the latest fashion (the clothing purchased on credit) "to show the home folks how well we were getting on in Chicago."[52]

Ade and McCutcheon's prodigal son act was a performance in cultural one-upmanship that rested on long-established resentment and admiration of metropolitan ways. In flaunting their clothes, the young men seemed to acknowledge the ready-made, temporary quality of their new city selves, suggesting to friends and acquaintances in Lafayette that they, too, could cross the barrier separating provincial and urban life—if they had the will and desire. Here, as in many stories of American self-making, the possibility of taking on a new identity and letting go of the old was both a challenge and a threat.

This performance continued at the *Morning News,* where Ade and McCutcheon found an ideal vehicle for developing their perspective on urban-rural relations. As the morning edition of the newspaper owned by Victor F. Lawson, the *News* was not only the largest daily in Chicago, and arguably the most important, but many of its readers came from outside the city. By 1893, the *News* had more than 200,000 subscribers spread throughout the Midwest, an audience whose hinterland perspectives were often matched by the journalists who wrote for them.[53] Indeed, some of Ade and McCutcheon's most successful contemporaries in the newspaper business—Ray Stannard Baker, Will Payne, Brand Whitlock, and others—likewise grew up in small midwestern towns and drew upon these backgrounds in developing their careers. Along with journalistic luminaries like Finley Peter Dunne, Eugene Field, and Opie Read, they wrote in a vernacular style that, according to one historian, "urbanized an already existing frontier newspaper genre."[54] Distinguished by their attention to concrete detail, characterization, humor, and slang, they treated Chicago as if it were part of the provinces and addressed their audience as a village newspaper might, assuming that Chicagoans were interested in the daily goings-on in their neighbors' lives.[55]

In Chicago, as in other nineteenth-century cities, the modern newspaper's broader cultural relevance grew out of its readers' need to know and understand the changing urban landscape around them. By reflecting and commenting upon the facts of city life, by authenticating all that was new and strange—from crime statistics to consumer and leisure culture—newspapers gave their readers a common discourse, addressed their "longing" for identity, and, in a sense, made a community of them.[56] In Chicago, this distinctly modern process took a decidedly ironic turn when reporters interpreted the expansive industrial landscape in a language that provincial newcomers could understand, and all that seemed urban was turned upside down for inspection by small-town and rural onlookers. Although glimmerings of a less personal, perhaps more scientific journalism were evident in the global, sociological perspectives necessitated by the sheer complexity of city life (some of Ray Stannard Baker's reporting moved in this direction), in the 1890s, journalists like Opie Read, whose frontier humor appeared regularly in The Arkansaw Traveler, had the latitude to explore both the objective and subjective dimensions of urban life.[57]

In demeanor and attitude, the journalists who constituted Ade and McCutcheon's social circle affected a seasoned worldliness. As a character in one of Brand Whitlock's novels puts it, Chicago reporters viewed journalism as a "business" rather than a profession and disliked their work for the demands it made on their time and the compromises it required of their writing. Nonetheless, they fairly reveled in the knowledge they gleaned as reporters in Chicago, and took a strange pride in being exposed to the outlandish incidents, whether it was criminal behavior or political corruption, which they regularly witnessed in their work.[58] Reporting the news in late nineteenth-century Chicago led naturally to a tough-guy, philosophical detachment—similar to the noir sensibilities that emerged in the 1930s—which, for a young journalist recently arrived from the sticks and eager to see beyond the supposed pieties of small-town life, could be quite appealing. Although the perspective of the cynical big-city reporter is now something of a cliché, in late nineteenth-century Chicago it offered a compelling way of relating to a disordered urban world.

This style was at the center of the Whitechapel Club, an assortment of Chicago journalists who gathered informally between 1887 and 1894 to drink, tell stories, sharpen wits, criticize literature, and acknowledge the surreal extremities of their working world. Named for the district in London that Jack the Ripper prowled, the group surrounded itself with various death-related artifacts and trophies and, in the most dramatic of its over-the-top activities, cremated the body of a man (at his request) after he killed himself. Ade was a member of this group, and so were Brand Whitlock and Opie Read (McCutcheon was not). At the very least, their participation signified an effort to acknowledge the daily realities of Chicago in a way that they could not in their official duties as reporters. More ambitiously, the Whitechapel Club was about making art and incorporating these realities in some rhetorical structure or transcendent performance. In this respect, its purposes resembled those of the more genteel Little Room and Cliff Dwellers, though its materials—taken from the city streets, and unapologetically realistic—were very different.[59]

Although the Whitechapel Club had nothing to do with hinterland migration, its relentless turning over of accepted truths was consistent with the probing of regional origins that distinguished Ade's and McCutcheon's explorations of city life. True to the spirit of the club, Ade was especially capable of playing the unrepentant hayseed and challenging the pretensions of urban society. At the same time, he was comfortable moving in bourgeois circles, and as his membership in both the Whitechapel Club and the Little Room suggests, he was also able to see Chicago's development through drawing-room windows.

Among this group of journalistic newcomers Ade and McCutcheon stand out, both for their collaborative portrayal of small-town migrants and for their increasingly self-conscious view of themselves as participants in, and observers of, a migratory culture. While their journalistic work was not limited to portraying hinterland-urban relations, Ade and McCutcheon established their journalistic reputations in part by describing this migratory experience to an audience who had participated in it. Both claimed that their sensitivity to the texture and drama of urban life was due to their small-town roots and, by implication, their ability to see the city in terms of small-scale human interaction. The column they began working on in 1893, roughly three years after their arrival at the *News*—entitled Stories of the Streets and of the Town—shows them adopting this perspective in carefully drawn explorations of urban culture. With Ade writing the prose and McCutcheon contributing the illustrations, the column became a centerpiece in Chicago's golden age of journalism.

In the City but Not of It

It was entirely fitting that Ade and McCutcheon's professional work together began at the 1893 Columbian Exposition. For the thousands of midwesterners (and countless Americans) drawn to the phantasmagoric landscape by the lake, the fair dramatized the wonders of civilization—and

Chicago. Assigned by the *Record*'s managing editor, Charles H. Dennis, to cover the fair during and after its construction, McCutcheon viewed the finished landscape as "the most beautiful man-made spectacle the world had ever seen, complete, serene, and incomparably lovely." More beautiful than the Indiana State House, the Court House in Lafayette, or the artificial wax flowers he purchased during his visit to Chicago as a college student, and more grand than "the long converging gas lamps that met at a vanishing point far down on Michigan Avenue" (which he beheld during his first attempt to settle in Chicago) or "the 36 seater Barber Shop at the Palmer House," the fairgrounds were a fitting culmination of a Hoosier boyhood spent dreaming of faraway lands. Proudly, McCutcheon took his younger brother, Ben, on a tour of the fair when he visited the city, but was disappointed "that he passed by these wonderful buildings more beautiful than the world had ever seen assembled in one place and never uttered a single gosh." Like the urban "pinhead" that Henry Blake Fuller praised Ade for portraying, Ben was "determined not to be a jay, or to act like one, or show astonishment at anything he saw." [60]

Ben, however, was finally not so different from his brother. For it was resistance to jaw-dropping awe and his determination to see the World's Fair as not altogether different from what he had seen back in Indiana that allowed John McCutcheon to make himself at home in Chicago. This resistance, which ironically was but another manifestation of wonder, exemplifies the proprietary pride that fairgoers and migrants shared. If the fair represented the civilization that Americans deserved by right, then Chicago belonged to the Midwest—to anyone who wanted to migrate—not just to Chicagoans per se. Though McCutcheon later acknowledged his sentimental attachment to the wonders of the fair, at the time, he played the part of the streetwise reporter to his younger brother.

Although the two columns of print that the *Record* set aside each day for the two young journalists to cover the exposition—aptly titled "All Roads Lead to the World's Fair"—appeared anonymously, Ade wrote most of the copy and McCutcheon contributed many of the accompanying illustrations. The "Roads" column regularly assumed the visitor's point of view; for instance, its May 13, 1893, report portrays a rural tourist who seemed to have been "oppressed" by the sights.

To sympathize with the old gentleman in the electric train you must remember that he had been for a good many years taking in a daily landscape of stubble-field, orchard and straight country roads. His experience had taught him that a red

two-story hay press was a big building. To him the huddle of huckster stands at the
county fair made a pretty lively spectacle. Then he was put on a train and rushed
into Chicago. With the roar of wheels still in his ears and the points of the compass
hopelessly mixed he found himself being fed into the 60th Street gate with a lot of
strange people. A few minutes later the entire Exposition fell on him and he collapsed. He couldn't carry it all at one load and keep up a conversation at the same
time. To-day he will be able to feel the ground under his feet and locate some of the
principal buildings.[61]

Additional stories in the *Record* indicate that the old gentleman's reaction to the fair was more typical than not. There is the "homesick" immigrant who finds comfort in visiting the German village "to recall halcyon
days in the Fatherland." There are the hundreds of midwesterners who
end up at their own state buildings looking for some sign of home. The
Indiana people who visit their state building "are pleased with the homelike arrangements for their comfort"; they read hometown newspapers and
find "a pleasant loafing-place for hoosiers." At the South Dakota State
Building, citizens of that state chat in rural dialect—"I swan, is that you?
What are you doin' here?"—without having to worry about being "sand-
bag[ged]" and robbed. Each visitor gains "a peculiar satisfaction to know
that the state building belongs to him as much as to any one else. He has a
right to take a nap on the sofa or sit tilted back on the veranda all day long.
Then when he looks in the register and finds that other people from his
county are in town it takes away that lonely feeling."[62] With varying degrees
of displacement and nostalgia, the sightseers described in these reports
ironically find signs of home in a landscape that initially appears inaccessible
to human-scaled encounters. In the "All Roads" column, Ade offered a view
of the Fair with which migrants to the city, permanent or not, could easily
identify.

   In fact, the column was so successful that when the fair concluded,
Charles Dennis informed Ade and McCutcheon that "they might use [the
editorial page] every day, subject to my supervision, in any way they
liked."[63] So began Stories of the Streets and of the Town: two Hoosiers set
loose in the city to continue their roving accounts (fig. 7).

   Ade established a voice that was both personal and detached. Although
his attention to mundane details seemed to place him on the scene as an intimate observer, he invariably adopted an omniscient, third-person point of
view within a narrative structure that resembled fiction, thus endearing him

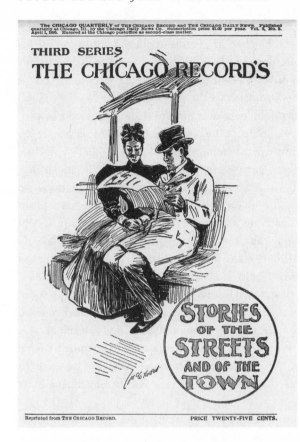

FIGURE 7
John McCutcheon's
cover design for the
Chicago *Record*'s
book version of the
column Stories of the
Streets and of the
Town (1895). (From
John McCutcheon,
*John McCutcheon's
Book* [Chicago: Caxton
Club, 1948]; author's
collection)

to writers such as William Dean Howells, Henry Blake Fuller, and Theodore
Dreiser, who were likewise concerned with developing realistic portrayals of
urban life.

While these articles are too numerous and varied to be easily summarized, many point to the dynamic, frequently ironic presence of "country"
in the city. One early story, "Her Visit to Chicago," focuses on the visit of
a Mrs. Latimer to her son John and his wife, who live in Chicago.
Mrs. Latimer is visiting from John's hometown of Birdville, Ohio (a real
place), which Ade describes as "neither village nor city, although possessing
the virtues of each." John Latimer represents a type that appears frequently
in Ade's reporting: an "eminently respectable" migrant who has thrived in
Chicago but whom the city has not "spoil[ed]." He has a family, a good
job, and a social position. "Therefore," Ade observes, "he was more than

willing that his mother should come and investigate and learn just what her
son had accomplished. He had a feeling that Birdville did not appreciate his
success." Although John does not long for home, he nevertheless brings
Birdville to Chicago in order to claim the fatted calf that goes to local boys
who have made good in the outside world.

Ade makes it clear that John measures the world and his success by provincial standards—expectations, as his very coming to Chicago suggests,
that begin with the promise of urban migration. But his mother's visit does
not have the desired effects, since she refuses to be impressed by any display
of urban pretension or to acknowledge that Chicago has anything on
Birdville. When her daughter-in-law—a Chicago native—takes her into society and Mrs. Latimer mentions she is from Birdville, her hostess (a society
"leader") condescendingly calls it a "charming place" and says she "dearly
love[s] the country." Bridling at the idea that Birdville is "country"—it has
twenty thousand inhabitants, old families, colleges, and literary societies—
Mrs. Latimer asks her hostess where she grew up. This is a bold question,
Ade explains, as "Everyone in society knew that the leader had romped
away her girlhood around the country stores and jack oaks of an Illinois way
station, but not one ventured in ordinary conversation, to go more than ten
years back into history." The leader's answer underscores her amnesia: "It
was some queer little place, I believe. Really, I can hardly remember a thing
about it."[64]

This version of Chicago history in the making features selective genealogy and class power combining to create a heritage worthy of a great city. Especially worth noting is how this constructed past depends on the suppression of small-town/rural origins and how Ade's subjects negotiate, or fail to
negotiate, this suppression. Although not alone in drawing attention to
American migrants who left their past behind, Ade brought the tensions of
internal migration into public discourse, dramatizing for an extensive readership how regional connections figured in Chicago's emergent cultural hi-
erarchy. Like foreign immigrants adapting to American ways, Ade's newcomers strive to fit into the city. At the same time, he emphasizes the
persistence of small-town perspectives in the seemingly urban order. The
society leader in the Latimer story reveals her village background by disso-
ciating it from her present urban identity; John Latimer exhibits his by
dramatizing the distance he has traveled from his small-town origins; and
his mother reminds everyone of how close the provinces still are. Though
Mrs. Latimer's democratic attitude apparently distinguishes Birdville values

from urban culture, the story itself takes place in Chicago. In other words, this triangular drama— of a Chicago native (John's wife), a small-town resident (his mother), and two urban migrants (John and the hostess)—is less about the difference between Birdville and Chicago and more about the mix of regional tensions that constitutes urban identity.

Because Ade's subjects are often respectable, genteel, and democratic, scholars have stressed his representation of Chicago's burgeoning middle class.[65] Yet if he constructs hinterland migrants in class terms, he also inverts this relation so that class status becomes subordinate to regional identity. For instance, in "Effie Whittlesy," one of Ade's best-known articles, Ed Wallace, another successful small-town migrant, comes home from work one day to discover that the servant his wife has hired is a fellow townsman (and formerly his family's hired girl). To the dismay of his wife— a Baltimore native—Wallace treats Effie as a friend and equal. At first Wallace hesitates, but then "the panorama of his life was rolled backward" and the "democratic spirit" of his small-town upbringing asserts itself, leading Ade to wonder whether this was "an old settlers' reunion or a quiet family dinner." Although the moment does not last, the shared history of the small town levels class distinctions. Wallace remembers he is "a child of the soil, who worked his way through college and came to the city in a suit of store clothes"—in fact, he still subscribes to his hometown paper— and Mrs. Wallace recalls that this small-town outlook is what attracted her to him in the first place. As for Effie, her role as a catalyst of small-town democracy is left unresolved. Determined to underscore their connection to the hinterland and their hometown values, Wallace encourages her to visit her folks back home and, if she returns to Chicago, to come to his house as "an old acquaintance—a visitor, not a servant."[66]

The migrants featured in the Birdville sketch and "Effie Whittlesy" create communities that, though shaped by memory and emotion, have a dramatic, living presence in Chicago culture. Given concrete expression through Effie, the internal emotions that tie Ed Wallace to the provinces become the occasion for human exchange and action. Here nostalgia is a vital force, capable of undermining class barriers with face-to-face democratic values. In this respect, Ade's recognition of the emotional ties that unite people links his writing to what Sydney Bremer calls Chicago's "residential novels"—fiction that highlights the importance of community and family life. More often than not, Ades's migrants avoid the isolation of individualistic self-making by drawing on connections to their former provincial homes.[67]

In many ways, Ade's presentation of midwestern migrants as a distinct social group resembles the treatment usually accorded immigrant groups. But
even if he had the term at his disposal, Ade likely would have resisted calling
these transplants ethnics, since doing so would have qualified their Ameri-
canness. As McCutcheon observed of his own profession, the cartoonist "is
at liberty to lampoon Americans all he wishes, because Americans are a
rather uncertain mass that lacks cohesion" but must avoid targeting ethnic
groups, since they "are quick to resent any slur against their nationalities."
Certainly, Stories of the Streets and of the Town tended to be free of caricature; however, the claim that the native born are an "uncertain mass" does
not ring true, since McCutcheon here implicitly—and later in these remarks, explicitly—distinguishes the American "race" from other ethnic
groups.[68] More important, the apparent absence of definable features among
native-born citizens gave the cartoonist reason to find a discursive means of
transforming this uncertain mass into a recognizable group. Ironically, Ade
and McCutcheon's gentle brand of nativism led them to underscore the dis-
tinguishing characteristics of white Americans—in short, their ethnicity.

The subtext for these representations was Chicago's rapidly growing immigrant population. Ade wrote about the city's foreign-born residents but
not in a comprehensive or self-conscious manner. In the Stories column, migrants and immigrants remained mostly separate. *In Babel,* his 1903 collection of *News* and *Record* writings, reveals his scope; the dramas of one story
rarely intersect with those of another. Still, they sometimes parallel one another. For instance, in an early piece entitled "Several Square Miles of
Transplanted Poland," Ade suggests that the West Chicago Polish community (located in and around the streets of West Division, Noble, Blue Island,
Milwaukee, and Clybourn) was but an extension of the Old World. But the
limits of this optimistic vision are evident in "Cooped Up in Town," an 1897
column about an American-born small-town manufacturer who searches the
city for his migrant brother. When, after riding the cars to his brother's address, Greenlee Banford finds himself on the city's outskirts (in the middle
of the prairie) and stops at a house to ask for directions, according to Greenlee a "big, dark-complected woman" came out and "jabbered at me in some
language I couldn't understand."[69] Walking to the next house—a half mile
away—he sees his nephew Thaddeus, and thus discovers Silas's home.

These two pioneer households clustered together at the ragged edge of
an expanding city are separated by skin color, language, and culture. All
these differences separate Greenlee from the immigrant, align him more

closely with his migrant brother, and accentuate the story's point of view. Seen almost entirely through the eyes of Greenlee, who is describing his Chicago visit to the folks back home in East Sirocco, "Cooped Up in Town" underscores the ongoing connection between town and country while disrupting the hinterland's conventional view of Chicago. Silas's relatives believe he and his family will "never be happy in town," especially since they'll be "huddled in with the swarm of strangers in the new and wicked Babylon." But Silas likes his job in the electric-car barn, and while his wife is "lonesome," it is not because they are "packed into one o'them big flat buildin's like mackerel in a kit" and do not know "who or what [their] next-door neighbor is." [70]

In "Looking For a Friend," a Stories article published in 1895, Ade offers a textbook description of the anonymity that faced newcomers from places such as Mathersville, which, like "every other town with a radius of 500 miles from Chicago," had "contributed its colony to increase the growing population of the city." Friends back in Mathersville, Ade goes on to observe, could not understand how former neighbors could become "hopelessly lost and diluted in the mass of 1,500,000 persons." Although some Mathersville migrants eventually find one another, they discover that "the loneliest spot on earth is in the thick of a multitude of strangers." [71] In "Cooped Up in Town," Chicago's vast scale also impedes face-to-face interaction, but there Ade turns his previous notion of urban alienation inside out by suggesting that rural spaces, not urban crowding, are responsible for the wife's isolation. He leaves intact East Sirocco's condescending views of immigrants — and, like his narrator, does not push past superficial knowledge to challenge the urban-rural boundaries taken for granted by readers on both sides of the divide.

Ade's fascination with the tracts of open prairie within the city limits suggests that he, and perhaps some of his readers, were not quite comfortable with boosters' "windy" insistence on Chicago's metropolitan greatness. Greenlee Banford cannot believe he is still in Chicago when he rides the streetcar north from Milwaukee Avenue on the Oregon Avenue line. He tells the folks back home that "[t]he houses kep' gettin' farther apart, and for awhile we was runnin' right through the open prairie. Then there'd be a row of houses and then some more prairie. I begin to be suspicious." [72] Chicago's unfinished state is expressed in unsettling incidents, as for instance when a man is murdered on a street corner and his body later torn apart by prairie wolves. Such episodes dramatize the natural wildness of Chicago's urban frontier, the very shape of which, Ade suggests, is at odds with traditional notions of city space. For whenever a man travels north, south, or west on a streetcar, "he is seldom able to point out to his car-mate where the city leaves off and the country begins." He has no idea when he has left the city, since "the imaginary line has no artificial landmarks to show its course."[73] From this vantage point, late nineteenth-century Chicago was indeed nature's metropolis—a city whose rural hinterland often seemed very close at hand.

Thus exposed, the city limits seem to be a subjective, human contrivance rather than an authentic dividing line. Pushing inward from that boundary, Ade uses Stories of the Streets and of the Town to show the patchwork nature of Chicago's "urban" landscape and, in his most deconstructive perceptions, suggests that what seems to be town might really be country. On the other hand, Ade in no way claims that hinterland and city are interchangeable. Size, scale, and variety of human experience—the spectacle of urban life—clearly distinguishes Chicago from Lafayette or Kentland.

Time and again, Ade puts a face to urbanization by portraying migrants who cross the line into Chicago and inhabit a space that is *in* the city but not *of* it. Although he delights in portraying young men who suppress their hinterland backgrounds as they venture into society, he does not focus exclusively on the middle classes.[74] In "Clarence Was Not at the Station," Ade tells the story of a country girl who arrives in Chicago expecting to be met by a young man who, during a visit to her hometown, promised to marry her. Instead, she is befriended by a streetwise hack driver who buys her a ticket home. The more comical "How Jasper Swift Came and Saw and Went Home" follows a clueless jay who comes to Chicago but soon goes home. There, Ade narrates through a description of artifacts ranging from betting chits to a delinquent hotel bill to a railroad ticket home.[75] These stories run the migration narrative in reverse—toward pathos and failure—while still affirming the strong connections between Chicago and its hinterland.[76]

Beyond Realism

At its best, Ade's writing from the mid-1890s verged on a complex form of realism that reflected both the physical and social landscape of Chicago and the psychological experience of crossing into urban territory. Noting these emphases and the migratory perspective that shaped them, William Dean Howells confided to Ade that "Effie Whittlesy is the truest and humanest study of life I know" and praised him in print for showing how "the American small town which has often shrunken into the American City lives again here in its characteristic personality."[77]

Yet by the early 1900s, Ade and McCutcheon had both evolved toward a more exaggerated, expressionistic style. In this change, Ade was the leader—indeed, McCutcheon credited him with guiding his early work on the *News*—and the cartoonist followed him toward a more humorous form of representation, a shift that led Ade to his widely read column "Fables in Slang" and first taste of national fame.[78]

Describing the transition in typical fashion, Ade joked that "I went to bed a realist, wearing sack-cloth pajamas, and I awoke as the comical cuss who wrote snappy fables." Borrowing the fable pattern of Aesop and John Gay, and inserting slang and capital letters ("without reference to rules"), Ade created cameos of social scenes and types, which he always ended with a moral.[79] For example, "The Fable of Handsome Jethro, Who Was Simply Cut Out to Be a Merchant" begins like this:

An Illinois Squab came home from Business College with a pair of Tan Shoes big enough for a Coal Miner. When he alighted from the depot one of Ezry Folloson's Dray Horses fell over, stricken with the Cramp Colic. The usual Drove of Prominent Citizens who had come down to see that the Train got in and out all right backed away from the Educated Youth and Chewed the Tobacco in Shame and Abashment. They knew that they did not belong on the same Platform with One who had been up yender in Chicago for goin' on Twelve weeks finding out how to be a Business Man. By Heck!

This fable turns on familiar Ade material: a provincial youth discovers Chicago and returns home with cosmopolitan airs, which his townsmen simultaneously envy and scorn. Jethro gets his comeuppance at the climax of the story when, after refusing to do chores on his father's farm, he storms off to town and gets a job at a "Five and Ten-Cent Store," where he remains for the next ten years, accumulating only nineteen dollars in capital. Unable to balance his desires and his resources, Jethro unwittingly initiates a story of reverse migration, while Ade's conclusion—"Moral: *Drink Deep, or Cut Out the Pierian Spring Altogether*"—suggests what an urban migrant must do if he wants to remain in the city.[80]

That the fables are filled with such dramas of hothouse regional tension prompted Howells to observe that Ade found hinterland migrants in the city "striving for alien worldliness" and visited their "origins with the same un-sparing vision."[81] These subjects differed little from what Ade saw in Stories of the Streets and of the Town; but the scope and angle of the vision changed in his writing of the fables. In brief, Ade turned to caricature, exaggerating details that in his Stories he had been so careful to present in scaled relation to the urban landscape. In the case of figures like Jethro, this meant focusing disproportionately on the size and color of his shoes, not gratuitously, but rather to highlight his out-of-kilter search for metropolitan grandeur. Focusing in this way on physical features served, ironically, to emphasize the migrant's inner features: his desires, ambitions, and emotions. The fable became a kind of prose cartoon, its distortions comically illustrating abstract truths.

By the late '90s, McCutcheon's style, too, had changed, likewise moving closer to caricature as he gave up illustration for cartoon drawing. Significantly, he characterized this development as Ade did: "Up to that point I had been a realist. Now I had to be made over into something requiring whimsy and, if possible, humor." Expressed in the passive voice, McCutcheon's explanation alludes to his editor's request that he begin drawing cartoons for the *Record* and to the influence of Ade, who "helped materially" in the transition and "provided the excellent suggestions that gave my early cartoons whatever distinction they had."[82]

Not surprisingly, Ade offered concrete advice when McCutcheon was illustrating his prose. In a pencil-written note of December 1912—roughly fifteen years after the two had begun their move from realism to more stylized forms of representation—Ade describes the pictures his friend might draw for the fable he was writing. Sent to Chicago from Lafayette, where Ade was awaiting the completion of a new house, the letter exemplifies the nuance with which the two friends now discussed the migration narrative.

My Dear Mac:

I will send you the Fable by the end of the week. The story, briefly, will be as follows:

Young man living in small town (not village) starts to city. Parents burden him with advice and warnings. Picture might be a burlesque treatment of the familiar "Breaking home ties"—His parents think of the city as a net-work of traps and pitfalls. This might be a picture. Their conception of city life. He meets college friends in the metropolis and is drawn into the new movement for social reform, civic cleansing, settlement endeavor, bringing Maeterlinck to the masses etc. etc. One of his mad diversions is the symphony concert. This will make a picture. Showing him sitting entranced among the Brahmites and Peer Gynters. While he is in the city the small town becomes infected with the present provincial craze to assume metropolitan airs. A club is opened—also country club. Natives pride themselves on learning all the improprieties of urban life such as bridge for money, new mixed drinks, the tango and boisterous rag music. The pictures will suggest themselves. After a long absence he returns to find his parents all tangled up with the flesh-pots and the jack-pots. He gives up his job in the city and comes home to save them. One picture might show him horror-stricken at the Belshazzar cabaret in a drawing room back home. This is rather meagre but it may help you to get some ideas and pencil them. I will send the whole thing as soon as possible.—The house is coming on rapidly. Will keep you informed so that you may come and see it when it is ready.[83]

Even before Ade had written the fable, he envisaged the illustration: McCutcheon could juxtapose the parents' moralized, old-fashioned view of the city with the son's discovery of modern, Europeanized conceptions of urban living, and then he could return to the hometown and portray the parents' embrace of the new and the son's hysterical reaction to their conversion. In imagining the parents' corruption, Ade's proposal turns Jethro on his head—only to set him right side up by making him the prig and the butt of the fable's moral. Writing in 1912, Ade had little difficulty highlighting the impact of urban popular culture on the hinterland—in ironically comic terms—though he took pains to emphasize that this fable is set in a small town and not a village.

Ade's migration narrative thus turns back upon itself. But just as important as the actual plotting is how Ade communicates the story to McCutcheon. For one, he did not have to explain that he wanted McCutcheon's cartoons to dramatize abstract concepts; the references to Hovenden's famed painting and Materlinck make that point. Second, Ade's suggestion that McCutcheon "burlesque" Hovenden relies on a visual vocabulary for rejecting sentimental notions of breaking home ties. Closer to McCutcheon's craft than his own, the plan for illustration was itself a series of scenes caricaturing the progress of nostalgia: in short, Ade writing as a cartoonist.

In 1912, Ade and McCutcheon were clearly a long way from the realism they practiced in the 1890s. Their stylistic evolution had given them a new language for representing urban-rural relations. But style alone does not explain Ade's proposal to parody the breaking of home ties, nor does it account for McCutcheon's apparent willingness to caricature Hovenden's painting. Behind the evolution was a changed relation to the migration experience. Although migration had been Ade and McCutcheon's theme since arriving in Chicago, in the early years their proximity to the experience had disposed them to treat the process of home-leaving with sympathy and respect. Fifteen years in and out of Chicago had established a certain emotional distance, allowing them to aestheticize this subject and transform their documentary point of view.

Economic and social mobility had much to do with this new perspective. By the turn of the century, both men were independently enjoying successful careers. After McCutcheon's departure for the Philippines in 1897, their collaborative work on the *Record* ended. In 1900 Ade, too, left the *Record*; shortly thereafter, his fables went into national syndication, bringing him between $500 and $1,000 a week, and he began writing dramas and musicals. By 1904 he was splitting time between his rooms at the Chicago Athletic Club and a country home he had built in Brook, Indiana. In 1903, three years after returning from his prolonged stint abroad, McCutcheon had also vastly improved his position by moving over to the *Chicago Tribune,* where he made a beginning salary of $250 a week.[84] Both migrants had "made it," and their arrival was evident in the expressive work they continued to do together.

Consider, for instance, *Captain Fry's Birthday Party,* a play they collaborated on for the Little Room, a social club founded in the late 1890s whose members discussed cultural issues with a sense of humor. In 1903, the club included Chicago's social, artistic, and professional elite: Jane Addams, Henry Blake Fuller, Harriet Monroe, Will Payne, Melville Stone, Edith Wyatt, Ade, and McCutcheon. It brought together old and new Chicago, urban natives from prominent families as well as newcomers such as Ade, McCutcheon, Payne, and Addams.

Though Ade wrote the script for the play, *Captain Fry's Birthday Party* was based on a cartoon series that McCutcheon had begun at the *Record* and continued to publish in the *Tribune.* In the series, McCutcheon dramatized the daily goings-on of Bird Center, Illinois, a town name he borrowed from one of Ade's fables. Still, he maintained that the characters featured in Bird Center—for instance, the town minister, banker, Civil War veteran, and several eligible young ladies—are "types which I had known during my experience in a small town." They are "nice people, genuine and generous, and their social circle is one into which any one gifted with good instincts and decency may enter."[85] This claim of realism found support from his audience, in particular from Brand Whitlock, the journalist-turned-novelist who had returned to Ohio to practice Progressive politics. Whitlock wrote McCutcheon from Toledo, where he was serving a term as mayor and reading the *Tribune* daily, to say "you have caught the very essence and spirit of our life here in the Middle West, and have portrayed it with an honesty that appeals especially to a rabid realist like me. I have often wished that I could write a novel with such good, kind, provincial people in it as you get into the Bird Center series — such real human people — but I throw up my hands; you have already done the job." Whitlock also praised a set of cartoons — serially titled *The Boy in Springtime, The Boy in Summertime,* and so on — which had appeared in the *Record.* Whitlock compared these scenes to *A Boy's Town,* William Dean Howells's study of an earlier generation: "his boy and yours are pretty much the same, which goes to show the universality and truth of the realist's art."[86]

Despite Whitlock's claims of realism, the Bird Center drawings are closer to what McCutcheon called caricature. Although the images of the town green and parlor gatherings as well as the accompanying text identify Bird Center as a late nineteenth-century midwestern village, the human faces lack identifying features. More cartoonish than objectively realistic, they are icons whose meaning depends on what the reader brings to the image. This combination of realism and iconic abstraction made the town as much a concept as an identifiable place.[87] It allowed viewers to reconstruct their own hinterland lives — past or present — within a culturally familiar but geographically abstract environment (fig. 8). So for Whitlock, Bird Center was both a recognizable town and the very essence of midwestern life. It was also home to "good, kind, provincial people," that category of citizens which regionalists like Ade, McCutcheon, and Whitlock had worked to recognize and construct. To the extent that Whitlock's reaction — and audience response in general — derived from the memory of growing up in a small town, McCutcheon's retrospective vision had the potential of creating a community of readers based on nostalgia.

Chicago's cultural elite followed the instructions on their Little Room invitation and, on January 30, 1904, "metamorphosed into natives of Bird Center." Their guests also came "in the character and garb of Bird Centerites."[88] In assuming roles in this imagined community, the Little Roomers

FIGURE 8 From John McCutcheon's Bird Center cartoons (1904). (From John McCutcheon, *John McCutcheon's Book* [Chicago: Caxton Club, 1948]; author's collection)

drew upon symbols and rituals of small-town life that, simply by reading the newspaper, most Chicagoans would have recognized. When urban natives and newcomers donned costumes and performed their roles as Bird Centerites, they mimicked the ethnic identity that recent midwestern migrants routinely experienced, acknowledged the contributions that

FIGURE 9   Cast of *Captain Fry's Birthday Party*. (George Ade Papers, the Newberry Library)

small-town migrants had made to Chicago, and perhaps most important, designated Main Street as a touchstone of distinctly American values (fig. 9). Moreover, these nostalgic reenactments demonstrated how hinterland ethnicity—being white, native born, and of provincial origin—was hard to separate from issues of social and class power.

The Little Room drama signified the privileged place the small town would play in cosmopolitan twentieth-century American life. Located somewhere between the objectively rendered landscape of the small town and abstract, expressionistic parodies of that landscape, Bird Center, in all its renditions, emphasized the provincial antecedents of urban culture. Contrary to Whitlock's claims, its hold on reality was only provisional, since the Little Roomers enacted a social reality that migrant Chicagoans had already abandoned. Ironically, *Captain Fry's Birthday Party* resembled the ethnic literature of foreign immigrants, since its concept of "home" had more to do with what the migrant now longed to see than what home actually was. Although the comic antics that characterized the Little Roomers' performance may suggest that there was little at stake in these cultural politics, the humor affirmed the migrant's hybrid identity as a Main Street Chicagoan. At least for Ade and McCutcheon, the joke could be quite serious. The play was their life; performing in it was an autobiographical act. Behind the burlesque lay a commitment to Hoosier ties, which the play's generic picture of the small town both acknowledged and obscured.

Exiles in Suckerland

As provincials-turned-urban-insiders, Ade and McCutcheon celebrated their success with fellow Hoosiers in the Indiana Society of Chicago. Just how many hypothetical Hoosiers participated in these exercises is impossible to say, though the society thrived. During the first twenty years of its existence, at least three hundred people attended every annual banquet. In 1940, its twenty-ninth dinner, which celebrated McCutcheon's seventieth birthday, included 1,260 guests; thirty years later, the Indiana Society of Chicago held its fifty-sixth annual dinner and still seemed to be going strong. Along the way, the society generated hundreds of souvenir programs, gag pamphlets, and other ephemera; through Bobbs-Merrill, it brought out twelve volumes of original Hoosier literature (with works by Ade, McCutcheon, Marjorie Benton Cooke, Kin Hubbard, George Barr McCutcheon, James Whitcomb Riley, and Gene Stratton-Porter) as well as a directory of notable Indianans entitled *Who's Hoosier;* and it arranged the publication of sheet music for such songs as "Sleepy Little Town in the Brown County Hills!" which were performed at the society's annual celebrations.[89]

The purpose of these dinners, as Ade announced at the second annual banquet, held at the Auditorium Hotel on December 11, 1906, was "to glorify the state in which we were born, and to gloat over adjoining states." The Hoosiers managed this objective at the first meeting, also held at the Auditorium Hotel, by packing the speakers' table with such luminaries as publisher S. S. McClure, Judge Kennesaw Mountain Landis, Notre Dame president Father Cavanaugh, Purdue president Winthrop Stone, guest of honor Senator Albert J. Beveridge, and Ade and McCutcheon.[90] Echoing the drama played out by the Little Room and the village scenes depicted in McCutcheon's cartoons, Beveridge celebrated Indiana as the home of "the average American," while the writer Meredith Nicholson, who continued to live in the state, characterized it as a "home" where "American traditions *still* are realized in daily life and living."[91] Here Beveridge and Nicholson implied that the more the rest of the nation changed through modernization and immigration, the more Indiana became America's native "home."

As cofounders of the society and mainstays in the organization's early development, Ade and McCutcheon worked hard to promote the inherent—and paradoxical—virtues of being a Hoosier and a migrant. In this sense, their shared work, while lacking the intense self-consciousness of literary modernism, nonetheless marked a new note in the construction of Hoosier/urban identity. The creation of the society and the annual banquets and meetings suggest that the ad hoc gatherings of Hoosiers—similar to the groups of migrants described in Stories of the Streets and of the Town—eventually grew into a self-acknowledged community. Similarly, by embracing their Hoosier identity, Ade and McCutcheon affirmed their participation in the same migratory culture they represented. Together, authors and subjects collaborated in establishing the Indiana Society.

As for the gag invitations and stunts that highlighted the Hoosier ties of transplanted Chicagoans (the Fatted Calf invitation is only one example), in the end the Indiana Society seems cartoonish. Its identity was conceptual—flexible enough to contain the hyphenated contradictions of small-town and rural people living in, and helping build, modern Chicago. These tensions fueled the society's ironic, self-congratulating sense of having made it in the big city, prompted their campy, sometimes edgy assertion of being from the sticks, and informed the production of their annual spectacles, which were perhaps more like the Little Room's staging of Bird Center than any foreign immigrant society's celebration of ethnic roots. Wayward Hoosiers were more provincial than ethnic—more provincialized than ethnicized—since they had options that most immigrants lacked. Most important, they could go home.

As George Ade acknowledged at the Indiana Society's first banquet in 1905, smart men did leave Indiana—and they did so to make their fortune in a city whose opportunities were there for the taking. Speaking before the 375 transplanted Hoosiers, Ade recalled his arrival in a Chicago

surcharged with Hoosier exiles—men who were here not because they wanted to leave Indiana, but because the population up here could be worked more easily than the bright native article down home. You know it has been said that a great many men who are Hoosiers by birth are suckers by instinct. And so we who are true to the old State cannot blame you for remaining here in Chicago, although

I trust that all of you are following my example and if you succeed in separating the Chicago public from any part of its revenues, that you will invest your ill gotten gains in Indiana.[92]

According to this view, the exiles who comprised the Indiana Society were ambitious men who had no choice but to leave home, so hemmed in were they by canny Hoosiers, so drawn were they by Chicago's economic opportunities, its gullible citizenry, and, of course, their own desire to succeed. This notion of migrant identity has less to do with roots back home (though Indiana-ness remains an inherent virtue) than with a process of self-making that linked Main Street to Chicago at the very moment of the migrant's birth. According to Ade, Hoosier migrants did indeed possess a hyphenated identity; they were "Hoosier-Suckers."[93] In uniting these terms, he referred both to the economic snares facing greenhorns in the city, and to a long-standing nickname for Illinois residents. As early as the 1830s, state settlers were called "suckers," after the migrating fish that flourished in Illinois rivers. Not exactly a compliment, the term also implied that settlers were easy marks. It is this sense of the word that Ade evoked and then reclaimed.[94] On the one hand, Chicago Hoosiers were to be admired for separating Illinois residents from their cash. On the other hand, having now become residents of Suckerland, they ran the risk of turning native—and becoming fools themselves.

No fool himself, George Ade went back to Indiana 1904, using the farm he purchased in his home county of Newton and his status as a successful prodigal son to conduct further prose explorations of faraway lands and small-town landscapes. Still, Ade never really left the orbit of Chicago, often returning to his adopted city while maintaining a busy travel schedule.

For his part, John McCutcheon stayed in Chicago and became a figure beloved by Suckers and Hoosiers alike. In 1917, at the age of forty-six, he married Evelyn Shaw, daughter of architect Howard Shaw, and moved to the northern suburb of Lake Forest, commuting into the city and his position at the *Chicago Tribune*. Just months before his wedding, McCutcheon had realized one of his lifelong fantasies when he purchased a small island in the Bahamas, which he called Treasure Island.[95] Still, like Ade, he remained a son of the middle border to the end, always making it clear in his art that the origins of his success and the longing that drove his success lay somewhere in the hinterlands.

5

THE PLACE OF NOSTALGIA

In 1899, Theodore Dreiser took a passage from George Ade's *Fables in Slang* and pasted it on his own manuscript. Years later, when a reporter told him that Dreiser had plagiarized his work in writing *Sister Carrie* (1900), Ade responded with characteristic wit and generosity. "While some of us have been building chicken coops, or possibly, bungalows, Mr. Dreiser has been creating skyscrapers." He was honored to be part of Dreiser's work and "simply flattered" that the novelist thought well enough of his writing to use it. After all, Ade noted, "Theodore Dreiser was born in Indiana and we other Hoosiers are very proud of him." [1]

This was not the first time Dreiser had turned to Ade for help. Shortly after he began working on the *Chicago Globe* in 1892, Dreiser was assigned to cover local social venues, one of which was the Washington Park Race Track. New to the job, Dreiser arrived at the track with little idea as to how he should proceed. But as chance would have it, Ade was there also, working the event for the *Chicago Daily News*, and Dreiser asked the already established reporter for advice. "I'll tell you what to do," Ade said. "Look back in the files of your paper and find the last race meeting at this park. Then see how that was done. They're all the same. All you have to do is write in the names of the horses running today and their owners' names. That will be what your copy reader will want anyway. Besides, you can get it all out of the first afternoon edition of the *News*. I am going to telephone that. Besides it will be in plenty of time for your paper." [2]

While Ade's response was both a measure of his own generosity and the product of a journalistic culture characterized by cooperation, it also flowed from the migratory stream that brought the two men to Chicago. However much Dreiser's "borrowing"—of race results and, later, from Ade's popular column—exceeded the bounds of professional courtesy, his plagiarizing was mediated by his Indiana affiliations. In 1892, Theodore Dreiser was twenty years old and had come to the *Globe* after several unsatisfying petty business jobs and a short stint at Indiana University. A self-described "dreamy cub" with virtually no experience as a newspaper reporter, he was a legitimate greenhorn and an understandable object of sympathy for the five-years-older, relatively well-established Ade.[3] While it is unclear how prominent a role their common Indiana ties played in this initial conversation, Dreiser was likely too eager, too ambitious, not to have mentioned them. Eight years later, however, there was no doubt but that Ade had claimed Dreiser as a fellow "exile in Suckerland" and Indiana writer whose work benefited from the Hoosier perspective.

Even Dreiser, a writer who often appeared to be a "cold-blooded analyst" of emotions, seemed to maintain a strong affection for his home state of Indiana.[4] In 1896, he collaborated with his brother Paul Dresser to write the first stanza and refrain to the deeply nostalgic song, "On the Banks of the Wabash." Like other popular ballads that Dresser wrote during the 1890s and 1900s, the song conjures up images of childhood homes and of a beloved, aged mother. Essentially a regional variation of "Home, Sweet Home," it makes Indiana "home" to these youthful scenes and emotions, thereby expressing the longing that many adult Hoosiers felt for a simpler, bygone era and tugging on the hearts of small-town migrants who had left their home states to make lives in the nation's cities. So evocative was this combination of setting and sentiment that in 1899 the sheet music for "On the Banks of the Wabash" was a best seller (fig. 10). Fourteen years later, in 1913, Indiana adopted it as the official state song.[5]

'Round my Indiana homesteads wave the cornfields,
In the distance loom the woodlands clear and cool.
Oftentimes my thoughts revert to scenes of childhood,
Where I first received my lessons, nature's school.
But one thing there is missing in the picture,
Without her face it seems so incomplete.
I long to see my mother in the doorway,

As she stood there years ago, her boy to greet.
[CHORUS]
Oh, the moonlight's fair tonight along the Wabash,
From the fields there comes the breath of new mown hay.
Through the sycamores the candle lights are gleaming,
On the banks of the Wabash, far away.

Echoing the poetry of James Whitcomb Riley and some of the Indiana Society of Chicago's more sentimental rhetoric, Dreiser's lyrics raise questions about the place or impact of nostalgia in his fiction and literary realism in general. In light of his borrowing from Ade, these questions also go to the nature of the city's literary community and the extent to which Chicago's hinterland writers understood themselves joined and their work informed by

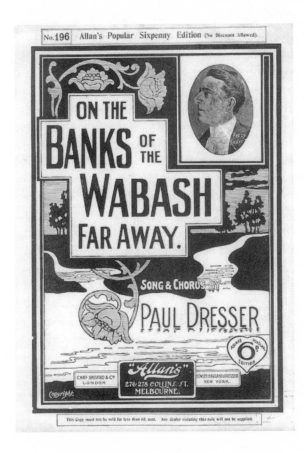

FIGURE 10
Sheet music cover for
"On the Banks of
the Wabash" by Paul
Dresser. (By permission
of the National Library
of Australia)

their shared hinterland background. Most of all, this particularly lachrymose expression of loss and longing for home, from a writer whose representations of metropolitan self-making generally seem resolutely antinostalgic, suggests that the structures of feeling that shaped turn-of-the-century Chicago literature—and urban identity in general—were marked by contradictory, yet complementary desires. In other words, Dreiser and other writers who came of age in small, hinterland communities had difficulty imagining metropolitan culture outside the familiar framework of their original homes.

These contradictions are epitomized in *Sister Carrie,* Dreiser's debut novel about a small-town girl who leaves Columbia City, Wisconsin, to find success in Chicago. From the beginning of the novel, when she departs for Chicago, Carrie Meeber appears determined to forget the past and shed her small-town upbringing. Roaming amid pleasures and staring longingly into palaces, she spends much of her time in a state of suspended amnesia, anxiously or blissfully fantasizing about the diversions she hopes to enjoy, but giving little thought to the world she left behind. Almost always in the process of migration, Carrie is swept along by the force of her longing, an emotional condition that inevitably leads her to the brighter lights of a bigger city—New York—at which point Chicago begins to seem like a small town.

To the extent that Dreiser describes the "drift" toward city life as a one-way ticket out of small-town America, *Sister Carrie* thus contains valuable career advice for would-be migrants: homesickness and ambition do not mix. But Dreiser's novel is not simply antinostalgic. For while it is true, as Daniel Aaron has noted, that *Sister Carrie* was the first American novel to present urban life in sympathetic terms, its modernity cannot be separated from its provincial sources or, for that matter, the migration experience. Locating Carrie's origins in Columbia City—a small town that in real life was located not in Wisconsin but on the railroad lines just west of Fort Wayne, Indiana, and not too far from his hometown of Warsaw—was one way in which Dreiser acknowledged these antecedents. Plagiarizing Ade's *Fables* was another. To put these contradictions in the novel's own language, Carrie is set afloat on a sea of mixed emotions: the stronger currents lead to cities, charting a narrative of urban migration, while a comparatively weaker, yet significant undertow pulls the action back home to the provinces. Though she tries to forget where she is from—the cardinal sin of anyone who rises to fame in modern America—her bad dreams, waking blues, and endless rocking recall her origins.[6] Indeed, the very title of the novel insists on the notion that the urban and the rural are connected by family ties.

Like his heroine, Dreiser longed for metropolitan success and moved steadily away from his impoverished Indiana upbringing in search of it. And geography gave shape to ambition. As Dreiser notes at the outset of his novel, "Columbia City was not so very far away, even once she was in Chicago. What, pray, is a few hours—a few hundred miles away?"[7] The question is ironic, since Carrie never returns home; but it suggests how important provincial sources and perspectives were to Dreiser as he searched for a literary form suitable for representing his own career ambitions. In the late 1890s, when he wrote *Sister Carrie,* Warsaw was not that far behind him. To the extent that similar places were at the backs of other Chicago migrants, Dreiser's hugely "felt" novel is more than a single life history; it is a collectively authored migration narrative. Thus when Dreiser borrowed from Ade or when the humorist forgave the novelist's "theft," each recognized a fellow traveler who had crossed the border from province to city, and whose small-town background was part of a common experience that made kinfolk of all wayward Hoosiers.

More than a matter for literary historians, Dreiser's assumptions about the importance of home and place are consistent with Ade and John McCutcheon's observations of Chicago's hinterland migrants: though the urban landscape made relentless demands on newcomers and its physical and social differences required some measure of assimilation, the provincial *domus* remained a potential cornerstone for individual and group identity. As undifferentiated as "the old country home" may seem when compared to the cultural landmarks that distinguished Chicago's foreign-born communities and neighborhoods, members of the Indiana Society and other such groups wore this affiliation on their sleeves. Antagonistically disposed to any attachments based on nostalgia, Sister Carrie suppresses her hinterland antecedents (rejecting her "sister") in order to assume a cosmopolitan, urban identity. Still, her submerged past resembles what political theorist James Scott has called a "hidden transcript": a latent, culturally charged discourse that seldom comes into clear view but nonetheless shapes her emotional life and her movements in the novel.[8]

The image that epitomizes Carrie's longing for home is, not surprisingly, one of motion. Seated in a rocking chair, usually looking out a window, she moves the chair back and forth and dreams of a better life. In his reading of the novel, Philip Fisher compares Carrie's rocking to the enormous Ferris wheel that was first unveiled at the Columbian Exposition, arguing that their circular motions symbolize Chicago's status as the "anticipated city" of desire.[9] This reading catches one side of her desire-driven movements but leaves out the other, which Dreiser illuminates at the end of novel. Carrie, once again shown in her rocking chair, is adrift in nostalgic reverie: "Whether it be the tinkle of a lone sheep bell o'er some quiet landscape, or the glimmer of beauty in sylvan places, or the shadow of soul in some passing eye, the heart knows and makes answer, following." [10] As the signposts for nostalgia come into view—the lone sheep bell and the rural landscape serve as conventional markers in nineteenth-century Romantic literature— her rocking chair appears more like a symbol of American domesticity than a vehicle for urban mobility. Like the chair—and echoing Henry Blake Fuller's advice to Hamlin Garland, to put one foot in Wisconsin and the other in Chicago—Carrie is taken by her longing in two different directions. Impelled back by the same force that sends her forward, she recapitulates her migration as a cycle of desire that leads beyond her home and back again. In literally rocking it to 'em, Dreiser arguably created the Chicago novel that Fuller was calling for: a narrative attuned to both the geographic and emotional dynamics of this as yet unfinished provincial city.

What difference does this view of Sister Carrie's interior life make for our understanding of the novel and of Dreiser's standing as a Chicago/ hinterland writer? At the very least, the emotional undercurrents present in *Sister Carrie* suggest that the novel's meaning derives more from its broader regional frame than its urban setting might first suggest. Although Carrie's desires are principally aimed at the city's expansive consumer and leisure activities—her erotic drives apparently sublimated by economic forces— the idea that her movement forward may be determined in some way by a latent nostalgia turns the novel's metropolitan economy on its head and positions the hinterland as an active agent in the novel.

In what follows, I push off from *Sister Carrie* to consider the role of nostalgia in three Chicago novels written in the wake of Dreiser's groundbreaking book: Will Payne's *The Story of Eva* (1901); George Barr McCutcheon's *The Sherrods* (1903); and Brand Whitlock's *The Happy Average* (1904). All these stories are migration narratives, and each of them is concerned with how its protagonist has internalized hometown values and what sort of claim, if any, provincial culture has on Chicago. They are also romances, and so are generically focused on the sentiments and rituals of courtship; but in every case the conventions of love and plot are mediated by urban-hinterland relations. Like Garland's *Rose of Dutcher's Coolly*, these novels assume the city's capacity to attract ambitious migrants, but more so than this work, they grant cultural power to the postmigration pull of the hinterland, thus setting in motion a complicated, and sometimes volatile, transferal of "home feeling" to Chicago.

Although there is little evidence to indicate that these writers explicitly intended their novels to be responses to *Sister Carrie,* their stories speak to one another, and to the tensions dramatized by Dreiser, with remarkable similarity. This is not surprising, as the three writers, all migrants, were professionally or socially connected. Raised on a farm in Whiteside County, Illinois, Will Payne worked for a bank in the small town of Harvard, Nebraska, before moving to Chicago in 1890 and launching a career as a newspaper reporter. While in Chicago, Payne worked for the *Daily News,* the Chicago *Chronicle,* and the *Economist* while writing popular fiction. He was also a member of the Little Room, as was George Barr McCutcheon; in fact, both men had acting parts in *Captain Fry's Birthday Party.* Like his older brother John, McCutcheon began his career as journalist, serving as a city editor in Lafayette, Indiana, where he wrote novels at night. He arrived in Chicago flush on the success of his best-selling novel, *Graustark* (1901), a costume romance set in contemporary Europe. Brand Whitlock, on the other hand, no longer lived in Chicago when he published *The Happy Average.* By 1904 he had returned to Ohio to work in the office of the mayor of Toledo, Samuel "Golden Rule" Jones. However, throughout the early and mid-1890s, he covered the political scene for the *Chicago Herald,* regularly attended meetings of the Whitechapel Club, and wrote short stories set in a fictional version of his hometown of Urbana. A friend of Ade and McCutcheon's, he may or may not have known Payne. Like Ade, he knew Theodore Dreiser slightly and admired *Sister Carrie.*[11]

Reading these novels together as texts linked by their common preoccupation with the romance of migration brings us back to Fuller's call for a provincial perspective in Chicago fiction, but with a slightly different sense of what it means to look at the formation of metropolitan identity from the hinterland. In his letters to Ade and Garland, Fuller acknowledges that the migration experience gave hinterland writers an emotional as well as a cognitive understanding of Chicago that natives like himself lacked. Having crossed the threshold from small-town to metropolitan life and participated in a similar rite of passage, they understood—or perhaps more important, they *felt*—what it meant to look at the world from a hinterland perspective.

As Willa Cather notes at the outset of her novel, *My Ántonia* (1926), the special knowledge gained from growing up in a small midwestern town meant that small-town exiles belonged to "a kind of freemasonry." [12] Essentially, this was a nostalgic vision—a view based on a longing for, and appreciation of, the distinctive features of life on the prairie; a view that could be acquired only by those who left their small-town home for city life and then were able to look back on that once-familiar landscape with new eyes. However, Cather's view is not nostalgic in a manner that the term ordinarily implies. It is not simply a static reflection of past circumstances or a retrograde emotion that exists in opposition to modern life. As Svetlana Boym has observed, "Nostalgia, like irony, is not a property of the object itself but a result of an interaction between subjects and objects, between actual landscapes and the landscapes of the mind." [13] In this respect, Cather achieved literary power through her consciousness of, and ability to shape, the emotions that draw her back home. She escapes censure for writing overly sentimentalized portrayals of Nebraskan life because the small-town world that she depicts is a dynamic, changing entity rather than a fixed, unchanging object that she seems intent on preserving. Still, her representations of provincial life gain lyrical and emotional intensity from the yearning for home that focuses her aesthetic gaze; moreover, these representations assume another layer of meaning when they become occasions for Cather to reflect on the memories and affections that link her to her former home. So nostalgia serves as a powerful source of expression. This, after all, is a central point of the story that picks up where the frame chapter to *My Ántonia* ends; as told by Jim Burden, the story of Antonia Shimerda and Jim's life on the Nebraska prairie is a creative act of memory and recovery.

Broadly speaking, the example of Cather fits into a history of American writers who have moved from the so-called peripheries of the culture to established centers for literature and art where they have built careers by reimagining the homes they left behind. The key words or terms that might be used to designate some of the chapters of this history (such as "revolt from the village" and "lost generation") point to the deficiencies of provincial life, but home almost always remains a site of origins and negotiations to which writers return. Ernest Hemingway's portrayal of childhood landscapes in northern Michigan provides a good example of a literary migrant's antagonistic embrace of his provincial origins, while F. Scott Fitzgerald's gloss on *The Great Gatsby* (1925), that "this has been a story of the West, after all," suggests that even the most relentless quest for status and legitimacy cannot escape the (geographic) past. [14] For these writers and others, the movements from province to metropolis and the nostalgic reconstruction of former landscapes have been defining features of their literary renown.

I emphasize nostalgia in this context—instead of memory, for instance—because of the links it establishes among geography, emotion, and retrospective vision. Although nostalgia's primary definition (homesickness) has yielded to a temporally based meaning (longing for past circumstances), the concept's usefulness as an analytic tool has much to do with the spatial dislocations that the term initially addressed. Critics have pointed out that nostalgia is a historical emotion, whose meaning varies according to local circumstances, the force and direction of one's yearning depending on the apparent gaps in culture and space that prevail at the particular moment of displacement.[15] However, scholars also agree that nostalgia is an especially modern emotion, whose emergence coincided with the development of mass culture and linear notions of progress. As Boym notes in her illuminating account of the emotion's place in early modern Europe, nostalgia was one of the "side effects" of progress, which expressed a longing for more intimate spatial experience at a time when the "new horizon of expectations" was constantly expanding.[16] During the early nineteenth century, amid the dramatic cultural and spatial manifestations of progress—rapid urbanization, steamship and rail travel, industrial manufacturing, and significant population shifts—the highly personal, backward-looking experience of nostalgia constituted a widely shared form of Romanticism.

As this brief overview suggests, thinking of nostalgia as a culturally constructed affliction of "provincial origin" leads in two somewhat contradictory directions.[17] First of all, it is clear that one strain of nostalgia went hand in hand with the process of self-making that was at the heart of Western modernization. In this instance, nostalgia was the provenance of the middle class—literally, those geographically mobile segments of the population who were able to leave home for the sake of individual economic development. The intensely emotional, even erotic nature of nostalgia also marked it as a prime condition of the bourgeoisie and a precursor of the therapeutic ethos that has more recently distinguished the middle class.[18] That nostalgia was a vital topic in nineteenth-century European Romantic literature, that its emotional effects are usually expressed in printed language, reinforces the notion that it was chiefly the affliction of the literate and educated classes.

On the other hand, the nostalgia that ensues from the unsettling of provincial communities by economic and political transformations suggests a different kind of reading. For instance, Raymond Williams prefaces his examination of nineteenth-century pastoral literature in *The Country and the City* (1973) by observing that nostalgia "can mean different things at different times" and emphasizing the need to analyze the "successive stages of the criticism which the retrospect supports: religious, humanist, political, cultural." [19] Williams's examination of the ideological and class dynamics that shaped rural-urban relations and informed the development of English literature proceeds from the assumption that political positions and cultural values may be teased out of the "structures of feeling" that animate texts, especially literature. Reading beyond the (typically elite) class status of a given poet or novelist, he works outward from these expressive moments toward an analysis of larger social structures and movements. Although the rural poor and working-class men and women whose ways of life were undone by absentee landlords and urban elites did not write literature, Williams nonetheless finds them present in these texts.

Notwithstanding Williams's significant influence on literary and cultural studies, *The Country and the City* has not inspired a parallel study of American urban-rural relations. England's smaller size and relative unity, its longer literary history, and the centralization of metropolitan power in a single city—London—suggest the challenges of scaling Williams's model to fit the American setting. While American cities have certainly developed in tandem with their hinterlands, often establishing the terms of provincial development, only in a handful of cases can these relationships be said to have evolved along literary lines. Moreover, in regions where urban centers exercise relatively little cultural influence—the antebellum South, for instance—it is not always clear whether the city or the country should be considered "provincial."

Another aspect of Williams's analysis that has not fared so well in the American context is his use of nostalgia as a critical lens. In contrast with Britain and Europe, where allegiance to place and region figure prominently in the "long *durée*" and the difference between metropolis and province has been settled for centuries, American literary and historical traditions appear less tied to place; time, not geography, has been the crucial determinant of change. And when Americanists have considered the cultural place of nostalgia, they have tended to follow a temporally based definition of the concept, such as the one offered by historian Christopher Lasch. According to Lasch, nostalgia is "the abdication of memory." Whereas memory sees history as continuous and treats the past as a "formative influence" on the present, nostalgia has no interest in continuity. "Strictly speaking, nostalgia does not entail the exercise of memory at all, since the past it idealizes stands outside of time, frozen in unchanging perfection." [20] Ironically, Lasch acknowledges the original definition of *nostalgia,* even showing how the term's spatial, usually pastoral dimensions began eroding in the 1920s, but he does not address the historical antecedents of that definition.

In other complementary considerations of the term, Americanists have treated nostalgia as a kind of antimodernism, a compensatory emotion that serves to legitimate and accommodate dramatic changes in the status quo, but remains outside the principal mechanisms of cultural transformation.[21] While the urban-rural divide remains a critical marker in American studies, and though scholars regularly underscore the resiliency of Jefferson's vision of pastoral republicanism as a stay against industrial expansion and the monopolistic abuse of power, the emotional map of nostalgia—as a map of country and town relations—remains largely unexplored. At the same time, "home" has been marked by students of nineteenth-century domestic and sentimental culture as a touchstone of affective, ideological powers. It would stand to reason, then, that nostalgia factored prominently into nineteenth-century efforts to understand the shift from rural to urban life and that it had a significant place in Chicago literature.

Even so, assessing the place of nostalgia in literary discourse is not a matter of hunting down one-on-one correspondences. We may agree that urban literature, like the modern city itself, is saturated with desire, but to account for these longings simply by identifying their objects ignores the lessons of daily life as well as the conclusions of psychological theory. Whether redirected or sublimated, desire does not typically run a straight course. This is especially true of nostalgia, since its presumed object is at a geographic and historical distance, and may never be attained. Consequently, the effects of nostalgia may be indirect—as Boym notes, nostalgia is "never literal, but lateral. It looks sideways"—and, especially in literature, ironically expressed.[22]

Because nostalgia was enabled by the ideologies of self-making and the physical fact of migration, its status and meaning were relative. However, this contingent status did not necessarily mitigate its full-throttled expression in Riley's poetry, songs such as "On the Banks of the Wabash," or pictorial representations of rural homes such as the photograph that appeared in a 1902 issue of *The Inland Printer,* over the title "How Dear to My Heart Are the Scenes of My Childhood" (fig. 11).[23] These portrayals assume and obscure the causes of the sentimentality that they express. Alternatively, Ade and McCutcheon's work and many of the Indiana Society's activities reveal the historical (and enabling) context for nostalgia, often commenting on its ironic place in the culture. Adelina Patti's 1887 performance of "Home,

FIGURE 11 An homage to rural childhood at the turn of the century. (Baker Old Class Collection, Baker Library, Harvard Business School)

Sweet Home" in the Chicago Auditorium is unreservedly nostalgic but suggests multiple sources for its ceremonial, public display of sentimentality. Is "home" the city of Chicago? The American nation? Each listener's birthplace? Home life in general? All these things? Nostalgia's sideways movements suffused the hall with unspecified longing, providing emotional ballast to Chicago's civic identity.

As I argue in the previous chapter, these sentiments had a life beyond expressive forms and ceremonial occasions. Through organizations like the Indiana Society, migrants developed identities based on their provincial homes that resembled the ethnic identities typically associated with immigrant communities. Besides the Indiana Society, there were at least half a dozen other voluntary associations based on sentimental attachments to state or town origins, some of them quite well established by the turn of the century. As Bessie Louise Pierce notes, these societies provided opportunities for members "to extol the past while looking toward the future." In the 1850s, migrants from the East Coast established the New England Society of Chicago and the Bay State Union, while in 1877 a group of prominent

Chicagoans organized the Illinois Association of the Sons of Vermont, which included over two hundred members.[24] Perhaps the best-known home society in nineteenth-century Chicago was the Old Settlers Society of Chicago, which was established in 1855.[25] Although other organizations stressed their commitment to preserving the memory of their original homes, the Old Settlers implicitly honored such origins while also celebrating the members' role in founding Chicago, a mission that epitomizes the reciprocity between city-building or self-making and nostalgia. This duality was likewise reinforced by many of the homeland societies established by Chicago's immigrants.[26] In all these organizations, newcomers established communities and created links with one another that benefited their work and family lives.

Awash in the nostalgia emanating from a thousand hometowns and a dozen homelands, turn-of-the-century Chicago was thus a city in search of home. Although this characterization may appear to be at odds with Chicago's reputation in the nineteenth century as a frenetic, present-minded business city, it was in fact the logical corollary of the town's boosting ethos. Over time, as the city's pioneer roots receded into history and a modern ur-banscape covered those rural patches where the prairie's indigenous character shone through, this search doubled back on itself and Chicagoans developed a nostalgia for itself, for those moments in "old" Chicago when it appeared that the city could be whatever it wanted to be.

For instance, Mary Ann Hubbard, who came to Chicago from Massachusetts in the 1840s with her husband, Gurdon, explained in the 1900s that "Chicago was a much pleasanter place to live in then than it is now, or has been since 'The Fire.' The people with whom we associated were all friendly and kind, sharing each other's joys and sorrows, and enjoying simple pleasures. . . . If we wanted to give a party, we borrowed lamps of the neighbors, sometimes spoons, and as we had to make all our own ice cream, those of us who kept cows would send cream, others, flowers in their season, and kind and neighborly acts were offered and often accepted and reciprocated."[27] One of several recollections of Chicago's early years that appeared at the beginning of the twentieth century, Hubbard's account, which she wrote especially for her niece, collapses the distinction between genealogy and civic history. As suggested by the title of another, like-minded collection—*Chicago's Yesterdays: A Sheaf of Reminiscences* (1919), "garnered" by Caroline Kirkland (Joseph's Kirkland's daughter)—these reminiscences speak in an intimate, often familial manner about the dramatic pace of change in Chicago.[28] This personal approach to history was later incorporated by journalist Herma Clark in her hugely popular Sunday *Tribune* column, "When Chicago Was Young," which began its more than twenty-year run in 1929. In letters written by a fictional narrator to her friend in New York, Clark indulged her readers' fascination with local history.

Like the many midwestern county histories written during the 1890s and early 1900s to celebrate the region's settling, these retrospective accounts literally bring history home, providing a familiar context for understanding dramatic social transformations.[29] In this regard, Mary Hubbard's nostalgia for Chicago's original home spirit and the widespread interest in how Chicago used to look and feel, particularly among older citizens, are hardly surprising; both served to place the city's startling growth on familiar ground. However, they also suggest a brooding over intimacy and space that was distinctive to the city's migratory history. At first glance, Hubbard's implicit longing for an earlier period in Chicago history would seem to be a variety of time-based nostalgia. A closer look, though, suggests that her nostalgia revolves around the domestic and communal spirit that she and her neighbors presumably brought to Chicago from New England, and which had now disappeared. Mary Hubbard is homesick—not for the city that she never left but for the home she internalized, idealized, and carried with her from Massachusetts. In short, her nostalgia for Chicago's past is mediated by her longing for her original home.

A similar irony pertains to Herma Clark's representations of "young" Chicago. While Clark's columns were filled with details about nineteenth-century urban culture, she presented her information anecdotally, as a small-town newspaper might speak to its readers, thus following in the journalistic tradition of Ade and McCutcheon. Advising would-be reporters on small-town newspapers to write "local history," Clark followed her own counsel by ransacking the files of the *Tribune* and the collections at the Chicago Historical Society for stories of human and social interest. Born in 1871 on a farm near Princeton, Illinois—what she called her "Beloved Little Home Town"—Clark was as interested in Chicago as the most eager migrant.[30] However, practically by her own admittance, her nostalgia for her adopted city's past was filtered through her abiding love of her provincial home.

In the eyes of migrants, especially those who were writers, turn-of-the-century Chicago was seldom just itself but instead an unresolved picture of what the city could be or a haunting reminder of what once was. Moreover, the conditions of its growth were such that these two images often overlapped, blurring together as in a doctored photograph or film. European architects and city planners who visited Chicago during the nineteenth century frequently commented on the speed with which its denizens designed and constructed buildings, particularly in the Loop; forging ahead with barely tested design principles and construction techniques, America's hurry-up city seemed to have little regard for tradition and historical precedent.[31] Yet as Dreiser suggests in his description of Chicago's outskirts, which Carrie sees through the train window when she first approaches the city, the meaning of these changes depended on one's point of view. Was the sight of one or two houses and a half-finished sidewalk, all but surrounded by prairie, the image of a city yet to be or of a midwestern village left behind? When Chicagoans encountered open spaces and grazing cows and gardens within the city limits, did they see empty building lots or were they reminded of their provincial homes?

Even before the fire of 1871, Chicago's capacity to hold these contradictions in balance was part of the urban future described in such boosting literature as *Biographical Sketches of the Leading Men of Chicago* (1868). In this celebratory history, the authors wistfully note that the city's "early landmarks have been swept outwards by the swift-advancing tide of settlement" and express their disbelief "that so little time has elapsed since the old block house [part of Fort Dearborn] was 'all and singular' of the scene above the water." As these changes glide by as in a dream, the authors indulge their nostalgia for a Chicago that no longer exists and acknowledge that further progress will change the face of the city again. However, they coyly refuse to discuss this future, instead "preferring that the million of people who will ere long claim Chicago as their home, should tell of their own greatness."[32] Shaped both by the pull of nostalgia and the drive to establish Chicago's domestic foundations, "home" was a moving target.

The emotional tug-of-war over the status and meaning of home that accompanied the shift from rural to urban culture was central to the general development of literary realism, and played an especially prominent role in Chicago fiction written during the 1890s and 1900s. Among the historical tensions that preoccupied realist writers, none was more obviously broached in the fiction itself than the apparent differences in culture between metropolis and province. The town-country divide offered a useful structure for registering the impact of industrial capitalism, consumer culture, new immigrant populations, and other economic and political movements that, in the decades following the Civil War, transformed American society. Although the most discerning writers resisted the impulse simply to attribute such changes to the overbearing power of "the city"—and instead explored the cultural traffic between town and country—the rural home typically served as the default repository of traditional and moral values, and the migration narrative, the best format for dramatizing the internal transformations in the culture. In these literary representations of a changing culture, nostalgia exercised considerable influence.

Consider, for instance, William Dean Howells, whose novels of the 1880s and '90s were early important models of American literary realism. In contrast with Dreiser and other, younger realists, Howells has long seemed the embodiment of genteel decorum; as critics have noted, his writings seem aimed at containing the potential disorder of the new city and suppressing the desires of consumer culture.[33] But these readings give short shrift to the affections for home that sustained his continued interest in provincial culture and informed his ongoing commitment to the political, moral, and creative values of small, face-to-face communities. In his third-person autobiographical account, *A Boy's Town* (1890), Howells claims to have returned as a young man to the Ohio village in which he grew up "wholly cured of that longing for his former home that had tormented him before he revisited its scenes." By visiting his hometown, Howells presumably found the antidote for an acute case of nostalgia. Though he continued to love his hometown, he now "fully gave himself up to his new environment, and looked forward and not backward." Having realized he could not return to the past, he was able to "cherish" his memories of it.[34] While Howells outgrew his homesickness, his nostalgia did not simply disappear; rather, he learned to reflect on his emotional attachment to home and draw upon it in his writing.

For instance, in his landmark novels of the 1880s, *A Modern Instance* (1882) and *The Rise of Silas Lapham* (1885), as well as in *The Minister's Charge* (1887)—all migration narratives—Howells struggled with imagining how his migrating protagonists could remain in Boston and still uphold traditional moral values. Ultimately rejecting urban culture, Silas Lapham and Lemuel Barker (of *The Minister's Charge*) return to northern New England and an apparently stable moral universe. Provincial standards likewise prove a critical benchmark in *A Modern Instance,* as the central crisis of that novel—Bartley Hubbard's reprehensible treatment of Marcia Gaylord and their subsequent divorce—also reveals a cleavage in their village upbringing: though Bartley's moral fall takes place in Boston, his roguish behavior emerged in the hometown he shares with Marcia. Howells's recognition that small, provincial communities do not have an absolute purchase on moral rectitude complicates and deepens his portrayal of metropolitan-hinterland relations. Nonetheless, that in such later works as *The Quality of Mercy* (1892), *A Traveler from Altruria* (1894), and *The Son of Royal Langbrith* (1904) he consistently shifts the site of moral arbitration from city to provinces suggests that he continued to place emotional stock in his Ohio upbringing.

In mapping his own emotional geography onto Yankee culture, Howells earned his place in New England literary history as perhaps only a midwesterner could. This is not to say that the relation between metropolis and province was a uniquely midwestern subject, but only that Chicago's rapid rise to prominence during the 1880s and '90s gave special meaning to the region's cultural importance and perhaps galvanized Howells in his portrayal of Boston and its northern territories. Certainly, Howells followed the development of Chicago literature with a degree of hometown interest, and noted the representation of provincial migrants. In the mid-1890s, he wrote a highly complimentary review of George Ade's "Stories" and "Fables," remarking that "the prey of Mr. Ade's keen wit is the eternal snob, man, woman, and girl (rather especially girl), and he seizes these in their infinite variety as he finds them in a metropolis striving for alien worldliness with the persistent consciousness of its heart, of the farm, the village, the country town where it was native."[35]

Later, he praised Ade, Edith Wyatt, Henry Blake Fuller, and Will Payne, among others, in a *North American Review* article entitled "Certain of the Chicago School of Fiction," for "doing rather more than their share of the best literary work in the country," in particular for their sense of equality and justice, which is "the really valuable contribution of the West, and of that Chicago in which the West has come to its consciousness."[36] In his appraisal of Chicago literature, Howells offers a subtle variation on Hamlin Garland's judgment that Chicago, as the capital of the West, is "splendidly American," since its "dominant population" is "drawn from the immediate States, Indiana, Illinois, Iowa, Wisconsin, Kentucky, and Ohio."[37] Without explicitly addressing the provinces' contribution to Chicago, Howells leaves little doubt that the Middle West had come to understand itself—in the fullest emotional and intellectual sense implied by the term *consciousness*—by coming to Chicago.

If, as I am suggesting here, Howells saw in the development of Chicago literature something of the nostalgic energy that animated his own fiction, he underestimated, overlooked, or had yet to see the emotional energies that

inform the novels of Dreiser and his contemporaries. Payne's *Story of Eva,*
McCutcheon's *Sherrods,* Whitlock's *Happy Average,* and of course *Sister
Carrie* are great with feeling and emotionally divided over the lure of the city
on the one hand and the prerogatives of nostalgia on the other. To the extent
that the hinterland migrants portrayed in these novels come to consciousness in Chicago (and not all of them do), their epiphanies—about their relation to Chicago, and Chicago's place in the region—are based on the protagonists' adhesion to home and the values and commitments associated
with home. Nostalgia works laterally or relationally in all these novels, suf-
fusing the migrants' interactions with the world but not necessarily establishing the departed home as a fixed object of desire.

In differing ways, these novels serve as emotional barometers for the
city's relentless growth. Written at the century's turn, they offer views of
what Chicago looked and felt like after its reputation as an ambitious, striving metropolis had been established through relentless boosting, rapid economic growth, and a variety of civic accomplishments, in particular the success of the 1893 World's Columbian Exposition. To think of Chicago in the
terms set by the fair's White City, as an imperial metropolis, may be to overestimate the agency and power of the city's elite classes. Nonetheless, there
is little question but that by the mid-1890s Chicago was a significantly different city than it was ten years earlier, and that it in broad, symbolic fashion
could claim to have achieved much of what its most fervent boosters desired.
At this very moment of success, these novels found provincial Chicagoans
still dreaming—not necessarily of additional metropolitan power and further self-making but rather of the dreams they had developed in their small-
town and village homes and of the costs that they paid to fulfill those dreams
in Chicago. At bottom, these novels all suggest that turn-of-the-century
Chicago was still a provincial town.

Will Payne's Reconciliation of Home and Desire

In *The Story of Eva* (1901), Payne tells the story of Eva Soden, a transplant
from Hopeville, Nebraska, who comes to Chicago after the breakup of
her marriage to a traveling salesman who has been unfaithful to her. Eva's
journey to Chicago is actually a repeat performance, since she first moved to
the city with her husband to be near his business headquarters, but then
went back to Nebraska after discovering his infidelities. The novel opens

with Eva's return to Chicago, where she is determined to find a job and live independently. She is helped in this endeavor by her relative and friend "Little Sarah" White, who also a small-town migrant—from Indiana. Sarah helps Eva get a job at the publishing company where she works, and together the two women set up house at a boardinghouse near Union Park. Eva's ambitions extend beyond her menial job, and she eventually takes a position as the cashier at a new lunch-counter restaurant in the Loop. At the same time, she falls in love with Philip Marvin, a college-educated New Englander who works as a literary advisor at her former workplace. Believing that her salesman husband has obtained a divorce in another state, Eva "marries" Philip and gives up her job, and the couple moves into a luxurious residential hotel on the North Side. After a series of social mishaps and misunderstandings in which Eva's morally forthright, if naive, provincial character is contrasted with Philip's more sophisticated but weaker character, the couple becomes estranged—only to be reunited after the cathartic return and death of the salesman husband and a fire at the hotel during which Eva rescues a child and figuratively "saves" her husband through her stronger, heroic nature. The novel concludes with the couple returning from a visit in Hopeville to begin their lives again in Chicago—in a more reasonably priced apartment and anticipating the birth of their first child.

In *The Story of Eva* as in his other fictional work, Payne blurs the edges of Chicago's urban landscape while emphasizing the internal dynamics that pull his protagonists back to their rural homes. *Jerry The Dreamer,* which Payne published in 1896, describes the city's ragged edge through the eyes of an "intelligent young countryman" whose conceptions of urban life are derived from Charles Dickens. Jerry, like Payne, is a journalist, and he hopes to describe his initial encounter with Chicago and sell the account to a newspaper. However, he is bewildered by the city's uncertain boundaries: "the little communities of frame dwellings, citified by macadam streets and gas-lamps, set out in the wide, flat, green, prairie, with considerable stretches of meadow and truck-garden between them." Payne's description of this liminal zone—citified but not yet city—parallels the accounts that George Ade wrote in the early 1890s, but assumes another layer of meaning when Jerry's bewilderment leaves him feeling "strangely flattened out and inconsequential" and unsettles his expectations of achieving great success in Chicago (that is, "life, fame, money, joy!"). Although Jerry's initial disorientation stamps him as a greenhorn, Payne implies that Chicagoans in general find these semi-rural spaces notoriously hard to read. To wit, residents on the outskirts of town place signs in front of vacant lots and buildings informing streetcar passengers that "they were going through villages once having a distinct life, but now merged in the huge outspreading metropolis."[38]

These opening qualifications — of Jerry's dreams and Dickens's usefulness as a literary model — suggest Payne's intention of writing a novel based more on Chicago's particular historical conditions and Jerry's perceptions of them than on inherited narrative conventions. Typically, the modern urban novel takes shape around a narrator or protagonist whose subjective impressions of the city are the key to his psychological development and the basis of the city's meaning in the text. As Richard Lehan notes, the narrator's response to the city "moves us from an objective to a subjective realm, as well as from a shared to a private reality." The problem for Jerry, and for the novel as a whole, is that once he is separated from the naive dreams of self-making that prompted his migration from his dreary hometown of Tampico (Illinois), he is unable to recover a new way, or a new narrative, for achieving success and developing himself. Although he gains a place on a Chicago daily newspaper, falls in love, and marries, the sense of comfort he achieves is fragile and short lived. Cut off from any meaningful community and alienated from his wife's upper-class family, he is never far from being flattened out by the city's oppressive economic conditions and feeling like an "atom."[39]

Ostensibly, Jerry develops an alternative urban narrative that explains his alienation, literally by writing articles for a small leftist newspaper — based on Henry George's theories of agrarianism and land ownership — that criticize prevailing labor conditions and Chicago's class structures. Yet Payne shows these efforts to be relatively ineffective in redressing Chicago's social ills or filling the gaps in Jerry's emotional life. When Jerry most feels the need to recuperate himself and regain his connection to a community, he dreams of home. Not surprisingly, these "failing moments of hunger for Tampico — for the quietness, friendliness of it" punctuate his first days in the city; however, they persist into his fourth year there when, despite his professional success, Jerry dwells on "the great, foolish dreams he had indulged" back home. Indeed, his dreams never seem so real or his emotions so vivid as when he is gripped by nostalgia at the end of the novel, when he "thought again, as he had often done, of going off into the country somewhere. The still shade of Tampico, the peaceful stretches of grass and grain, came before him, and his heart burst for them."[40]

Barely theorized, these eruptions of usually unarticulated longing constitute a potential substrate for the narrative and a possible leverage point for

Payne's criticism of Chicago's commercial ethos. However, like the little communities of frame dwellings on the edge of Payne's Chicago, they are submerged into the metropolitan ethos of the novel and left undeveloped. Ultimately, Jerry is reunited with his wife, and his dreams of Tampico remain unanswered.

By contrast, in *The Story of Eva*, these little villages have moved in from the outskirts to occupy a central position in the novel. The shabbily genteel neighborhood where Eva and Sarah board is filled with provincial newcomers like themselves: "a floating population of under clerks, mechanics, stenographers, agents, canvassers, and the like, poorly paid, hopeful in proportion as it was young, and as it drew from the inexhaustible country which kept pouring its youth into the hive of the city." Though by lounging on the front stoops during the summer and conducting romances in their shirtsleeves, they exhibit the sort of familiar, rustic manner that so bothered Henry Blake Fuller, Payne presents them as the city's emerging middle class—hardworking, honest, and passionate. They also represent Chicago's future, a picture of which comes into focus when Eva and Sarah meet a young family who came to the boardinghouse from a country town ("for which the wife pined") but now have the means to "venture upon a little flat of their own, far out on the western edge of the town, where they would see stretches of grass in the summer." This inside-out view ironically places Chicago's provincial migrants (and their longing for prairie space) at the forward edge of the city's expansion.[41]

Although Eva's Union Park neighborhood no longer is fashionable and has "decayed" physically, it serves as the concrete embodiment of the cultural standards that guide her behavior in the novel. By her own estimation, Eva is "rather rustic in her views of propriety," even "vulgar" in outlook, yet this lack of urban sophistication serves as a prime indicator of her moral and emotional strength. Time and again, Eva's winning traits—her "air of friendliness" and "neighborly wish to please" as well as her independent nature and practical sense—are referred to her Hopeville background and favorably contrasted with the city's grinding atmosphere and its opulent excesses (24, 219, 39, 133). These qualities serve her well in her job and at home in her neighborhood. Most of all, they enable her to redeem and guide her more aristocratic suitor, Philip Marvin, who suffers from an apparently congenital inability to act and take charge of his life, a weakness that Payne explicitly ties to his stagnating Massachusetts home and family. Philip recognizes these weaknesses and leaves home for Chicago because of them, but he cannot escape them in himself. Consequently, it is up to the more vital midwestern migrant, Eva, to direct him and to establish their home in Chicago, based on her provincial values and perspective.

All but neglected in studies of Chicago literature, *The Story of Eva* warrants examination if only because of its similarities to Dreiser's *Sister Carrie*. The resemblances are striking. A small-town girl yields to the blandishments of a flashy traveling salesman, struggles to make a life for herself in Chicago, and ultimately establishes a relationship with a more respectable man whose intense attraction to the girl is offset by apparent weaknesses in his character. Plot variations aside, both novels examine the relation among desire and urban migration and metropolitan culture, placing at risk the respectability or moral stature of the woman adrift. Although Garland's *Rose of Dutcher's Coolly* also examines these issues, Rose's reputation never comes into question; in other words, her desires as a sexual being and ambitious migrant do not conflict with, or threaten, the values that she is expected to uphold as a respectable woman.

Of course, this conflict is missing from *Sister Carrie* as well. Indeed, that Carrie's moral "fall" seems to go unpunished has bothered some readers since the novel first appeared. The conflict is not entirely absent from *The Story of Eva,* and how Payne addresses its potential impact reveals the role of desire, or more specifically, nostalgia, in the novel.

In short, Eva's ongoing, felt connection to Hopeville values holds in check her attraction to Philip Marvin and causes her worry after she agrees to live with him (unmarried) in a plush lakefront hotel. This is Eva's fall—from moral rectitude and the frugal social traditions of small-town Nebraska—and her eventual rejection of these circumstances, along with her criticism of Marvin, reveals the extent to which nostalgia grounds her in the democratic values of her home. In this regard, Payne develops Eva's nostalgia as a form of cultural criticism, to highlight the economic inequalities and excess for which late nineteenth-century Chicago was famous.

Compared to Dreiser's representation of Carrie, who seems free of domestic restraints, this portrayal appears deliberately conservative; that is, Eva's nostalgia truly seems to tie her to ideological imperatives of home. On the other hand, she is acutely conscious of the desires that shape her self and life. When, for instance, she meets a former, considerably older suitor who comes to Chicago to find a job, his physical presence activates a corresponding emotional response within her: "To her inner sense, in a strange way, her world seemed to be rising up around her, to becoming vitally into her life again on all sides,—the world of simple things, of getting a job, of daily earning the daily bread, of small, careful economies; the world in which one lived so simply, so near to the ground, so near to his fellow workers" (302). However earnestly this passage presses the case for honest labor, it also emphasizes the self-conscious way in which Eva is able to feel and reflect upon her nostalgia.

Eva's awareness of her past and of how her connection to Hopeville frames her life is evident throughout the novel. It forms the primary context in which she thinks back upon her failed marriage and considers a future life with Philip Marvin. Eva knows herself, knows where she is and has been, in a way that Carrie Meeber never does, and that knowledge gives her actions a sense of purpose that Carrie lacks. Eva's reflective nostalgia also distinguishes her from Philip, who has strong emotions but does not know what they mean or how to act upon them. Not surprisingly, Payne presents Philip's emotions as the feelings of a man who is falling in love but does not know it. Yet there are also passages in the novel where Payne's treatment of Philip conjures up the emotional isolation of modern urban life. Once, for example, he describes Philip's departure from the office and his idle walk up the street, noting that "he had felt lonely,—so lonely that it was a kind of nostalgia; but he could not tell what he longed for. It was nothing definable and everything indefinable. He glanced at the lake, at the buildings, at the people, with a kind of sad, idle discontent" (41). Even when loneliness or its surrogate, nostalgia, goes unrealized, it haunts the city.

George Barr McCutcheon and the Failed Romance of Migration

If *The Story of Eva* represents the integration of nostalgia in Chicago culture, then George Barr McCutcheon's novel *The Sherrods* (1903) dramatizes the incompatibility of longing for urban success and remaining true to one's love of home. Like *The Story of Eva*, *The Sherrods* is a romantic tale that addresses the dynamics of migration through a marriage plot. More so than Payne's novel, however, it eroticizes the lure of the city and the nostalgia for home, and makes the two conflicting desires the occasion for violent melodrama.

The older brother of John T. McCutcheon, George Barr McCutcheon was only a sometime migrant to Chicago, beginning his writing career as a newspaper reporter in Lafayette, Indiana, and completing it as a novelist in New York City. McCutcheon's best-selling novel, *Graustark* (1901), a costume romance set in medieval Germany, established him as one of the country's leading writers of popular fiction. *Brewster's Millions,* published in 1902, eventually brought his talents to Hollywood, where that novel and several of his other books were made into films. *The Sherrods* was published in 1903, two years after *Graustark* and one year before the sequel to *Graustark, Beverly of Graustark,* appeared. However, as George Ade later suggested, the sequence in which McCutcheon's novels were published was not necessarily the order in which they were written. Throughout his tenure on the Lafayette *Courier,* McCutcheon wrote novels in his spare time, and *Graustark* was just one of several manuscripts he was ready to publish.[42]

Regardless of when it was written, *The Sherrods,* McCutcheon's first and only fictional representation of themes that dominated his brother John's cartoons, took its place next to his popular tales of European conquest and romance. While it and the *Graustark* stories are set in very different places, each of the novels is concerned with the progress of empire and the emotional and ideological energies at stake in colonization.

In contrast with John McCutcheon's work, *The Sherrods* takes a fairly negative view of urban migration. Set in rural Indiana and Chicago, the novel follows the fortunes of Jud Sherrod, a rustic youth whose artistic talents take him to the city, where he embarks on a fast-track career as a newspaper illustrator and painter. As in *Rose of Dutcher's Coolly,* Jud's aptitudes and his departure for Chicago soon become entangled with his romantic interests. However, here the love interest develops before the migrant hero has left home. In fact, the novel opens with Jud's marriage to Justine Vann, his childhood sweetheart. Jud and Justine are both poor—a financial crisis impoverished their parents and led to their deaths—but they are young, beautiful, resilient, and in love. After settling down to a hard but contented existence on a farm, their lives change dramatically when Celeste Wood, a beautiful Chicago socialite, sees one of Jud's sketches when passing through the area. She recognizes his artistic genius and encourages him to come to Chicago to develop his talents. At Justine's urging, Jud moves to Chicago by himself with the understanding that she will join him when he is established in his work. Like John McCutcheon, Jud secures a job as an illustrator on a Chicago daily newspaper, and he thrives. Initially embarrassed by his inability to support Justine and later unwilling to disrupt his status as a solitary young man on the rise, Jud neglects to tell anyone in Chicago that he is married and gradually slips into a double life in Chicago and Indiana. The novel then takes a decidedly lurid turn when Jud encounters Celeste Wood again in Chicago. They fall in love and marry, Jud's double life having paralyzed his ability to act and leading him to commit bigamy. The novel ends when a worried Justine—leaving her newborn at home—comes to Chicago to look for Jud. When she finally reaches his new home, Jud sees his two wives together and kills himself in despair and shame. In the aftermath, the scandal is hushed up, Jud's body is returned to Indiana for an honorable burial, and Justine and Celeste leave for Europe, committed to sharing their tragedy and raising Jud's child together.

With hardly a trace of irony, satire, or humor, *The Sherrods* ratchets up the cost of urban migration in a story that is more concerned with instinctual desires and dramatic spectacle than reasoned motives and social analysis. Jud is not so much a villain as an "honest fellow" who lacks the maturity, sophistication, and strength of character both to satisfy his own ambitions and honor his love for Justine. Faced by the high cost of living in Chicago, he cannot imagine a way to bring his wife to the city, little realizing—McCutcheon points out—that "selfishness was the weight which drew his intention out of balance."[43] Paradoxically, Jud's self-absorption is reinforced by his rigid idealism. He views his wife as a paragon of rural virtue: too innocent, too beautiful, and too good to live a hardscrabble life in Chicago. Jud conducts his own life with the same idealistic fervor. Once in Chicago, he lives humbly and eschews all vices, remaining loyal to his wife and his crystalline vision of urban success. This vision is epitomized by Celeste Wood, who is not only beautiful and wealthy but also generous and kind—precisely the sort of woman that, in a happier version of this tale, a promising young man like Jud would deserve to win. Even Justine is smitten by Celeste. Struck by her fairy-princess-like appearance in the woods, she urges Jud to take seriously her words of encouragement and to look for her in Chicago. And at the novel's end, McCutcheon implies that she has transferred at least some of her passion for Jud to Celeste.

Given Jud's seemingly unconscious turn toward bigamy and the overblown, violent conclusion, it is difficult to argue for *The Sherrods'* realism, though McCutcheon's representation of quotidian details—from clothing to regional dialect to economic conditions in Clay County, Indiana (located in the southwest part of the state)—indicates a commitment to historical authenticity that the larger movements of the novel support. His portrayal of Judd's arrival in Chicago, for instance, includes details that are typical of other migration narratives: the train "rolled" into Dearborn Street Station, and he "stumbled out into the smoky, clanging train-sheds among countless

strangers" as "rebuffs, amused smiles, and sarcastic rejoinders met his innocent queries as he wandered aimlessly about the station." Not surprisingly,
the portrayal of the Chicago newspaper business seems particularly aimed at
documenting the real, workaday world of journalism. So when Judd enters
the newspaper artist's office, there "was no halo of glory hovering over the
[artist's] rumpled head, nor was there a sign of the glorious studio his dreams
had pictured. He found himself standing in the doorway of what looked like
a junk-shop. Desks were strewn with drawing-boards, cardboards, pens,
pads, weights, thumb-tacks, unmounted photographs, and heterogeneous
assortment of things he had never seen before" (92, 97).

All this detail provides colorful scaffolding for a melodramatic conflict
between county and city, between two irreconcilable desires to live in two
different places at the same time—a novel, in other words, that deals symbolically with the sentiments of migration. Driven both by his desire to realize his full artistic potential in Chicago and an (almost) equally strong desire
to uphold rural virtue, Jud implodes under the pressure to satisfy both aspirations. The roughly commensurate pull of these two claims on his affection is reflected in his bigamy and the intimate relationship that he establishes with two equally attractive women. Or, as McCutcheon notes of Jud's
two loves, "On one hand, Justine was his ideal; on the other hand, Celeste
was an ideal. . . . Both were made for him to adore" (187).

Although George Barr McCutcheon's cartoonish handling of this conflict
seems at odds with responsible cultural criticism, that his brother John
rewrote this plot in *The Restless Age,* a novel he published eighteen years
later, suggests that *The Sherrods* was taken as serious commentary in some
quarters. *The Restless Age,* too, tells the story of an ambitious young man
who leaves rural Indiana for Chicago and, almost forgetting the childhood
sweetheart at home, gets drawn into a compromising relationship with
a wealthy socialite in the city. In John T. McCutcheon's story, though,
the protagonist corrects his mistake, returns to the farm, and marries his
Indiana sweetheart. Moreover, in telling his version of this story, the
younger McCutcheon eschews torrid melodrama and instead editorializes,
in Progressive-era fashion, about the importance of revitalizing rural life
through the adoption of scientific farming techniques and the expansion of
cultural activities in the hinterland. Thus, the Chicago cartoonist (ironically) lent his support to all reasonable strategies for keeping would-be
migrants at home.

The lesson of *The Sherrods,* however, is that logic alone cannot explain
why migrants such as Jud Sherrod leave home for Chicago. Instead,

The Sherrods engages the "lure" of the city on its own terms, highlighting the irrational forces that draw young people to the city. McCutcheon's eroticizing of this demographic shift and his representation throughout the novel of virile bodies and hot-blooded romance underscore the importance of desires in urban migration while also acknowledging that unconscious forces—resistant to reasonable analysis—might be compelling migrants to forsake home and family. Absurd though McCutcheon's bigamy plot may appear, it is worth noting how often late nineteenth-century writers depended on it, or a similar crime of passion, to get at the conflicts and anxieties shaping the issue of urban migration (*The Story of Eva* being only one example).

In the novel's calculus of desire, urban life outweighs rural life—otherwise there would be no conflict—and McCutcheon reveals the deficits of remaining at home by caricaturing the residents of Clay Township. At the same time, once Jud arrives in Chicago, he begins to feel the contrary pull of nostalgia. Indeed, his initial recoil from city life, in Dearborn Station, describes the trajectory of the novel's ensuing drama: he "saw the people and novelties of a great city through dim, homesick eyes, and thought only of the old, familiar, well-beloved fences, lanes, and pastures, and Justine's sad face. His ambition waned. He realized that he did not belong in this great, unkind place" (93–94). By collapsing Jud's nostalgia with his love for Justine, McCutcheon eroticizes Jud's homesickness and presents his love for Justine as part of the rural scenery. Although one might argue that McCutcheon has conveniently blurred the distinction between love and nostalgia, the novel seems to argue that the two cannot be separated; that love of home, family, region, and wife draw from the same emotional well. Unlike Carrie, Jud cannot, over the long term, sustain his urban identity—he cannot "pass" as a Chicagoan—nor can he successfully suppress his nostalgia. Though he seeks to rid himself of his emotional attachment by sneaking home to kill Justine, this largely symbolic rite of passage into urban citizenship fails: he acknowledges his love of Justine and, by extension, the Indiana home that is so much of a part of their identities. Jud's nostalgia-ridden guilt takes its course like a disease, progressively altering his ability to function so that by the time Justine discovers his infidelity, he is already on the brink of a psychological collapse.

In discussing *Graustark*, critic Amy Kaplan has argued that McCutcheon's popular novel was one of several historical romances written in the 1890s that reinforced imperialist interests abroad by redirecting American nostalgia for the now-closed frontier onto foreign lands. According to

Kaplan, these "swashbuckling" romances "offer a cognitive and libidinal map of American geopolitics during the shift from continental conquest to overseas empires. By looking back at a lost wholeness, they create fanciful realms on which to project contemporary desires for unlimited global expansion."[44] In this context, what is striking about *The Sherrods* is its failure to imagine a seamless shift from rural to urban society. Whereas works like *Graustark* reimagine virile male bodies performing noble tasks in exotic lands, thereby accommodating for the loss of suitably masculine work at home, *The Sherrods* highlights the disintegration of the male body and domestic tranquility in an equally spectacular fashion. Read against *Graustark*, *The Sherrods* thus seems like a compensating afterthought, a fictional window on the empire at home that McCutcheon forgot to cover in his first novel. However, the libidinal map provided by this novel, though filled with bright color, leads nowhere; though McCutcheon concedes Chicago's overwhelming capacity to attract, he clings to the hinterland's cultural and emotional powers. In the end, the internal conflict between urban self-making and rural nostalgia melts down, leaving the impression of violent paralysis — a different version, one might say, of the back-and-forth movement signified by Carrie's rocking chair.

Brand Whitlock's Middle Ground

The title of Whitlock's book *The Happy Average* (1904) presumably refers to the balance of urban and provincial cultures that the novel's two lovers reach in trying to make a life for themselves in the late nineteenth-century Midwest. The protagonist, Glenn Marley, has just graduated from Ohio Wesleyan and returned to his parents' home in Macochee, Ohio, with the hope of reading law and then establishing a law practice there. Marley is disappointed to discover, however, that the prospects for career advancement in Macochee are very poor, since business there is "dead." As his law preceptor tells him, Macochee "was nothing but a country cross-roads before the railroad came, and since then it's been nothing but a water-tank; if it keeps on it'll be nothing but a whistling-post, and the trains won't be bothered to stop at all." Marley's disappointment heightens and eventually reaches a crisis point when he falls love with Lavinia Blair, the daughter of the local county judge. Determined to establish a career so that he can marry and support Lavinia, Marley goes to Chicago, where he eventually finds success as a newspaper reporter. The novels ends with his triumphant return to Macochee and his marriage to Lavinia, who will return with him to Chicago to set up house; Marley, they hope, will resume his study of the law. Although the couple would prefer to live in Macochee and while Marley does not really like Chicago, they understand that their "dream" of being together can only be realized in the big city.[45]

This dream is also the happy average of Marley's career ambitions and the couple's shared love of home. In other words, the novel affirms the value of nostalgia without diminishing the self-making energies that living in Chicago enables. To do this, Whitlock stresses the prospective power of nostalgia. This does not mean that homesickness is completely deferred, only that its full capacity to effect change is acknowledged and set aside for some day in the future, when, after prospering in Chicago, Glenn and Lavinia decide to come back to Macochee. In *The Happy Average,* to dream of Chicago is also to dream of Macochee.

Although it is not clear when the Marleys will return from Chicago, Whitlock sets the novel almost entirely in Ohio, grounding Glenn and Lavinia's dreams in the everyday, provincial world of Macochee. Glenn does not leave for Chicago until nearly two-thirds of the way through the book, and when we do learn about his progress in the city, it is chiefly through the letters that he writes back home to Lavinia. She reads these to her family and friends, an exercise through which those who hear Glenn's accounts "felt their own fortunes somehow bound up with his." When Lavinia worries aloud to Glenn's mother that one of his letters is filled with witty, high-spirited descriptions of Chicago, Mrs. Marley tells her that "the poor boy is dying of homesickness; that's what makes him write in that mocking vein." Encouraging Lavinia to believe that Glenn is lonely rather than happy, she explains that he "has a long hard battle before him" and "in a great cruel city. We must help him all we can" (274, 262, 263).

Given the audience, it is not at all surprising that these letters are received in such a traditionally sentimental vein. The female recipients of Glenn's correspondence serve to underscore the conventional functions of nostalgia, the bonds of piety and love that link the absent young man across time and distance to his real home. Mrs. Marley, in particular, represents the traditional, pietistic claims of home. Her husband, Glenn's father, is a Methodist minister, so when she urges him before his departure for Chicago to remember "there's a strong Arm to lean upon," or when Glenn acknowledges how much it means to him that his mother has packed a Bible in his trunk, Whitlock seems to be carrying forward the imperatives of an older Protestant tradition, the values, for instance, upon which the YMCA was built. Whitlock presents these scenes of maternal power without irony, though it is worth noting that when Lavinia selectively reads Glenn's letters to a close friend and her suitor, who is also Glenn's friend, the suitor humorously demands that she recite the romantic passages so he can evaluate how he "handles the love interest" (245, 262, 292).

This playful treatment of a scene that would have been handled much more earnestly fifty years earlier highlights Whitlock's commitment to literary realism, a stake that he also acknowledges in the novel through the character of James Weston, a Chicago reporter who becomes Marley's best friend. Not only is Weston an avid realist (and, not coincidentally, a champion of William Dean Howells's *A Modern Instance*) but, like Marley, he is a provincial migrant. Indeed, he seems remarkably like George Ade: "a Sig. from an Indiana college" who, realizing he could not find a job in his small-town home, set off immediately for Chicago.[46] Whitlock's suggestion—reinforced by Marley's own realistic descriptions of city life in his letters home—is that this new literary generation now has the responsibility for interpreting the relationship between city and country.

Allegiance to home is clearly a significant aspect of this relationship, but as Weston suggests to his friend, ambitious young men like themselves have no choice but to acknowledge the historical forces before them and leave their provincial homes if necessary. The title of the novel that Weston has just written, *The Clutch of Circumstances,* provides a rationale for Marley's migration to Chicago—he has no choice—and describes the context in which Marley now feels his connection to home. Indeed, he mordantly refers to the emotional relationship that circumstances have dictated when he writes to Lavinia after having secured his first stable job in Chicago as a bill clerk for a railroad: "Today I wrote a bill for freight to Cook and Jennings, Macochee, Ohio, and you can imagine my sensations. It made me homesick for a while" (280).

Marley's attention to the sensations of nostalgia and the circumstances that inspire them frame the last third of the book as well as his and Lavinia's decision to return someday to Macochee. When he first thinks about going to Chicago, "his throat ached with the pain of parting" and "he had a sense of being the mute and helpless victim of forces that were playing with him." On the day of his actual departure, he tours the town and realizes that after he leaves, people will "be going on with their concerns just the same, and he would have disappeared out of their lives and out of their memories" (235, 239). At home, he feels his impending absence even more acutely and invests each little landmark—woodshed, ax, and saw—with emotional significance. Finally, putting his arms around the family horse, he begins to cry. Later, after he arrives in Chicago, Marley pays tribute to his home and these emotions by deciding to live in a boardinghouse on Ohio Street.

Despite the self-absorbed, sometimes comic side of Marley's nostalgia, these emotions track his gradual maturity and coming-to-terms with what Whitlock identifies as stable, enduring values. As he thrives in his work as a reporter and comes to be comfortable in Chicago, his letters home focus more on his present life in the city and less on the world he left behind in Macochee, and so Marley seems to relinquish his longing for home. As "on a palimpsest," Whitlock writes, "the old impressions were erased to make way for new ones." But this older emotional transcript remains active, surfacing when Marley comes to Macochee a successful, urbanely dressed journalist, and his heart swells at the sight of the "old mill-pond." Ironically, Whitlock treats these nostalgic undercurrents as the basis for future emotional growth and maturity rather than childish emotions. For example, during his return trip home, Marley dwells for a moment on his failures in Macochee, telling Lavinia that he does not "need" the town anymore, that "it is little and narrow and provincial, and the real life is to be lived out in the larger world." Although by virtue of his outward migration Marley has earned his cosmopolitan perspective on Macochee's provincial character, Whitlock chides him, in his narrator's voice, for this "immature" judgment on his hometown—for failing to remember, as Weston has reminded him, that his failure to obtain employment was beyond anyone's control. Marley seems to grant this larger truth moments later when he admits to Lavinia that he would be willing to return someday to Macochee to live (274, 314, 335).

Just how sincere this offer is may be judged by Whitlock's own decision in 1897 to leave Chicago and his job as a reporter and return to Ohio to practice law in Toledo. He never went back to live in his hometown of Urbana— the small town on which Macochee is based—but he continued to believe, at least for a while, in the "good, kind, provincial people" of the Midwest, who were appearing in John T. McCutcheon's *Tribune* cartoons at the same time Whitlock was writing *The Happy Average*. Whitlock, as we know, admired those cartoons for their realism. By the same token, he must have been pleased when William Dean Howells wrote him, praising *The Happy Average* for its "absolute fidelity . . . to the facts."[47]

More than Will Payne and McCutcheon, Whitlock imagined the mid-western small town as a vital and ongoing model for social and political relations. Whether it was the small size and face-to-face community, the pastoral setting and rural economy, or simply the absence of all those elements that distinguished Chicago, the vision of Urbana (or Macochee) sustained Whitlock's nostalgia so that, in novels like *The Happy Average,* the hinterland is conceived as a potentially viable place to live. Macochee, it should be noted, is not Tampico, Illinois, or Hopeville, Nebraska; despite its relative stasis and the lack of opportunities for Glenn Marley, Macochee is more than a whistle-stop; and Whitlock's portrayal of it, when seen comparatively, serves as a reminder that not all fictionalized small towns are the same.

Still, for all the emotional stock Whitlock placed in the provinces, Chicago remained the catalyst for his desires and was the place that he instinctively deferred to when he considered his own dreams of success. Although he disliked much about the city, the brutish, relentless Chicago that Whitlock recalled in the passage quoted at the end of chapter 3 represented the beginning of his literary career and provided the metropolitan perspective from which he was able to construct his vision of Macochee and become a realist writer. In his autobiography, he notes that when he was boy growing up in Ohio, Cincinnati was "the City" that represented the "larger world"; and in *The Happy Average,* Glenn Marley also briefly considers going there to make his fortune.[48] However, in the end Whitlock and his surrogate entered "the gates of Chicago" and, eventually, Chicago itself became an object of nostalgia for an older Whitlock, who mourned the loss of opportunities that the city once provided. In 1911, he complained to his friend Clarence Darrow—also a migrant from Ohio—that he feared that he had made a mistake by leaving Chicago, as it is "the most significant, in some senses, the most interesting city in America." Placating him as only a fellow provincial could, Darrow replied that "Toledo is as big as Chicago and a country cross-roads is as big as either." But Whitlock could not get over feeling that in leaving Chicago he had forgone the wealth and fame that friends like George Ade, and perhaps even Clarence Darrow, now enjoyed.[49]

While throughout the nineteenth century Chicago boosted its reputation as a city where dreams of individual advancement might come true, Whitlock seems to have internalized, personalized, and, in effect, refantasized that image so that it serves as the benchmark of quite another dream—one tinged with regret and disappointment. Although Whitlock was not quite thirty when in 1898 he recalled his experience starting out in Chicago, his longing for that moment when his future was still ahead of him suggests the brooding of an older man.

Whitlock was not alone in his desire to measure his career against the growth of Chicago. For Payne, George Barr McCutcheon, and Dreiser also—who, like Whitlock, were born between 1865 and 1871—Chicago was a young man's city, a place where careers could be made. The nostalgia that informs much of their fiction might therefore be seen as a kind of emotional stay against unrestrained professional ambitions. This would also help explain the role played by some of the female protagonists, who, as domestic figures, ensure that masculine desires are finally contained within the middle-class home. Significantly, though, the women in these novels are seldom presented as subjects of nostalgia, perhaps because they cannot represent the power of homemaking and at the same time mourn the absence of something they are responsible for creating (Carrie Meeber being the critical exception here). In theory, they instead figure as wives and mothers, as vessels for a home-spirit that is missing in Chicago. Nostalgia, in this sense, is a male affliction, while the city and narrative itself are conceived as masculine subjects anticipating the restoration of home—which in the migration novel is usually somewhere else. Accordingly, the Indiana homestead sentimentalized in "On the Banks of the Wabash" is seen through the male gaze as that place in memory where the mother comes out to greet the missing son. The mirror image of the urban magnet depicted in the opening pages of *Sister Carrie,* this vision is as suffused with anticipation as any prospective view of Chicago—except, of course, that it derives from a sense of loss.

Important though these gender roles are to illuminating the place of nostalgia in Chicago migration literature, they do not address the geographic and cultural terms by which these four writers sought to mitigate or compensate for the loss of their provincial home. While Whitlock hedged his bets by privileging the virtues of Macochee and settling for Chicago, Payne underscored the cultural benefits of integrating provincial values in urban society, and McCutcheon imagined an apocalyptic outcome to urban self-making, all three wrote novels in which the course of nostalgia is limited to the Middle West. Only Theodore Dreiser moved beyond the region to show how the desires first evoked by Chicago had a life in the nation as a whole.

Moving from Columbia City to Chicago to Montreal to New York City, Carrie Meeber spends enough time in places other than her original destination to raise the question as to whether *Sister Carrie* should even be called a Chicago novel. In his 1913 survey of Chicago fiction, Floyd Dell flirts with a negative answer to this question when he refers to the Chicago "that lives in the minds and imaginations of young people all through the Middle West . . . and that begins to die with their first sight of the town."[50] A literary migrant himself, Dell agreed with other Chicago writers that provincial fantasy and urban reality are not the same thing, but he stopped short of saying that the dreams that brought migrants to Chicago ended at the city limits. Rather, given Dell's own journey from Davenport, Iowa, to Chicago to New York City as well as the migrations in Dreiser's novel (which Dell briefly discusses), one might say that the "death" of Chicago's image signaled the onset of new desires, and new destinations.

Indeed, the effect of Carrie's moving to New York is to create a hierarchical relationship between America's first city and its second, and to suggest that Carrie's unquenchable longing for urban excitement has taken her to a larger, older, wealthier, more powerful metropolis. Although she does not intend to move to New York—her married lover, Hurstwood, elopes with her—there is no doubt once she has settled there that she finds the city's glamorous commercial culture more appealing. In editorial asides, chapter headings, and through his handling of Hurstwood's decline, Dreiser underscores New York's heightened "atmosphere." As he says of Hurstwood's job prospects in a chapter entitled "The Kingdom of Greatness: The Pilgrim Adream," "Whatever a man like Hurstwood could be in Chicago, it is very evident that he would be an inconspicuous drop in a ocean like New York."[51] Whereas all roads from Columbia City and other points west lead to Chicago, Dreiser shows New York to be the nation's true imperial city, an American Rome. Chicago, on the other hand, becomes to New York what Columbia City initially was to Chicago: a provincial crossroads. To wit, Hurstwood's failure in New York and his brooding nostalgia for the success he once enjoyed in Chicago suggest the declension of a small-town migrant who is unable to make it in the city.

The map that Dreiser draws in *Sister Carrie* is a weave of railroad corridors, urban streets, and domestic and commercial spaces—all connected, one might say, by a thick red line of desire. Although Carrie migrates from one place to another on this map with little conscious regard for the places she left behind, her movements are united by her always emotional, subjective engagement with the world. As critics have noted, her instinctual attraction to the commercial pleasures of Chicago and New York reveals the sensual, even fetishistic, response that mass consumer culture elicits from consumers. However, that Carrie is impelled by these desires whether she is in Columbia

City or Chicago suggests, from Dreiser's perspective, that urban culture was well on its way to becoming delocalized during the late nineteenth century.

Yet if Dreiser's migration narrative shows the force of Carrie's desires going forward, it also suggests that the strength of her emotions—and the momentum that carries her—is due in part to the retrospective movement of her feelings—in short, her nostalgia. In his discussion of the novel, Thomas Riggio argues that Carrie's periodic sadness or "blues" may be traced to her unhappy family life in Columbia City, bits and pieces of which Dreiser reveals to create a subtle portrait of psychological distress. As Riggio sees it, Carrie moves through the novel fruitlessly (and unconsciously) searching for the emotional experience that she missed growing up. Consequently, she is drawn like a child to her rocking chair and the rhythm that she associates with the nurturing mother she never had.[52] Although Riggio does not discuss nostalgia, his account of Carrie's longing brings to mind a central feature of the concept: the perpetual quest to recover origins that are out of reach.[53]

Yet Carrie's search for home and family takes place in such a way as to argue for a broadly expansive understanding of home. When at the end of the novel Dreiser describes her rocking-chair daydream by invoking pastoral imagery, he returns to the beginning of the novel and the "familiar green environs of the village" that she is about to leave. Here, at the outset of Carrie's journey, Dreiser notes that she is "lightly" bound to her home and that while she weeps when she says good-bye to her mother, her ties to Columbia City were soon "irretrievably broken." The word *irretrievably* emphasizes the inaccessibility of the home and childhood that Carrie has just left, but Dreiser does not say she will never have any desires—conscious or not—to recover this part of her life. His cyclical return to her origins at the end of the novel, via nostalgia, suggests that she does, and that in her continual migrations she is fated to search for such happiness that she may never feel.[54]

However bleak this ending may be, the conclusion that Carl Sandburg reaches in his poem "Mamie" (1916) is much darker. In it he tells of a woman in a little Indiana town who feels imprisoned by her life and dreams of a romantic existence in Chicago. So she goes to the city. But in Chicago she feels just as dissatisfied as she did at home. Still determined to improve her life, she "beats her head against the bars in the same old way" and wonders if there is yet another, bigger place where there are "real dreams that never go smash."[55]

"Mamie" bears an unmistakable resemblance to Dreiser's story, as Sandburg captures the resurging, unsatisfied desires that propel one woman's migration out of the hinterland. Yet as much as Sandburg verges on the territory and imagery explored by Dreiser, Ade, and even Fuller (in his notion of rocking it to 'em), he strikes a new note in translating the rhythm of Carrie's desire into frustrated violence and self-destruction. In thus revising the erotic lure that characterizes his more famous poem, "Chicago," and highlighting the desperation that underwrote some versions of Chicago dreaming, Sandburg took the fellow feeling that distinguished Chicago's literary migrants to a different place.

PART THREE

THE POLITICS OF BEING NATIVE

[P]ragmatists think the question to ask about our beliefs is not whether they are about reality or merely about appearance, but simply whether they are the best habits of action for gratifying our desires.

RICHARD RORTY (1999)

6

JANE ADDAMS

Like two flagpoles stuck in the ground, "city" and "country" served as rallying points throughout much of the nineteenth century for a fierce national debate over the changing nature of American society. During the 1880s and '90s, the relationship between town and country became more complicated, shaped by both the experiences of urban migrants and the representations of those experiences by writers, reformers, and other social commentators. By constructing the terms of urban modernity around the prospective and retrospective desires of hinterland migrants, and by linking the city's unfinished status to the identities of its provincial citizens, Chicago's writers helped to loosen the categories of "rural" and "urban" and expand the discourse of spatial and economic mobility. With the emergence of more self-consciously innovative writing in the 1910s—for instance, the fiction of Willa Cather and Sherwood Anderson—Chicago became known as a place where American literature was being made new.

But the impulse to make it new was not limited to literary culture. One of the most vivid examples of Chicago's provincial modernity was Jane Addams's attempt at Hull-House to create an intimate face-to-face community based on values that she strategically identified with her hinterland background. Addams's provincialization of urban culture was particularly evident in two areas. First, she accorded Chicago's foreign-born citizens the pioneer status typically reserved for the native-born Americans who settled the midwestern frontier and early Chicago. Though primarily rhetorical in expression, this equation had tremendous implications for Addams's understanding of democratic community. To think of immigrants as having the same desires, goals, and privileges as white, native-born citizens was a radical act that confirmed the notion that Chicago was an urban frontier, but challenged the idea that America's fastest-growing city belonged principally to the native born. Second, Addams drew explicitly on her hinterland upbringing in formulating her theories about how urban children should be raised. Guided by her "free-ranging" childhood in Cedarville, Illinois, she came to believe that city living conditions imperiled the health and future of poor children, and thus strived to bring the boys and girls of Hull-House closer to the world of her youth.[1]

As scholars have noted, Addams's efforts at Hull-House were vitally connected to her rural background. According to Morton White and Daniel Levine, she drew upon the "spirit" of small-town life to compensate for Chicago's "unnatural environment which prevented natural human goodness from manifesting itself." Motivated by nostalgic idealism to transplant the roots of prairie democracy, her settlement work was, in Robert Crunden's words, the "great catalyst to progressive social science," the key link between "the rural protestant past" and the modern discipline of sociology that was just beginning to flourish at the University of Chicago.[2]

However, this summary of Addams's accomplishments offers too neat an account of her transition from hinterland to city. It also presupposes a conceptual separation between rural and urban that she herself did not hold, determined as she was in all her work to create unity from diversity and draw connections across cultures. Though keenly attuned to the factors that distinguished Cedarville from Chicago, Addams did not dwell on those differences until she was well launched at Hull-House and ready to import the provincial qualities that she thought would enhance urban life. When, in the early 1900s, Addams affirmed the virtues of hinterland culture, she did so with a pragmatic view of the political and social gains that she hoped to achieve. Her restraint does not necessarily mean that she cared or felt less about her hinterland home than more outwardly sentimental migrants, only that she wanted her abiding belief in the virtues of small-town life to serve a higher cause.

By the turn of the century, Addams appeared quite comfortable sorting out the distinctions between rural and urban values or ways of life. For instance, in 1907 she published an article entitled "The Difference Between City Boys and Country Boys" in the *Dallas Daily Times Herald*. In it she explains that urban youngsters "have been brought up on the false excitement which the street offers" and have "NOTHING WHICH WAS NATURAL AND NOR-MAL from their youth." This is in contrast with the "old-fashioned country boy, who seems to have carried off all the honors of the past generation" by virtue of his more natural, rural upbringing, which fosters the "HABIT" of courage and initiative. Although she was probably not responsible for the sensational presentation of her prose—in capital letters—or the byline that identified her as "JANE ADDAMS, Sociologist, Chicago," the article correctly sketches the social scientific framework that now supported her international reputation and guided her subsequent more fully developed endorsements of the benefits that derived from country living.[3] When Addams describes these advantages in *The Spirit of Youth and the City Streets* (1909) and "The Play Instinct and the Arts" (1930), she notes that many urban youngsters, particularly the children of immigrants, suffer from the lack of open, natural surroundings that were usually available in the country. Yet even though she underscores the salutary effects of the natural, she avoids the opposition between country and city that distinguished so much nineteenth-century rhetoric and treats those effects not as essential values but as human attributes that could be more easily nurtured in a rural environment. Through this relativistic perspective and her use of scientific terms like *instinct* and *habit*, Addams showed just how much her own migration from Cedarville to Chicago was mediated by her experience at Hull-House and exposure to contemporary thinkers such as William James, John Dewey, and G. Stanley Hall.

In the 1890s, however, Addams seldom mentioned the rural-urban divide in published writings. She moved to Chicago in 1889. Having determined, along with Ellen Gates Starr, to live without prejudice on Halsted Street among the poor and foreign born, she resisted thinking about her immediate surroundings in dichotomous terms. Whether those terms meant dividing the poor from the rich, the urban from the rural, or the native born from the foreign born, she apparently set aside cultural assumptions in order to see the world through the eyes of her neighbors, and to underscore the "subjective necessity" of democracy. This charge was consistent with the doctrine of good works (the Golden Rule) that informed Addams's upbringing, but it was also a work in progress that bore the imprint of her intellectual growth and her wariness of dogma and either/or solutions.

During her first decade or so at Hull-House, Addams also distinguished her work from conventional notions of "settlement"—for example, western

pioneer efforts that Frederick Jackson Turner described in "The Significance of the Frontier in American History," his address given at the
World's Columbian Exposition of 1893. In her purpose-defining article,
"A Function of the Social Settlement" (published in 1899), Addams says
nothing of urban frontiers, but she criticizes the prevailing belief in "geographical salvation," which caused people to move "from country to town,
with the conviction that they are finding more fullness of life." Addams
questions whether such movements — even changing neighborhoods within
a city — brought happiness and claims that they missed the central objective
of settlement, which was to enhance social relations. A settlement house,
for instance, "touches to life the dreary and isolated, and brings into a
fuller participation of the common inheritance," enabling residents of the
neighborhood to make connections among one another and see the world
anew.[4]

Pragmatic Turn

Although Addams eschewed the ritualistic pulling up of stakes typically
associated with the American pioneer tradition, her notion of settlement
reflected her embrace of pragmatism, a philosophy of learning and belief
that was itself always in motion. And in "A Function of the Social Settlement," she quotes John Dewey and William James, whose writings seemed
to reflect her own experiences at Hull-House. "Beliefs," Addams recites
from James's path-breaking address on pragmatism, "are really rules of action, and the whole function of thinking is but one step in the production of
habits of action."[5] What, after all, was a settlement house but the concrete
embodiment of pragmatic thinking, an environment where beliefs are not so
much transplanted from other places but rather transformed and generated
though interpretation, action, and synthesis?

The thrust of Addams's pragmatism, as Charlene Siegfried has emphasized, was to enact a democratic way of life based on the "interdependency
of all persons in societies, from the local to the global." She resisted doctrinaire political stances — like socialism — not because she disagreed with
their stated goals, but because she realized how polarizing and ultimately
self-defeating contentious political agitation could be. Focused always on
the whole, on the process of building unity, Addams instead recognized the
value of multiple identities and coalitions of diverse individuals.[6]

To think of Jane Addams in these terms, as a pragmatist committed to the ongoing generation of beliefs and community, is to understand more clearly her ambiguous treatment of town and country relations, and the distance she sought to put between her role as head resident of Hull-House and any assumptions people might have had about her status as a middle-class, female reformer come from the provinces to work with Chicago's immigrant population. Particularly in the early years of her career, Addams contended with what Victoria Brown calls "the media image of her as a selfless maiden who had sacrificed personal wealth and happiness to live and work among the poor." [7] Add to this image her provincial antecedents, and Addams's task of explaining why she was in Chicago becomes even more complicated.

For example, any suggestion that her small-town background uniquely qualified her to introduce American values to the foreign born was a potential barrier to the mutual relations that she hoped to establish with neighborhood residents. Also, the idea that she was a homegrown provincial bringing Main Street to Halsted Street is inconsistent with Addams's upbringing and education. Her father, John Addams, was a prominent businessman and politician whose entrepreneurial leadership—in the 1840s, he spearheaded a successful effort to bring the Galena and Chicago Railroad to nearby Freeport—served to modernize the region. [8] And her stepmother, Anna Haldeman Addams, was ambitious if not successful in her aspiration to move in more sophisticated social circles. By the time Jane Addams arrived in Chicago in 1889, she had a college degree from Rockford Female Seminary, had toured Europe twice, and had lived in Baltimore on two occasions. Moreover, her decision to establish Hull-House grew out of an accumulation of world-broadening experiences that transcended geographic and cultural differences. Addams's cosmopolitan perspective did not stop her from emphasizing her hinterland background and love of home when it was advantageous. But it did foster her conviction that beliefs and wisdom were not tied to any one place or vantage point but rather were the product of being and acting in the world. Although it would be several years before Addams consciously adopted the language of pragmatism to explain her mission at Hull-House, she was already thinking pragmatically when she came to Chicago.

As articulated by William James and his contemporaries, pragmatism sets aside the essential truths that govern traditional metaphysics in favor of an experience-based philosophy of knowledge and morality. By questioning the idea that foundational truths lie outside the human experience in some transcendent form, and referring instead to how people test and derive their beliefs through their engagement with the world, pragmatism's chief articulators brought Darwin's theories of biological selection to epistemology. As Louis Menand has shown, pragmatism's radical antifoundationalism and its vision of humans as thinking and desiring animals striving to measure belief against a swiftly changing environment stemmed largely from historical transformations that made belief in eternal verities seem untenable. For example, Oliver Wendell Holmes and Charles S. Peirce—who, along with James, developed the beginning theories of pragmatism—came to the new philosophy through their discovery of life's contingencies, Holmes by having his faith in human goodness shaken by fighting in the Civil War, and Peirce by realizing that scientific inquiry cannot measure naturally occurring phenomena with absolute precision.[9]

One upshot of pragmatism's reshuffling of the relation between truth and reality was the understanding that philosophical theory is "just one of the ways we make sense of our needs." Pragmatism's difference from other ways of thinking, Menand notes, may be explained in this way: "We wake up one morning and find ourselves in a new place, and then we build a ladder to explain how we got there. The pragmatist is the person who asks whether this is a good place to be. The nonpragmatist is the person who admires the ladder."[10]

Though Addams's movement from country to city did not have the same cataclysmic effect on her as the Civil War did on Holmes, she recognized that urban migration was a large-scale social transformation with disruptive implications for the culture as a whole. More to the point, she understood that this shift would turn upside down stereotypical notions of rural and urban life (that one was moral and virtuous, and the other was not). She rejected these seemingly essential dualities, and instead worked to effect the transfer (and continuity) of values typically found in small places—in effect, building a ladder from Cedarville to Chicago to create a more supportive civic culture.

This view of Jane Addams as a pragmatic migrant strategically drawing on the resources of her provincial background to support her work at Hull-House is consistent with the history that Victoria Brown gives of her early career. As Brown has shown, young Jane Addams longed to pursue a life of action and service, to emulate the stories of heroism her father told her as a child. Growing up in a family that valued ethical conduct but was not settled on orthodox religious questions, Addams gradually developed the spiritual framework that later distinguished her work at Hull-House, undergoing a process of self-education that led her to a relatively secular vision of human interdependence.[11]

Crucial to the development of the youthful Addams's views was her growing dissatisfaction with the idea that books alone are the source of wisdom. In 1879, when still a student at Rockford, she wrote her friend and classmate, Ellen Gates Starr, to tell her that she was reading Thomas Carlyle's *Sartor Resartus* and enjoying it. But, she complains, "I am sort of disgusted with general reading . . . my admiration for a well-read person is mingled with just a bit of contempt that they had to READ to find out all about it." Significantly, this pitch for experiential learning—Addams sounding like John Dewey a decade before meeting him at Hull-House— came in a letter in which Addams discusses Starr's plan to leave Rockford early and teach school in Chicago. Addams expresses enthusiasm for this proposal as well as her confidence that "you will gain a good deal more than if you had been that time in our noble institution. There is something in being in a big city, in giving somewhat as well as taking all the time, in gaining the ability not to move in ruts—that will give you self-reliance and an education a good deal better than a boarding-school will, and I think that you have a pretty prosperous outlook."[12]

This Emersonian assessment of city life offers an interesting preview of Addams's subsequent decision to move to Chicago. Without the evangelical call to good works, the nineteen-year-old Addams almost sounds like an urban booster: Chicago is bigger and more expansive than Rockford; most important, it will give Starr the freedom to move—literally and figuratively— beyond the "ruts" (or prescribed social roles) that limit the opportunity for individual growth in the hinterlands. A decade before her own migration, Addams recognized that Chicago might be a good place for self-making.

But she did not come to Chicago directly. Leaving Cedarville for the big city might end the drift in her life, but it was not clear—at least not yet—that such a choice would be hers alone to make. There were familial responsibilities that she felt obliged to meet, including the genteel domestic life that her stepmother had planned for her. Moreover, even though John Addams's death in 1881 left her with roughly $60,000 in assets (an income of $3,000 a year) and considerable financial independence, these same resources also made her a more attractive prospect for marriage. Little wonder that she approached her future with caution, or that she later called these years a "Snare of Preparation."[13]

As a migrant, Addams was thus something of an incrementalist, focusing on her dream of playing a significant role in the world outside Cedarville while gradually enhancing her understanding of urban life through trips to Europe and stints in Baltimore, where she had her first face-to-face encounters with life-threatening poverty. Though she yearned to leave her hometown, she was also resigned to her role as a spinster, which involved addressing a wide variety of family problems.[14] In fact, her movements in the months leading up to her second trip to Europe suggest that she was just as likely to stay in Cedarville as move elsewhere. Writing from Baltimore in January of 1887, she confided to her sister, Alice, that "I think I have grown older this winter and have discovered among other things that it is well to hold fast to the place in which you were born and placed as it were. I enjoyed Stephenson Co. very much last fall and have all sorts of plans for my farm house in the dim future."[15]

However, Addams's impulse to "hold fast" to her native ground did not simply spring from an unqualified love of home; it was also a reaction to her life in Baltimore, which she laments in a letter that she sent to her sister-in-law, Laura Shoemaker Addams, a month earlier. Asked to attend a Rembrandt exhibit by a well-educated Baltimore woman, Addams worries that the invitation was based on the incorrect assumption that she knew a good deal about art and complains that "in a city, people are always rushing to one extreme or another, they won't let you [go] quietly along and take you for what you are worth, they insist upon your declaring yourself."[16] Echoing the advice that she offered to Ellen Gates Starr in 1879, a more seasoned Addams realized that urban society also produced "ruts" and that even in cities, social pressure could make it difficult just to be yourself.

Yet Addams's views were in flux. That summer, while visiting Alice in Girard, Kansas, she again reflected on the meaning of home and this time felt the lack of freedom. Now surrounded by the prairie landscape and the small-town routines that she had missed in Baltimore, and with family responsibilities pressing on her at every turn, she sent Laura a detailed itinerary of the route she would take back home — by train, steamboat, and train again — and an account of the friends and family she would see along the way. All in all, she tells Laura, "Alice and I have had a very pleasant visit together, the baby of course being our chief point of interest. I have some pictures of her which are to go to you. I have various calls to make and then will leave in proper social shape. I do think little towns are more exacting and trying than big ones."[17] The final sentences encapsulate Addams's conflicting sentiments—of feeling drawn to loved ones but also hemmed in by village life and familial obligations. It was a conflict that she could not escape so long as she remained in Cedarville, which the rest of the letter demonstrates. Even while traveling across the great Middle West, her way was guided by familiar faces.

Five months later, Addams was on a ship bound for England, on the brink of making a decision that would resolve the drift in her life. In *Twenty Years at Hull-House* (1910), she highlights the moral drama that led to this decision. Referring first to the European tour that she took in 1883, she describes the galvanizing impact of watching poor people scramble for garbage in the Whitechapel District of London, their "myriads of hands, empty, pathetic, nerveless, and workworn." [18] Moving then to her 1887–88 trip, she underscores the inspiring example of Samuel and Henrietta Barnett's settlement work at Toynbee Hall in London which served as a model for Hull-House. And, later in the chapter, she explains how, after seeing a brutal bullfight in Madrid (which actually took place a month or so before her Toynbee Hall visit), she resolved to change her life and invited Ellen Gates Starr to join her in establishing a settlement house in Chicago.

But what Addams does not fully disclose in her dramatic account of visiting Europe is the extent to which her decision to go to Chicago was the final step in a series of calculated movements and educational moments—her second visit to Baltimore being especially affecting—that drew her closer to a life apart from Cedarville and the immediate press of family responsibilities. In the end, her decision to migrate was a pragmatic one, born of her clarifying desire to make a difference in the world and her gradual back-and-forth movement away from her home. [19]

Seeds on the Prairie

The initial chapters of *Twenty Years of Hull-House* evoke this fluid movement between hinterland and city by presenting Addams's experiences in Chicago and Cedarville side by side. This arrangement downplays the sense of anticipation found in other migration narratives and emphasizes the reciprocal relation between home and city, past and present, native and foreign born. The link between these dualities is Addams's own experiences, or rather her recollection of them. At the outset of her autobiography, she explains that "[n]o effort is made in the recital to separate her own history from that of Hull-House," because "the mind is pliant under the pressure of events and experiences, [and] it becomes hard to detach it."[20] At first glance, this seems to mean that Addams will subordinate her self to the larger forces around her and that her life story will be an objective history of the settlement movement. Later in the book, when she writes about the activities at Hull-House, this is largely the case: she blends into the larger story. However, when she looks back on her childhood and family history, her mind appears "pliant" in two different ways. For one, we see the younger Addams adapt to the world around her, her mind responding to the changes she observes and thereby shaping her "formless character" (19). Second, we see the older Addams interpreting the past in light of her experiences at Hull-House—providing an account of her own evolution that both leads to the present and is colored by it.

Addams's description of her hinterland background in *Twenty Years* bears out her tendency, as she describes it in *The Long Road of Woman's Memory* (1916), "to interpret racial and historic experiences through personal reminiscences."[21] Like other American autobiographies, *Twenty Years* is a representative life history aimed, in this case, at showing the nation's shift—or evolution—from small-town culture to a more complicated urban society. And, like other autobiographies, it is not accurate in all respects, as Addams sometimes bends the facts and details to accentuate her composite portrait of a culture adapting to the needs of urban industrial life.

At the outset, she establishes the framework for this exercise in interpretive memory by subtly linking her work at Hull-House to the pioneer traditions of her provincial home. "These early recollections," she muses in the first chapter, "are set in a scene of rural beauty, unusual at least for Illinois. The prairie round the village was broken into hills, one of them crowned by pine woods, grown up from a bag of full of Norway pine seeds sown by my father in 1844, the very year he came to Illinois, a testimony perhaps that the most vigorous pioneers gave at least an occasional thought to beauty." This picture of John Addams planting foreign seeds in American soil figures in genealogical terms as a precursor to the younger Addams's equally pioneering efforts to cultivate ethnic diversity on Halsted Street in Chicago. Suggesting that the democratic beliefs that guided Hull-House were tested and embraced by her father's generation, Addams linked her mission to midwestern frontier traditions.

Addams gives further gloss to this tradition when she contrasts the summer games that she and her stepbrother enjoyed—"as only free-ranging

children can"—with the street play that took place near her current home at
Hull-House. The latter "is sure to be rudely destroyed by the passing
traffic," so that "even the most vivacious [children] become worn out at last
and take to that passive 'standing round' varied by rude horse-play, which
in time becomes so characteristic of city children." [22] Addams's message is
clear: in order to become active and engaged citizens, urban children need
access to the same natural freedoms that rural youngsters enjoy. However,
instead of assuming, as some nineteenth-century reformers did, that urban
immigrant children be systematically exposed to native values and practices—that they be "Americanized"—Addams stands this proposition on
its head and instead implies they have a right to the same freedoms that she
enjoyed during her childhood.

While the lyrical tone of these reminiscences highlights Addams's poetic
sensibilities, the mixed rhetoric of *Twenty Years* underscores the challenge
of writing a developmental history—of her own life and that of the settlement house movement—within the generic confines of a literary autobiography. When Addams uses terms like *organism* and *overdifferentiation,* her
admiration of Auguste Comte, Charles Darwin, Herbert Spencer, and scientific thought shines through (92, 98). Such language signals her intention
of recounting her own intellectual evolution while also alluding to her position as a world-renowned social theorist—the destination that the younger
Jane Addams ultimately reached. One idea in particular marked her arrival
as a serious if not radical thinker: "the theory that the dependence of classes
on each other is reciprocal," and that social relations acquire a "peculiar
value" by virtue of the fact that they are reciprocal in nature. Though
Addams states at the beginning of *Twenty Years* that she arrived in Chicago
"without any preconceived social theories or economic views," she clearly
believed that working across class lines would give her great personal satisfaction. It took time for this longing to connect with others to develop into a
theory or social policy that might reform civic conditions, but the desire was
there from the day that Hull-House opened (xvii).

Addams's insistence that the cultural and political value of social reciprocity can only be realized through experience is at the heart of her famous
1892 lecture, "The Subjective Necessity of Social Settlements" (excerpted
in chapter 6 of *Twenty Years*), which serves as a theoretical action plan for
Hull-House's experiment in cooperative living and democratic society. As
articulated by Addams, the Hull-House mission rests on the belief that a
"higher civic life" is possible only through "common intercourse," which

social settlements achieve by bringing people of different backgrounds and classes "into juxtaposition" with one another. The goal of this process is not to highlight differences, but rather to build on what they share — a realm that includes "all that is noblest in life" and (evoking William Wordsworth and perhaps following G. Stanley Hall's work on racial memory) "memories and glimpses of that long life of our ancestors which still goes on among so many of our contemporaries" (92). To build a community founded on reciprocal social relations, a settlement must be flexible, spontaneous, tolerant, and "ready to experiment"; it must think and act pragmatically, with a commitment to interpret(ing) democracy in social terms (98). In short, there could be no boundary between theory and practice.

Social reciprocity's importance at Hull-House can hardly be overestimated, as it sketched a common ground that enabled the poor and the middle class, the native and foreign born to learn from one another. Equally important are the sentiments behind the theory. All told, the words *longing, desire,* and *crave* appear more than half a dozen times in "The Subjective Necessity of Social Settlements," each occurrence underscoring the spiritual yearning — a "primordial," almost biological, necessity — that prompted young women and men to improve living conditions for the poor and enhance the quality of civic life (92). The implication of Addams's discussion is that emotions are an integral aspect of the social landscape that constitutes the settlement house movement.

Significantly, Addams includes in this otherwise rather scientific discussion a vignette that personalizes these longings and provides a poetic, historical context for examining her motivations, as well as those of her audience.

You may remember the forlorn feeling which occasionally seizes you when you arrive early in the morning a stranger in a great city: the stream of laboring people goes past you as you gaze through the plate-glass window of your hotel; you see hard workingmen lifting great burdens; you hear the driving and jostling of huge carts and your heart sinks with a sudden sense of futility. The door opens closes behind you and you turn to the man who brings you in your breakfast with a quick sense of human fellowship. You find yourself praying that you may never lose your hold on it all. A more poetic prayer would be that the great mother breasts of our common humanity, with its labor and suffering and its homely comforts, may never be withheld from you. You turn helplessly to the waiter and feel that it would be almost grotesque to claim from him the sympathy you crave because civilization has placed you apart, but you resent your position with a sudden sense of snobbery. Literature is full of portrayals of these glimpses; they come to shipwrecked men on rafts; they overcome the differences of an incongruous multitude when in the presence of a great danger or when moved by a common enthusiasm. They are not, however, confined to such moments, and if we were in the habit of telling them to each other, the recital would be as long as the tales of children are, when they sit down on the green grass and confide to each other how many times they have remembered that they lived once before. If these childish tales are the stirring of inherited impressions just so surely is the other the striving of inherited powers (92–93).

Although it may going too far to claim that the "you" who feels estranged in the big city is an urban migrant, Addams's retrospective view parallels fictional accounts of the newcomer set adrift in the bustling, anonymous streets. [23] "You" experienced all the emotions that Addams once felt, probably during one of her trips to Europe: loneliness, empathy for the working class, homesickness, and above all, an intense desire for human fellowship. In attributing these emotions to a mirror self, Addams assumes that her audience underwent a similar migratory passage before taking up settlement work. Yet there is a second and even third order of feelings that grow out this complicated identification with the "great mother breasts of our common humanity." After the moment of arrival passes and "you" has become a communal "we," Addams characterizes these sentiments in explicitly literary terms as the emotions felt by characters that have been shipwrecked. But— and here Addams follows her emotions down to what seems to be their primary source—the longing for fellow feeling is also the stuff of everyday life, and as rich and mysterious as the fanciful stories that children tell one another. In this last analogy, which connects adult intuition to juvenile storytelling, Addams seems to lose her thread. On the other hand, her apparent return to the "green grass" of her own pastoral childhood underscores the most important lesson of the vignette: that the desire to forge community among social unequals is an inherited attribute and as natural and pure as child's play. Here, and in other passages dealing with her early years at Hull-House, we see her striving to join individual habits of desire to a larger collective purpose.

It is difficult, after reading this passage, not to be drawn back to Addams's accounts of childhood, in particular her description in chapter 1 of a recurring nightmare in which she found herself alone in the world and faced with the responsibility of making a wagon wheel. Addams interprets this dream as a symptom of girlhood anxiety, brought on by her "excessive sense of responsibility" and "compounded" by images from *Robinson Crusoe* and the doomsday rhetoric of Second Adventists.[24] However, the dream is also a darker rendition of the yearning for fellowship that Addams (and "you") experienced in the city hotel and that literary characters (like Crusoe) have when they are shipwrecked.

Hull-House was Addams's answer to this yearning. In *Twenty Years,* she goes out of her way—not as a social scientist but as a poet or writer of fiction might—to show that the desire to forge human connections is an inherited instinct that is as compelling for Italian peasants as it is for Addams and other settlement workers. This is the moral of her epiphany in "The Subjective Necessity of Social Settlements," and also a key point of her early "impressions" in *Twenty Years,* where she joins past and present in an effort to show, as in the wagon wheel dream, the settlement movement's deep cultural and emotional roots. Metaphorically, these conjoinings bring Addams's hinterland background into the evolution of Hull-House and give Chicago's immigrants a stake in the history of antebellum Illinois.

The links between Addams's experiences at Hull-House and her early life are numerous, and extend well beyond her comparison of childhood play in Cedarville and Chicago. She stresses her father's friendship with Abraham Lincoln, and implies that her work with immigrants is an extension of their unswerving commitment to all citizens. She also describes her father as a model for intercultural exchange and community involvement, emphasizing his admiration for the Italian republican Joseph Mazzini. And, evoking yet another dreamlike memory, she dramatizes his role in developing her sense of civic responsibility. As he came out of his bank one day onto the main street of town—"a veritable whirlpool of society and commerce"—John Addams greeted his daughter and "lifted his high and shining silk hat and made me an imposing bow." This "totally unnecessary identification among a mass of 'strange people'" struck the girl as surreal, but in the context of the relations she later established with many "unknown" Chicagoans, the incident seems instructive. Just as her father's grief over the death of Mazzini convinced Addams that people of different languages and cultures can share "large hopes and like desires," so her lessons on the streets of Freeport taught her to feel connected to the strangers around her (32, 35). Whether or not John Addams ever greeted his daughter in this fashion is almost beside the point. More important is Jane Addams's construction of him in *Twenty Years* as a heroic figure determined to pass on the value of civic responsibility and democratic community.

John Addams is also the touchstone of a story that Addams tells about Stephenson County's annual Old Settlers' Day. A featured speaker at a celebration held in the 1870s, her father praised a local German-born woman for her "heroic fortitude" in supporting the Galena-Chicago railroad venture. As Lois Rudnick points out, the incident serves to dramatize the pioneering spirit of foreign-born immigrants and, by implication, their American character. Jane Addams later reproduced these celebrations of frontier success with a Pioneer Day at Hull-House honoring older immigrants—"so like the men and women of my earliest childhood"—for their courage as well as their contributions to Chicago's civic culture.[25] Given small-town midwesterners' fondness for celebrating Old Settlers' Days during the 1880s and '90s, Addams's equation could hardly fail to resonate with her audience. Chicago readers likely responded on yet another level, since the Hull-House Pioneer Day paralleled the annual celebrations held by the Calumet Club, the Old Settlers Society, the Indiana Society of Chicago, and other organizations for native-born newcomers.

Such episodes achieve much of their persuasive power by highlighting the intersection of Addams's life story with larger, historical forces—in this case, her ability to match her commitment to multiethnic democracy with the prairie democracy of her father's generation. However, as a number of scholars have pointed out, the details that make up *Twenty Years at Hull-House* are not always accurate.[26] Addams herself signaled the memoir's potential for historical discrepancies when she titled the first chapter "Earliest Impressions," underscoring her intention of sketching and interpreting the past, rather than documenting it.

The description of Old Settlers' Day is a prime example of Addams's impressionistic approach. Beginning with a discussion of Lincoln's influence on Stephenson County's original pioneers, who were determined to govern themselves and their resources without outside help, and ending with a nod to the Illinois president's importance at Hull-House, the account moves in a circular fashion to underscore the legacy of democratic ideals. The crux of the portrayal is Addams's recollection of the Old Settlers' celebration, which took place in 1875 when she was about fifteen years old. This meeting, particularly her father's exchange with the German woman who supported the railroad plan, stands out in her memory because it convinced her that "the people themselves were the great resource of the country."[27] She claims that the episode undermined her enthusiasm for Thomas Carlyle's *Heroes and Hero Worship,* a book that she was reading at the time and had planned to give to friends. That gift no longer seemed appropriate, since she now understood that ordinary people were capable of accomplishing great things on their own. She also notes that the event shaped the development of her political beliefs, for she explains in closing that she later gave some Hull-House boys copies of Carl Schurz's book on Abraham Lincoln. Not incidentally, Schurz was a German immigrant.

Addams's artfully symmetric prose shows, rather than argues, that American democracy depends on the foresight, common sense, and hard work of ordinary citizens, foreign and native born alike. However, in bringing this belief to life, she seems to shape her own history to fit the message. For instance, she asserts that this incident prompted her skepticism of Carlyle's model of heroic leadership, but her biographers suggest that she did not question Carlyle's teaching until after she left Rockford Seminary two years later.[28] This timeline is also consistent with the date of the letter that Addams sent Starr in 1879, expressing her interest in Carlyle's writings and her impatience with abstract book learning. Although Addams eventually distanced herself from Carlyle's thinking, during the late 1870s she was still reading him with interest.[29]

Another hint that this account may be more impression than objective reality comes from Addams's publishing history. While large portions of *Twenty Years* were printed or presented elsewhere before being revised and incorporated in the book, she did not publish anything on Old Settlers' Day prior to the autobiography's appearance in 1910. She did, however, write an article called "A Village Decoration Day" for an 1883 issue of the *Rockford Seminary Magazine*. An expository portrayal of how a rural community honored Civil War veterans (Decoration Day being the precursor to Memorial Day), the essay resembles Addams's treatment of Old Settlers' Day in several significant ways. It, too, focuses on a hometown ritual that took place one summer in Addams's past, likewise highlighting the "power" that "memories and experiences . . . yet exert in quiet country places." It also underscores memory's claim on Addams herself, foregrounding her nostalgic impulse to recover examples of heroism from the provincial world of her youth. Finally, just as the *Twenty Years* account salutes the common sense of Stephenson County's residents, so the article begins with the recognition that the "simple-hearted people" of the village "do not seek culture from books or artificial means, but take whatever Experience offers them, with such seriousness and depth of feeling that their lives are radically deepened and steadied."[30]

All these factors raise questions about the veracity of the *Twenty Years* account, and suggest that Addams took poetic license in treating Old Settlers' Day as a coincidence of personal epiphanies. That her description of Old Settlers' Day may actually be a reconstructed version of "A Village Decoration Day" does not alter its persuasive power or its broader, impressionistic truth. However, it does reveal Addams's determination to present hinterland culture as the seedbed for ethnic pluralism and pragmatic thinking. And it suggests the intensity of her desire to bring her nostalgia for home and love of father into alignment with her mature but no less fervent commitment to her extended family at Hull-House.

"A Village Decoration Day" was not a suitable vehicle for striking this balance. It says nothing about the foreign born—in fact, the village seems dominated by native-born Protestants—and the slow-moving, rural atmosphere that Addams describes is at odds with the economically progressive stance that she later ascribed to Stephenson County. Of course, she could have revised the article for inclusion in the autobiography, but it would have been difficult to reorient the solemn tone and grave subject matter to accommodate both the diverse readership and the vibrant pragmatism that she had in mind in 1910. To be sure, "A Village Decoration Day" includes a boost for experiential learning. However, this endorsement, like her 1879 letter to Ellen Gates Starr, is an example of what in *Twenty Years* she calls "premature pragmatism" and "callow" writing.[31] These gropings toward pragmatism are premature (and perhaps also immature) not simply because they lack the philosophical sophistication of the older Addams's writings, but also because they baldly state the virtues of experiential learning without showing that such learning is part of the experience of living. Addams's portrayal of Old Settlers' Day, on the other hand, is aimed at revealing the seamless connection between experience and knowledge, and at dramatizing the cultural advantages of a pragmatism shared by all citizens. Almost a century in advance of Richard Rorty's endorsement of pragmatic democracy, Addams showed how experiential learning helped a diverse American community "achieve" their country.[32]

Tightly woven into a chapter that forms a bridge between the land of Lincoln and Great Britain, Addams's account of the Stephenson County Old Settlers' Day is the rhetorical high point of her portrayal of hinterland culture. It enables her to claim in a succeeding passage, once again invoking the legacy of Lincoln, that Toynbee Hall's initiatives "could not but seem artificial to a western American who had been born in a rural community where the early pioneer life had made social distinctions impossible." This is a far cry from her eye-opening response to the poor people she saw scavenging garbage in the Whitechapel District, but ironically, it is not so far from the fifteen-year-old girl's disillusionment with Thomas Carlyle. With that disillusionment so close at hand, Addams was well poised to characterize her perspective during this English tour as that of "the rustic American" who "looked on in detached comment." Although she is generally determined in *Twenty Years* to blur the differences between provincial and cosmopolitan—between native and foreign born—here she underscores her "dual consciousness" and the discomfort she felt in being an American provincial in Britain.[33] This sense of divided self, more akin to W. E. B. Du Bois' notion of double consciousness (described several years earlier in *The Souls of Black Folk* [1903]) than Benjamin Franklin's shrewd frontier personae, led Addams, uncharacteristically, to drop her veil and fall back on her Cedarville antecedents.

A Free-Ranging Childhood

Ultimately, Jane Addams's divided consciousness was a Chicago frame of mind—a reflection of the same tensions that George Ade, John McCutcheon, Will Payne, Henry Blake Fuller, and others engaged in their portrayal of urban-hinterland relations and, in varying degrees, negotiated in their own transition to city life. As a highly involved citizen of Chicago, a member of the Little Room, and a provincial migrant herself, Addams was surely aware of contemporaneous literary treatments of urban migration, though she left no record of her impressions. When her fellow Little Roomers performed *Captain Fry's Birthday Party*, she was not part of the cast, but given the play's emphasis on native-born Americans and its burlesque tone, her lack of participation is not surprising.[34] When Addams did draw upon her provincial background to support her work at Hull-House, she was in full control of the rhetoric.

However, she demonstrated more than a rhetorical interest in her hinterland past. Beginning in the early 1890s and continuing with greater conviction in the 1910s and '20s, Addams developed an instrumental use of rural and small-town values that helped her advocate for specific reforms that would improve the lives of urban children. Her accomplishments in this area focused mostly, but not exclusively, on the children of immigrants, because their desultory play on the streets of Chicago appeared to lack the free-ranging spontaneity that she and her stepbrother enjoyed as children growing up in Cedarville.

Tangible signs of Addams's desire to improve/enhance the play environments of immigrant children appeared in the mid-1890s, when she began taking large groups of them on extended stays in the country. Renting a tract of land in Michigan or Wisconsin, Hull-House residents pitched tents and set up camp for between fifty and one hundred children, who stayed in these makeshift facilities for two weeks. At about the same time, Addams also turned her attention to the neighborhood around Hull-House and convinced a local property owner to tear down several dilapidated buildings and establish a playground in their stead. This collaborative project, the first public playground in Chicago, was ready for use in the spring of 1892.[35]

Both these initiatives were aimed at improving the health and well-being of urban children, and each had lasting consequences for Hull-House, the city of Chicago, and Addams's evolving sense of civic culture. Although her contribution to the national playground movement has been widely noted by historians of the Progressive era, her determination to establish a permanent summer camp for city kids is less well known.[36] And yet when Addams reflected on her second twenty years at Hull-House, she noted that the Joseph T. Bowen Country Club—the summer camp that she established in Waukegan, Illinois, in 1912 with the financial support of her good friend Louise De Koven Bowen—"really illustrates perhaps better than anything else Hull-House has been able to achieve, the results of the play instinct coming to flower in a sheltered place where beauty and decorum are cherished."[37] This statement is remarkable not only for its superlative praise of the camp's success, but also because it unequivocally endorses the aesthetic and developmental benefits of country living. Here, as opposed to *Twenty Years at Hull-House*, Addams has a concrete idea of how provincial values should serve urban society.

Addams's thinking on the relationship between "play" and urban society can be followed in three of her works: *The Spirit of Youth and the City Streets* (1909), *A New Conscience and an Ancient Evil* (1912), and the essay "The Play Instinct and the Arts" (1930), which also appears, in a slightly expanded version, in *The Second Twenty Years at Hull-House* (1930). Taken together, these writings sketch a theory of desire and creativity that looks toward the "natural" development of youthful energies and the foreclosure of unhealthy and immoral behavior.

Although it would be a mischaracterization to say of these three works that they deal explicitly with the differences between rural and urban life, the distinctions that they draw between harmful and healthy behavior tend to follow geographic fault lines. In *The Spirit of Youth and the City Streets,* Addams associates destructive behavior with the traditional temptations of the city—liquor, dance halls, and various other urban amusements that serve as unhealthy outlets for "the insatiable desire for play." And in *A New Conscience and an Ancient Evil,* she targets prostitution as the worst of these outlets, illustrating its dangers with examples of innocent country girls who have been lured to metropolitan areas to traffic in sex.[38] Finally, in the "The Play Instinct and the Arts," Addams comes close to reifying the perils of city life (in psychological terms) when she theorizes that "the very size of the city throws any attempt at social intercourse into a pathological condition."[39]

The language that Addams used to describe this breakdown in social relations varied in its allusions, but the cause of the breakdown was always the same: the modern industrial city's diminished community structures and its unruly size. Sounding like a historian and an anthropologist in *A New Conscience,* she explains, "social relationships in a modern city are often so superficial, that the old human restraints of public opinion, long sustained in smaller communities have also broken down. Thousands of young people in every great city have received none of the lessons in self-control which even savage tribes imparted to their children when they taught them to master their appetites as well as their emotions."[40] Without explicitly identifying these "smaller communities," the book contains enough references to rural life to make the connection for most readers. How could the protective structures of these smaller communities be restored to urban society? The more "literary" *Spirit of Youth* contains a partial and negative answer, which evokes the cultural legacy of the small town and country village: "We certainly cannot expect the fathers and mothers who have come to the city from farms or who have emigrated from other lands to appreciate or rectify these [urban] dangers. We cannot expect the young people themselves to cling to conventions which are wholly unsuited to modern city conditions, nor yet equal to the task of forming new conventions through which this more agglomerate social life may express itself."[41]

In short, Addams conceded that urban conditions were inimical to the development of a "protective code which reminds one of the instinctive protection that the free-ranging child in the country learns in regard to poisonous plants and 'marshy places.'" Her rhetoric illustrates the complicated mix of ends and means that lay before her. Deploying the same term that she used in *Twenty Years* (published the year after *The Spirit of Youth*) to describe her own childhood play—"free-ranging"—she implied that city children ought to aspire to the same ideal state of freedom with learned limits. Yet Addams was careful to suggest that children acquired this sense of limited freedoms not through social structures but through natural, universal processes. Children learn by instinct, and when conditions are right, they internalize "protective codes" naturally. This is a nostalgic vision, but carefully framed by important qualifications. Borrowing language from G. Stanley Hall—in *Adolescence* (1904), Hall argued that play "is the ideal type of exercise for the young, most favorable for growth, and most self-regulating in both kind and amount"—she implied that children typically learn by organic means. Citing legal terminology ("protective codes"), she suggested that urban youth were capable of developing the social restraints that legislators often tried to establish through laws and regulations. Addams was not opposed to legal guidelines (in fact, she advocated for governmental regulation in many areas), but when it came to young people she was most of all concerned that they develop their own, internal discipline—that is, "freedom for the young people made safe only through their own self-control." [42]

Freedom, in other words, depended on one's ability to control and channel the "insatiable desire for play." In terms that critics such as William James praised for their honesty, Addams did not argue for the denial and suppression of sensual energies, or condemn them as lurid. Instead, she acknowledged their universal force—insatiable for *all* young people, regardless of origin—and underscored their potential good, urging that they be redirected toward competitive sports and various educational and cultural activities. Her claim that the desire or "instinct" for play (like Thorstein Veblen's "instinct for workmanship") could be turned to positive habits was a pragmatic argument, and James recognized it as such, famously observing in his review of *The Spirit of Youth and the City Streets* that Addams "simply inhabits reality, and everything she says necessarily expresses its nature." [43]

In content and approach, *The Spirit of Youth and the City Streets* and *A New Conscience and an Ancient Evil* qualify as pioneering treatises in civic policy, written by an experienced social reformer. However, the drift of these two books also speaks to the issues and themes engaged by other Chicago dreamers. What, for example, is Addams's discussion of the "insatiable desire for play" but a consideration of the very same longings that brought ambitious young migrants to Chicago? And in urging young people to exercise "self-control" of their desires, was she not suggesting yet another version of middle-class self-making? What's missing, of course, from her analysis is a sharply articulated view from the hinterland, revealing Chicago's lure for prospective migrants. Addams highlights a similar kind of desire, and presents it much as Carl Sandburg does, as an internalized energy that helps power the city lights; but her perspective is so generally retrospective and her portrayal of the differences between rural and urban culture so relative that her provincial perspective can be hard to spot.

Yet it is there, even in *The Spirit of Youth* where Addams claims that the older conventions—the Cedarville way of enforcing social order—will not work in the modern city. For while Addams looks hard for new conventions, her analysis is informed by a nostalgia for the social controls of small-town life and a yearning to transform the desires of young people into good works.[44]

Both these impulses were present at the founding of the Bowen Country Club, a project that was arguably even nearer to Addams's heart than *The Spirit of Youth and the City Streets,* which was her favorite publication. After all, the club was an extension of her home at Hull-House, while *The Spirit of Youth* was just a book. Moreover, it was a community capable of evolution and change—and of enacting the very spirit represented in the book.

Located on the shores of Lake Michigan in Chicago's northern suburbs, the Joseph T. Bowen Country Club opened in the summer of 1912 and closed in 1963, when the Waukegan Park District acquired it. During the years of its operation, the club honored its original mission of providing a natural retreat for economically disadvantaged children who would otherwise spend their entire summer in the city. In an overview of the camp that she gave in 1946, Louise De Koven Bowen said that the idea for the club grew out of Addams's long-held concern with "getting the boys and girls of the neighborhood off the hot summer streets where they played, [and] got into all sorts of mischief."[45] For Addams and her colleagues, the club was closely allied with their efforts at Hull-House to improve the living conditions and provide additional educational opportunities for the children of immigrants. In later years, after Addams's death, this focus shifted, but only slightly, to meet the changing needs of the neighborhood's population. For instance, by 1946, the club included African-American children, and its staff sought to show camp residents—according to one counselor—"how people of every nationality, race and creed can live and work together entirely free from prejudice."[46] In 1954, the camp promised to give Halsted Street kids the experience of "living with others in the American pattern of life, as lived in normal uncrowded ways."[47] Although it is debatable whether Addams would have approved of a mission that explicitly reinforced the value of "normal" living conditions, she would certainly have endorsed the camp's interest in civil rights, since the goal at Hull-House since the early 1890s was to have people of all nationalities and races work together harmoniously.

But in the 1910s and '20s, Addams could not have been more pleased with the Bowen Country Club. Its seventy-two acres of woodland, ravines, gardens, and cottages, which Louise Bowen purchased and endowed for the Hull-House Association, represented the culmination of Addams's search for an environment suitable for experiential learning, a place apart from the "pain and confusion" of city life where the energies and talents of immigrant children could develop naturally.[48] With separate facilities for boys and girls, the club offered a variety of recreational and educational activities: swimming, hiking, basketball, outdoor games, gardening, handicrafts, photography, domestic science, art classes, and drama. These activities were similar to those offered by early twentieth-century summer camps, promoting what Peter Schmitt has called the "back to nature" movement.[49] However, the Bowen Country Club differed from other summer camps in that most children who attended it were also participants at Hull-House, which meant that their experiences in both places were often purposefully linked. Indeed, the *Hull-House Yearbook* highlighted these overlaps when it reported in 1916 that the children at the club "utilized their winter training" when they staged musicals and theatricals.[50]

Theoretically, the country club encouraged the constructive expression of the play instinct, whose misguided application in the city led, in Addams's view, to gang fights, prostitution, and other social problems. In this respect, the organic coming to flower of sensual energies that Addams prized about the camp was linked to the cultivation of orderly behavior—what she called "decorum." The children who attended the Bowen Country Club were usually not old enough to be involved in the illicit activities that Addams condemned in *The Spirit of Youth and the City Streets* and *A New Conscience and an Ancient Evil*. However, campers were permitted to attend through their eighteenth birthday, and the club's educational philosophy was based on the assumption that a supportive social atmosphere and ongoing exposure to nature and art would build lasting friendships and the habit of creative production. Tied by memory to the beauties and vicissitudes of nature, veteran

FIGURE 12 Girls pausing from play at the Bowen Country Club (date unknown). (JAMC neg. 4976, Jane Addams Memorial Collection, Special Collections, The University Library, University of Illinois at Chicago)

campers "remember when the tall trees were little, the summer when we had no raspberries because the rabbits had eaten the bark from the bushes during a winter of incessant snows, and all the natural landmarks which collect about a country house."[51] Because they were in a better position to see themselves as part of the natural world, these campers were better equipped to build a life apart from the sensational amusements and mechanized tasks of urban society.

There was, to be sure, little in these formulations that differed substantially from what Addams and her colleagues had already sought to accomplish at Hull-House itself. However, the very founding of the Bowen Country Club indicated that Hull-House alone was not enough for Addams to achieve her most cherished goals. "Sheltered" from Chicago, the club's natural surroundings provided a haven for "collective living" where the romance of city could be challenged and the children of Halsted Street given another outlet for their desires (fig. 12).[52] Equipped with several cottages and a Commons dining hall, the club likewise gave various Hull-House groups a place for repose. During the summer of 1912, the Outing Committee held its annual picnic on the grounds, and the Jane Club celebrated its twentieth anniversary there; in 1915, both the Boys' Sketching Class and the Italian Circolo traveled out from the city for weekend parties at the club.

And every June, like Old Settlers returning home, former campers who had recently married were permitted to honeymoon in one of the cottages.[53]

For Addams as well, spending time at the Bowen Country Club felt something like a homecoming. In 1929, Louise De Koven Bowen constructed a large cottage that she regularly shared with Addams and Mary Rozet Smith, Addams's life partner. Addams was so comfortable there and at the camp that when she wrote about the Bowen Country Club in *The Second Twenty Years at Hull-House,* she was reminded of her father's "unalterable affection"—and the secure place he made for her in Cedarville and the world.[54] Forty years after she left Cedarville for Chicago, Jane Addams was still holding fast to the place she was born.

7

AMONG IMMIGRANTS

Despite its historical importance, Jane Addams's pragmatic vision of multi-ethnic America found few parallels among the writers who comprised the first generation of the Chicago literary renaissance. Hamlin Garland fashioned hinterland protagonists in opposition to foreign-born immigrants; one group was "American," while the other was not. In their portrayal of Hoosier migrants as ethnic types, George Ade and John McCutcheon came close to acknowledging a kinship between the native and foreign born, but found little overlap between the two. Although Henry Blake Fuller (not a migrant himself) sensed that the provincial newcomer's assimilation into urban culture resembled that of the immigrant, he nevertheless presented Chicago's "foreign" citizens as objects of curiosity.[1] In short, most turn-of-the-century hinterland writers had difficulty incorporating self-making immigrants in their vision of Chicago.

This shorthand summary gains in significance when one considers the limited field for ethnic literature in turn-of-the-century Chicago. For instance, between 1890 and 1920, the city's large foreign-born communities produced few, if any, literary works written in English. In contrast with New York City's multiethnic Lower East Side, where an English-language literature had emerged by 1900, Chicago's Anglophone ethnic literary tradition—however limiting that category may be—did not take root until the 1930s.[2] Just how much foreign-language literature was written in late nineteenth- and early twentieth-century Chicago is a question that deserves further research.

Scholars have further complicated matters by narrowly defining the field of ethnic literature so that it excludes writers who enjoyed mainstream success or moved comfortably in dominant cultural circles. So while Theodore Dreiser and Carl Sandburg were both second-generation Americans (of German and Swedish ancestry, respectively), critics have typically not considered them "ethnic" writers. This classification is problematic on a number of levels, since, as Werner Sollors has noted, it presupposes the existence of an ethnic identity that many American writers, native or foreign born, were actually in the process of constructing.[3]

That said, this chapter is less concerned with ethnic literature per se than with how provincial writers represented foreign-born Chicagoans and their children. Although hinterland writers varied in their portrayal of immigrants, they generally relied on their provincial backgrounds to dramatize and assess the place of the foreign born in urban society. That they often assumed the provincial Midwest to be the special provenance of mainstream American values means that their writing was also implicitly nationalistic in orientation. In this regard, hinterland writing about multiethnic Chicago was involved in the construction of multiple, interlocking identities based on region, class, and national origin.

The writers highlighted here—Edith Wyatt, Elia Peattie, and Carl Sandburg—looked at Chicago's foreign born from different places on the social map. While Wyatt focused on the interactions between middle-class ethnics and the native born and Peattie portrayed the immigrant poor through the eyes of a middle-class social worker affiliated with Hull-House, Sandburg envisioned a prairie democracy in which foreign- and native-born workers had an equal share. Although each of them published these views after the bitter xenophobia of the 1880s and '90s had abated, their representations of ethnic Chicago are nonetheless utopian in reach and together show how thinking provincial was an aid to creating a multiethnic metropolis.

Hard Times

Seeing Chicago in all its human aspects was no easy task, especially under duress. Consider the beginning of Ray Stannard Baker's journalism career. Among the provincial writers who made their way to Chicago, none was

more committed to social justice than Baker. Arriving in the city in the spring
of 1892 from the University of Michigan Law School, the twenty-two-year-
old eventually landed a job with the *Chicago News Record* where, as a colleague of George Ade and John McCutcheon, he covered political news for
six years. Intensely idealistic, Baker later achieved national renown with
McClure's Magazine as a muckraking journalist who helped shape public
opinion on labor conditions, economic policy, and race relations. "[A]lways,
at heart," a "countryman," Baker traced his idealism to his upbringing on the
Michigan frontier and what he called "the religion of my youth," the idea that
each person is a distinct individual (a soul) who deserves the full support of
his family and neighbors.[4] Like Ade, Baker believed that his provincial demeanor gave him certain advantages as a newspaper reporter. "I had come
out of the frontier, where many practices of the city were quite unknown," he
recalled in his 1941 memoirs, *Native American: The Book of His Youth*.
"When I wanted to cross the street I crossed it: when I wanted to stop a man
to ask a question, I stopped him. I was suspicious of 'no admittance' signs
and tempted to find out whether they meant what they said. I had had little
practice in the art of living in a crowded world." In fact, Baker found his faith
severely tested by Chicago's oppressive living conditions, its unforgiving labor market, and the air of anonymity that generally pervaded the city. Living
hand to mouth as he looked for a job, he was able to see Chicago's poverty
from the inside, an experience that "influenced my entire attitude toward
life." During his early days in the city, Baker took comfort in visiting Hull-
House and watching Addams—"that saint of the slums"—"pioneering toward a new method of living together in a crowded world." Addams "was
not preaching a doctrine: she was living a life," and for Baker the difference
revealed the limitations of his frontier brand of self-reliance.[5]

Baker's recognition that Chicago's social ills—and those of industrial
capitalism in general—required a political solution that went beyond the
sturdy individualism of his youth crystallized in an encounter that he had in
the winter of 1892–93. Now on staff at the *News Record,* he had spent the fall
investigating the "tramp problem"—even spending several nights in a flop-
house—trying to understand the circumstances that brought thousands of
indigent men to Chicago. The problem was not new. In 1891, *The Rights of
Labor* (formerly *The Knights of Labor*), the weekly newspaper representing
the working class, complained that the Carpenters and Building Association
had published false advertisements "lur[ing]" workers to the World's Columbian Exposition, which was then under construction. The promise of

employment at the fair was empty, since "for every vacant job in any trade or calling in Chicago there are at least ten men to fill it." The upshot was that 25,000 "able-bodied" men, some with families, many from small towns, were now encamped in the city without work, food, or adequate housing. The editors wanted to know, who would take care of this "army of starving workmen?" And "what will be the result if these hungry stomachs are not provided for?"[6]

In a series of *Record* articles that extended for more than a year, Baker asks the same unanswerable questions, with similarly alarming implications. In a piece written in November of 1892, entitled "Filled With Tramps," he reports,

Tramps, vagabonds, paupers, maimed and crippled beggars with hungry children are flocking to Chicago in hundreds. Some of them are criminals by choice and some by dire necessity. They come — men, women, and children — like the mighty vanguard of the sight-seeing army soon to visit the World's Fair. There is no gala-day parade for them. Like a deadly, infectious disease, they creep silently, insidiously into our midst. Every daybreak sees them gnawing closer to the heart of public morals and personal safety. Every road leading to Chicago is lined with them; they come in the night by railroad, steamboat and peddler's wagon. Fabulous stories of the opportunities which the World's Fair will offer have come to their ears, and they are hastening to the new El Dorado.[7]

Baker's description of the Black City that was developing alongside the unfinished White City is a vision of Chicago dreaming flipped over. Although in subsequent articles he toned down his apocalyptic rhetoric, he consistently offered a foil to the civic image favored by boosters, pointing out that not every migrant who was drawn to Chicago was able to succeed. On the threshold of the much promoted and highly anticipated Columbian Exposition, and as an economic depression began to set in, this story of migratory failure was important news. Still, Baker had no comprehensive explanation for why this army of paupers had come to Chicago or what the city should do with them beyond administering ad hoc relief through charitable organizations headed by civic leaders. According to Baker's reports, some of the migrants were well-intentioned men looking for work, some were indigent drifters, some had been recently discharged by jails and hospitals, and some were professional vagabonds and con men who had been sent to Chicago by municipal officials in other cities and small towns in the region.[8]

As Baker struggled to see more clearly into this shifting human landscape, he maintained his "native" perspective, sounding by turns like an upright republican, dismayed by the spectacle of healthy men asking for handouts, or a frustrated idealist, angered that the American way had failed so many people.

Baker's bewilderment peaked one frigid night when he walked into City Hall and saw—and smelled—hundreds of ragged, dirty bodies lying on the floor. His instinctive response (which he later identified as the reaction his father would have had) was to grab one of the sleeping men and angrily ask him what he was doing there. In the hours and days that followed, Baker fed the man, paid for his bed, and tried to find him a job. And he learned that the man—really a boy—had come to Chicago from his Iowa farm on a freight car filled with potatoes. "You see," the boy told Baker, "I thought that if I could only get to Chicago, I could better myself. I could get a good job." Yet not even Baker, after deciding to make the case a personal "test" of the economic conditions in Chicago and his inherited faith in self-reliance, could find the boy a job. Finally, he ended up at Hull-House, where he asked Jane Addams what he should do. She advised him to send the boy home. So Baker arranged for his travel back to Iowa, conceding that his test had ended unsuccessfully.[9]

The experience was not a complete failure. Soon after the boy's departure, Baker realized the dramatic potential of the incident and vowed to write a novel about it, using what he learned as a reporter to enhance his understanding of the nation's political economy. Yet after traveling with Coxey's Army to Washington in 1894 (a venture aimed at dramatizing the plight of the unemployed) and reporting on Eugene Debs's involvement in the Pullman labor strikes (even testifying on his behalf in Chicago), Baker did not feel he was any closer to understanding the larger problems. Uncomfortable with the systematic fixes promised by socialism and the single-tax movement, both of which gathered momentum during the 1893–94 depression, he grew increasingly wary of his own impulse to write the definitive fictional account of the era. "It was not only the complication of the problems themselves," Baker notes in his autobiography, "it was the complexity and perversity of me, the observer. . . . I found my own eyes colored by my background; my observations blurred by my education, and complicated by my loyalties; warped by my selfish interests; short-circuited by my emotions. I was myself, in some sort, the potato-car boy!"[10] Marked by a determination not to sacrifice the principles of his trade—honesty, skepticism, and objectivity—his retreat from this first attempt at fiction writing instead became an object lesson in his own intellectual and political development.

In one sense, Baker's account of these events in the final chapter of *Native American* constitutes an ironic postscript to his Chicago education: the mature journalist reflecting on how the younger reporter came to understand his personal implication in a major news story. Eventually, he did fictionalize the potato-car boy's story—not by dwelling on the boy's failed migration (which, of course, spoke to Baker's own fear of failure) but by developing the authorial persona of David Grayson, a prosperous businessman who leaves the city and retires to a farm to write books extolling the virtues of rural life. As Robert Bannister has pointed out, creating Grayson enabled Baker to speak from an idealized, genteel, provincial perspective, providing a counterbalance to the politically engaged writing that he pursued as a Progressive journalist. For instance, in the 1920s, it gave him a forum for advocating unrestricted foreign immigration, a policy that Baker the journalist began to question during World War I, when "the apparent disloyalty of many hyphenated Americans had given him pause." The roots of this divided position, though, went back to Baker's experience in early 1890s Chicago, when he sensed that the depression had placed the interests of unemployed native Americans in conflict with those of the foreign born. Hardly a nativist, Baker was an advocate of free immigration, especially to the degree that it promoted democratic self-making and allowed immigrants and their children to become part of the American middle class.[11] Still, when it appeared that economic and social conditions threatened the upward mobility of native Americans—as it did the potato-car boy—he had difficulty incorporating ethnic Chicagoans in his vision of self-making.

The Foreign Problem

Remarkable on several levels, Baker's account of the steps that led him from his first encounter with Chicago's brutish poverty to his reflections on the potato-car boy also stands out for its typicality. Like many literary migrants who launched their careers in late nineteenth-century Chicago, he disliked the city that he found so fascinating. Like Brand Whitlock, he worked from his visceral reaction to the city's extremes to a more considered perspective as a Progressive. This political position, though not unique to hinterland migrants, was inseparable from Whitlock's and Baker's experiences as newcomers to Chicago. Representative of the "Progressive impulse" that Richard Hoftstadter traced to the small-town or rural perspective, such positions emerged from the principled confrontation of midwestern republican ideology with the exigencies of the modern industrial city: widespread poverty, oppressive labor conditions and wages, inefficient services, corrupt politics, and the influx of European immigrants.[12] But, in contrast with Jane Addams, whose decision to live among immigrants was the defining feature of her life in Chicago, Baker had little to say on this last subject. This, too, was typical, though for reasons that had little to do with the reform impulse.

What is striking is how Baker's silence about immigrants dovetails with nineteenth-century literary portrayals of Chicago's foreign born. Although Chicago writers certainly did not ignore immigrants, they tended to present them in stereotypical terms, often associating them with "swarms" or the sound of "babel" (both popular literary figures for foreignness) or subordinating them to roles in fiction that reinforce the natural rights and powers of the native born. An especially didactic example of this second practice is E. P. Roe's best-selling novel, *Barriers Burned Away* (1872), which tracks the relationship between an atheistic young German woman and her pious, natural-born suitor during the Great Fire of 1871. Concluding with their romantic union and the woman's religious conversion, the novel dramatizes the assimilation of the foreign born into Chicago's cultural mainstream and the rebirth of the burned-over city. Not incidentally, the catalyst for this transformation—the morally upright suitor—also happens to be a provincial migrant.

The anxiety captured by Roe's novel persisted as middle- and upper-class Chicagoans—white and native born—struggled to understand the meaning of the city's expanding population of foreign-born residents. In 1890, more than three-quarters of Chicago's million-plus population were either born outside the United States or the offspring of parents who were. Among the city's "older" immigrant communities, the Germans were the largest, totaling a quarter of the entire population, followed by the Irish, who literally helped build the city in the 1830s. Though smaller in numbers, Chicago's Swedes, Norwegians, and Danes represented the largest Scandinavian community in the nation. The city's "newer" immigrants, from eastern and southern Europe (Poles, Slavs, Bohemians, Greeks, and Italians), who began arriving in the late 1880s and increased in number during the 1890s and early 1900s, were generally poorer and looked and sounded much more "foreign" than Chicago's other immigrant groups.[13] For many "American" citizens, they also seemed more threatening.

The city's legacy of labor unrest, punctuated by the 1886 Haymarket tragedy and the Pullman strike of 1894, fueled native-born Chicagoans' worries about the ideological orientation of the city's foreign born. Given its heavily industrial economy, Chicago was a natural venue for union organizing and radical political activity, and because the working class was dominated by the foreign born (and their children), the ongoing battles between labor and capital often assumed a distinctly ethnic flavor. The anxiety, even fear, which these conflicts inspired in many middle- and upper-class residents can hardly be underestimated. By 1890, persuaded by almost twenty years of social disorder dating to the Great Fire, Chicago elites greeted each new outbreak as evidence that "something was fundamentally wrong" with the city.[14]

Outside the labor arena, native-born Chicagoans found additional reasons to be concerned about the foreign born. For instance, German and Swedish immigrants, who belonged to conservative branches of the Catholic and Lutheran Churches, were more likely to follow their religious convictions than the American state, whose liberal orientation and emphasis on individual freedoms challenged their belief in patriarchal authority and corporately organized communities and families. While the consequences of these beliefs were perhaps more visible in ethnic enclaves of the rural Midwest, where civic leaders sought to maintain these traditional social structures by controlling the mechanisms for marriage and property entailment, the German-American community in Chicago likewise sought to reinforce group identity in the late 1880s by pushing for German-language instruction in the public schools, consequently alarming "Americans."[15]

But Chicago's ethnic communities were a good deal more "American" than many native detractors of the "foreign" presence may have realized or cared to admit. As historian Orm Overland has shown, the "filiopietistic rhetoric" with which ethnic Americans honored their ancestry was rarely an argument for "separatism," but rather part of a "homemaking myth" that demonstrated a particular nationality's distinctive connection to American culture. So, for instance, in 1904, when Italian Americans in Chicago successfully petitioned to have a public school named for Giuseppe Garibaldi (prompting angry protests from the Irish- and Swedish-American communities), they highlighted their ancestral history in order to honor the republican spirit shared by Italy and the United States.[16]

Thus while immigrants faced hostility from native Americans and rival ethnic groups that provincial migrants seldom encountered—indeed, one of the homemaking myth's primary goals was to overcome such resistance—many of them (like provincial migrants) forged "complementary identit[ies]" based on their nostalgia for the homes they left behind and their commitment to their new homes in Chicago.[17] Furthermore, many ethnic Chicagoans were every bit as committed to self-making as their native counterparts. For example, the city's prosperous German Americans (gentile and Jewish), some of whom were celebrated in books like *Chicago and Its Distinguished Citizens* (1881), occupied positions of influence in a variety of industries, including banking, distilling, and brewing.[18] As the economy expanded, the foreign born and their children benefited from the increased opportunity for advancement by moving into a variety of white-collar professions.[19]

These opportunities are prominently featured in *Sister Carrie,* a novel largely free of the categorical separation between the native and the foreign born that characterizes so much nineteenth-century Chicago fiction. In fact, Dreiser conflates the two categories and presents a third, calling Carrie "a fair example of the middle American class—two generations removed from the emigrant."[20] His idiosyncratic description of this status—separating "middle" from "class"—softens the economic connotations of the phrase and locates Carrie at the center of a broadly envisioned social landscape (rather than halfway up a class ladder). The second phrase expands and clarifies this middling position in terms of Carrie's ethnic origins, implying that her movement away from the cultural perspective of her immigrant grandparents and her father's vaguely working-class status (Dreiser reveals only that he works in a flour mill) now places her that much closer to the mainstream of American experience. Briefly, but pointedly, Dreiser suggests that Carrie's migratory ambitions, as well her status as a representative American, are connected to her ethnic history.

At the same time, Carrie's ethnic origins, like her hinterland antecedents, remain suppressed, part of the shadowy personal history that compels her to leave Columbia City. In ways that Dreiser suggests but never fully explains, they inform the choices that she makes in Chicago. One such choice takes place when Carrie, having lost her factory job, decides to leave her sister Minnie and brother-in-law Sven Hanson's apartment and accept Charles Drouet's offer of financial assistance. In this episode, her desire for material happiness and longing to remake herself are in full force. And to move ahead, Carrie elects to bypass the grinding sacrifices made by Sven and

Minnie, and distance herself from their dreary, working-class existence. Ironically, Hanson, the son of Swedish immigrants, is a more likely candidate for upward mobility than Carrie. Employed at the stockyards cleaning refrigerator cars, he is determined to rise through hard work and frugality. While the Hansons' current living situation—a flat in a neighborhood filled with clerks, laborers, and recent migrants to the city—lacks distinction, Sven has mortgages on two West Side building lots and plans for the future. However, for Carrie, this method of self-improvement is too slow moving, so she affiliates herself with Drouet, whose family, the salesman tells her in a bit of unintended comedy, "was French, on my father's side."[21]

Given these details of descent, Carrie's ongoing migration begins to look like an assimilation drama, with Carrie determined not to make her sister's mistake and settle for a working-class man only one generation removed from the immigrant experience. Unlike Hanson, Drouet presents himself as a fully assimilated American, while Carrie's married lover, Hurstwood, with his Anglo-American surname, appears practically aristocratic. Carrie's successive relationships with these two men reinforce the sense that her migration away from small-town Wisconsin and her family's ethnic, working-class background (in both its provincial and metropolitan forms) toward the wealthier confines of Chicago and then the bastions of New York is bringing her closer to an older, more established America. Throughout this process of self-making, she remains unaware that what she is determined to erase—her regional, class, and ethnic origins—is the impetus for her forward movement.

Blurring the separation between native and foreign born, provincial and metropolitan, and working and middle class, *Sister Carrie* thus questions one of the primary assumptions of late nineteenth-century Chicago fiction, that a hinterland migrant must be a white, native-born American. However, Dreiser does so in a fairly limited manner. As his biographers have stressed, his impoverished upbringing—as one of ten children born to a German Catholic immigrant father and a second-generation Moravian Mennonite mother, who moved their household from one small Indiana town to the next in search of better living conditions—made him painfully aware of the various ways in which class status was constructed in nineteenth-century America. This sensitivity is particularly evident in *Sister Carrie,* where Dreiser suggests a complicated subtext for his heroine's movement, including her ethnicity, only to underscore the cultural power of Chicago's native-based narrative of self-making. In this respect, he made a decision as pragmatic in its way as any that Jane Addams (or Carrie) made.

Thus Dreiser's novel, like Ray Stannard Baker's story of the potato-car boy, affirms the assumption—held by many middle- and upper-class Chicagoans—that the city's opportunities for self-advancement belonged principally to the native born, particularly ambitious young migrants. To tell a different story about Chicago, one that embraced the foreign born and their children as full participants in the city's future, required a different understanding of self-making and a visionary grasp of what the city's pluralistic community might be.

Practically speaking, this vision belonged to Jane Addams and her colleagues in the settlement house movement. In literary terms, it found expression in the fiction of Edith Wyatt and Elia Peattie, and the poetry of Carl Sandburg. Of the three, only Sandburg migrated to Chicago as an adult, and then it was after years of wandering which led him from his hometown of Galesburg, Illinois, where he was born in 1878, to Milwaukee, where among other jobs he worked as an organizer for the Wisconsin Social Democratic Party. In 1912 he moved to Chicago, where he settled in as a journalist and poet. Wyatt, born in Tomah, Wisconsin, in 1873, spent much of her childhood in the small-town Midwest (her father was a civil engineer with the railroad) before moving with her family in 1884 to Chicago, where she developed a career as a teacher, writer, and Progressive activist. Peattie, the oldest of the trio, grew up in south suburban Chicago, and during her career as a journalist, which included several years on the Omaha *World-Herald* and more than twenty on the *Chicago Tribune* (where she served as literary editor), she developed a wide-ranging understanding of the city's role in the region. Like Wyatt, Peattie was a member of the Little Room, and closely affiliated with Chicago's newly forged literary institutions. And, like Wyatt, who taught classes at Hull-House between 1905 and 1920, she was a regular presence at the Halsted Street settlement house.[22]

The timing of these writers' mostly positive representations of Chicago's ethnic residents—all published after 1900—suggests that the general climate surrounding native- and foreign-born relations had eased somewhat since the mid-1890s. Of course, from the perspective of a Socialist like Sandburg, the industrial system continued to oppress working men and women, especially ethnic laborers, making Debs an ever more popular political figure. Nonetheless, for the native-born middle and upper class, the local threat once apparently posed by the foreign anarchists associated with the Haymarket affair had diminished considerably. Second, the discourse of urban-rural relations which had developed over the previous decade and, in particular, the example of Jane Addams and Hull-House provided a rich context for conceptualizing the status of ethnic Chicagoans.

Edith Wyatt and the True Midwest

The first sentence of Edith Wyatt's best-known work, *True Love: A Comedy of the Affections* (1903), suggests the vibrancy of her social vision: "The straight white street was checkered with brilliant squares of green." The description of sky, sprinklers, swaying treetops, and a sightseeing carriage, which follows this abstract beginning, designates the setting as residential Chicago. As the novel spreads out beyond the city to the downstate town of Centreville, where much of the action takes place, Wyatt's straight checkered street gives way to the larger prairie— of "serried corn-bottoms and banks of green," striated vistas of foliage, hills, grain, sky, and townscapes— large "clean" interiors swept by "long beams of sunlight."[23] Through the repetition of such layered images and a romantic plot in which characters are drawn back and forth between Chicago and the hinterland by love and desire, she integrates city and country, but not without judgment. Whether the brilliant green squares represent the power of *Urbs in horto* (City in a Garden, the motto Chicago adopted in 1837), rhythmically felt, or mirror the symmetrical landscape created by the Northwest Ordinance of 1787, they gather force in the remainder of the novel as the look and feel of midwestern democracy. So at the end the novel, when the protagonist, Emily Marsh, looks out from Centreville at the spreading valley, contemplating her marriage to the unpretentious Dick Colton, "the best traditions of her life fused to her with her future, now to be so free and democratic." Emily's marriage to a Centreville native truly "centers" the social energy in the novel, confirming that the source and model for a democratic Chicago lie in "commonplace" values (exemplified by Colton) and common places (small-scaled, rural communities).[24]

Wyatt's outlook in *True Love* is shaped by nostalgia, but unlike Will Payne's *The Story of Eva* and Brand Whitlock's *The Happy Average,* it presents hinterland culture as a positive force to be discovered and revealed as the action unfolds. Whereas in Payne's and Whitlock's novels nostalgia figures principally as an emotion of loss emanating from the migrant's departure from home and then guiding the effort to nurture provincial culture in Chicago, here it seems remarkably free of the past. Because *True Love* is not a migration narrative organized around an individual's longing to go to Chicago (in fact, most of the movement in the novel is back toward the hinterland), it lacks a sentimental division between urban life and a provincial home. Instead, the novel insists on an emotional continuity between city and country, deriving its sense of home from familial connections sustained across the region and over time.[25]

In this, her most fully realized work of fiction, Wyatt lays out a model for democratic culture based on these continuities that illuminates her view of native-foreign relations. I refer to democratic "culture" rather than community, because even though Wyatt's fiction is always about social relations and groupings, she is most interested in exploring how people treat one another, and whether their openness and tolerance of one another is democratic in nature. Like her friend Jane Addams, Wyatt worked most effectively in the pragmatic mode, which is to say that in the working-out of relationships and situations, her characters are frequently involved in testing, abandoning, and developing their beliefs and ideals. In her fiction, this process, while implicitly philosophical, takes place through human conduct rather than intellectual debate; in fact, characters more interested in ideas than people are often the object of her satire.

Wyatt's faith in human interaction translates democratic ideals into fictional technique and earned her high praise from William Dean Howells and William James, who met Wyatt socially in Massachusetts in 1900. After reading her short-story collection *Every One His Own Way* (1901), James marveled to a friend that he spent "more than 24 full hours close to that paragon of genius, and never divined her." He noted the book's "good humor, philanthropy, observation, humorousness, the admirable style, modesty, etc., etc., etc" and praised Wyatt's "sense of limits" and "feeling for human nature." "But where," James wanted to know, "did she learn so much of life?"[26] Given the scope of the book—a series of fables that focus on relations between Chicago's native-born and ethnic middle class—the question was understandable.

Half a dozen years later, James again commented on *Every One His Own Way,* this time in an address given at the Association of American Alumnae, in which he notes Wyatt's description of a couple "who stand for culture in the sense of exclusiveness." The couple—Richard Elliott and Margaret Alden—are "feeble caricatures of mankind, unable to know any good thing when they see it, incapable of enjoyment unless a printed label gives them leave." Embroidering on the social value of democracy, James goes on to assert, "Real

culture lives by sympathies and admirations, not by dislikes and disdain—
under all misleading wrappings it pounces unerringly upon the human
core."[27] For James, as for Wyatt, culture was a pragmatic, democratic enterprise, dependent on the feelings and ideas generated through vigorous
human interaction.

James's characterization of Wyatt's literary turf meshed with her own, except that she stressed the Midwest's importance in shaping her perspective
and fostering the kind of culture that James prized. In a lecture entitled "The
Poor Old Past" (1935), Wyatt discusses her aesthetic concerns in autobiographical terms, beginning with her childhood home on LaSalle Street,
which she calls "a place of fresh, green grass-plots and beautiful, drooping
elm-trees, of white, clean-scrubbed curbs and steps and horse-blocks and
long rows of cream-colored stone houses." In this description, so much like
the opening of *True Love,* she marks her literary territory as comfortably domestic and conventionally middle class. Moreover, she acknowledges that
she does not mind speaking as "an un-sophisticated member of the bourgeoisie," or "from the standpoint of that still more out-cast figure, the Old
Lady from Dubuque." Ten years after the *New Yorker*'s famous (or infamous)
first issue stipulating that the magazine was not edited for the "old lady in
Dubuque," Wyatt turns the conventional notion of cosmopolitan on its
head, claiming that her aesthetic approach (and, by implication, much modern literature) derives from her experience as a middle-class provincial. For
example, whereas critics traced the modernists' use of strong colors to the
Russian dancer Serge Diaghileff, Wyatt notes that she first became aware of
how colors might be used in art when she was a child in Dubuque. "The
thing I noticed was the magical charm of the portulaca beds which still spread
their brilliant mosaic of silk petals over Iowa every summer—mosaics of a
myriad, vivid, delicately-clashing and chording colors—magenta, and scar-
let and pale pink, lemon and yellow and rose-flecked and crimson like and
bisque and orange." In designating this scene from her provincial childhood,
she argues that a premigration perception reoriented her view of the natural
world and eventually influenced her literary aesthetic. In that moment, she
realized that what seems to be discord may in fact be part of a creative process
yielding a larger synthesis. Turning then to the present, Wyatt goes on to
note that "we" have all learned to see color "dynamically" and "to make our
sense of this aspect of existence a natural power in the ways of our lives." For
Wyatt, this new understanding of color as mosaic had broad, hopeful implications. "For one would like to look at all truth dynamically—the truth of the

past as well as the truth now and truth to come. People who have their minds closed to truth about the past will have their minds closed to truth about the future also." [28]

Wyatt's model of dynamic creation—a pragmatic method of deriving truth—suggests that the prairie green and city pavement illuminated at the outset of *True Love* is a portent of the truths that will emerge from the novel's blending of provincial and urban cultures. Philosophically, this view of hinterland-city relations was quite close to Jane Addams's, though Wyatt expressed herself in aesthetic rather than sociological terms. As literary criticism, Wyatt's remarks on naturally occurring mosaics offer a realist rebuttal to modernist pretension (since Wyatt claimed to have learned from experience what others picked up from Diaghileff), while also implying that *True Love*'s imagist beginning (like Ezra Pound's "In a Station of the Metro" or a Piet Mondrian painting) might herald a modernist narrative. Just as crucial here, though, is Wyatt's identification with the old lady in Dubuque, by which she connected her intellectual and aesthetic development, as well as the modernist innovations associated with Diaghileff, which she associated with her experience as a middle-class woman. In featuring the garden as a source of creativity—an image frequently invoked by nineteenth-century American women writers to signify female powers—Wyatt thickened her lineage as a provincial writer. Just as important, she suggested, by way of metaphor, how a democratic culture might be made of native- and foreign-born perspectives.

The twenty-odd stories in *Every One His Own Way* approach this possibility optimistically, describing a multiethnic Chicago united by common sympathies and admirations. Structurally and thematically, Wyatt's book is indeed a mosaic, as the stories are interlocked by individuals and families who appear and reappear throughout the volume. Wyatt even anticipates the writing of *True Love* by introducing characters that go on to play a key role in that novel (for instance, Dick Colton's sister, Fanny) and by establishing familial links between Chicago and Centreville. Most important, however, the notion of a mosaic is reinforced by the web of connections— marriages, friendships, common feelings, and beliefs—that her native and ethnic Chicagoans establish through serendipitous and cultivated encounters. Interestingly, she pictures this web much as she did in her 1935 address, describing on the first page of the book a yard cultivated by a prosperous German and "filled with little flower-beds shining with petunias, portulacas, and zinnias." [29]

The conflict and resolution of Wyatt's opening story, "Two Citizens," set the tone for the book. Together with his "amiable German wife and a beautiful German daughter" and "many fat little boys," Wyatt's German, Mr. J. Hoffman, lives a rich, comfortable existence marked by a love of gardening, food, and music. Although Hoffman "sold beer and distributed jobs in return for political influence," she treats this deviation from political idealism as a fact of Chicago life and no bar to family happiness. By contrast, she introduces "an American" who lives in "the same city with J. Hoffman," but "in very moderate circumstance." This citizen is Richard Elliott, the character singled out by William James as a "caricature" of humanity. Elliott is a literary critic who holds stiflingly conventional ideas about art and culture and disdains middle-class life as "painfully hideous." Also, Elliott tells a friend, "most middle-class Americans are foreigners"; consequently, when he walks by the Hoffmans' home and sees the family enjoying themselves, he is "sickened." Unable to accept "that kind of person," he cannot see the Hoffmans' happiness. However, his younger brother, Thomas, a newspaper reporter, can. And, after meeting the Hoffmans' daughter Lulu at a Lutheran church event (which he is covering for his newspaper), he falls in love with her and the Hoffmans' "easy and affectionate goodness," which seems "like the natural and unsought goodness of the Golden Age." Without ever meeting the Hoffmans, indeed without knowing that he once walked by their home, Richard Elliott tries to dissuade his brother from marrying Lulu. But he fails, and Thomas marries happily. Years later, after Elliott's brand of criticism has gone out of style and he loses his job, he goes to live with his brother and sister-in-law. While living there he writes "some juvenile versions of the Greek myths, which were much enjoyed by many ladies" but ignored by his nephews and nieces, who "much preferred the amusement of being chased and poked by their young uncles, Otto and Maxie" (10, 9, 11, 13, 17, 21).

The gap in this story between inflexible, short-sighted natives and more tolerant, open-minded citizens (both ethnic and native-born) establishes a divide that runs throughout the book, separating a hidebound Chicago from the cosmopolitan, democratic city it could become. Wyatt draws this line of separation implicitly, showing rather than stating what a progressive, multiethnic community it is. Yet the stories' occasionally stilted, fablelike language and morals also give her representation of this human drama an ethical dimension.

Although it is true that the intolerant characters are all native-born Chicagoans determined to judge life by an unyielding "Standard," Wyatt emphasizes the importance of human capacities—for love, joy, kindness, compassion, and pleasure—rather than ethnic differences (93). Because the stories deal principally (though not exclusively) with middle-class life, she does not have to explain how working-class or poor immigrants are to be included in this civic democracy. Instead, as the title suggests, every character is free to go his own way, and live with the consequences of his actions. Combined with the book's loosely linked, episodic structure, this approach gives Wyatt's imagined city a democratic ethos. As in George Ade's column Stories of the Streets and of the Town, her Chicagoans are shown in their homes, on the streets, at concerts, or otherwise abroad in the city. More than Ade, however, Wyatt is interested in bringing Chicago's native and foreign born together and dramatizing the impact of their shared histories.

So in "Joy of Life," a follow-up to "Two Citizens"—Margaret Alden, of "'Mayflower' immigrant tradition" and as prejudiced as her friend, Richard Elliott—happens to meet Lulu Elliott while walking and arranges to visit her friend's sister-in-law in order to improve her, only to find that the call has no effect on her already happy life. "The Fox and the Stork" reaches a similar standstill when Tom Taylor invites a former schoolmate and his wife—both of whom are Jewish—to dinner after his old friend prevents a robber from mugging him on the street. Although the event brings the friends together again after years of living in different social circles, the outcome is ambiguous. Fred Einstein's "tremendous piece of Jewish good-nature," his anecdotes about "Dutchmen" and "Dagos," and his wife's luxuriant wardrobe present insurmountable cultural differences for the Taylors. In these stories, Wyatt realistically shows how good intentions do not simply lead to happy conclusions (50, 72).

These acts of reaching out resolve more positively in other stories. In "Beauty and the Beast," a "young American gentleman" named Nicholas Harris falls in love with Bertha Rinklemann, who lives across the street with her aunt and uncle Flora and Fred Einstein. Even though his sisters believe "he could never be happy with any one so different," Nicholas marries Bertha—happily. Then, over several stories, Wyatt traces the movements of Henry and Elsie Norris, siblings whose diverging attitudes toward ethnic Chicago initially mirror the demeanors of Richard and Thomas Elliott. While Elise enjoys spending time with her music-loving friend, Ottilie Bhaer, and sees in her marriage to Sigurd a "lovely democracy characteristic of the most advanced spirits," Henry (a friend of Richard Elliott's) dismisses the German music that Elsie and her friends like so much. After trying and failing at a Theodore Thomas concert to convince her brother that Schubert's romantic "Erlkonig" is great art, Elsie realizes that "his Standard was as inevitably a part of him as the very color of his eyes" (154, 103). However, Wyatt is unwilling to permit this judgment-by-biology to stand, and in a subsequent story, aptly titled "Trade Winds," she shows how Henry helps a failed store owner, John Wollfe, find a new job. Wollfe's ethnicity is unclear and he has been working in Chicago for more than fifty years, but his store is on Halsted Street and his daughter, who later drowns in an accident with her Irish suitor, attends classes at the nearby settlement house (taught, not incidentally, by a friend of Norris's). Without confirming Henry's conversion to a more tolerant, open-minded position, the story shows his sympathies moving toward a change in beliefs.

The importance of hinterland culture in *Every One His Own Way* is less obvious than in *True Love*, but it is nonetheless critical for Wyatt's vision of a pluralistic Chicago. She does not address the city's provincial underpinnings until the second half of the book, but when she does, the small-town Midwest appears as the benchmark for tolerance and democratic civility. Rich in genealogical detail, two stories in particular resemble *True Love* in how they link native-born Chicagoans to family members located in the agricultural Midwest. "The Peacock's Tail" introduces the Porter family, whose male head of household, Major Dan Porter—"a boyish old man" and "a little countrified"—grew up in Peru, Illinois, and settled in Chicago, where he married a woman with eastern ties. A second story, "Daffy-Down-Dilly" (named after the Mother Goose rhyme about a daffodil that "comes to town," or blooms), begins with the arrival of a letter from the major's sister-in-law, announcing that her sons will be arriving in Chicago with a delegation of young people (including Fanny Colton from Centreville) to visit a livestock show at the Columbian Exposition. Deputized to meet his cousins— referred to as "Brother Bill's boys"— the son, Tom Porter, serves as Chicago's host to the hinterland, a job he chooses instead of visiting with Margaret Alden (a more distant cousin on his mother's side), who is planning to visit with the Porters that afternoon (181, 188).

Into both these stories, Wyatt inserts already established characters— like Elsie Norris and Richard Elliott, as well as Margaret Alden—and plays them off the down-to-earth sensibilities of the Porter clan. This is by no means a straightforward comparison, if only because the female side of the Chicago Porter family represents a refined, and more limited, notion of culture. However, Wyatt demonstrates her preference for the "Peruvian" side of the family through the alignment of her characters. For instance, in "The Peacock Tail," Major Porter determines to hold an "honest, democratic little dance" for his grand-niece, but she holds herself aloof from the festivities. "As for Brother Bill's boys, these Margaret Alden could not permit to remotely touch her perception." On the other hand, Elsie Norris enjoys the dance and parts "reluctantly" from the major. Also signaling his attraction to provincial ways in "Daffy-Down-Dilly," Tom Porter finds the rural, family atmosphere at the Exposition building "lively, cheerful, and almost domestic," and when his cousins and the other "Peruvian" young men devote all their attention to Fanny Colton—"the country-town belle"—he "jubilantly" joins the "following," even though he is not "sufficiently adaptable to be able to join in the repartee and badinage with success" (189, 188, 189, 252, 253, 255). Unlike Margaret Alden, he is open to having his perceptions touched and changed.

Wyatt's ongoing dramatization of such emotional and cognitive movements—the shifts in admiration and sympathy that William James associated with "real" culture—is central to her literary vision. It provides a narrative thread that joins the Porter family stories to the earlier portrayals of ethnic and native encounters, revealing the cultural energy that Thomas Elliott, Lulu Hoffman, Tom Porter, Ottilie Bhaer, Elsie Norris, and others have in common: a desire to reach across socially constructed boundaries to know other people. If, as James claimed, this sympathetic impulse is more real than its oppositional force, that is because he believed cultures are evolving entities whose success depends on the adaptability of peoples' emotions and attitudes. The stories in *Every One His Own Way* suggest that Wyatt also believed that native-born Chicagoans must accommodate to a multiethnic society, or, like Richard Elliott, become obsolete. However, as her portrayal of Tom Porter's trip to the Exposition building suggests, the willingness to extend oneself is much more important than the actual capacity to adapt.

Short of explicitly designating Centreville as the source of this democratic spirit (as she does in *True Love*), Wyatt presents the midwestern small town as the cultural example most worth emulating. *Every One His Own Way* includes Germans, Italians, Jews, Irish, and southern and eastern transplants, but offers little information on cultural antecedents other than those of provincial migrants, whose democratic traditions Wyatt believes are a vital part of Chicago's own heritage. These traditions are especially important for the native-born middle class, who in Wyatt's social world bear the primary responsibility of reaching out across ethnic divisions to revitalize civic culture.

Like Jane Addams, though, Wyatt avoids the patronizing suggestion that these democratic sympathies are more native than ethnic. In fact, her tongue-in-cheek portrayal of the "Peruvian" relatives as foreign exotics implies a kinship between ethnic Chicagoans and provincial midwesterners. "Queen for a Day"—positioned in the second half of the book, along with Wyatt's other migratory stories—makes this connection explicit. Set in the factory town of Batavia, Missouri, it describes the romance that develops between Ottilie Wolfgang and Sigurd Bhaer when Ottilie comes from Chicago visit to her German aunt. Suffused with forget-me-nots, blue cornflowers, and roses (Ottilie herself is a "blooming rose"), their courtship is distinguished by the vivid flora of Wyatt's provincial youth (225). At the conclusion of the story, Sigurd returns with Ottilie to Chicago to be married, and Mr. Wolfgang finds his daughter's musician husband a job in a theater orchestra. Thus "Queen for a Day" resembles a migration narrative, adapted by Wyatt to show yet another way in which desire and self-making can shape Chicago culture.

Elia Peattie and the "Silvertree Method"

Published in 1914, Elia Peattie's novel *The Precipice* dramatizes Chicago's social workers assisting needy immigrant families while celebrating and occasionally criticizing the twenty-five-year-old legacy of Hull-House. Its heroine, Kate Barrington—modeled on Hull-House worker Kate Ostrander, and probably inspired by the example of Julia Lathrop, who helped establish the first national Children's Bureau—comes to Chicago from the downstate village of Silvertree to attend college and later returns to the city to practice social work and help make a "great home" of Chicago, capable of supporting all children. Like other protagonists of Chicago fiction, Kate Barrington is a self-maker, but as Sidney Bremer has argued, her accomplishments are strongly gendered, marking *The Precipice* as a "suffrage novel." [30]

The integration of domestic and occupational duties in Peattie's protagonist distinguishes her from the strong female characters envisioned by male writers—for instance, Hamlin Garland's Rose Dutcher—since it acknowledges women's distinctive cultural work as mothers and wives, and relocates it in the public sphere. Kate's fierce independence and commitment to enfranchising all citizens also suggest Peattie's interest in showing how the spirit of small-town republicanism has been translated to Chicago. This genealogy is also heavily gendered—and ironic—since Kate leaves Silvertree after the death of her mother and a quarrel with her overbearing father, who is the town physician. However, despite rejecting her father—and his adopted home—she extends and adapts his authoritative caretaking to Chicago.

Throughout the novel, Peattie stresses the connection between Kate's professional success and her small-town background. In explaining her effectiveness as a spokesperson for the Children's Protective Association, Peattie credits her direct, commonsense approach. Unlike other social workers, who are "more skilled in the dreary and often meaningless science of statistics," Kate tells stories.

She talked in personalities—in personalities so full of meaning that, concrete as they were, they took on general significance—they had the effect of symbols. She furnished watchwords for her listeners, and she did it unconsciously. She would have been indignant if she had been told how large a part her education in Silvertree played in her present aptitude. She had grown up in a town which feasted on dramatic gossip, and which thrived upon the specific personal episode. To the vast and terrific city, and to her portion of the huge task of mitigating the woe of its unfit, Kate brought the quality which, undeveloped, would have made of her no more than an entertaining village gossip.[31]

In this, as in other valuations of urban-hinterland relations, small-town culture—its more accessible scale and democratic forms of communication—is the source of humanity in the anonymous city. As Peattie notes elsewhere in the novel, Kate's ability to bring social problems to life and inhabit them captivates people other than settlement house workers and women's club members: "Children loved her, and the sick and the bad." When, on a crowded streetcar, a friend cannot understand her ease among "foreign faces" and asks why she won't stick with "your own kind and class," she tells him she likes the human "variety" while accepting the close proximity to ethnic laborers as part of her life and work (49, 175).

Peattie's interpretive asides further clarify the relative importance of her protagonist's small-town background. For starters, her criticism of social workers too caught up in statistics and jargon indicates that she aims not simply to recognize the accomplishments of an emergent professional class of women, but to draw even finer distinctions within that class and stress the value of her provincial heroine's straight-ahead powers and plain-spoken honesty. At the same time, one of Kate Barrington's most attractive traits is her lack of self-consciousness, which here means that she is oblivious, or at least resistant, to the idea that her small-town background may have had any positive influence on her professional work. Consequently, it falls to her Irish-American friend and musician, Marna Carton, to classify her working style as the "Silvertree method"—in other words, an approach that comes directly from her small-town upbringing (107). This is ironic in two ways: Kate Barrington acknowledges no "method," and Peattie herself seems to prefer a profession unencumbered by self-conscious, scientific approaches. From this perspective the essential thing is to foster a homelike city for all Chicagoans through caring and building trust. Fortunately, Kate Barrington is skilled in both providing primary care and talking about her work, so that when she speaks—as directly as she acts—she and her words become symbols of the child advocacy movement.

The vision that emerges in *The Precipice* is of a social welfare system rooted in the ethos of the small town and unmediated by bureaucracy and superfluous specialization. At several points in the novel, Peattie even suggests that the Silvertree method is superior to the Hull-House approach.[32] For instance, when Kate is invited to become a resident of Hull-House, she declines, since she is afraid it offers "too much community of interest," preferring instead the "variety" of the cooperative housing where she currently lives. As for Jane Addams, Kate "sometimes" gave Addams "whole credit" for her success. After all, Addams was a "genius for inclusiveness" and the leading spokesperson for the idea that a city should be "a great home." However, in one of her authorial asides, Peattie notes that Kate had "added her own interpretations" and "said things that Jane Addams would have hesitated to say."[33] Her reports, too, on Kate's interactions with children and immigrants suggest that Kate is able to accomplish things that Hull-House residents cannot.

As opposed to Edith Wyatt's depiction of middle-class ethnics, Peattie shows little of this drama. Kate's attraction to the city's human "variety" begins when she enrolls at the University of Chicago and discovers her interest in students who are "alien to her—in the Japanese boy, concealing his wistfulness beneath his rigid breeding; in the Armenian girl with the sad, beautiful eyes; in the Yiddish youth with his bashful earnestness" (5). Kate's social work takes her well beyond this initial infatuation with the exotic otherness of ethnic Americans, so that she appears on the street "with a baby in her arms and two miserable little children clinging to her skirts" and, later, establishes a getaway home in the Wisconsin woods for Polish mothers and their children to "go and forget the belching horror of the steel mills, and the

sultry nights in the crowded, vermin-haunted homes" (31, 97). But the novel
never moves beyond these vivid illustrations of hands-on care and pastoral
respite (similar in theory to the Bowen Country Club) to present Kate's sustained involvement in Chicago's ethnic communities. She is among immigrants, but remains only a symbol of engagement, representing rather than
enacting the work of community building and human interaction. Certainly,
her relationships with the other residents at the Caravansary (her cooperative living community)—Irish- and German-American artists and intellectuals—provide her with variety, but they do not approach the vision of civic
home that Kate's own role suggests. In this sense, the novel seems cut off
from its protagonist's dreams in a way that Wyatt's most-desiring characters
seldom are.

   In her discussion of the novel, Sidney Bremer suggests that the lack of detail on Kate's work life is due to Peattie's journalistic habit of reporting rather
than dramatizing events.[34] Another reason, I would argue, may be found in
the fractious history that precedes Kate Barrington's decision to pursue a career in Chicago. This account, which reveals the waning vitality of her
hometown and the tensions in her parents' marriage, is at odds with the
more idealized Silvertree vision of community and family that Kate, consciously or not, seeks to realize in Chicago.

   When Kate returns home from college at the outset of the novel, she is
moved by familiar images—the sawmill, the livery stable, and her mother—
to forget everything she learned at the University of Chicago and think of
"only the things which were from the beginning." But this nostalgic reverie
lasts only a moment, as Peattie quickly shifts to current time and shows Kate
to be caught between a tyrannical father and her passive, highly feminized
mother. This division, Peattie stresses, is imbedded in Silvertree's social order and its past. For instance, Kate understands that her father's self-esteem,
and to an extent his overbearing treatment of her mother, are tied to Silvertree's decline: "To insult Silvertree was to hurt the doctor in his most ten-
der vanity. It was one of his most fervid beliefs that he had selected a growing town, conspicuous for its enterprise. In his young manhood he had
meant to do fine things," driven by his "one holy passion, that of the physician." Now "the torpor of the little town had taken the light from his eyes and
reduced the tempo of movements." Kate has an equally vivid sense of her
mother's character and connection to these changes, and before leaving college she sees in her mind's eye "a moving-picture show" of her mother's role
in Silvertree: "Now she was pouring the coffee from the urn, seasoning it

scrupulously to suit her lord and master, now arranging the flowers, now feeding the goldfish; now polishing the glass with tissue paper" (10, 14, 12, 9).

In these glimpses of a single marriage, Peattie contains the emotional history of midwestern bourgeois society, capturing both the isolation and the hopes implicit in separate but linked gendered roles. Inasmuch as Kate has internalized this history, and resents her father's treatment of her mother, it paves the way for her revolt from him—and Silvertree—when her mother suddenly dies. On the other hand, to the extent that Kate inherits this history—as parts of her own personality—it shapes her life in Chicago. Indeed, Peattie invites this reading while explaining Kate's professional success: "A psychologist would have said there was much of the man about her"—that is, independence and assertiveness—"but all this was more than offset by this [her] inherent impulse for maternity" (49).

This psychological and cultural diagnosis creates a dilemma that Peattie is unable to overcome in the exposition of Kate Barrington's career as a social worker. For while the novel implies that the best model for the inclusive civic family that Kate and her colleagues wish to develop in Chicago is the small-town polity, Silvertree and the Barrington family as well—the representative realities—are exposed to withering critique. The ideal of the small town persists in symbolic form, or as a "method" to be deployed on an ad-hoc basis; but the seamless, beloved community capable of sustaining native and foreign born alike is never brought down to earth and tested. Despite glimpses of Kate's individual work with immigrant children and families, the novel fails to grapple with the reality of a civic home. A vision of it emerges, perhaps, when Kate describes her plan for a national Children's Bureau, and the president embraces it as a viable governmental agency (with Kate as director), but it is still only a theory—and, ironically, a bureaucracy. Moreover, Peattie implies that people find Kate's "propaganda" appealing, not because of the plan's merits, but because they delighted in the newspaper reports of "the country girl who had come up to town, and who, with a simple faith and courage, had worked among the unfortunate, and the delinquent" (108).

Peattie's shrewd insight into Americans' sentimental interest in the drama of urban migration offers yet another possible explanation for Addams's refusal to make much of her hinterland origins when she arrived at Hull-House: she knew that her story would distract Chicagoans from her primary purpose. More important, and in a way that Peattie may not have intended, her recognition that this traditional drama appealed to readers suggests why her own migration narrative stops short of showing how natives and the foreign born might live together. Caught in the bind of simultaneously criticizing and idealizing the small-town home that its heroine rejects, the novel falls back on the drama of self-making and devolves the resolution of Silvertree's problems on Kate's career and personal life. Indeed, the novel ends, not with a vision of Chicago as civic home, but with the drama surrounding her decision to marry a man who finally accepts her idealistic career ambitions. While this deflection of larger communal questions onto stories of individual striving characterizes Chicago migration novels and midwestern novels of the 1910s and '20s that deal with the "village virus"—Sinclair Lewis's work being a prime example—it obscures *The Precipice*'s larger ambitions.

Big Shoulders and Prairie Winds

Arguably the best-known American poet of the twentieth century, Carl Sandburg began to gather his audience in 1916 with the publication of *Chicago Poems*, a collection of verse that brings together vividly drawn images of Chicago, the agricultural and small-town Midwest, working-class life, and ethnic culture. Based only on *Chicago Poems*, Sandburg's subsequent reputation as the People's poet would be well deserved. As Philip Yanella and Mark Van Wienen have shown, the Sandburg of this period was a Socialist, and his Populist sensibilities extend to his dramatization of inequities suffered by working-class Americans as well as his creative use of vernacular language.[35] The "City of the Big Shoulders," the image that sets the context for many of the collection's more political lyrics, identifies this political agenda as essentially urban in nature, with Sandburg celebrating the vitality of Chicago's working class—native and foreign born—and protesting its diminishment under industrial capitalism.

However, if the working-class "myth-man" whose torso looms over the city depicted in "Chicago" is urban, he also draws strength from the prairie, butchering hogs and stacking wheat with a lusty, primordial power.[36] The poet who figured Chicago in these terms was a citizen of the hinterland as well as the city, and his political vision—of a democratic community, inclusive of foreign- and native-born workers and committed to social justice—was sustained by the same hopes and dreams that attracted small-town and rural migrants to the city. This Sandburg was a poet of desire as well as politics, and in *Chicago Poems* he describes a city of unfulfilled dreams, shared by migrants and immigrants alike.

A good place to examine these dreams is "Population Drifts," which begins with the scent of summer hay being blown into the city.

New-mown hay smell and wind of the plain made her a woman
whose ribs had the power of the hills in them and her hands
were tough for work and there was passion for life in her
womb.

She and her man crossed the ocean and the years that marked their
faces saw them haggling with landlords and grocers while six
children played on the stones and prowled in the garbage
cans.

Evoking the agricultural life that the couple led before immigrating to the United States, the smell of hay recalls a time from their youth when, passionate and hopeful, they dreamed of a new life. Now, the poem goes on to say, after years of economic hardship in Chicago, including the death of two children, these hopes are gone. Two of their children now work in a box factory, and as they "fold the pasteboard, they wonder what the wishing is/and wistful glory in them flutters faintly when the/glimmer of spring comes on the air or the green of summer/turns brown." Although the upsurge of desire, in sync with seasonal changes, suggests that the parents' passions have continued into the next generation, the children are confused by longings for which they have no reference. They do not know, Sandburg notes in the poem's ironic final line, that the scent on the prairie wind is "praying for them to come back and take hold/of life again with tough hands and with passion." [37]

The ostensible meaning of "Population Drifts" is that people move or migrate with the undulations of the earth, compelled by internal desires to answer the call of nature. In fact, the poem shows how such desires, and the expectations born of them, drift away from all that is natural. It is not only unnatural, it is criminal, Sandburg implies, that conditions in Chicago have killed one of the couple's children (it "coughed its lungs away"), crippled two others, pushed one into jail, and left two in grinding jobs with no escape. The problem here is not with nature but with a class system that thwarts the realization and regeneration of American immigrant dreams.

"Population Drifts" parallels the movement of "Poems Done on a Late Night Car," whose dialectical structure traces the evisceration of hinterland desires. The first section of the poem gives voice to "The Great White Way

of the city," which, when asked "what is my desire," responds, "Girls fresh
as country wild flowers." The second part, entitled "Used Up," pictures
these girls—now with "painted faces," riding in a streetcar at night—as
"Roses,/Red Roses,/Crushed" and "Beaten by the fists of/Men using
them." The final part, called "Home," defines its subject as "a thing my
heart wishes the world had more of."[38] Circling back (as "Population
Drifts" does) to the original scene and emotion that launched the poem (and
the migration), the poet mourns the city's lack of maternal spirit.

Both these poems—one focused on European immigrants, the other on
provincial migrants (of unnamed ethnicity)—follow the course of desire and
migration to failure. Both poems embody this failure in the female form, underscoring the corollary loss of family and home through images of sickness
and violence (in "Poems Done on a Late Night Car," the city-as-perpetrator
is specifically male). Although these poems stop short of the self-inflicted
battering dramatized in "Mamie"—which also follows a trajectory of expectation, migration, and loss—the subjects depicted in them turn inward with
their desire, abandoning hope of happiness and community in moments of
wistful resignation.

This is a common end point in several poems in Sandburg's collection:
the poor and broken (often women and children) become the victims of a
hard city whose natural setting—the prairie—should have been a refuge. In
"They Will Say," the poet observes of "my city" that "the worst that men will
ever say is this:/You took my little children away from the sun and the dew."
The narrator of "Cripple" sees a man with "hollow eyes" in "the dark and
dust of a house down in a slum" and concludes, "I would rather have been a
tall sunflower/Living in a country garden." Conversely, moments of happiness or strength in *Chicago Poems* are punctuated with pastoral references: a
fish crier "with a voice like a north wind blowing over corn stubble in January"; a dancer whose flurried movements evoke "a million green leaves."[39]

That Sandburg generally does not identify the ethnicity of these figures
reinforces the sense that nature's power is universal, that it plays no fa-
vorites—an impression that does not hold true for his portrayal of social
forces, which nearly always favor the well to do. Over the course of his long
career, Sandburg's repeated portrayal of the prairie's mythic force became a
hallmark of his writing, leading some critics to condemn his saccharine
treatment of midwestern life.[40] However, this charge makes little sense in the
gritty context of *Chicago Poems*. Here, the trope serves as a call for common
decency; since all Chicagoans live on the prairie, they should acknowledge
their shared humanity. Sandburg imparts this lesson in "Skyscraper," where

he presents the people in the building—from janitors "talking in foreign tongues" to corporate lawyers—as a potential community. Office girls as well as "master-men" go into "the soul of the building," and the soul derives its "dreams and thoughts and/memories" from the "Prairie and valley, streets of the city," which funnel people in and out of the skyscraper.[41]

Elsewhere, Sandburg offers a less sanguine view of this potential community. Striking a militant pose in "I Am the People, the Mob," he identifies the narrator as a representative of the working class and a harbinger of social justice:

I am the audience that witnesses history. The Napoleons come
from me and the Lincolns. They die. And then I send forth
more Napoleons and Lincolns.
I am the seed ground. I am a prairie that will stand for much
plowing. Terrible storms pass over me. I forget. The best of me
is sucked out and wasted. I forget. Everything but Death
comes to me and makes me work and give up what I have.
And I forget.
Sometimes I growl, shake myself and spatter a few red drops for
history to remember. Then—I forget.[42]

Sandburg's *über* prairie espouses a doctrinaire Marxist theory of history, but with a distinctive local resonance. His reminder that a slow-to-arouse working class can sometimes spill blood conjures memories of Chicago's history of working-class violence while also prompting a comparison to Upton Sinclair's novel *The Jungle* (1906), whose Lithuanian-born protagonist, Jurgis Rudkus, eventually becomes a Socialist. Yet if the People (a designation that absorbs both native- and foreign-born workers) "learn to remember" and, like Rudkus and his peers, become an educated mob, Sandburg's characterization of them—as a prairie—is a distinctly midwestern image. According to him, politics is a thing of the soil, something worth plowing and seeding for, and revolutionary figures like Lincoln (and even Napoleon) are homegrown heroes. On these grounds, *The Jungle* seems out of touch.

By this I do not mean to suggest that Sinclair's politicized representations of Chicago's immigrant workers lack authenticity—either because he was not a midwesterner or because he was native born. Rather, I offer *The Jungle* as a point of contrast with the provincial perspective that hinterland writers, regardless of their politics, insisted upon—even when their subject matter appeared to take them off native ground.

PART FOUR

BORDER CROSSINGS

The impact of *Chicago*? Will the younger reader believe that my father seldom, if ever mentioned New York? Never, to my knowledge, London, Rome, or Paris? If you were born, like Anderson, in the sprawling Midwest, Chicago was the place to go and where you went. Those faded maps on the walls of small railroad stations illustrated this mindless movement at a glance: all the lines led to Chicago. There they stopped. As every rail traveler knows, that is also true today — except for hogs.

Only a novel will convincingly suggest the draw of such a town on the dreaming provincial, and the energy generated by the actual confrontation.
Many have been written.
WRIGHT MORRIS, INTRODUCTION TO SHERWOOD ANDERSON'S NOVEL WINDY MCPHERSON'S SON *(1965)*

My first glimpse of the flat black stretches of Chicago depressed and dismayed me, mocked all my fantasies. Chicago seemed an unreal city whose mythical houses were built of slabs of black coal wreathed in palls of gray smoke, houses whose foundations were sinking slowly into the dank prairie. Flashes of stream showed intermittently on the wise horizon, gleaming translucently in the winter sun. The din of the city entered my consciousness, entered to remain for years to come. The year was 1927.
RICHARD WRIGHT, AMERICAN HUNGER *(1944)*

8

FLOYD DELL, SHERWOOD ANDERSON, AND TENNESSEE MITCHELL

On June 2, 1913, Floyd Dell wrote poet Arthur Davison Ficke of Davenport, Iowa, from the studio apartment he had recently leased on Fifty-Seventh Street near Jackson Park on Chicago's South Side. One of several hastily constructed buildings that had served visitors to the Columbian Exposition, Dell's storefront flat placed him in the midst of an artists' colony — a collection of writers, sculptors, and actors drawn together by the cheap rents and promise of community. Although Dell's marriage had all but ended and a concurrent affair was coming to a close, he addressed his friend in a tone of heightened excitement. "Do you know what it is," he prods Ficke, "to have the horizons of your life, burst open and admit you to a new country, a wonderworld. No you don't; or at least you don't know what it is to determine to stay there, to settle, to take out naturalization papers in paradise. Well, until you have done that, you don't know what a great thing it is to be alive." Teasing his friend about his social status (Ficke was a Harvard-educated lawyer who came from a wealthy family) while also acknowledging his artistic talents, Dell imagines returning to Davenport and asking, "Where is my old friend Arthur Ficke?" only to be told by "the greybeards" that he was elected mayor long ago. So Dell wants to know, "When are you coming to Chicago? I need your advice as to where to hang the Nude Lady and other masterpieces which will adorn my walls."[1]

Dell's ironic humor was typical of his temperament and his friendship with Ficke, which lasted for most of their adult lives. In 1908, the twenty-one-year-old Dell had left Davenport for Chicago, where his precocious literary talents earned him an editorship at the *Friday Literary Review*, the literary supplement of the *Chicago Evening Post*. Back in Davenport, Ficke maintained a legal practice and wrote poetry on the side, indulging his sophisticated literary and artistic interests with periodic trips to Chicago and visits with friends. In his letter to Ficke, Dell urges his friend to break free and make another trip to the city—an invitation prompted in part by Dell's own relocation to the Fifty-Seventh Street studio and his current emotional state. Three days later, Dell tried to clarify those feelings as well as his move to Fifty-Seventh Street by telling Ficke, "It is really a Lake Isle of Innisfree business."[2] In William Butler Yeats's 1892 poem, Dell presumably identified with the speaker's intention to "arise and go now, and go to Innisfree, / And a small cabin build there, of clay and wattles made," where "I shall have some peace." This migration toward Walden-like solitude, Yeats indicates in the last stanza of "The Lake Isle of Innisfree," symbolizes an internal journey, for no matter where the poet is or what time of day it is, he will hear "lake water lapping" in his "deep heart's core." A provincial migrant himself, Yeats wrote the poem in a moment of piercing homesickness, after a store sign he saw on Fleet Street in London reminded him of his home in Sligo County, Ireland. But though Dell treats Yeats as a kindred spirit in this exchange, the motivating emotion for the reference was not nostalgia but a finely measured (and mediated) desire for artistic independence.[3]

Midwestern literary culture never sounded so cosmopolitan, or so modern. Without expressly urging his friend to leave Davenport for Chicago, Dell summons familiar cultural longings—the desire to escape small places for the splendors of metropolitan life—in playfully allusive terms. The reference to Yeats adds another layer of significance to the dialogue, revealing the two writers' familiarity with the poetic language of romantic alienation and enabling Dell to mean more than he actually said.

It also provides an explicitly literary context for the letter Dell had sent Ficke a week earlier, describing in some detail his Fifty-Seventh Street studio. There, Dell gives a fuller account of what his "new country" looked and felt like, and what his reference to "The Lake Isle of Innisfree" actually meant.

It is 11:30 P.M. I have just returned from the north side, where I have been seeing the Carys, to my ice-cold studio, where I have built a fire with scraps of linoleum, a piece of wainscoting, and the contents of an elaborate filing system of four years creation. I am writing at a desk spattered with kalsomine, and lighted by four candles. The room contains one bookcase and nine Felo-Naptha soap-boxes—full of books—counting the one full of books I am giving away to get rid of them—a typewriter stand, a fireless cooker, a patent coat and trousers hanger, and a couch with a mattress and a blanket. In this blanket I roll myself securely and sleep till 5:30 A.M., when I am awakened by the flood of daylight, also by the fact that my shoulders are cold. I wrap myself tighter, and sleep till 8 o'clock, when I get up, take a sketchy bath at a faucet, and go around the corner for breakfast. In the window seat, along with my shirts, is a great bundle, containing a magnificent & very expensive bolt of beautiful cloth, for curtains for the windows. If I am ever able to pay for that, and for my new suit, I shall give you a party, and you shall come and see the combination of luxury and asceticism which will be the charm of my studio. At present its only luxury consists in that same asceticism. I have been rather unhappy this evening, because of some troubles at the office, but as soon as I entered my studio, a balm descended upon my spirit. I had intended writing you to say that I have been indulging in the folly of falling in love again—or of re-falling in love. But now I cannot but speak in simple and un-ironic terms, and say that I am glad to be young and intelligent and on the spot when a certain beautiful woman looks about for a beloved. For that happy accident I rejoice, and I am by no means certain that that accident is not the most important thing about me.[4]

Pictured here as a refuge from urban life (coincidentally located near the shores of Lake Michigan) and a spur to creative freedom, Dell's studio figures as a kind of Lake Isle of Innisfree while still remaining tied to the workaday world. In describing his new home, Dell fairly revels in the details that make it a threshold for literary production, lovemaking, and luxurious self-abnegation. However, what struck Ficke about this account were not the details but rather the self-consciousness with which Dell reported them. Observing with a glint of humor that the letter "was a small gem which I suppose you wish me to preserve for posterity," Ficke compliments Dell on his literary performance.[5]

The savoir-faire with which Floyd Dell constructed his artist's garret suggests both a familiarity with trans-Atlantic literary antecedents and a connoisseur's appreciation of avant-garde living conditions. Not surprisingly, scholars have pointed to Dell's studio letter as evidence of the bohemian culture that in 1913 began to flourish on the city's South Side, largely due to Dell's dynamic presence. The description bears out Christine Stansell's recent definition of bohemia, showcasing in miniaturized form a "liminal zone in the city" designed to usher young rebels across the "boundary" between bourgeois respectability and the urban avant-garde.[6] As Stansell and others have argued, in early twentieth-century America the geography of bohemia was most fully realized in New York's Greenwich Village, which emerged as the primary destination for the American avant-garde at precisely the moment that Dell was forging his way in Chicago. In fact, less than six months after describing his Jackson Park studio to Arthur Ficke, Dell left for Greenwich Village, where he helped edit the *New Masses* magazine and became one of his generation's best-known radicals.[7]

That New York reaffirmed its status as the nation's premier cultural hub during these years is important to Chicago literary history if only because the East Coast metropolis played a leading role in the midwestern city's dwindling reputation in the arts. As critic Samuel Putnam observed in an *American Mercury* article, "Chicago: An Obituary" (1926), the midwestern city seemed likely to become the country's "literary capital" in the 1890s and then again in the middle 1910s, only to see its aspirations cut short by departing writers: Sherwood Anderson, Floyd Dell, Theodore Dreiser, Hamlin Garland, George Barr McCutcheon, Will Payne, and Brand Whitlock, among others. According to historian Neil Harris, Chicago's writers went to New York on the promise of additional money, expanded career options, greater celebrity, and a more supportive cultural environment—all factors that conspired to make Chicago "a way station rather than a terminus" for artistic talent.[8] Putnam found the specific causes of Chicago's literary "death" harder to pin down, but natural nonetheless: "The small town youth with a hankering for print is attracted first to the neighboring provincial metropolis rather than to the distant and overaweing glamour of New York. And so, from his home in Des Moines or Kokomo, he comes to Chicago to get his breath and look about him before hiking on to (speaking contemporaneously) the painted purlieus of Greenwich Village or the penumbra of the Algonquin."[9]

Chicago literary histories mostly follow this rise-and-fall trajectory, tracing the city's emergent culture through two phases of a literary "renaissance" that concluded in the early 1920s. But however useful this periodization is for tracking the evolution of the on-the-ground literary community, its emphasis on the city itself—its internal resources—risks obscuring some of the social energies most responsible for Chicago's literary "rise." In his important study, *The Chicago Renaissance in American Letters* (1954), Bernard Duffey alludes to these extrametropolitan energies when he attributes the "dispersal" of Chicago writers not to New York's attractions but to shifts in the political mood and changing notions of artistic liberation, which loosened the writers' attachment to the city.[10]

Both Dell's homemaking letter to Ficke and his subsequent move to New York City were part of these broad transformations in Chicago's literary culture. However, these shifts, including Dell's journey toward bohemia, can only be fully understood in the context of the hinterland migrations that had shaped Chicago's literary aspirations since the 1880s. Marking a significant change in how literary migrants felt, thought, and wrote about the relationship between the hinterland and the city, Dell's self-dramatizing dialogues are filled with the anticipation of personal and cultural liberation, a sense informed by the literature of the modern era but figured primarily in the image of migration, of crossing over from one home to another. As Dell described it, his Jackson Park studio was indeed a threshold for change—and desire—but it was also an extension of the migration that had brought him to Chicago five years earlier and would carry him on to New York a few months later. Bohemia, in this sense, was as much a process as an actual place, and its emergence in Chicago during the 1910s hinged on the cultural crossings that brought Dell and other migrants to the city.

The literary bohemia that developed around Dell's Fifty-Seventh Street studio and, before that, the North Side apartment that he occupied with his wife, Marjory Currey, was short-lived in comparison to what emerged in Greenwich Village. Yet historians who find the Chicago experiments lacking in staying power and relative importance generally give short shrift to the migratory roots of both the Chicago and New York communities and underestimate the bohemian work—radical politics, the talk and practice of free love, and the commitment to avant-garde representations—that migrants such as Dell and Margaret Anderson had already accomplished before arriving in Greenwich Village. Much of the "work" in Chicago was rhetorical and—as Dell's letter to Ficke suggests—involved setting the stage for literary efforts that took place elsewhere. For instance, it was through the Jackson Park circle that Sherwood Anderson met Dell, who praised Anderson's writing and helped him publish his first novel, *Windy McPherson's Son*. And it was at a Dell-hosted party that Margaret Anderson announced her plans to establish the modernist-leaning *Little Review* and found a donor to pay for its first issues.

These gatherings were mostly about cultivating a style—of "living like the hard gem-like flame," as Margaret Anderson remembered—but this bohemian style reflected and encouraged a growing tendency in the region to join the spirit of modern rebellion with a distinctly midwestern literary voice. By 1921, these efforts received a name and seemed to become a movement when critic Carl Van Doren (who grew up in rural Illinois) suggested that the ongoing "revolt from the village" in midwestern literature was synonymous with the search for artistic liberation.[11] Sinclair Lewis's *Main Street* (1920) became the most famous example of Van Doren's thesis; however, small-town rebellions were not new to Chicago literature, and Sherwood Anderson as well as Floyd Dell transformed their significance by developing migration narratives that established provincialism—that is, a hinterland upbringing—as the basis for modernist thinking.

Here and in the next chapter, I want to argue that the literary community that evolved in Chicago between 1905 and 1920 fostered a climate of innovation and experimentation—call it a modernist style—that derived in large part from that community's migratory nature. Distinct in several ways from the migrations that brought Chicago's first generation of provincial writers to the city in the 1880s and '90s, this movement resembled the cultural "border-crossing[s]" that, according to Raymond Williams, encouraged the development of modernist literature and art in Britain and Europe during the 1910s and '20s. Williams notes that the modernists "were exiles one of another," provincial migrants or immigrants whose journeys into the cities of the twentieth century enabled the development of new artistic and intellectual communities and generated the conditions for revolutionary angles of vision. The strange look and sound of the city (especially if the migrant's language was foreign) and the cobbled-together nature of the trip as well as the "baffling unfamiliar" aspects of the people met along with the way "raised to the level of universal myth this intense, singular narrative of unsettlement, homelessness, solitude and impoverished independence: the lonely writer gazing down on the unknowable city from his shabby apartment." In this modern, urban myth, "the artist as necessarily estranged" became a popular, somewhat romantic figure—precisely the image that Floyd Dell self-consciously evoked.[12]

Drawn from a series of essays published about the time of his death in 1988, Willliams's speculations on the historical-geographic dimensions of modernism show him returning to the themes of his previous work, *The Country and the City,* and striving to theorize the flow of emotional and creative energies from province to metropolis during the modern era. But while in the earlier book Williams had been preoccupied with the sense of loss that pervades much pastoral literature, in this later investigation he found little nostalgia for the hinterland culture. On the contrary, his urban migrants are aggressively inventive, ironic, and, at least until their writing becomes a highly marketable commodity, decidedly antibourgeois. The chief difference, as Williams suggests in his dialectical survey of mass culture's emergence, lay in how the dizzying expansion of urban-based, technology-driven media—newspapers, photography, cinema, radio, and so forth—shaped the artist's conception of his work. On the one hand, this new array of expressive forms made the metropolis that much more attractive for artists and writers. On the other, it marked a "new imperialism" which threatened to squelch other forms of artistic expression. Writers and artists living on the peripheries of metropolitan culture and skeptical of the very forces that attracted them to places like London and Paris responded by positioning themselves against the status quo and becoming Socialists, misanthropes, and iconoclasts.[13]

Though not directly transferable to the turn-of-the-century Midwest, Williams's insight into the edgy, even subversive attitude generated by a provincial existence may help explain why so many midwesterners—from T. S. Eliot to F. Scott Fitzgerald—became expatriated modernists. The sense of being isolated from the cultural mainstream, which living in the middle part of the nation can foster, was perhaps the single most important reason for ambitious intellectuals to leave home. Chicago promised a solution to this feeling of marginality, but it was a solution that evolved and did not mean the same thing in 1905 that it meant in 1890.

For starters, Chicago was a larger, denser, more socially complex place than the city that John McCutcheon and Jane Addams encountered in the late 1880s. The population was just under 2 million people, roughly twice what it was in 1889; the ethnic composition, more diverse. The city's manufacturing and business sectors had also grown substantially, as had the cultural resources available in libraries, museums, and universities. Although this expansion confirmed and reinforced Chicago's status as a destination for hinterland migrants, it also had the paradoxical effect of eroding the mythic stature the city enjoyed in the 1880s and '90s. No longer contending with New York to be the number-one metropolis and now a familiar presence on the horizon of opportunities, Chicago's extraordinary promise waned.[14]

Second, while Chicago still dominated the region, the same forces that once made the city distinct—for instance, commercialized entertainment and leisure activities—were now a significant influence in other places.

Sociologists Robert and Helen Lynd document this drift toward mass urban society in *Middletown* (1929), their study of Muncie, Indiana, but the shift away from localism toward national cultural standards and values was already a topic for journalists in the 1890s and 1900s. Poet Vachel Lindsay, a Springfield, Illinois, native and booster of small-town life, commented on this trend in 1908, in a letter to editor Richard W. Gilder, lamenting his town's inability to stem the departure of talented people. "The really able people have their interest centered elsewhere," Lindsay observes, and "the network of civilization makes them almost as interested in the remotest part of the land, as their own city." As Lindsay suggests through the term *network,* his fellow townsmen were not necessarily drawn to any one city's example; rather, they looked to several "centers of culture or finance in the big cities" and dispersed their intellectual and economic interests accordingly.[15]

In subtle but significant ways, these developments complicated Chicago's place in the region, in effect skewing its status as a magnet for desiring migrants. Moreover, the economic and political events of the 1890s, particularly the 1893 depression and its impact on the city's labor market, but also the growing appeal of populism, with William Jennings Bryan as its standard bearer, and the striking popularity of Eugene V. Debs's socialism, placed Chicago's booster ethos in a less favorable light. At least for emerging hinterland writers and intellectuals who grew up in the 1890s with some exposure to radical politics or avant-garde literature—like Walter Pater's injunction to live like a hard, gemlike flame—the world must have seemed bigger than the Midwest or Chicago.

I would not want to overestimate the extent to which Chicago's lure diminished in the first two decades of the twentieth century. After all, Carl Sandburg did not publish his desire-filled "Chicago" until 1914, and provincial midwesterners continued to come in droves to the city to seek jobs and start new lives. On the other hand, it is possible to think of Sandburg's poem and even Dell's ecstatic description of his Fifty-Seventh Street studio as baroque evocations of desires that had shaped the city throughout the nineteenth century, not so much belated as mediated by decades of similar representations. Given this history, there was a peculiar logic in the fact that the Jackson Park colony was located on the outskirts of what had once been the Columbian Exposition—Chicago's most ambitious civic moment to date.

But the social gatherings that took place at Jackson Park in 1913 were more than an addendum to Chicago's past glories. Alive with the language of a new era, they served as a focal point for the avant-garde community and a gateway to Chicago's literary resources—people and institutions. Although this loose affiliation of writers and artists was not purposely organized to accommodate hinterland migrants, one of its primary effects was to galvanize Chicago's provincial writers and speed their intellectual and aesthetic development toward some still undefined notion of modern, cosmopolitan literature. With the possible exception of Sherwood Anderson, Chicago's bohemians did not, critics have argued, contribute much toward modernism's formal development in literature or art; rather, theirs was a movement in attitude and style.[16] Yet this movement identified the lure of the big city with the inward passion of artistic liberation and placed midwestern Chicago fiction at the headwaters of a crucial change in American literary culture.

In the rest of this chapter, I examine the social context for this reorientation, focusing on the early careers of Floyd Dell, Sherwood Anderson, and Tennessee Mitchell Anderson. I pay particular attention to Dell for two reasons: first, his hinterland upbringing and migration to Chicago vividly dramatize the political and aesthetic possibilities that Raymond Williams associated with provincial life and modern border crossing; second, he played a leading role in establishing a bohemian literary community in early twentieth-century Chicago. Dell touched on a theme important to both these phases of his life when, in his autobiography, he wrote of his adolescent coming-of-age in Davenport, Iowa, "I had to manufacture a Bohemia for myself."[17] Although he recognized the guidance and support he had received as an intellectually precocious teenager, he nonetheless foregrounded his singular drive toward literary and political independence— that is, his self-making. The unfolding of this familiar theme in migration narratives of restless youths who assert their individual desires before actually leaving for the city is one of the more interesting developments in early twentieth-century Chicago fiction.

Bohemian before He Left

When Floyd Dell arrived in Chicago in 1908, he was twenty-one years old and had been working full time for almost five years. In Davenport, Iowa, he had worked at a candy factory and then as a reporter for two different newspapers. Before Davenport, Dell lived in Quincy, Iowa—with a population of thirty thousand, it was somewhat smaller than Davenport—where he spent his adolescence and began to think of himself as a poet and a Socialist. His rapid intellectual development, which set him apart from his peers and most adults, was decisively shaped by his family's financial situation, which had begun to deteriorate even before his birth in 1887 in Barry, Illinois, a small town a few miles east of the Mississippi River. A veteran of the Civil War and a strong supporter of the Republican Party, Dell's father went into business for himself as a butcher after the war but during the 1870s slid gradually from the ranks of middle-class "respectability" and struggled to hold a variety of working-class jobs. Realizing at the age of five that his family was poor, the young Floyd Dell became a careful student of social status. As a teenager, he embraced socialism, believing that systematic political change could bring back his father, who, Dell later reasoned, had been taken by "American respectability." At the same time, reading and writing literature, especially poetry, provided a refuge from his family's straitened circumstances (56).

As described in his memoirs, *Homecoming* (1933), Dell's self-education redefined the ideological and emotional boundaries of his hinterland background. In reading Ralph Waldo Emerson, Thomas Carlyle, and H. G. Wells, he discovered how a career in letters could be a vehicle for social change. As he followed his interests in socialism to Marx and Engels, the Russian anarchist Peter Kropotkin, and other European revolutionary writers, which he read alongside such native radicals as the Peoria-born freethinker Robert Ingersoll and Minnesotan Ignatius Donnelly, he expanded the heroic political tradition—including Lincoln and John Brown—which he had absorbed from his father. When Dell discussed these texts with his republican father, he sidestepped their possible connection to Chicago-style anarchism and the Haymarket episode (which his father deplored) and instead presented the Russian Nihilists' search for freedom as an idealistic adventure set in "a kind of Slavic Forest of Arden, or Sherwood Forest, where Robin Hood and Maid Marian robbed and killed the rich and helped the poor." His subsequent discovery of poetry's expressive power "at the rate of one great poet a week"—Housman, Keats, Shelley, Whitman, and Wordsworth, among others—likewise brought his emotions into new territory, giving him a distinctly individualized language for understanding and communicating his romantic yearnings (63, 81).

The prevailing view among literary critics and historians is that Dell's brand of radicalism did not become culturally significant until the 1910s, when a generation of urban intellectuals, from Dell to Van Wyck Brooks to Mabel Dodge to H. R. Mencken to Emma Goldman, fashioned a critique of

American "genteel" traditions and modern industrial society that recast the role of the politically informed critic. But this view only begs the question of how such attitudes began to emerge in places like Quincy and Davenport, Iowa. It does not explain, to paraphrase historians Drew Cayton and Susan Gray, how the "the ideal of republican independence" that dominated the midwestern small town could support both "the conformity of George F. Babbitt" and the radicalism of Eugene V. Debs (who grew up in Terre Haute, Indiana).[18]

In Dell's case, his recollection of the dream life that he developed in Barry, Illinois, provides a clue. Deprived of Christmas gifts because of his family's poverty and determined to renounce all future desires, the five-year-old Dell developed elaborate fantasies about what might happen in private spaces sheltered from public view and the economic pressures at home. For instance, when he walked through the town square on the way to and from school, he passed by groups of boys telling stories or playing marbles. In the middle of the square was a bandstand with an upper loft where he knew older boys went to read dime novels, which were "forbidden" literature. As he explains, "This escape from the world of people fascinated me, and may have had something to do with my attic fantasies, which presently began." Meanwhile, along the edge of the square were retail establishments, including a blacksmith shop and a retail store, where Dell loitered, "studying its changing display of 'Diamond Dick' and 'Nick Carter' and 'Frank Merriwell' novels, on the cover of which some new and exciting episode was displayed in picture every week." Dell knew the books were off limits—he could not afford to buy them—nonetheless they commanded his interest, just as the knives and toys in the hardware store did. "Sight aroused no motor impulses," he recalls, since wanting to touch them or own them "might have been a painful reminder that I was poor. . . . Always there was an invisible plate-glass window separating me from the things I looked at. My hands hung at my sides, and I touched things only with my gaze."[19]

Significantly, this account immediately precedes Dell's description of how he discovered Barry's "Free Public Library," a realm apart from the commercialized pleasures of the square and the impoverished circumstances of home, where he was truly "free" to explore the pleasures of reading, sometimes with his father. At the age of seven, he read children's adventure stories and struggled with Hugo's *Les Misérables.* But soon Dell could read even that, and so "years pass quickly in public libraries, and one may grow as old as Rip Van Winkle in that enchanted cave, while remaining a child in the outside world" (17). Engaging his desires at the most elemental level, these excursions sped Dell's literary education and provided the foundation for his career as a writer and critic.

The private, even erotic nature of this inward literary turn was clear to the middle-aged Dell, who associated his discovery of romantic fiction with his reclamation of the attic space above his bedroom (a prototype of the artist's garret he would construct at Jackson Park), where he went to dream about the fifteen-year-old girl who lived next door. But the political and social implications of reading were also clear, as Dell associated both his father and the small-town landscape—for instance, he felt "privileged" to go with his father to Barry's town green to hear Fourth of July speeches—with midwestern republican traditions (7). As exemplified by his attraction to Hugo's story of a poor French worker who goes to prison for stealing a loaf of bread but later redeems himself, the young Dell dreamed of freeing himself and his family from the tyranny of poverty.

Reconstructed thirty-five years after the fact, Dell's discussion of his hinterland upbringing is an attempt to explain how a poor but gifted midwestern boy manufactured a Bohemia for himself. Most of Dell's abiding interests are at work in this interpretation of the past: his commitment to individual expression; his belief in the power of literature to change lives; his allegiance to social democratic politics; his materialist understanding of history and culture; and his long-standing familiarity with psychoanalytic theory, including his own therapy. To argue, based solely on *Homecoming,* that Dell's emergence as a literary radical happened just as he described it or that it could not have happened in any other place than Barry, Illinois, and Quincy and Davenport, Iowa, would be wrongheaded. On the other hand, there is little question that small-town culture—its class structure, social landscape, and republican traditions—gave Dell the vocabulary, if not the social experience, to present his movement into the avant-garde as the distinctly American "quest for life, liberty, and happiness" (55).

In Davenport, Dell found the community, the intellectual resources, and the employment opportunities that allowed him to think of himself as a politically committed aesthete. In 1903, when his family moved to the hub of Iowa's Tri-City region, Dell was sixteen years old and very much aware that his family's economic status and his developing literary interests were at odds. Although his parents believed that their son's intellectual talents would ultimately secure his future, Dell felt obligated to help support his family (as his brothers had) and figured that his immediate future would be spent working in a factory and writing poetry on the side. In fact, he dropped out of high school his senior year to work in a candy factory; when he was fired from that, he took a job in a printing shop.[20]

However, Dell's ongoing political and intellectual development cut short his career as a laborer. Since arriving in Davenport, he had met several people who encouraged him to pursue a different path. At the Davenport Public Library, he met Marilla Freeman, the head librarian and a graduate of the University of Chicago. Besides appealing to Dell as a woman, she encouraged his intellectual growth, and introduced him to Charles Banks, a poet and English teacher at the high school, who in turn schooled him in the craft of writing poetry. Meanwhile, through attending meetings of the Davenport Social Democrats, Dell met a postal worker named Fritz Feuchter—to this point, "the most important thing that had happened in my life," he remembers—who guided his enthusiasms and urged him to quit his job at the print shop and pursue a position at one of Davenport's newspapers.[21] At the age of eighteen, Dell began a career as a journalist and man of letters.

The story of Floyd Dell's rise—told by his biographers and himself—resembles an Algerian tale of extraordinary talent justly rewarded, rewritten from a bohemian perspective. By the time Dell left Davenport for Chicago in 1908, he was in a sense already made. At eighteen, the waifish boy-poet-Socialist took his literary cues from Henrik Ibsen and Bernard Shaw, was able to recommend the writings of New York avant-garde art critic James Huneker to fellow reporter Harry Hansen (a slightly older resident of Davenport who also migrated to Chicago and later profiled Dell in his *Midwest Portraits* [1923]), and showed up for poetry readings in Davenport drawing rooms with a black silk scarf wrapped around his collarless shirt.[22] And for all of Dell's native gifts, his new hometown set the terms of his success. Although he and his contemporaries subsequently referred to Davenport as a "small town," its proximity to Moline and Rock Island, Illinois, a well-developed industrial base with extensive retail and wholesale trade and sizable banking interests, gave the town the feel of a larger city. The population was quite diverse and included a substantial German-American community interested in European culture and Socialist politics, as well as a cosmopolitan upper class who, through Marilla Freeman's introductions, took an interest in Dell's literary talents. Accustomed to living in working-class neighborhoods and taken now to "poetic prowling" at night, Dell also discovered Davenport's dance hall and red-light district, which reinforced his understanding of the town's several sides.[23]

Moving from one side of Davenport to another and negotiating the class differences that distinguished one social group from another—talking politics, literature, and art, and fashioning himself as an idealist on the edge of important change—Dell developed the bohemian style that served him well in Chicago and New York. Three decades earlier, in Springfield, Ohio, a city whose economic and demographic character resembled Davenport's, John Glessner served a similar apprenticeship—in essence, learning in a smaller-scaled city the lessons he would practice to more dramatic effect in Chicago. Though their migrations led them to different places in the social and political spectrum, their frequent boundary crossings prepared both of them for success in the city.

The final phase of Dell's apprenticeship revolved around his friendship with George Cram ("Jig") Cook, an acquaintance of Marilla Freeman's who would later establish the Provincetown Players. Cook was older than Dell (by fourteen years) and came from a well-to-do Davenport family, but he was a credentialed intellectual, having published a novel and, during his twenties, lived for several years in the bohemian quarter of San Francisco. After moving back to Davenport, Cook continued his iconoclastic ways. When Dell met him, he was in the process of divorcing his wife so that he could marry Mollie Price, a young anarchist from Chicago whom he met through Charles Banks; then, soon after he married Price and she became pregnant, he began an affair with Susan Glaspell, also a writer and resident of Davenport. Between 1906 and 1908, the individual relationships that helped launch Dell in Davenport had evolved into a loosely knit community—including Cook, Glaspell, Freuchter, Freeman, and William Fineshriber, a rabbi in town—which met regularly to talk about a range of radical subjects, from socialism to sex.[24] To these intellectually and erotically charged discussions, Dell brought a quick mind and a command of Socialist theory that outpaced his older peers. From it, he gained confidence in his own abilities and a clear sense of the pleasures that derive from creating a bohemian community.

In the winter of 1907, Dell's position in this web of relations shifted somewhat when he was fired from the *Davenport Democrat* for insubordination and joined Cook at his farm about ten miles from town.[25] There, Dell became close friends with Mollie Price, attempted a romance with Freeman (she limited its scope), and that summer met Margery Currey, an English teacher at Davenport High School. A friend of Price's, Currey was from Evanston, Illinois; and as Dell considered his next move—and the lack of employment options in Davenport—she recommended Chicago, even inviting Dell to spend Thanksgiving with her family. In November of 1908, carrying a letter of introduction from Marilla Freeman, Dell took a train to Chicago, where he was met at the station by Dr. Graham Taylor, a friend of Freeman's and the director of the Commons settlement house, who helped Dell get his bearings before he went to board with Mollie Price's anarchist father.[26]

In succeeding years, Dell characterized his time in Davenport as a key transition in his life. When Cook died unexpectedly in Greece in 1924, Dell wrote his friend Ralph Cram that before Cook left, he had proposed that they all go back to Davenport and transform it into "another Athens." Cook's proposition, made in all sincerity, reminded Dell of Vachel Lindsay's vision for Springfield, Illinois — and of the poetic dreams he and his friends once shared. According to Dell, there was "something of old Athens in Davenport," but, he observes, "I am not sure how much of what we found existed in objective fact and how much in our own hearts. Only, when I hear about the drab life of the middle west, I think to myself, 'Davenport was not like that!'" Instead, Dell remembered it as a place where he discovered the "splendor of ideas" and the beauty of friendship and love. "I wonder what Davenport is like now," he continues, and if "there are boys and girls growing up there who dream wild, foolish, beautiful dreams; and if there is anyone like Jig to assure them there is wisdom in their folly and bid them not be discouraged or afraid." Forty years later, he explained to literary historian Dale Kramer that Davenport (and Chicago, too) remained in his memory as "a romantic city."[27]

Dell's "romantic" hinterland was the same Midwest that he identified in the two-part discussion of Chicago in fiction that he wrote for *The Bookman* in 1913. There, Dell pays tribute to "the Chicago of all the Sister Carries who come up from Indiana and Iowa towns, ignorant and adventurous," a Chicago "that lives in the minds and imaginations of young people through the Middle West, a Chicago that exists by virtue of their aspiration and their need, and that begins to die with their first sight of the town."[28] In this formulation, the boundary separating the small-town Midwest and Chicago is hard to discern, since the city is so clearly the projections of dreams developed and nurtured in places like Davenport. Here, as in his letter to Cram, Dell is not denying the "objective" reality of Chicago or Davenport, but rather underscoring the "poetry," or romance, through which provincial migrants sought to fashion transcendent realities of their future lives. This idea was hardly new; indeed, it is implicit in a large portion of nineteenth- and early twentieth-century Chicago literature, especially (as Dell noted) in

Sister Carrie. However, Dell was the first critic to state so clearly that the city was in some elemental way the product of individual fantasy and desire.

This insight, as we shall see, had important consequences for the development of Chicago fiction in the 1910s. But it also related to Dell's efforts to create a bohemian culture in Chicago, for, as he suggests in his letter to Ficke—written at roughly the same time that Dell was composing his *Bookman* articles—his artist's studio was simply another iteration of the romantic impulse that had brought him to Chicago. The studio objectified what Dell's letter expresses by way of poetry, that he was struggling to transcend the mundane realities of city life and start afresh, Innisfree style, in a new home.

Yet despite this vision of romantic alienation, Dell was not really alone with his art. From the moment he left Davenport for Chicago, he had been buoyed in his efforts to make his mark on the world. Not only had Marilla Freeman linked him to Graham Taylor, but she also had written him a letter of introduction to Charles Thomas Hallinan, an editor with the *Chicago Evening Post* who helped him find a job. Back home in Davenport, Susan Glaspell dunned Dell for news of his progress: "Now sit down to your machine and write us a letter. Tell us the things you ought to have sense enough to know we want to know.—Work hard—that is hard enough to keep your job—and avoid the pitfalls of a great city."[29] Though Glaspell humorously invoked the prodigal son parable, her note reflects the interest of Dell's extended family in his ongoing development.

Moreover, when Dell married Margery Currey in August of 1909 and the couple moved to Rogers Park, a neighborhood on the city's Far North Side, Currey gave his editorial career her full support, helping to create an atmosphere that attracted Chicago's writers and artists to their apartment. Margaret Anderson, who established *The Little Review* and ate frequently with the Dells, noted that Currey "created a sort of salon for Floyd who was so timid he would never have spoken to anyone if she hadn't relieved him of all social responsibility and presented him as an impersonal being whose only function in life was to talk."[30] These dynamics continued in Jackson Park, even as the couple's relationship foundered and they gravitated toward a "modern" marriage that allowed them more freedom. For while Dell lived by himself, Currey's studio adjoined his—an arrangement that signified the contingent nature of Dell's individual bohemian status. In dress as well, Dell had help, too, as he began sporting a high collar, black stock coat, a walking stick, and gloves, after a lunch at which writer Charlotte Perkins Gilman and

FIGURE 13
The bohemian Floyd
Dell, as painted by
Bror Nordfeldt in 1913.
(Floyd Dell Papers,
the Newberry Library)

stage designer Michael Carr decided with some amusement that such an outfit would dramatize his antibourgeois sentiments (fig. 13).[31]

Dell's Chicago experience bears out sociologist Claude S. Fischer's contention that modern cities "generate alternative subcultures" not by "breaking down social ties and releasing people's deviant instincts" but rather by "encourag[ing] social ties in the small sectors of society" that foster values and behavior "that mainstream society considers aberrant." Furthermore, Dell's migration to Chicago and the network of friends and acquaintances that enabled this move suggest that his place in the city's literary and intellectual enclave was largely self-selected, in a way that would not have been possible when Chicago's literary community was beginning to form in the 1880s and early 1890s.[32] Community rather than anomie sustained his bohemian identity, and his realization of this fact accentuated the irony with which he effected his individual "revolt from the village." At the same time, if his migration to Chicago had in some sense developed as an extension of the community he knew in Davenport, Dell brought these antecedents forward, hiring Jig Cook as his assistant editor on the *Friday Literary Review* after he assumed the editorship, and enlisting Arthur Ficke as a book reviewer.[33] He also made new friends, establishing contacts through his work at the *Review* and in Jackson Park, which moved Chicago literary history in new directions.

All this was clearly on Dell's mind when, in October of 1913, he left Chicago. Writing en route to his old Davenport friend, Rabbi William Fineshriber, he noted,

now I am on my way back to New York to commence all over again the adventure of life. It is curiously like the beginning of my Chicago adventure. Now, as then, I have apparently exhausted all the economic possibilities of my hometown. Now as then I have been advised, and urged, and pushed into making the break. Now as then, I do it with great reluctance and regret, thinking far more of the friendships I am leaving behind than of any possible satisfaction which the new environment may afford.[34]

Thus Floyd Dell crossed over—again.

Leaving Business for Literature

In February of 1913, Sherwood Anderson returned to Chicago for the third time, renting a room on Fifty-Seventh Street, not far from the Jackson Park artists' colony.[35] He had first moved to Chicago in 1896 from the small town of Clyde, Ohio, with strong, but ill-defined dreams of making his fortune. After a year and a half of work as a factory hand—and no fortune—he returned to Ohio to serve with his National Guard unit in the Spanish-American War. After the war, Anderson went back to Ohio, finished high school, and then moved again to Chicago, where he remained for almost six years, launching a successful career as an advertising copywriter and, in 1904, marrying Cornelia Lane, who came from a well-to-do Toledo family. When he retraced his steps to the city in 1913, his marriage and business career were in disrepair. He had recently failed as the president of a paint manufacturing company in Elyria, Ohio, and left that position following a psychological breakdown during which he was found wandering the streets of Cleveland without any idea of his identity. In returning to Chicago—alone, at first— Anderson resumed his former job as a copywriter so he could support his family and have time to write fiction, a practice he had begun in Elyria but which he now hoped to take up in earnest. He was thirty-six years old.

Spanning three discrete stages in the first half of his life, Anderson's relocations to Chicago yielded a layered, complex understanding of the city's possibilities, which informed his portrayal of the migration process in such works as *Windy McPherson's Son* (1916) and *Winesburg, Ohio* (1919). If, in 1896, he was uncertain about his career prospects and bewildered by what the city's frank display of sexuality meant for his own identity, then in the early 1900s his urban experience was marked by his successful assumption of middle-class manhood: a white-collar job, marriage, and family. By 1913, however, this sense of earned confidence had eroded, supplanted by another hoped-for milestone: literary success. As Anderson emphasized in terms that assumed near mythical status as his literary career took off, this last transition—his reinvention of himself as a great writer—meant rejecting the very desires that prompted his initial migration to Chicago and fueled the city's rise.

In "When I Left Business for Literature" (1924), a *Century* article (which also appears in his autobiographical *A Story Teller's Story*), Anderson portrays his Elyria breakdown as a middle-class rebellion, suggesting that he had buckled under the pressure of "the American dream" in order to assume his natural role as an artist. Among the critics reinforcing this image of dissent, Harry Hansen notes in his popular *Midwest Portraits* (1923) that in Anderson, "we have stumbled upon an American writer to whom revolt is not an empty phrase but an actuality, lived through in suffering and silence." Yet Anderson's "revolt" was more complicated and drawn out than this picture of the long-suffering artist would suggest. According to Kim Townsend, his most recent biographer, his lapse from reason was not a nervous breakdown or amnesia but rather a "fugue state" brought on by conflicting demands and a desire for single-minded focus. Anderson, Townsend notes, "was a man who wanted to get out of his business, to leave—if not destroy—his wife, but in his imagination, all he wanted to do was live in writing, be a writer." [36]

In this dream of self-transformation, the Jackson Park colony played a crucial role. Not only did the circle of writers and artists encourage Anderson's literary progress—with Dell in particular working to find a publisher for his first novel, *Windy McPherson's Son*—but it helped him imagine what life as a literary bohemian might be like.[37] Anderson had something of a model for a life in art through his older brother, Karl, a painter then living in New York City, but the relationship between the two was not especially close. Yet it was through his brother that Anderson met Margery Currey, who was reporting on an exhibition of Karl's for the *Daily News*. While staying with Sherwood, Karl Anderson had borrowed a copy of his brother's novel and then passed it on to Currey, who after reading it sent Sherwood a note urging him to stop by one of their studio gatherings. Currey then passed the manuscript on to Dell, who went on to write glowingly about the unpublished novel in the *Friday Literary Review*.[38] With some nervousness, Anderson followed up on Currey's invitation, believing, as he recalled, that his life was about to change: "Now I was to go into a new world, men and women whose interests would be my interest, the curious feeling of loneliness and uncertainty broken up. I thought of the nights when I could not work, the hours spent walking the city streets, great projects forming in my mind, these coming to nothing."[39]

Over the summer of 1913, Anderson became part of the Fifty-Seventh Street group, attending parties, going on outings, and meeting a good portion of Chicago's literary avant-garde, including Dell, Currey, Carl Sandburg, Margaret Anderson, poet Eunice Tietjens, critic Lucian Cary, journalist Ben Hecht, and visitors such as Arthur Ficke and Theodore Dreiser, who attended the Jackson Park gatherings when they were in town. That Anderson found his new world in proximity to Dell and Currey is not surprising. Though Dell was more than ten years younger than Anderson, he was far better read in contemporary literature. When Dell held forth on Chekhov, Turgenev, and Freud, Anderson paid attention. As a critic, Dell was astute and well connected, and for having placed *Windy McPherson's Son* with the British publishing house of John Lane, deserved the title of "literary father" that Anderson gives him in his *Memoirs*. Also, because Anderson's relationship with Cornelia was under strain, he found Currey and Dell's "modern" companionate marriage a model worth studying.[40]

The effect of this heady atmosphere on Anderson was electric and, scholars agree, the catalyst for his forthcoming literary career. As Irving Howe observed half a century ago, in a judgment consistent with other critical opinions of the Chicago Renaissance, Anderson was drawn to the Fifty-Seventh Street group for the companionship it offered among other provincial migrants, who were likewise attracted to the creative possibilities of the city. Anderson "needed" the company and support of this group. Moreover,

Howe concluded, the conversations and interactions "stimulated and released him for *Winesburg*, his most significant work; his flight to Bohemia was a condition for this creative recovery of the town."[41]

In fact, one could go further and say that the flight itself—from Clyde to Chicago, and from middle-class respectability to literary bohemia—is inseparable from *Winesburg* and served as the motivating theme for much of his fiction. That is, when Anderson portrayed Clyde in his groundbreaking work, as he already had in *Windy McPherson's Son*, he was not only stepping back from his Ohio upbringing in order to present it anew from his newly found perspective in the urban avant-garde, he was also writing about the migratory process that led him one state of mind to another. Similarly, as he became increasingly comfortable with the Fifty-Seventh Street group and more confident about his literary talents, he adopted the bohemian style as his own. He let his hair grow and took to wearing scarves; and when Dell left for New York and replaced his black stock outfit with a proletarian flannel shirt, Anderson, after visiting him in Greenwich Village, assumed the black garb of the literary aesthete—a decision Dell understood to be "symbolic" of his friend's change in status (fig. 14).[42]

These earnest attempts at self-fashioning were dramatized by Anderson's provincial antecedents and business background. Among fellow migrants like Dell and Margaret Anderson (who grew up in Columbus, Indiana), his small-town origins were a point of connection that assumed even greater weight when Dell confirmed that Anderson had written an excellent novel about that background—something that no one in their cohort (Dreiser, who no longer lived in Chicago, being the model of success) had yet accomplished. Anderson underscored this truth himself by telling stories at parties about his business career and hinterland upbringing.[43] That this gifted storyteller was an advertising man by day only enhanced the drama of his crossing over into Chicago's bohemian community.

By the 1920s, Anderson was adeptly playing the role of the authentic, heartland writer who had escaped his false life as a businessman to pursue a higher calling. This presentation seemed to work especially well with New York intellectuals like Van Wyck Brooks, Waldo Frank, and Paul Rosenfeld, who as editors of the *Seven Arts* periodical had published Anderson's fiction and saw in it a like-minded concern with the negative effects of American industrial culture. Writing to Brooks in 1918, for instance, Anderson claimed an authorial kinship with Mark Twain (about whom Brooks was writing at the time) and noted that, like Twain, "he was alone on that stream sometimes."

FIGURE 14
Echoing Floyd Dell's
fashion statement,
Sherwood Anderson
poses circa 1922.
(Chicago Historical
Society DN-0009914;
Chicago Daily News
photograph)

Three years later, in a letter to Paul Rosenfeld, he referred again to his similarity to Twain and, perhaps reflecting his disappointment that Brooks had
not made the connection in *The Ordeal of Mark Twain* (1920), spelled out his
own representative status: "I have in my inner consciousness conceived of
what we roughly speak of as the Middle West, and what I have so often called
Mid-America, as an empire with its capital in Chicago," he explained. "When
I started writing, my conception wasn't so clear. Then I went only so far as to
want health for myself. I was a money-getter, a schemer, a chronic liar. One
day I found out that when I sat down to write, it was more difficult to lie." At
that point, Anderson gave up the "American trick" of "putting it over" and
became a writer.[44]

Nearly identical to Dell's conception of midwestern desire in the *Bookman,* Anderson's internalization of Chicago's imperial powers was the key

gambit in his modernist retelling of the urban migration narrative. The Middle West, as Anderson describes it here, is an imaginative realm of his own making, similar in design to William Faulkner's mythic Yoknapatawpha County, which would appear later that decade (and, it is worth noting, bearing Anderson's influence). Moving well beyond Henry Blake Fuller's suggestion that the migrating writer was in an ideal position to capture the construction of ambition and identity in the rising city, Anderson abandoned the distinction between objective and subjective realities—the framework for realism—and took authorial responsibility for creating and representing center and periphery by himself. Significantly, too, Anderson identified this authorial vision with his rejection of profit making. Leaving business for literature gave him license to represent the migration from small town to Chicago; in this sense, his rebellion against middle-class culture and the revolt from the village against were one and the same.

While in 1913 Anderson was virtually unknown to the world of literature, the persona that he describes in his 1921 letter to Paul Rosenfeld was already beginning to form. That figure—a robust, untutored, hinterland storyteller—was certainly at odds with the middle-aged businessman who had lived in Chicago for half a dozen years and worked around urban commercial culture for more than a decade. Still, Anderson's success in reinventing himself revealed a facility with image and language that was consistent with his work as a salesman and copywriter. And he had been writing fiction in his spare time since his Elyria days.[45] In this respect, his career path resembled that of Edgar Lee Masters, who had moved to Chicago from Lewiston, Illinois, in 1892 to launch a career as a lawyer; until the success of *Spoon-River Anthology* (1915), Masters had pursued poetry as an avocation. However, Anderson was eight years younger than Masters, and proved more adaptable to the new era.

Thus Sherwood Anderson crossed into bohemia, evoking in his *Memoirs* a self-conscious connection between individual creativity and liminal urban space that recalls Dell's letter to Ficke. "It was time of a kind of renaissance, in the arts, in literature," Anderson remembered, "a Robin's Egg Renaissance I have called it in my mind since. It fell out of the nest." This notion of rebirth, of a group of writers and artists creating something new by pushing out through a shell and from a nest, suggests a community living apart, in cocoonlike insularity from the rest of the city. Indeed, in characterizing the "devotees of art" with whom he spent time after returning to the city, he underscores their efforts "to find, in the huge undisciplined city, little nooks, quiet places, little restaurants, where we could sit, as we imagined it might be in some old world city." As for the Fifty-Seventh Street group, they generated "a feeling of brotherhood and sisterhood," the "gayest and happiest" time Anderson ever knew. Later, when the group broke up and Anderson moved to a rooming house on Cass Street on the city's North Side, he formed a new nest, surrounded by boarders who were likewise involved in one creative struggle or another. Anderson called them "Little Children of the Arts," and they "seemed to me to live, most of them, in a little closed-in world of their own." Here, Anderson wrote *Winesburg, Ohio,* and when he finished the book, he felt "as though I had little or nothing to do with the writing. It was as though the people of the house, all of them wanting so much, none of them really equipped to wrestle with life as it was, had in this odd way, used me as an instrument" and told their stories "through the lives of these queer small town people of the book."[46]

Anderson's Innisfree style of homemaking had implications both for the creation of his best-known work and for how Chicago writers could, or could not, represent the city in literature. Whereas in the 1890s George Ade and Hamlin Garland noted the city's unruly, expansive nature, they nonetheless endeavored to portray its character in whole. By the 1910s, a different sensibility had emerged, one that conceded the city's sprawling size and "undisciplined" nature, and aimed for a more limited perspective within metropolitan culture that focused on the inner lives of Chicagoans. This approach had complements in the inward-looking, self-conscious writing style that developed at this time and in the bohemian communities that, nested within the city, fostered the deliberately artistic desires of the migrants who comprised them. No less attentive to the ambitions that fueled the city's rise than their nineteenth-century counterparts, the provincial writers who initiated Chicago's robin's-egg renaissance eventually took their dreams elsewhere. In doing so, they helped make the world they knew best—the Midwest and the Chicago they had imagined—home to the nation's desires.

Up in Michigan

At roughly the same time that Anderson was reconstituting himself as a bohemian writer and easing out of his marriage, he met Tennessee Claflin Mitchell. A native of Jackson, Michigan, Mitchell migrated to Chicago in the late 1890s, taking a job as a piano tuner while also pursuing her interests in dance and, over time, developing friendships with many artists and writers. In 1909, she began a year-long affair with Edgar Lee Masters, and by the time she encountered Anderson at a party held by the Dells at their Fifty-Seventh Street studios, she was good friends with Margery Currey. A talented artist in her own right, who made a name for herself as a sculptor, Mitchell is generally linked to the Chicago Renaissance through her relationship with Masters and marriage to Anderson.[47] Mitchell herself was conscious of her primarily supportive role and of the forces, both cultural and familial, that shaped her position as a female artist and provider. This awareness features significantly in the autobiography that she began in 1928.

Assessing Mitchell's own understanding of this work is complicated, since she died in 1929 and never finished the narrative. What remains are seventy-seven handwritten pages and a note to Sherwood Anderson explaining that a publisher had asked her to write a "book of memoirs" and asking him if he had "any feeling against it." Mitchell notes her uncertainty regarding how she would "use" him in the memoirs, "because I don't know. All I do know is that I wouldn't want to exploit myself through you. I also know that the world wouldn't be losing a masterpiece if I never took my own pen in hand. Why can't they let me keep at my clay pail? So please be quite frank."[48]

Here Tennessee Mitchell Anderson (she retained her married name, though the couple divorced in 1924) seems to acknowledge her subordinate role by downplaying her literary talents and anticipating her ex-husband's discomfort with the project. But Mitchell's sensitivity to their mutual exploitation, as she humorously describes it, hints at another way in which her creative work was linked to his. In describing her Jackson, Michigan, childhood and relocation to Chicago, Mitchell's unfinished autobiography resembles Sherwood Anderson's chosen literary genre: the migration narrative. Furthermore, it illuminates the psychological and sexual dimensions of Tennessee Mitchell's small-town upbringing, a theme that Anderson pursued with great success in *Winesburg, Ohio*. It is not clear whether Mitchell deliberately modeled her memoirs on Anderson's fiction, and there is no record of Anderson responding to her inquiry; but like other first-person accounts of literary culture in early twentieth-century Chicago, hers locates the origins of bohemian rebellion in the provinces and establishes them as the precondition for urban migration.

At the same time, Mitchell distinguishes her life by emphasizing the particular challenges that she faced as a woman. So while Floyd Dell writes of

leveraging his working-class roots to create a bohemia for himself in Davenport, Mitchell explains how she was compelled by necessity and gender to
seek a life for herself beyond her middle-class upbringing. It would be an exaggeration to say that her self-making took place against her will; nevertheless, she shows how her departure from Jackson and search for work sprang
from her responsibilities as the oldest daughter in an unsettled family.

    From the initial description of making social calls with her mother in
Jackson to the final sentence in the manuscript, where she notes her naive involvement with a circle of homosexual men in Chicago (an experience she
claimed to understand better when she read Edward Carpenter's book *The
Intermediate Sex: A Study of Some Transitional Types of Men and Women*
[1912]), the memoirs highlight the shift from nineteenth-century mores to a
self-consciously modern self. However, like Dell, Mitchell examines her
past through a contemporary interpretive lens, which means that the adult
analyst frequently seems present in the narrative. For example, she explains
that when she accompanied her mother during a round of neighborhood
calls wearing "a leg horn hat and a pink sash," she eventually lost patience
with the grown-up conversation and during the final visit stood up on a cro-
cheted stool—surrounded by floral displays and photograph albums—and
said, "Now let's talk about me." This anecdote, arising from the rich domestic interiors of bourgeois life, serves as the prompt for the memoirs, for
as Mitchell goes on to explain, "Ego will out. A few years ago after being saturated with many of the current autobiographies I had a dream. I dreamed
that I was writing my autobiography and the first sentence read 'I was a vir-
gin until my fourth year.' It made an amusing story but had no historical
connection in mind with the fact for I retained that pearl of great price until
maturity if not years of discretion" (ibid.). Mitchell's purposefully witty
conflation of her precocious histrionics and sexual identity sets the tone for
the literary performance to follow: an exposition of the circumstances, both
cultural and highly personal, that led to her "liberation" from home.

    The term *liberation,* though, deserves qualification in two respects. One
is that Mitchell's departure from Jackson took place under duress when her
widowed and financially reduced father remarried and his new wife forced
Mitchell out of the home that she had managed since her mother's death
during her teenage years. In this sense, the autobiography is more a story of
displacement than liberation, with Mitchell—now alienated from her father's affections and her middle-class estate—going to Chicago to fend for
herself and one of her younger sisters, who later died of meningitis there.

The impact this uprooting had on Mitchell's sense of herself is felt throughout the narrative, as she strives to balance this melodramatic account—so
common in nineteenth-century domestic fiction—with the story of her
emergence as an independent New Woman.

The latter plotline touches on the second reason for approaching Mitch-
ell's "liberation" advisedly, and that is her family's unconventional character.
Named for Tennessee Claflin, the famous or infamous advocate of free love
and spiritualism, who visited her mother when she was pregnant, Tennessee
Mitchell bore the expectations of her family's radical ambitions. In the autobiography, she recalls being dandled on the knee of Robert Ingersoll—
"Uncle Bob Ingersoll"—a friend of her freethinking maternal grandfather's.
Her mother carried on this radical tradition through her devotion to spiritualism (the family regularly attended séances) and such causes as the Anti-
Cruelty and Anti-Vivisection Societies. Though embarrassed by the teasing
that her name brought, Tennessee also admired her mother's iconoclastic
stance and proudly notes that when a neighbor criticized her mother's relationship with Claflin and claimed that not even she would name a child for
her, her mother retorted, "I like the name. I admire the woman. I dare and
I will" (ibid.).

This example of maternal daring and will, with antecedents flung back to
Tennessee Claflin and Victoria Woodhull's provocative agitation for free
love and their unprecedented careers as stockbrokers in New York City,
lingers in the autobiography as Mitchell describes how she established a life
for herself and her sisters when their mother and grandfather died and her
father relinquished control to a cold and unsympathetic second wife. Compared to Sherwood Anderson's artistic self-invention, the development of
Mitchell's "ego" appears less flamboyant not only because she lacked economic power to give up—for the sake of art—but also because she presents
her history as a series of decisions mandated by her need to make a living.
Bypassing a chance to marry a wealthy and "haughty" young man from
Jackson, she built on her musical training and instead became a piano tuner,
an occupation that gave her a foothold in Chicago despite her initially being
shunned by the profession for being female.

Significantly, Mitchell's description of leaving home is almost a stock image of the urban migrant: "Taking my violin once more under my arm, this
time in the hope of selling it, with some of my mother's jewelry as a last re-
sort and the two hundred dollars that my father had given me, confident that
in a short time I would rescue my younger sisters and that Life awaited me,

I started for Chicago." Yet "Life," as Mitchell defines her career choice, is not about self-making and upward mobility but instead "the bringing of accord to the jangling pianos of the world" (ibid.). Inspired by her reading of Ralph Waldo Trine's New Thought ode to self-realization, *In Tune With the Infinite: Fullness of Peace, Power, and Plenty* (1897), this vision of promoting musical and spiritual harmony cleverly suggests that her supporting role as a piano tuner—as opposed to a performer—grew out of a realistic appraisal of her life circumstances and a need to ameliorate her radical legacy.

Still, the memoirs repeatedly show Mitchell in the performance mode, stuck in positions that expose her vulnerable ego. At her first and only piano recital, her drawers slip as she is walking onstage and she has to pull them up; later, as an adult, she attends a beach party in Maine wearing false breasts (because she is concerned about her figure), only to find them slipping out of place when she goes for a swim as everyone watches. While on the one hand these scenes convey, as in a bad dream, a sense of acute embarrassment and anxiety, on the other they also criticize, in a comical way, the social norms that conspired to make her the center of attention. By underscoring her debasement, Mitchell worked to undo it. She adopted a similar strategy in visiting Helen Masters after the poet's wife discovered Mitchell was having an affair with her husband. Kneeling at Helen Masters's feet, Mitchell asked for forgiveness in a dramatic reenactment of a scene from a play that Edgar Lee Masters had recently written in which the working-class mistress of an upper-class man begs for his wife's sympathy.[49] This performance, best understood in light of the power differential that governed bourgeois gender relations at the turn of the century, was Mitchell's effort to stay in tune with the status quo by ironically (and humorously) assuming a role imagined (in advance) by the adulterous poet.

In describing her move from Jackson to Chicago, Tennessee Mitchell recalled that she felt a sense of "complete at-homeness" that she doubted she would have felt in any other large city. Given Chicago's relation to its hinterland, this was hardly a surprising response. After all, the city was built on the ideological assumption that it was the natural home of white, native-born midwesterners. However, as we have seen, the experience of making a home in Chicago or, to be more precise, the representation of this experience in literary and nonliterary texts, reveals the tensions surrounding this assumption. The examples of Mitchell and (for instance) Jane Addams suggest that unmarried women negotiated the process of self-making and homemaking with some care, simultaneously accommodating and subverting the prerequisites of true womanhood as their migrations led them further into urban culture. Underwritten by desire, these negotiations assumed a frankly sexual nature in the bohemian literary circles that emerged in early twentieth-century Chicago. Margaret Currey, a native of Evanston who migrated back to the city after teaching high school in Davenport, Iowa, agreed to an open marriage with Floyd Dell, a self-declared feminist. Margaret Anderson, who came to Chicago from Columbus, Indiana, to escape a boring middle-class existence and make a "beautiful life," sold "a calf-skin Ibsen and two exquisite silk negligées" to make ends meet and staked her claim to the avant-garde by publishing in the *Little Review* not only experimental works of literary modernism but also cartoons dramatizing her life with lover and coeditor Jane Heap.[50]

Because Tennessee Mitchell Anderson did not finish her memoirs, we cannot know how she would have tied her role in the Chicago literary renaissance to the preceding history of her life, and whether her peculiarly modern account of growing up in Jackson, Michigan, led beyond jangling pianos to her own Lake Isle of Innisfree. For a full-length story of artistic and sexual liberation, beginning in the hinterlands and passing through Chicago, we must turn to fiction.

9

CHICAGO DREAMING

Following the publication of *Winesburg, Ohio* in 1919, Sherwood Anderson boasted in a letter to his friend, psychoanalyst Trigant Burrow, that the book was getting "remarkable recognition," even from "those who have fought me before." Though the reluctant businessman complained about not making enough money from writing fiction, he still hoped to quit his job at the Long-Critchfield Agency. "I want something of leisure to develop in leisure my impressions of life," Anderson wrote. "Having made myself an artist by infinite labor, I want to lead my life and do the work of an artist and not have to spend my days writing stupid advertisements."[1] This declaration came with some irony, since Anderson had progressed as an artist by writing about young businessmen who dream of leaving their small-town homes and making a fortune. From "The Man of Affairs," a sketch he wrote for *Agricultural Advertising* in 1904, to *Windy McPherson's Son* (1916), the road to *Winesburg* was paved with migration narratives, written in the Chicago tradition of self-making.

How Anderson moved from the boosting realism of *Agricultural Advertising* to the lyrical introspection of *Winesburg* is the story of desire's evolution from a widely shared attraction to Chicago as a city of opportunities to a more internally oriented yearning for artistic expression. The gist of this evolution may be seen in the differences between Peter Macveagh of "The Man of Affairs" sketch or Sam "Jobby" McPherson in Anderson's first novel and George Willard of *Winesburg, Ohio.* While Macveagh and McPherson direct their passions toward the accumulation of money and the economic rise of Chicago, Willard (a newspaper reporter) discovers in the process of leaving home "the background on which" he can "paint the dreams of his manhood."[2] Similar to the impressions that Anderson notes in his letter to Burrow, this self-conscious merging of the artistic impulse with the emotional experience of migration constituted a new note in the history of Chicago literature.

But not entirely new. Published four years before *Winesburg,* Willa Cather's *Song of the Lark* (1915) also traces the artistic awakening of a provincial migrant from the inside out. Strictly speaking, Cather's heroine (a would-be opera singer named Thea Kronborg) is not from the midwestern hinterland—she comes from Moonstone, Colorado—but in order to realize her musical talent she must cross over to Chicago. Kronborg's recognition of the primordial desire that propels her singing emerges through a maturation process that parallels her movement away from Moonstone. At the age of thirteen she senses "that there was something about her that was different" and knows, without fully understanding her gifts, that she will eventually leave her hometown. When she is fifteen she drags her mattress over to her bedroom window on summer nights and lies awake, "vibrating with excitement" and feeling life "rush" in on her; though "in reality," Cather explains, life "rushes from within, not from without." Thea's awakening is both a sexual and an artistic experience, for there "is no work of art so big or so beautiful that it was not once all contained in some youthful body, like this one which lay on the floor in the moonlight, pulsing with ardor and anticipation."[3] In this gendered portrayal of art waiting to be born, Cather implies that the same romantic yearning that led young people to believe in a transcendent Chicago—as Floyd Dell described in his 1913 *Bookman* article—also drives the creative process. Here, great art stirs in Moonstone, not in New York, Paris, or Rome.

This final chapter shows how the cultural and literary conditions of hinterland migration gave rise in the 1910s to a different kind of migration narrative, marked by modernist sensibilities and, most important, a self-conscious treatment of desire. The critical discussion of literary modernism is vast, and I have no intention of summarizing it here or of conducting modernist readings of selected migration novels. Rather, I want to highlight the ways in which texts such as *Song of the Lark* and *Winesburg, Ohio* departed from their predecessors, stressing where appropriate the characteristics that make them seem more like works of literature written after 1920 than before.

Connected by their subjects to nineteenth-century midwestern culture, *Song of the Lark, Winesburg, Ohio,* and to a lesser extent Floyd Dell's *Moon-Calf* are transitional works that reaffirmed the linkages among migration, desire, and art at the very moment that the romance of hinterland migration was beginning to wane as a theme in Chicago literature. Although none of these texts detail the city's shortcomings as a cultural center (in fact, *Song of the Lark,* the only narrative in this group to focus on Chicago itself, actually highlights its creative vitality), their representation of desire—as an artistic force that exists apart from Chicago's civic identity—suggests why the ambitions that drew migrating writers and artists to the city also led them away. The idea that desire is the wellspring of creative power was new to Chicago literature, and its development in fiction that features migrants as artists brought an element of self-consciousness typically associated with modernism. Another indication of these texts' modernist leanings, vividly illustrated by Cather's reminder that life "rushes from within, not from without," is the movement toward a subjective narrative point of view based on the protagonist's developing understanding of desire. Whereas in *Song of the Lark* this movement is synonymous with Thea Kronborg's artistic growth while Cather herself maintains an omniscient perspective in telling the story, in *Winesburg, Ohio,* Anderson assumes George Willard's impressionistic view of his small-town upbringing as his own authorial voice. Finally, all three of these texts more or less turn Chicago's mythic reputation on its head by stressing the primacy of individual artistic imagination instead of the city's capacity to absorb the creative talents of hinterland migrants. This turn, resembling the "arbitrary" reworking of Western myths in high modernist texts such as Eliot's *Wasteland* and Joyce's *Ulysses,* suggests both the revisionist ambitions of modern Chicago writers and the richness of the history that they hoped to revise.[4]

Like the eastward movement of Chicago's literary bohemians described in the previous chapter, the migration narratives examined here may well have reinforced the impression that this city was a stop along the way to greater intellectual and artistic achievement. Yet even while writers such as Willa Cather stressed the artist's need to move beyond Chicago, she illuminated the aesthetic benefits of a provincial background and—lending weight to Raymond Williams's speculations on the politics of modernism—stressed the necessity of crossing the border between hinterland and city in order to develop an artistic consciousness. In this sense, migration—from province to cosmopolitan center—dictated the geography of modernist literature.

The Moonstone Scale

In Willa Cather's novel *Song of the Lark* (1915), Thea Kronborg leaves the small town of Moonstone, Colorado, for Chicago to pursue her education in music, a journey that ultimately leads her to Europe and New York, where at the novel's end she emerges as one of the world's outstanding opera singers. Set in the 1880s and '90s and similar to other stories of Chicago self-making, *Song of the Lark* stands out for its multifaceted portrayal of Thea's emerging talents. For instance, though Thea's musical gifts mark her as a special child, they do not separate her from the rest of Moonstone so much as they set the terms by which her remarkably diverse hometown informs her artistic development. Her Swedish ancestry, represented by her Methodist minister father and her stoic, matter-of-fact mother—both born and raised in the Midwest—account for her phlegmatic temperament and physical expressiveness. But Thea's upbringing is also shaped decisively by other townspeople: Dr. Howard Archie, a local physician with cosmopolitan interests who brings her into the world and guides her education; Professor Wunsch, a German immigrant piano teacher who recognizes her gift and introduces her to the European musical tradition; Spanish Johnny, an itinerant singer from Moonstone's Mexican community, whose fervid emotionalism serves as a touchstone for her musical growth; Ray Kennedy, a freethinking, "deeply sentimental" railroad conductor whose insurance policy (with her listed as the beneficiary) pays her way to Chicago after he dies in a train accident.[5] In a thoroughly romantic effort to achieve the girl's destiny, Thea's advocates strive (though not always in concert) to enable her passage out of Moonstone into the wider world.

However, the romance of Cather's novel derives not simply from Thea's triumphant passage but also from the ongoing traffic between Moonstone and the rest of the world. This movement is implicit in the town's ethnic diversity, which sparks Thea's interest in music and her sense of being connected to the forces that have drawn people to Moonstone (the name itself connotes mysterious powers), a feeling of anticipation signified by her vibrating body in the scene noted above. She derives a vision of what her life might be from people like Dr. Archie, whose Moonstone existence is subtly wrapped up in his contemplation of possibilities that lie beyond the town. An early supporter of Colorado silver mines, he ultimately becomes a wealthy man and relocates to Denver; but his first investment is in Thea's future, which Cather cleverly forecasts in a scene in which Thea finds him reading Balzac's *Distinguished Provincial in Paris*. Dr. Archie tells her that the several volumes of *The Human Comedy* "aren't exactly books," but rather "a city," which she will eventually want to read. Professor Wunsch makes a similar point when he says to her, "The world is little, people are little, human life is little. There is only one big thing—desire. And before it, when it is big, all is little. It brought Columbus across the sea in a little boat, *und so weiter* [and so forth]."[6] More expansive than Dr. Archie's remarks, Wunsch's formulation—that longing is the animating force of most human movements, even the discovery of America—locates Thea's artistic instincts and her prospective migration on a worldwide map of emotions.

Cather's signal achievement as a writer, Joseph Urgo has argued, was to illuminate "the cultural mode of thought produced by migratory consciousness." In *Song of the Lark*, he explains, Cather shows the correspondence between migration and imperialism, as Thea's quest for individual success—across the continent and then to Europe—takes place as a form of manifest destiny, with the railroad serving as the vehicle by which she lays claim to her artistic potential.[7] However, the empire of feeling that finally constitutes her vocal artistry includes more than the desire for self-making; emotionally and ideologically, the mature Thea Kronborg is equally capable of expressing feelings of loss, defeat, and sorrow. Thus, at the end of the novel, when Thea has the chance in New York City to play Sieglinde in Wagner's Ring Cycle and sings "All That I have lost, / All that I have mourned / Would I then have won," Cather emphasizes her ability to express tragic sadness. This sadness, Cather makes clear, is also an important component of the music that Thea learned as a child from the immigrant Wunsch. His "lost hopes" and inveterate homesickness are reflected in his love of Christophe Gluck's opera, *Orpheus* (the migration narrative as myth), which dramatizes the hero's loss of his beloved Eurydice to the underworld. Wunsch's melancholy, as well as other losses that Thea encounters in her hometown, are part of the "the Moonstone scale" that informs her life and shapes her art. As the adult Thea tells Dr. Archie, paraphrasing Richard Wagner, "art is only a way of remembering youth. And the older we grow the more precious it seems to us, and the more richly we can present that memory."[8]

More than any other hinterland writer we have considered thus far, Cather provides a finely textured explanation for how provincial culture, or to be more precise, the memory of that life, factors in the creation of art. While several voices in *Song of the Lark* speak to the nostalgic undercurrents in Cather's writing, the nod to Wagner suggests that these emotions are mediated by the aesthetic process, and connected to other feelings, attitudes, and experiences associated with the past. Art offers a way of framing history, of viewing a past that is enriched as the artist's perspective and craft evolve over time. Cather's self-aware heroine understands that her Moonstone upbringing continues to affect how she lives in the world—the small town's scale is the measure by which she evaluates her adult experiences—but she does not mistake her view of the past as art. Instead, her art is an interpretive singing of mythic stories, by Wagner and others, that sweep across a wide spectrum of human endeavor and emotion. Musically speaking, the Moonstone scale is a register of historical experiences that determine the pitch and key of Thea's singing. Like George Willard's growing-up years in Winesburg, it becomes the canvas on which she can paint her dreams.

Despite the air of timelessness that Cather brings to these themes, the novel suggests that the small town supplies an ideal foundation for Thea's artistic growth. It also implies that in order to build on this foundation, Thea must migrate to Chicago, where her talents will be developed and her desires sharpened.

In her portrayal of Moonstone, Cather acknowledges the ethnic diversity that characterized much of the nineteenth-century Midwest, while in Thea she introduces a character with clear ethnic roots, the first such protagonist to appear in the Chicago migration narrative (nearly all the others being old-stock "Americans"). Although Moonstone is not part of the Midwest, scholars have argued it is a reconstruction of Cather's hometown of Red Cloud, Nebraska. Cather herself suggests this midwestern connection through her characters' antecedents: Thea's father grew up in a Scandinavian community in Minnesota, and attended divinity school in Indiana; her mother was born and raised in Nebraska by Swedish immigrant farmers; Dr. Archie comes from a small town in Michigan. Recently settled and boomed by the railroad, Moonstone reflects the spirit of the new West, yet this spirit is tempered by the townspeoples' awareness of the places they left behind—an ambivalent sense of starting anew that Cather highlights in a narrative aside: the town, if seen from the air, would look like a "Noah's ark town set down in the sand" (36).

Indeed, in many ways Moonstone seems like an extension of the midwestern small town, with the migratory energies that settled the Old Northwest now trained on the West. The town's intimate scale and gridlike topography, along with the close-knit, hierarchical social structure—animated throughout by a sense of history and the possibility of leaving home—follow the blueprint of Main Street culture laid out in so much midwestern literature (including Cather's subsequent portrayals of small-town Nebraska). Mr. Kronborg's position as the town's Methodist minister places the family literally at center of this milieu. Located one street west of Main Street, on a half-developed block not far from the depot, their home faces "the backs of the brick and frame store buildings and a draw full of sunflowers and scraps of old iron" and is a stopping place for many of the town's railroad men, who pause to chat with Thea and her mother on their way to and from work (31). It is this rough-hewn openness and, more important, Thea's gradual awareness of the natural and cultural forces linking Moonstone to the broader world, that create the occasion for Cather's reminder that life rushes from within, not from without.

Cather's description of Thea's body — erotically charged and bathed in moonlight — weds the town's romantic sense of possibility to Thea's identity as an "unconscious and unawakened" artist (86). The tension here between "within" and "without" marks the difference between artistic potential and artistic realization, between latent talent and liberated expression. It also describes a separation between inner and outer space that is reflected in the larger movements of the book. Just as voice and talent emerge from within, so Thea herself moves from Moonstone to Chicago to Europe and finally to New York, progressively migrating to more expansive artistic spaces. The animating force for this boundary crossing is her desire.

Cather's representation of Thea's pulsing body thus does more than forecast the distance that the singer travels in the novel: it highlights the desire and ambition fostered by life in Moonstone. Like the image of Sister Carrie rocking and looking out the window or Hamlin Garland rocking it to his readers, Cather's picture is finally about the dreaming that occurs in the space between provincial life and urban culture. Obviously, this is a figurative landscape, a place for fantasizing about what might be, but Cather, like other hinterland writers, gives it a specific locale. As in Floyd Dell's autobiography (and his novel *Moon-Calf*), Thea learns to dream in a room of her own — a loft set apart from her family and the workaday world. Her move into this new room is "one of the most important things that ever happened to her." Here, in cocoonlike seclusion, reading books, her "internal fires" stoked by quilts and blankets, she can escape "the clamor about her [that] drowned the voice within herself." Here, "her mind worked better" and "plans and ideas occurred to her which had never come before." As a result, "Thea began to live a double life," balancing her workaday existence in Moonstone with dreams that, after moving to her new room, bring her to the window trembling with desire. Although these episodes of longing reflect the fervor of adolescent sexuality, Cather stresses their importance for Thea's artistic education. For on these nights, she "learned the thing that old Dumas meant when he told the Romanticists that to make a drama he needed but one passion and four walls" (52, 53, 122).

The decision that Thea should go to Chicago to study music takes place as the inevitable coming together of plans aimed at achieving her artistic destiny. Several individuals play key roles in this resolution: Ray Kennedy provides the financial means for Thea to leave Moonstone; Dr. Archie argues for her artistic future; and the senior Kronborgs, recognizing their daughter's talent, accept the doctor's logic. What is especially striking about this combination of factors is Cather's determination to make Chicago a key destination in Thea's migration narrative. Though Cather was obviously familiar with Chicago's reputation, she is unique among writers of Chicago fiction for not having lived in the city herself. Moreover, the figure upon whom Thea Kronborg is modeled — the internationally acclaimed opera singer Olive Fremstad — never lived in Chicago either, but rather went directly from her small-town home in Minnesota to New York City, where she continued her musical education. Cather describes Fremstad's rise to success in "Three American Singers" (1913), an article she wrote for *McClure's Magazine.* Two years later, she reworked the story for *Song of the Lark,* this time integrating Chicago's desire-filled culture into the account.

That Thea's own desires and ambitions make her a likely migrant to Chicago is clear from her disposition and openness to change. Ray Kennedy, whose railroad view of the nation dominates the first third of the novel, concludes that she is "bound for the big terminals of the world; no way stations for her." As for Thea, she has none of the "priggishness" that distinguishes her sister, Anna, who is preoccupied by the "wickedness" of Chicago; or her father, who "believed that big cities were places where people went to lose their identity and to be wicked." In fact, one of the reasons she likes Dr. Archie is because he is " 'fast,' " a characterization that measures attraction to urban culture by speed and anticipates Thea's journey by railroad to Chicago, during which she is "surprised that she did not feel a deeper sense of loss at leaving her old life behind her." Significantly, she does not feel like she is losing anything when she leaves Moonstone, because she is completing rather than reinventing herself. Indeed, as she imagines during her return train trip to her hometown after her first year in Chicago, it "was as if she had an appointment to meet the rest of herself sometime, somewhere. It was moving to meet her and she was moving to meet it" (128, 116, 134, 116, 136, 184).

Thea meets this other part of herself—the unawakened artist—through her exposure to Chicago's brutal economy of satisfaction and despair, the currency for which is desire. As Cather notes in a philosophical aside worthy of Dreiser,

The rich, noisy city, fat with food and drink, is a spent thing; its chief concern is its digestion and its little game of hide-and-seek with the undertaker. Money and office and success are the consolations of impotence. Fortune turns kind to such solid people and lets them suck their bone in peace. She flecks her whip upon flesh that is more alive, upon that stream of hungry boys and girls who tramp the streets of every city, recognizable by their pride and discontent, who are the Future, and who possess the treasure of creative power (223).

This assessment, though broadly urban in scope, pertains especially to Thea's movement through Chicago, and the painful frustration that she experiences while pursuing her dream of becoming a musician and artist. While around her mediocre or cynical musicians, like her voice instructor, Bowers, compromise their art yet thrive commercially—and therefore appear satisfied in some crudely sensual way—Thea suffers the contrast and her own relentless ambition. After her second year in Chicago, she feels "goaded by desires" and an "enslaving" ambition "to get on the world" (207, 248). But her despair, or what Cather calls the whiplash of Fortune, also figures as a necessary phase of her artistic development, a form of disciplining that later allows her to understand the hardness of life and express it in music. The metaphors of embodiment in this passage recall Max Weber's image of Chicago as a flayed human body, and tie in with Thea's status as an artist whose form of expression is distinctly physical.

The depiction of Chicago in these organic terms, whether by Cather, Weber, or Carl Sandburg (and his notion of the broad-shouldered city), underscores the ongoing effort to find an objective correlative for the longings that moved migrants and Chicagoans to and through the city. Even with their distorted, dreamlike visions (of gigantism and corporal punishment), these images contrast with descriptions of Chicago as a dark, industrial machine, a trope that essentially denies the city's humanity.

Cather's contribution to this imagery was to highlight the ethnic diversity of Chicago's human forms and show its effect on Thea's artistic development and desires. Compared to other Chicago novels on this period and earlier, *Song of the Lark* is an unabashedly ethnic novel, emphasizing the interweaving of European culture on American ground. The Chicago sections of the novel extend the ethnic mixing that takes place in Moonstone: when Thea arrives in town, she lives with two German-American women, a mother and her daughter, who "is a Swede by marriage"; her first music teacher, Andor Harsanyi, comes from Hungary; the Nathanmeyers, wealthy patrons who help advance Thea's career, are German-American Jews; and Fred Ottenburg, who becomes Thea's lover (and eventually marries her), is a German-American "beer prince" with highly informed tastes in classical music. In presenting this cross section of cultural interests, Cather follows the designations of the era — ethnic Chicagoans are not hyphenated Americans, but usually "Swedes" or "Germans," while white native-born citizens are "Americans." She complicates these designations for Thea's family in a manner that reinforces the distinctions along nationalistic, racial lines. For example, according to Mrs. Kronborg, Thea's priggish sister Anna is "American," while Thea retains Swedish traits. As narrator, Cather amplifies these distinctions in explaining that the "Scandinavian mould of countenance" was hardly noticeable in Anna (144, 225, 115).

Similar physical descriptions fill *Song of the Lark,* many of them subtly tied to ethnic cultural differences. So Harsanyi is a "softer Slavic type" with "graceful shoulders" and a "delicately modeled" head; Ottenburg is "a gleaming, florid young fellow" with an inherited talent for business and recognizing great music; and Madison Bowers (Thea's talented but cynical voice teacher) comes from "a long line of New Hampshire farmers; hard workers, with good minds, mean natures, and flinty eyes."

This typing is especially strong in Thea, whose Scandinavian heritage and physical bearing (strong jaw, etc.) are continually linked to her singing abilities. Paradoxically, these inherited qualities give her the capacity to express, in music, a wide range of emotions and ideas. When Thea sings, her body transcends categories. Watching her from behind, Bowers sees "a very slight and yet very free motion, from the toes up. Her whole back seemed plastic, seemed to be molding itself to the galloping rhythm of the song." Later, as she sings at the Nathanmeyers' home, Ottenburg notices that her "flesh seemed to take a mood and 'to set' like plaster" (155, 225, 213, 227, 243). The embodiment of artistic talent, this plasticity also reflects the dynamism and movement inherent in American culture, the freedom to act on desires and dreams that brought Thea to Chicago and drew immigrants to America. No wonder that when Thea goes to the symphony for the very first time, the orchestra plays Dvorak's *From the New World,* a performance that leaves her trembling with excitement and desire, and thinking of home and her journey through the West. The performance, like her own singing, seems to embody the whole of the culture while also evoking the rich differences.

Although Thea's professional advancement takes place in the bourgeois, artistic climes of the city, the forces that awaken her artistic consciousness emanate from Chicago's grittier side. Cather dramatizes this self-awakening in a remarkable chapter organized around at least two epiphanies. One of these centers on Thea's experience attending the symphony at the Auditorium, and her immersion in Dvorak and Wagner's emotionally and historically resonant music. Another involves her visit to the Art Institute, where she sees *The Song of the Lark*, Jules Breton's 1885 painting of a European peasant standing in the middle of a field. Nearly fifteen years before the publication of her novel, Cather noted that "hundreds of merchants and farmer boys all over Nebraska and Kansas and Iowa"—visitors and migrants to Chicago—embraced this picture as a representation of their own place on the landscape, transformed to art.[9] Thea likewise sees her life reflected in this painting; in other words, her cathartic encounter with high art is inseparable from her migration experience.

Cather presses this point at the outset of the chapter when she explains that four months after leaving home, Thea knew very little of Chicago and lacked "city consciousness." Yet when she leaves the Auditorium after hearing Dvorak's symphony, she becomes "conscious of the city itself, of the congestion of life all about her, of the brutality and power of those streams that flowed in the streets, threatening to drive one under." Crossing these streets, Thea is propositioned by two men, a young man coming out of a saloon and later an older man, who leans over and whispers in her ear. Upset, she asks herself why these men "torment[ed]" her, blocking out the emotional residue of the music, and concludes that there "is some power abroad in the world bent on taking away that feeling."[10] This realization prompts further illumination and a resolution. Cather writes,

Everything seemed to sweep down on her to tear it out from under her cape. If one had that, the world became one's enemy; people, buildings, wagons, cars, rushed to crush it under, to make one let go of it. Thea glared round her at the crowds, the ugly, sprawling streets, the long lines of lights, and she was not crying now. Her eyes were brighter than even Harsanyi had ever seen them. All these things were no longer remote and negligible; they had to be met, they were lined up against her, they were there to take something from her. Very well; they should never have it. They might trample her to death, but they should never have it. As long as she lived that ecstasy was going to be hers. She would live for it, work for it, die for it; but she was going to have it, time after time, height after height. She could hear the crash of the orchestra again, and she rose on the brasses. She would have it, have it,—it! Under the old cape, she pressed her hands upon her heaving bosom, that was a little girl's no longer.[11]

Here, the girl who pulsed with anticipation in Moonstone now sees her ambitions in a richer, more complicated context, realizing in a flash of social Darwinian insight (and "goaded" by her feelings) that Chicago is filled with other desiring individuals, and that to realize her dreams of musical success she will have to rise above competing interests. Although Dvorak's and Wagner's music continue to wash over her, the catalyst for this coming of age is her exposure not to high art but to the two men who crudely proposition her. On the one hand, Thea's rejection of these propositions suggests, in explicitly gendered terms, the impediments and distractions that she will have to overcome as a female artist. On the other, these encounters underscore a crude, but elemental strain in the city's economy of desire, which is thematically linked to Thea's own desires and to her experiences at the Art Institute and the Auditorium. From the representation of desire in high art to its crude manifestation on the street, Cather shows us the spectrum of emotions that constitute urban life, and it is Thea's awareness of these emotions—her awakening "city consciousness"—that spurs the development of her artistic point of view.

Compared to other scenes of Chicago desire, Cather's description suggests a subtle, but important shift in the functions of emotion. While in the 1880s, Adelina Patti's performance in the Auditorium of "Home, Sweet Home" served to consolidate home feeling around an emerging civic identity, Cather uses this architectural monument as an important way station in Thea's individual artistic migration. Her portrayal of the urban space is consistent with (and may even draw upon) earlier visions of the restless, feverish city, but she is less interested than Garland and Henry Blake Fuller in exploring the possibility that Chicago's emotionally charged landscape could become the basis for cultural uplift. By 1915, this dream of redeeming America's Second City had lost its potency; and while Cather stresses the many ways in which Chicago continued to "unleash" desire (to use French sociologist Henri Lefebvre's phrase), and though she adopts the perspective of the provincial migrant in representing the city as a magnet of opportunities, she is intent on showing how these forces carry Thea Kronborg beyond the city to a position of heroic artistic heights.

Stylistically, Cather traces this movement in a novel that remains conventionally realistic in many ways. However, her portrayal of Thea Kronborg as an increasingly self-conscious artist turns the Chicago migration narrative in a new direction. As several critics have emphasized, Cather's erotic portrayal of how Harsanyi discovers her voice and later how Thea connects her vocal powers with the elemental natural forces that she encounters in an Arizona canyon positions her as a distinctly female artist, who gives birth through singing to a wealth of human emotions.[12] The link, therefore, between the image of Harsanyi touching his hand to Thea's throat and feeling her "big voice throb" like a "wild bird" and Thea's realization that the broken clay vessels she finds in Panther Canyon are "fragments of [prehistoric people's] desire" serves to highlight the ongoing human need for expression, and to make art. "Desire, in works of art," Judith Fryer has observed of these conjunctions, "must be concentrated within form."[13] Yet Thea's discovery of the appropriate form for expressing her longings—and indeed, her consciousness of the common threads that link all human desires—hinges as much on her movement through Chicago as it does on her trip to Arizona. Moreover, her physical ability to express her desires, and those rendered in operatic art, emerges in *Song of the Lark* as a gradual move inward—from her attic bedroom in Moonstone to the intimate spaces of her voice box—that parallels her migration to Chicago and elsewhere. In this sense, Chicago figured as a way station in Cather's effort to fashion a modern artistic form based on universal elements.

In "Three American Singers," Cather calls Olive Fremstad "A Worker, Not a Dreamer," who "fought her way toward the intellectual centers of the world."[14] In *Song of the Lark,* she describes a similar migration, except that she presents Thea as both a dreamer and a worker. In the novel's epilogue, Cather underscores the larger-than-life status of her transformed heroine by providing a snapshot of Moonstone in 1909 and noting that Thea had become an inspiration for young people with "dreams" of making an artistic mark on the world.

The Modern World and Sherwood Anderson's Dreams of Manhood

No single emotional stance distinguishes Thea Kronborg. At once ambitious, nostalgic, sensual, and pragmatic, she encompasses the variety of desires that constitute prior literary representations of the migration experience. That Thea is a performing artist suggests that her self-conscious, emotive nature derives from special talents that have little to do with her status as a migrant. However, I would say that Cather's delineation of the migratory forces that inform Thea's artistic growth also speaks to the changing nature of regional literature. Joined to a migration narration that opens up on transatlantic culture, Cather's sympathetic portrayal of small-town and prairie life — a distinctive feature in nearly all her fiction — illuminates an authorial perspective that in most nineteenth-century regionalism is hidden from view and generally less expansive in scope. The migration narratives written during the 1890s and 1900s suggest how a midwestern literary perspective was formed through the movement of creative energies from the hinterland to Chicago. In *Song of the Lark,* Cather acknowledges this construction; but by insisting on the provincial roots of American art and then connecting them to an avowedly cosmopolitan worldview, she adds an awareness of modernity that is missing the earlier fiction. As defined by Cather, and later Ernest Hemingway and Malcolm Cowley — who in *Exile's Return* (1934) argued that the "lost generation" of expatriated writers turned to the European landscape in the 1910s and '20s to rediscover and write about their provincial childhoods — modern consciousness was built around the emotions associated with crossing the border from one culture to another.

Sherwood Anderson's contribution to this trend stemmed not simply from the complicated psychological and social history that led him to a literary career, but also from the stylistic innovations that he brought to the migration narrative. Framed by the prefatory "Book of the Grotesque," *Winesburg, Ohio* reveals its retrospective literary vantage at the outset through Anderson's implicit association with the old writer who looks back and identifies his life experiences with many different truths. This frame gives the subsequent stories an air of transcendent authority that corresponds with Anderson's declaration to Paul Rosenfeld in 1920 that he held in his "inner consciousness" the entire Middle West. In *Spoon River Anthology* (1915), Edgar Lee Masters adopts a similar tack by representing in verse form — as epitaphs — the life histories of an entire town. In contrast with the omniscient point of view used by Masters, though, Anderson stresses the contrived nature of his perspective in *Winesburg* and, more important, suggests that this perspective grows out of the migratory experience by linking the old writer's dreamlike reminiscences to George Willard's determination to move to a big city and write about his impressions of life. Because the intervening stories are filtered through George's consciousness — as the town reporter he has a special knack for getting people's stories — he seems at times to be the

"author" of *Winesburg*. But "The Book of the Grotesque" serves as a reminder that the ability to see into peoples' hearts, to understand their dreams
and desires, requires age as well as something "young . . . inside," which the
old writer has.[15] So Anderson subtly points the way back to his own powers
as a writer, and orchestrates and consolidates the several narrative perspectives in the book.

The structure of *Winesburg* and the freedom it gave Anderson to examine the inner lives of his protagonists pushed American literature in innovative directions, offering younger writers like Hemingway, William Faulkner,
and Jean Toomer a framework for pursuing their own experiments in multiple points of view and psychological impressions. More to the point,
Anderson's innovations are framed by the work's migratory theme; that is,
George Willard's literary consciousness joins the narrative's retrospective point of view through his decision at the end of the book to leave
home. Significantly, the Washington, D.C.-raised Toomer emphasized
the influence of this migratory perspective on his own artistic growth when
he wrote to Anderson in 1922, praising *Winesburg* and the short-story collection *The Triumph of the Egg*. "The beauty, and the full sense of life that
these books contain are natural elements, like the rain and sunshine, of my
own sprouting," Toomer wrote from Georgia, where he had journeyed
to explore his origins. "My seed was planted in the cane- and cotton-fields,
and in the souls of black and white people in the small southern town.
My seed was planted in *myself* down there. Roots have grown and strength-
ened. They have extended out. I spring up in Washington. *Winesburg,
Ohio,* and *The Triumph of the Egg* are elements of my growing. It is hard to
think of myself as maturing without them." In the midst of writing *Cane*
(1923)—a modernist ensemble of stories with a circular design that incorpo-
rates several perspectives and moves back and forth between the North and
the South—Toomer found in Anderson's fiction a guide to crossing cultural
borders that helped him think through the structure of his own migration
narrative.[16]

Anderson's first attempt at the migration narrative appeared in *Agricultural Advertising,* the trade journal published by the Long-Critchfield
Agency. Covering a wide range of issues related to the region's farm economy, he touched frequently on the romance and longing that attracted small-
town midwesterners to big-city life. In "The Man of Affairs," one of many
profiles that he wrote for his regular Business Types column, he channeled
these energies into a story of an Indiana farm boy named Peter Macveagh,

who goes to Chicago "to make his fortune." This boilerplate treatment of hinterland self-making would barely be worth mentioning, were it not for Anderson's portrayal of desire and the account's similarity to *Windy McPherson's Son.* Macveagh is rough-hewn yet "clean, right down through his heart," and "like the fields and the woods, sort of kept clean by God and the seasons." Still, because he wants to "mix with men, and stretch his mental muscles," he leaves home for Chicago, where he takes a room in a boardinghouse and, finding work as a solicitor for a coal company, discovers he has a talent for business. "Here was a fellow of unusual vigor, and moral cleanliness," Anderson observes. "How could he help getting rich?" He cannot, but his "lust for power" and wealth ultimately leads to his "ruin," sullying the qualities that first brought him to Chicago. A "product of the times and the opportunities," Macveagh becomes a symbol of economic success, disliked and feared by his contemporaries.[17]

Windy McPherson's Son tells a similar story, but ends on a redemptive note as Sam McPherson overcomes an in-bred lust for money and power and settles down with his family. Anderson's preoccupation with moral purity speaks to the desires that drive the move to Chicago in both these texts, and the downfall that awaits the two migrants. Like Macveagh, McPherson is born with a talent for business, so when he decides to migrate from Caxton, Iowa, to Chicago, he seems to be following a naturally determined path. At the age of fifteen, "the call of the city came to him," and he "conceived of life in the city as great game in which he could play a sterling part." Sam's mentors have prepared him for this moment; the Caxton merchant who employs him has already recommended him to a Chicago firm, while the town's chief intellectual and artist (who once lived in New York City) has told Sam that he has "genius" in financial matters. Most important of all, Sam has spent his youth dreaming "with all of the ardour of his boy's heart" of making money and tracking his successes in a small account book.[18] There is never any question that Chicago is the logical destination for Sam. However, Anderson complicates this story by showing how Sam's unrestrained pursuit of fortune and adoption of the amoral practices of modern business degrade his spirit. In this sense, the desires that lead him inevitably to Chicago just as surely cause his corruption.

While this naturalistic portrayal of the migration experience connects *Windy McPherson's Son* to *Rose of Dutcher's Coolly* and *Sister Carrie,* Anderson also suggests the emergence of a narrative point of view that—like Cather's—stands outside the deterministic forces of desire. This perspective surfaces later in the novel, after Sam has become "one of the new kings of American business" and left Chicago in search of a new way of life. Anderson captures Sam's rueful sense of guilt as he wanders at night through a seedy neighborhood in Rochester, New York.

He thought of the weary, restless walks taken by young men from farms and country towns in the streets of the cities; young men believers in the golden vice. Hands beckoned to them from doorways, and women of the town laughed at their awkwardness. In Chicago he had walked that way. He also had been seeking, seeking the romantic, impossible mistress that lurked at the bottom of men's tales of the submerged world. He was like the naïve German lad in the South Water street warehouses who had once said to him—he was a frugal soul—"I would like to find a nice-looking girl who is quiet and modest and who will be my mistress and not charge anything." [19]

From Sam's boyhood longing for business success to his adult search for female companionship, the spectrum of desire in the novel constitutes a template for life's most vital dreams. The assumption here, as in most of Anderson's early fiction, is that the city—romantic and mysterious—is a place where such dreams can be realized. But the existential truth that follows from such searches also undermines those dreams, exposing the city's grimmer realities. Neither of these views, however, makes sense without the presence of desire to sharpen the city's promise and accentuate the sense of disappointment when the dream fails to materialize. Nor are these two perspectives likely to apply to urban natives. As the first sentence makes clear, in an image startlingly similar to Carl Sandburg's description of painted women, this understanding of the city belongs to the migrant-newcomer. In fact, as a young man in Chicago, Anderson himself spent hours at night tramping the city streets, drawn along by his anticipation of the adventures that could be around the corner.

This impression of the city's double-sided nature—its "golden vice"—is worth noting if only because it seems to summarize, and comment on, other literary representations of Chicago dreaming. However, I especially want to stress Sam's self-conscious examination of his role in this history of desire, as it begins to show how an authorial voice might break away from the naturalistic forces at work in the novel in order to comment on those forces. For Sam, this stance corresponds with the peace he seems to find at the end of novel. For Anderson, it pointed toward a new literary relation to desire, a way of positioning the narrator not as a product or creature of desire but as a sympathetic observer and chronicler of other peoples' dreams — a vessel, to use Cather's term, for other peoples' emotions. In Anderson's landmark migration narrative, *Winesburg, Ohio,* this narrator is George Willard.

Significantly, George works as a newspaper reporter for the *Winesburg Eagle,* chronicling the daily comings and goings in his small Ohio town (population 1,800). His literary ambitions are best served by his unaccountable gift for listening to other peoples' stories. Indeed, the text offers little explanation for why the citizens of Winesburg turn to George to discuss their failed dreams and secrets. Nonetheless, the stories themselves are filled with personal histories, some told directly to George, others simply presented by the narrator. In the opening story, "Hands," Wing Biddlebaum shares with George the troubled history that brought him to Winesburg, speaking "as one lost in a dream."[20] Wing's story, which revolves around his suppressed gay identity, introduces a poetic, psychological aspect to the text, and implicitly makes George the focal point for the revelations that follow in the subsequent stories, building toward an internal history of the community that complements the physical landscape depicted in the map of Winesburg at the front of the book (fig. 15).

Anderson's approach to all this is distinctly modern. The stories read like psychological case histories, and the language and imagery deliberately invoke Freud (Biddlebaum deflects his sexual anxiety in nervous energy; one woman has a "mad desire to run naked through the streets"; characters are "neurotic" or have an "overmastering" temperament). Moreover, Anderson is concerned throughout with the region's transition from an agricultural past to the modern, industrial present — a "revolution" in culture and consciousness that he summarizes in a shorthand history of mass culture (in the story "Godliness") and more subtly through his portraits of individuals caught up in the transience or pressures of the moment.[21] The sense that modernity encourages restlessness and even obsessive dreaming is reinforced by several characters who have ended up in Winesburg after failing to realize their ambitions in Chicago, Cleveland, or some other big city.

The idea that George Willard is *Winesburg's* principal narrator is suggested not only by his status as a particularly sympathetic reporter and his emerging interest in becoming a fiction writer (which his fellow citizens encourage), but also by how he leaves home in the last story, "Departure," with "a background on which to paint the dreams of his manhood." While seated

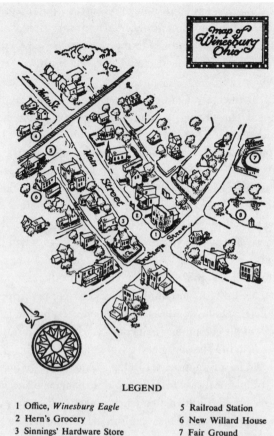

LEGEND

FIGURE 15
Map of Winesburg,
Ohio, published in the
first edition of the novel.
(Author's collection)

1 Office, *Winesburg Eagle*   5 Railroad Station
2 Hern's Grocery   6 New Willard House
3 Sinnings' Hardware Store   7 Fair Ground
4 Biff Carter's Lunch Room   8 Waterworks Pond

on the train and, like Thea Kronborg, going to "meet the adventure of his life," George's mind is "carried away by his growing passion for dreams" (246, 247). At first glance, this passion appears to underscore his similarity to other ambitious migrants. Indeed, for the conductor, George's departure is a "commonplace enough incident," for he has seen "a thousand George Willards go out of their towns to the city." Yet George is different from his peers. Unlike Dreiser's Sister Carrie, who is carried directly by her desires to Chicago, he is drawn by desire to the contemplation of other peoples' dreams as well as his own; in short, his awareness is that of an emerging fiction writer.

The penultimate story explicitly links this artistic consciousness to George's newfound understanding of the links between desire and mortality. "Sophistication," describes George's crossover into manhood, a threshold specifically marked by the death of his mother and his self-consciously passionate liaison with Helen White, the daughter of a prominent banker. Set against the backdrop of the town's now empty fairgrounds, the chapter is suffused with a sense of loss and anticipation, chiefly underwritten by George's decision to leave home. George's mood, Anderson notes, is "a thing known to men and unknown to boys," and while it encourages in him an air of self-importance—the impression that he is a "half-tragic figure"—it also illuminates his maturity. Anderson characterizes this moment as both a developmental milestone for all males and a basis for artistic insight.

The boy is walking through the street of his town. He is thinking of the future and of the figure he will cut in the world. Ambitions and regrets awake within him. Suddenly something happens; he stops under a tree and waits as for a voice calling his name. Ghosts of old things creep into his consciousness; the voices outside of himself whisper a message concerning the limitations of life. From being quite sure of himself and his future he becomes not at all sure. If he be an imaginative boy a door is torn open and for the first time he looks out upon the world, seeing, as though they marched in procession before him, the countless figures of men who before his time have come out of nothingness into the world, lived their lives and again disappeared into nothingness. The sadness of sophistication has come to the boy. With a little gasp he sees himself as a leaf blown by the wind through the streets of his village. (234)

Alternatively cast in the universal and subjunctive modes, the passage gives George's prospective departure a metaphysical heft. The "if" separates the typically developing eighteen-year-old from the imaginative analyst, who is able to see the contingencies of the moment in a broader historical context and connect his own mixed emotions about leaving home to those of other ambitious, desiring boys who have made similarly dramatic decisions. Without stipulating that George is such an analyst, Anderson notes that this "moment of sophistication" had now come to him, in effect bequeathing to him the sadness of retrospective vision, a way of feeling excitement, regret, anticipation, and nostalgia all at the same time. In contrast with Sam McPherson, George arrives at this moment relatively early in life and, significantly, with the expectation of becoming a writer. The trajectory of

Winesburg reinforces this last point, as George's apparent coming of age ties him explicitly to the old writer in "The Book of the Grotesque" who dreams and writes about "the long procession of figures" that appear before his mind's eye. Presumably, these grotesque figures are, or once were, the dreams of the aging writer's manhood (234, 235, 22).

Just after Anderson's death in 1941, Floyd Dell noted in his review of *Sherwood Anderson's Memoirs* that the events described in *Winesburg* were not "real memories; they were imaginative creations, centering around some core of memory. And Sherwood's was not a strictly realistic imagination; it was poetic, and sometimes fantastic—it exaggerated, it distorted, it went off into wild flights of caprice: but it was always trying for some truth of some kind, and most of its effects held some truth for our own memories. These stories evoked things forgotten, long buried in our minds—our own childhood experiences, fears, shames, blunders, curiosities, sexual interests." Similarly, the University of Chicago critic Robert Morss Lovett argued against the book's realism in a 1936 *New Republic* article, quoting Anderson, who denied *Winesburg* was an "exact picture of Ohio village life" and instead claimed that the characters were fictional versions of people he knew at the Cass Street boardinghouse in Chicago.[22] Ironically, this vantage point remains fuzzy in Winesburg, as Chicago figures principally as the terminus of the railroad line that George Willard takes on his journey to the unnamed "city."

Not surprisingly, Anderson's characterization of *Winesburg*'s regional focus—the hinterland as a reflection of urban emotional life—coincides with the social history of the "Robin's Egg Renaissance" that he gives in his memoirs. It is also consistent with Dell's assessment of the book's scope. For while Dell regretted the movement away from the objective realism of *Windy McPherson's Son*, which he admired "immensely" for its authentic portrayal of the life he had known in the provincial Midwest, he acknowledged the pathbreaking impact of Anderson's virtuoso performance in *Winesburg,* as it "ministered to a revolt against polite repressions and conventions."[23] The fragments of dreams collected and pieced together in *Winesburg* by several narrators—the old writer; George Willard, the reporter; George Willard, the once and future writer; and Sherwood Anderson, the presiding consciousness in the book—move toward a kind of literary art that Anderson continued to develop in the stories included *The Triumph of the Egg* (1921). There, as in *Winesburg,* Chicago hovers as the most modern of destinations—a background for illuminating personal fantasies and memories.

Dell and the Affirmation of Realism

Although Floyd Dell was not the last midwestern writer to fictionalize his movement out of the hinterland to the world beyond, his novel *Moon-Calf* and its sequel, *The Briary-Bush,* marked the end of the migration narrative as conceived in the 1890s and the conclusion of the so-called Chicago Literary Renaissance. To be sure, *Moon-Calf* does not present itself in these terms, but its publication in 1920 (after Dell's departure from Chicago) and the movement of its protagonist, Felix Fay, from Iowa to Chicago and then, in *The Briary-Bush* (1921), to New York, suggest Chicago's limitations as a destination for ambitious literary migrants. In fact, the plots of the two novels closely track Dell's own life—there are passages in *Moon-Calf* that he later reconstituted in his autobiography *Homecoming* (1933)—thereby dramatizing the shift from a nineteenth-century frame of reference to a deliberately "modern" perspective.

Yet if *Moon-Calf* and *Briary-Bush* provide a history of the revolt from the hinterland and the subsequent rise of a provincial literati in Chicago and New York, Dell's realism feels somewhat belated. In this respect, his impressions of *Winesburg, Ohio* are telling. Whereas Anderson indulges in "imaginative creation" and poetic exaggeration, in *Moon-Calf* Dell adheres to the historical record—as he remembered it—working from memory to describe Felix Fay's hinterland upbringing, his emergence as a writer and critic, and his eventual migration to Chicago. No less interested in Freudian analysis than Anderson and every bit as concerned with the ramifications of dreaming, Dell keeps the perspective tightly focused on Felix through a conventional, third-person narrative. Although Felix lives in "a world of dreams" and is disposed to believe in "new ideas," Dell traces his emotional and intellectual development in a bildungsroman whose sense of romance and adventure reflects the nineteenth-century literature he admired as a youth.[24] Felix's dreamy nature, epitomized in the novel's title through the image of a calf bathing in a stream of nocturnal light, points up Dell's debt to the Romantic tradition (in politics as well as literature). However, unlike Cather's Thea Kronborg, who also draws from the moon's power, Felix does not become a vessel for anyone else's desires or the gathering point for other stories. As a narrator, Dell resists the stylistic innovations that he associated with modernism.

In "The Portrait of Murray Swift," a short story that he wrote in 1913 but never published, Dell seems to inspect the reasons for this resistance. Swift is a brilliant but arrogant playwright who stops in Chicago on his way to

New York to meet a friend and visit the International Exhibit of Modern Art. He strides through the galleries discoursing wittily on Matisse, Cezanne, Van Gogh, and the dynamics of cubism—talking chiefly "for effect" but moved nonetheless by the bold experimentalism of the new art. Immediately afterward, his friend takes him to the studio of a postimpressionist painter, who invites Swift to sit for a portrait and quickly finishes it. As the paint dries and before seeing the picture, Swift goes for a walk with a beautiful female sculptor and friend of the painter; she fends off his flirtations and enigmatically warns him that he will not want to see her again after he has viewed the portrait. She is right. For when Swift returns, he sees himself "drawn with exquisite and mordant irony, with stick and cigarette, uncertainly halting before earth and sky, the head tilted back with a quirk of inquiry, the face curious and evasive, with something that was almost boldness in the eyes, something that was almost courage in the chin: Murray Swift, observant, indecisive, inadequate, against a rose-colored background."[25]

Although Murray Swift should not be confused with Dell himself, whatever insecurities Dell had about the limits of his intellectual acumen or of his capacity to sustain personal relationships (his relationship with Margery Currey was just ending) are amplified in this literary portrait of a writer who is prevented by his egocentricity from seeing himself as others do. Ironically, Dell glosses these anxieties in a story that deals topically but neutrally with the impact of postimpressionism on American aesthetic culture—ironic because during the mid-1910s Dell declared himself against the new art, telling his friend Arthur Davison Ficke in a 1915 letter that it "seems to have no aesthetic values at all."[26] In "The Portrait of Murray Swift," Dell gives this position a different think and wonders whether his personal deficiencies—the "almost" that distances Swift from boldness and courage—have kept him from becoming a more innovative writer and artist.

In *Moon-Calf,* however, he sets this question aside and joins his protagonist's individual dreams to the cultural myth of Chicago. At the end of the novel, as Felix Fay prepares to leave Port Royal, Iowa, to pursue a career as a journalist and writer in Chicago, he sees a railroad map in the town depot and commits the image to memory—and feeling. Moments later, he sees again "in his mind's eye" the

picture of iron roads from all over the Middle West centering in a dark blotch in the corner. . . .

"Chicago!" he said to himself.

And then the hurt came again—the hurt of lost beauty, of unforgotten, unforgettable love. Felix quickened his steps. Another mile. And water. And forgetting.

But his tramping steps went to the rhythm of a word that said itself over and over in his mind:

"Chicago! Chicago!"[27]

The last two words in the novel intone the faith that brought thousands of migrants to Chicago and thickened the dark blotches on so many maps of the region. Staged as an internal drama with a rhythm of its own, the conclusion of *Moon-Calf* suggests that Dell was determined to present the history of the Midwest not as a background for painting dreams but as an independent, living reality.

CODA

By 1920, all hinterland writers associated with Chicago's literary rise had left the city. Edgar Lee Masters, now living in New York City and struggling to keep his literary career alive, bitterly denounced Chicago to his friend Agnes Freer. Asked by Freer if he would ever return to the city, Masters explained that he would regard it as a "punishment" if he had to live there again.

Every writing artist or other artist who has been able to leave Chicago has done so; and for the matter of proximity might have chosen it as an abiding place. Dreiser was born in Indiana, but after a short experience in Chicago came to New York. Willa Cather was born in Nebraska. She passed Chicago for Pittsburg, and then came to New York. George Ade lives on his farm in Indiana, and when he goes away makes visits to Florida and abroad. Hamlin Garland tried his best to live in Chicago, and even with the peril ahead of failing to finance himself in New York made the hazard and came. Chatfield Taylor with a mansion at his command, and a social position too, which is so much valued in Chicago, won't live there. Booth Tarkington stays in Indianapolis or goes to Maine or abroad. Vachel Lindsay was kicked out of Springfield, by his own account made to me; but didn't locate in Chicago, but Seattle. He feared that he might be driven from Chicago also. Robert Herrick loathes Chicago and lives anywhere else that he can. George McCutcheon left Chicago long ago; as did Ring Lardner born in Niles, Michigan, and now living on Long Island. Sherwood Anderson betook him to New Orleans. These are conspicuous names; but the roll would run to thousands if there should be enumerated the painters, etchers, sculptors, and the beginning writers who have left Chicago to get freedom of life and congeniality of association; and to escape the village mind which curses Chicago in every department of life. Chicago is a clique ridden town, and the explanation may be that it is so recently populated by villagers, that the psychology of mass association has not been acquired.

Yet Masters did not endorse New York, where he sensed "a sterility in the air," nor did he wholly condemn the Midwest. In fact, he told Freer that his "preference would be to live in the west if I could manage it. I love Michigan for example — the blue water, the air, but not the people. I love the fields of Illinois; but the terrible summers and winters and the people I do not love." [1]

Masters's letter serves as a reminder of the complicated emotional geography on which the story of Chicago and its hinterland was based. Though Masters rejected Chicago and the parochial mindset that apparently characterized the city (and the Midwest), he could not escape the desires that drew him back to the scenes of his youth. Even as he staked out a postmigration position, he derived his authority as a cultural critic from his experience as a migrant. Indeed, throughout the 1920s in his fiction and poetry, Masters continued to write about the urban-rural continuum.

The same was true for other hinterland writers who left Chicago. During the 1910s and '20s, while living in a variety of places, Theodore Dreiser and Sherwood Anderson published novels and autobiographies in which they brood over their relation to the Midwest and Chicago. Long after his departure from the city in the 1890s, Hamlin Garland wrote *The Son of the Middle Border* (1917) and *A Daughter of the Middle Border* (1921), both of which highlight Chicago's significance for the region. In the mid-1920s, George Ade became the first playwright to have two Broadway hits running at the same time, *The College Widow* (1924) and *The County Chairman* (1924), each comedies set in small-town Indiana. And in 1935, the Virginia-born Willa Cather returned to the migration narrative in *Lucy Gayheart*, the story of a small-town girl's journey from Nebraska to Chicago and then back home, where she tragically dies. Thus while the moment for Chicago's hinterland-based literary communities passed in the 1910s, the link between city and country remained an important concern for migrating writers.

Meanwhile, the literary forms that developed in Chicago after 1925 also bore the imprint of the city's migratory cultures. Beginning with James T. Farrell's Studs Lonigan novels of the 1930s, which focus on the city's

Irish-American community, and continuing through the 1940s and '50s
with Nelson Algren's portrayals of West Side toughs, who are often the children of Polish immigrants, ethnic Chicagoans told stories dramatizing the
legacy of immigration. Equally important to the development of Chicago literature was the Great Migration of southern African Americans during and
after the First World War. The principal literary voice for black Chicago—
and black America—at midcentury, Richard Wright moved to the city from
Memphis in 1927, and wrote searingly of the Great Migration and its effects
in the North.

Because novels like Farrell's *Studs Lonigan* (1935), Algren's *Never Come
Morning* (1942), and Wright's *Native Son* (1945) take an unsparing look at
class, ethnic, and racial tensions, little seems to stand between the authors
and their subjects. However, as Carla Cappetti has shown, all three writers
followed the lead of University of Chicago sociologists, whose theories of
city life and migratory cultures promised a new sort of urban realism. So
Ernest Burgess's maps of Chicago, incorporating the city's immigrant communities in concentric bands around the Loop, helped Algren site the action in his novel, while Robert E. Park's essay "Human Migration and the
Marginal Man" (1928) gave Wright a conceptual basis for his migrating protagonists.[2] Apart from its intersection with urban literature, the Chicago
school had an enormous influence outside the academy, giving city planners, politicians, and assorted intellectuals a vocabulary and framework for
engaging the challenges of urban society. Indeed, few academic disciplines
have done more to promote the "urbanness" of the city than sociology, and
the studies launched at the University of Chicago during the 1910s and '20s,
using Chicago as a "laboratory" for understanding how cities work, were at
the leading edge of this consolidating vision.

Remarkably, of the two-hundred-plus sociology dissertations completed
at the University of Chicago between 1893 and 1930, not a single one deals
with hinterland migration.[3] The subject is also missing from the published
writings of Park, Burgess, W. I. Thomas, and Louis Wirth. Given the city's
history, this absence is startling but understandable. As sociology took root
in American universities, it expanded into subdisciplines that included
rural as well as urban sociology. This division was dimly reflected at the
University of Chicago, where several graduate students pursued research
projects on rural communities and small towns. However, it was plainly evident at the national level, in the split between urban sociologists such
as Park, and rural sociologists, employed mostly at large state universities,

who were focusing on the challenges faced by many rural and small-town communities. As rural sociologists carved out a niche within the American Sociological Society, they had to work around the profession's growing emphasis on urban issues. Hence, in 1925, when the society decided to concentrate on urban issues in its annual meeting, Charles E. Lively, a rural sociologist at the University of Missouri, wondered in a letter to a colleague at Cornell, "What have we to contribute to a program on The City?"[4]

Rural sociologists came by such anxieties honestly. Spurred by the 1911 report of the Country Life Commission appointed by President Theodore Roosevelt, the rural sociology movement grew out of concern about the declining quality of rural life: food shortages, unfair labor practices, health problems, the lack of social options, and, more generally, the "drift" of residents to the city.[5] Significantly, rural, not urban sociologists embraced the migration problem as their research agenda. In "The Drift to the City in Relation to the Rural Problem," (1911), an article published in the *American Journal of Sociology*, John M. Gillette of the University of North Dakota analyzes the phenomenon and suggests ways of improving the quality of country life. Although Gillette adopts a neutral, academic tone in acknowledging that rural social relations are "restricted" while "the kaleidoscope life of cities fascinates and allures," some rural sociologists went at the problem with moral conviction.[6] For instance, former clergyman Charles J. Galpin, who in 1911 at the age of forty-seven began teaching rural economics at the University of Wisconsin and later directed the Division of Farm Population and Rural Life of the U.S. Department of Agriculture, spoke frequently in the 1920s of the need to protect and conserve farm and rural culture. "Let us go the limit of concession and surrender the whole city to business," he urged a Utah audience in 1923, "and, as for ourselves, move out into God's country" and "live with trees at our door, with air to breathe, with God's sunlight pouring in, with space to move about in and quiet to cover us."[7] In this division of cultural work—with the city serving as a place for work and commerce and the country as a haven for moral regeneration—Galpin underscored the staying power of nineteenth-century rhetoric.

I offer this brief sketch of disciplinary change to highlight the paradoxical way in which hinterland migration did—or did not—claim the attention of sociologists. To be sure, the rural-urban continuum remained a live issue as the twentieth century unfolded, but its relevance as a topic shifted toward more specialized discussions. During the 1910s and '20s, while midwestern rural sociologists intently studied the effects of urban migration, their primary concern was with the long-term viability of hinterland communities. And though the Chicago school placed immigration and spatial mobility at the center of their research, they paid special attention to ethnic Chicagoans and African Americans—focal points that reflected the changing needs of the city.

Generally speaking, these disciplinary emphases paralleled the evolution of Chicago literature and the waning significance of the hinterland migration narrative as a representative civic story. Still, there is particular irony in that Robert Park and his colleagues did not elaborate on the narrative in their work at the University of Chicago, since most of them came from small towns located primarily in the Midwest. As a number of scholars have noted, this hinterland background had a significant impact on the development of the Chicago school. Henry Wu, for instance, has argued that being from a small town enabled the sociologists' understanding of themselves as "strangers to the urban community" and framed their view of the city as an exotic new society with its own set of rules.[8] At the same time, the Chicago sociologists aspired to disinterested social science and seldom acknowledged such influences in their professional writings, where the hinterland appears as a kind of trace element, lightly coating the depiction of city life.

These traces are especially pronounced in Robert Park's work. Born in 1864 and raised in Red Wing, Minnesota, Park made "the country" a regular touchstone in his writing about urban society, often juxtaposing the stasis of rural communities with the turbulent excitement of cities. In his essay "The City: Suggestions for the Investigation of Human Behavior in the City Environment" (1915), published in *The American Journal of Sociology*, he attributes the distinctive "temperament" of city dwellers to the demographic shift that drew "from the isolation of their native villages great masses of the rural populations of Europe and America." Although Park was particularly interested in why the city was home to unusual personality types, such as that of the criminal or "genius," the idea that the city fosters the development of "innate disposition"—in ways that the small town normally cannot—reads like a general proposition. For all migrants, the easy and rapid movement from one of the city's "little worlds" to another "tends to complicate social relationships and to produce new and divergent individual types. It introduces, at the same time, an element of chance and adventure, which adds to the stimulus of city life and gives it for young and fresh nerves a peculiar attractiveness. The lure of the great cities is perhaps a consequence of stimulations which act directly upon the reflexes. As a type of human behavior, it may be explained, like the attraction of the flame for the moth, as a sort of tropism."[9]

Boiled down to a stimulus-response model, Park's characterization of migratory desire bears a striking resemblance to the naturalistic imagery found in Garland's *Rose of Dutcher's Coolly* or Dreiser's *Sister Carrie*. In reprising the theme of self-making, it also offers a sociobiological explanation for how migrants from all small places, American and European, reinvent themselves in big cities. In short, while Park touches on the cultural-historical factors that gave Chicago its distinctive allure throughout the nineteenth-century Midwest, the thrust here is toward a generic theory of migration.

More than a decade later, Park refocused this theory to account for the impact of racial and ethnic identity on the migratory experience. In "Human Migration and the Marginal Man" (1928), the migrant stands at the center of modern urban culture, "free for new adventures" and ready to be "emancipate[d]" through "contact and collision with a new invading culture." Like Georg Simmel's "stranger," Park's migrant is an outsider in the culture, yet he updates the German sociologist's formulation by presenting his marginal man as an immigrant, a Jew, or a person of mixed race, whose alienation ultimately leads to "cosmopolitan" status. As in "The City," Park emphasizes the larger sociological processes these figures represent, moving toward the powerful, if somewhat abstract conclusion that the marginal man is a "new type of personality, namely, a cultural hybrid, a man living and sharing intimately in the cultural life and traditions of two distinct peoples."[10]

Given his career path—as a newspaper reporter in several cities, a doctoral student at the University of Heidelberg, and public relations director at Tuskegee Institute, where he worked closely with Booker T. Washington—this notion of hybridity appears to be the result of Park's own migratory education, beginning with his movement away from the small-town Midwest and encompassing contact or collision with several cultural traditions. Juxtaposed against the Chicago tradition of migratory self-making, Park's 1928 essay works in two ways. On the one hand, it shows Park, "a representative citizen of the old American stock of the Middle Border," redefining in sociological terms the yoked relationship between the provincial and the cosmopolitan. In an undated handwritten manuscript entitled "Notes on Human Migration," he acknowledged the provincial roots of this relationship when he cited Frederick Jackson Turner's essays on the frontier as proof of "the romantic temper" that has characterized the

American attitudes toward migration.[11] On the other hand, Park's published essay also suggests that Chicago could no longer be viewed as a frontier for native-born hinterland migrants. Now a destination for African
Americans as well as the foreign born, Chicago required a different sort of
narrative to account for the dreaming that prompted ambitious migrants to
build new homes in the city. In 1940, Richard Wright provided such an alternative when he published *Native Son,* a novel that both revises and criticizes the cultural expectations that underlie the Chicago migration narrative. I close therefore with Wright's version of Chicago dreaming.

Going to Smash in Chicago

Although in many ways the Mississippi-born Richard Wright defies catego-
rization as a midwestern writer, there is no doubt that his early writings,
especially *Native Son,* are deeply implicated in the reputation of Chicago as
a promised land for migrating southern African Americans. Indeed, as he
explained in the autobiographical *Black Boy* (1945), Wright came to the city
from Memphis in 1927 with hope born of his self-education but really "running more away from something than toward something."[12] The title of his
follow-up account, *American Hunger* (written in the 1940s but published in
1977), highlights the stark longings that compelled him to seek a better life
in the northern city. However, the autobiography as a whole shows how
these dreams failed to materialize, a point that Wright repeatedly dramatized during the 1930s and '40s to underscore the racist attitudes and economic barriers that greeted the more than two hundred thousand southern
black migrants that moved to Chicago between 1910 and 1940.[13] In *Native
Son,* Wright makes this argument with poetic ferocity as he describes Bigger
Thomas's futile efforts at self-making within a novel that, like earlier Chicago
migration narratives, is distinguished by its gritty realism and emotional
drama.

Born in Mississippi and brought by his mother to Chicago five years before
the novel starts, Bigger is to a considerable degree representative of the desires and ambitions that, according to Wright, defined the Great Migration.
Wright alludes to this representative status in the Guggenheim application
that he submitted to support his writing of *Native Son.* The "ultimate purpose" of the novel, Wright explains, is "to reveal the inner landscape of the
Negro mind, to show that under the Negro's strange and warped condition

of life that they, too, have an existence which is comparable to that of other people."[14] Wright makes a similar point about his protagonist's typicality in his essay "How Bigger Was Born," where he explains that "Bigger Thomas was not black all the time; he was white, too, and there were literally millions of him, everywhere." Arguing from a Marxist perspective that Bigger's poverty and lack of opportunity linked him to poor white "native son[s] of this land" who are also potential converts to communism or fascism, Wright notes that he had been unable to imagine his character in these terms before coming to Chicago.[15]

The self-described "pivot" of his literary and political life, Wright's conception of Bigger Thomas also turns on a vision of desire and mobility that links *Native Son* to Chicago's history of migration narratives.[16] But in contrast with the literary portrayals of white native-born migrants or the pragmatic stance adopted by Jane Addams, *Native Son* assumes that Bigger—because he is black and poor—cannot take advantage of the city's promise or fully satisfy his longings. Consequently, Wright's novel reads like an antimigration narrative that in tracing Bigger's movements exposes the racist and ideological underpinnings of the Chicago success story. As for Bigger's desires, the violence with which he expresses them serves as an extreme example of the damage that white Chicago has done to the African-American community.

In a particularly crude display of these desires, Bigger Thomas masturbates before watching the 1931 film *Trader Horn* in a Chicago theater. Excised from the first edition of *Native Son* but recently restored to honor Wright's original intentions, the scene echoes the rhythmic expressions of desire included in other migration accounts. In "polish[ing] his nightstick"—an urban slang term for *penis* that, in literal form, is a dark-colored instrument of police power and here becomes a symbol of black masculinity—Bigger recalls the rhythmic movements of Carrie Meeber in her rocking chair and Carl Sandburg's Mamie, who beats her head "against the bars" because her life does not measure up to her dreams.[17] Bigger's autoeroticism suggests both his alienated desire and his unwillingness to forego the satisfactions of modern urban life; a self-involved sexual act that Bigger jokingly associates with an image of power and suppression, it also points up the futility and violence of his restless striving.

Yet within the novel as a whole, it is not a solitary act. In the restored version of *Native Son,* defense attorney Max Boris explains during Bigger's murder trial that his client comes from an oppressed class whose desires have been tragically and dangerously misdirected. He tells the court in his own rendition of how Bigger was born, "This Negro boy, Bigger Thomas, is part of a furious blaze of liquid life-energy which once blazed and is still blazing in our land. He is a hot-jet of life that spattered itself in futility against a cold wall."[18] According to Boris, Bigger's potential—his life's seed—has been wasted, and his regenerating power spent in an angry collision with modern America. Boris's metaphor provides a sociopolitical explanation for Bigger's autoeroticism and suggests that the transformation of his desire into violence is symptomatic of a broader cultural phenomenon: the fruitless movement of African Americans into racist northern cities.

Boris's indictment resembles the figurative language that Wright used in his nonfictional writings about the Great Migration. In *12 Million Black Voices* (1941), he laments the rhythmic outpouring of African-American energies: "Our thirst for the sensual is poured out in jazz"; "We lose ourselves in violent forms of dance in our ballrooms"; or more harrowing still, "The kitchenette is the funnel through which our pulverized lives flow to ruin and death on the city pavements." Not even Freud, Wright comments in his introduction to *Black Metropolis* (Drake and Cayton's 1945 sociological study of Chicago), could find "a way to reconcile man's inordinate desires with a world that contained no feasible promise of their fulfillment." Hence, *12 Million Black Voices* documents the many unfulfilled, alienated migrants who "drift" from one place to another in unsuccessful efforts to establish satisfactory homes. Speaking for this unsettled community of migrants, Wright notes "we are filled with nostalgic melancholy, a blurred picture of many places seen and suffered in, a restlessness which we cannot appease."[19]

A primary antecedent for this kind of criticism was, of course, the slave narrative. Along with other twentieth-century African-American writers who wrote migration narratives, Wright used the structure of the slave testimony—*Black Boy* being the most vivid example—to chart the journey toward "freedom" and to criticize, bluntly and ironically, dominant white institutions and values.[20] At the same time, Wright acknowledged the homesickness that paradoxically drew some African Americans back to the South they had fled. This sense of nostalgia is likewise evident in the blues music that southern black migrants began playing in Chicago during the 1930s and '40s. In representing these emotions, Wright looked to a variety of sources. Particularly in his later fiction, he drew on Marx, Freud, and Sartre to fashion an anti-imperialist, antiracist critique of the black man's inveterate "homelessness." As Paul Gilroy has noted, this self-consciously global stance complicates any effort to see Wright as an indigenous or "authentic" African-American writer.[21]

Chicago figured prominently in Wright's emerging worldview, not only because it was the first stop in his journey out of the South, but also because his literary education, indeed his very decision to leave the South, was substantially informed by his reading of Chicago and midwestern writers. As he notes in *Black Boy*, it was through reading Sinclair Lewis, Theodore Dreiser, Edgar Lee Masters, Sherwood Anderson, and (Baltimore) critic H. L. Mencken that he developed the "hunger" for self-expression and political criticism that spurred his interest in writing and encouraged him to go to Chicago. Though Wright's situation obviously differed from these other writers', he identified with the ambitions and desires evoked in their work and found in their writing a way of using literature as a "weapon" to fight the ideological forces allied against African Americans.[22] In *Native Son*, this meant turning the promise of migration to an indictment of white Chicago and the imperial designs that the city represents.

The Regal Theater episode in *Native Son* is important, then, because it shows how Bigger's erotic fantasies and dreams of a better life are the products of a migratory imagination. In this respect, the film that Bigger and his friend watch warrants special mention. One of the most successful Hollywood adventure films made in the 1930s, *Trader Horn* follows the exploits of two white hunter-traders, who travel through the jungle to discover and rescue a beautiful white woman who has been raised by an African tribe and is now worshipped as a goddess by them (fig. 16). Shot in Kenya, it features more than thirty species of wild animals as well as two hundred black actors, some of whom speak "authentic" tribal languages.[23] Also, because the film was released before the revised 1934 Motion Picture Production Code took effect, the producers were able to depict the African women in their "natural" tribal garb. Presumably, this is what Bigger and his friend anticipate when they begin to masturbate: "pictures of naked black men and women whirling."[24]

This scene initially reads like a crude burlesque as Bigger and the comically named Jack Harding giggle while they masturbate to the tune of a theater pipe organ whose final sigh of music anticipates their orgasms and their "slumped" position in the theater seats. But the tone shifts as they listen to the organ "humming so low it could scarcely be heard," the music "mellow, nostalgic, sweet." The referent for this nostalgia is unclear, but as the film begins to unwind, Bigger hears "the roll of tom-toms and the screams of

FIGURE 16
Poster of the film
Trader Horn.
(Author's collection)

black men and women dancing free and wild, men and women who were ad-
justed to their soil and at home in their world, secure from fear and hyste-
ria." Spurred to longing by sound—here the African analogue of European
cowbells—Bigger briefly imagines the homeland he never had. And he
"frowned."[25] This yearning is the inverse of what Renato Rosaldo has called
"imperialist nostalgia," a term given to describe the sentimental affect that
underwrites the colonizer's desire to discover and then occupy a "traditional" culture or region.[26] For while the colonizer's longing for the exotic
underwrites his imperial position, Bigger suffers from the nostalgia of the
oppressed: an amorphous homesickness for a mythic ancestral land—
beyond the impoverishments of urban life, the horrors of his childhood, and
the legacy of slavery.

Bigger's reaction to *Trader Horn* is crucial to the direction the novel takes. As he watches the whirling bodies and listens to the drumbeat, Bigger frowns, Wright implies, because the free and easy life described on the screen is nothing like his own. Indeed, a major portion of Bigger's yearning involves dissatisfaction, and the upshot is an intensely felt determination to do something about it. In fact, Wright explicitly links the film's sensual imagery to Bigger's fantasies of a better life. Bigger first gazes at the portrayal of naked black bodies, but then

gradually the African scene changed and was replaced by images in his own mind of white men and women dressed in black and white clothes, laughing, talking, drinking, and dancing. Those were smart people; they knew how to get hold of money, millions of it. Maybe if he were working for them something would happen and he would get some of it. He would see how they did it. Sure, it was all a game and white people knew how to play it.[27]

These images of white affluence and sociability refer to the newsreel that played before *Trader Horn*, a film that shows Mary Dalton—the woman he will inadvertently kill only hours later—lolling on a Florida beach. Significantly, Bigger's anticipatory fantasy of working for rich white people is paired in this passage with the equally fantastic image of African sensuality. As one image gives way to the other, Wright suggests that Bigger's nostalgia and his capitalist desires are inseparable and that he must cross the color line to realize his dreams. This volatile combination of black and white bodies— sexuality and race—sets the stage for Bigger's migration from the Black Belt to the Dalton household.

What happens next begins to look like an inversion of *Trader Horn*, with Bigger pursuing his quest for "game" into deepest, whitest America. But soon after he starts his job as a chauffeur in the Dalton family, it becomes clear that he is the one who will be tracked down like prey. Throughout this hunt, Wright shows Chicago's racist authorities to be every bit as savage as the jungle worlds seen in Hollywood epics. At the same time, Wright leaves no doubt of Bigger's primitive nature, describing in lurid fashion his dismemberment of Mary Dalton and later his brutal murder of Bessie Mears. These scenes reveal how Wright revised Robert Park's notion of the marginal man, for while Park's migrant is emancipated through his contact and collision with urban culture, Bigger explodes with violence and is finally imprisoned for his actions. They also highlight the difference that Wright—and race—brought to the Chicago migration narrative. *Native Son* is indeed a narrative of desire and self-making; however, in Bigger's eyes, murder seems like a creative act. In dramatizing this last point, Wright shows what can happen when the doctrine of upward mobility is absorbed by people who are excluded by race from the economic and cultural opportunities that the city represents.

In this respect, the lure of Chicago, as expressed by Sandburg's image of painted women, spells nothing but trouble for Bigger. At the Regal Theater, he finds himself attracted to the rich white women shown in the newsreels—one of whom is Mary Dalton—and fantasizes about having sex with one and perhaps even marrying her. Wright uses this episode to show that Hollywood films now serve as a powerful vehicle for promoting and mediating desire and, more perversely, to illustrate how such erotic images of glamour and wealth can reinforce that long-standing racist assumption that African-American males are obsessively drawn to white women. This assumption seems borne out later that night when, during his first shift at the Daltons, Bigger carries the drunken Mary to her bedroom and cannot resist kissing her, fondling her breasts, and thrusting against her hips. When Mrs. Dalton walks in the room, Bigger covers Mary's mouth with a pillow to avoid detection and smothers her. Though inadvertent, the killing's placement in a series of sexually explicit scenes—beginning with the masturbation episode and the provocative film footage—suggests that Bigger's desires will keep him moving until he is imprisoned, and dead.

Bigger senses, but does not understand, the dangers he faces in bringing his desires into the Dalton household. Though Mary and her Communist boyfriend Jan clumsily welcome him to their world, his estimation of the situation mixes confusion and hate: "It was a shadowy region, a No Man's Land, the ground that separated the white world from the black that he stood upon. He felt naked, transparent; he felt that this white man, having helped to put him down, having helped to deform him, held him up now to look at him and be amused." As for Mary, Bigger's attraction is that of the oppressed for the oppressor; his hate slides easily toward sexual excitement, while his helplessness turns to violence. After Mary's death, Bigger himself recognizes the inevitability of this outcome, sensing that it "had not been accidental," that it "seemed natural," and even taking pride in finally dramatizing his long-felt "will to kill." Later, too, even before he is accused of the act, he reasons, after prompting from Bessie, that he had, symbolically if not literally, raped Mary, since "He committed rape every time he looked into a white face. He was a long, taut piece of rubber which a thousand white hands had stretched to the snapping point, and when he snapped it was rape" (508, 542, 658). Rape, as Bigger paradoxically figures, is both a willed act and something one commits without choice. Though he tragically works his way toward seeing his violent behavior as a creative act of will and a natural resolution of desire, the narrative shows that his actions are driven by cultural and political forces beyond his control.

The implications of this political reasoning for Wright's view of the Great Migration hardly can be underestimated. As far as Bigger is concerned, the journey from South to North, and out of the Black Belt to Cottage Grove Avenue, ends logically with the "rape" of a white woman and Bigger's own execution. If the goal of the Great Migration is some kind of freedom — better living conditions, political rights, and the chance to develop as a culture — then what begins in violence, in Mississippi or Africa, must end in violence. What is dramatized in the Regal as an individualized expression of black male desire takes shape again in an abandoned building on Chicago's South Side as a manifestation of sexual power, impotence, and rage. Bigger's rhythmic murder of Bessie, his arm "imaginatively swoop[ing] down to where he thought her head must be," is an act of "fancy" that carries his quest for freedom to its brutal extreme (667).

Max Boris is right: Bigger is indeed a furious blaze of liquid life energy that spatters against the cold wall of the city. But while Boris argues that Bigger's relationship to the world is a masturbatory one, he cannot understand — more important, he cannot feel — the desires that put Bigger on the road to violence. At the very end of the novel, when Bigger, speaking from his prison cell, tells Boris that "what I killed for, I am!" and that his killing must have gone toward something "good," the attorney backs away in terror, unable to follow Bigger in this leap of faith (849). Bigger's "I am" is a cry for identity and self-affirmation. Filled with nostalgia and fury, it is aimed at recovering the cultural ground lost through the Great Migration and stolen centuries earlier when Africans were removed from their homeland. However, as Wright makes clear when the steel door shuts in the last line of the novel, this is a cry that no one other than Bigger can really understand.

Neither the end of desire in Chicago fiction nor the culmination of the migratory perspectives that have infused the city since the 1830s, *Native Son* instead marks the limits of a narrative tradition that dominated midwestern literature between 1871 and 1919 and shifted American letters to the middle of the country. As I have argued throughout this book, the emergence of Chicago as a subject for writers and a center for literary activity was predicated on the city's connection to the hinterland and the migration of small-town and rural midwesterners toward the economic and cultural amenities of urban life. Above all, the literary construction of Chicago was based on the intangible emotions that this new, most brutally physical of cities evoked in its migratory population. Shaped by geography, class ambitions, gender, and ethnic tensions, the stories that literary writers told of Chicago dreaming were the distinctive product of a particular time and place. As the city, the region, and the web of relations that ties Chicago to its hinterland evolved, the stories changed as well.

Today Chicago remains the giant magnet that Theodore Dreiser encountered when he first came to the city in the 1880s. During the winter holiday season, tourists from throughout the Midwest join the throngs of shoppers in the Loop, many of them stopping to admire the Christmas decorations in Marshall Field's display windows. And on summer nights, the restaurant and bars in Lincoln Park become home to Big Ten college students and recent alumni. Now part of a sprawl of suburbs and industrial zones that extends north, west, and south, "Chicagoland" continues to be the Midwest's principal territory.

The city's status as a destination for desiring migrants is likewise apparent in more recent Chicago literature, though in terms that differ from the nineteenth- and early twentieth-century examples. *Native Son* underscores this difference, marking the next variation of the Chicago migration narrative as a meditation on the northbound movement of African Americans, a form of artistic criticism carried on by poet Gwendolyn Brooks and Delta blues musicians who registered the gap between migratory dreams and urban reality in emotional tones ranging from angry disappointment to bitter nostalgia. A migratory culture just as surely (if more indirectly) informs the fiction of writers such as James Farrell, Nelson Algren, Saul Bellow, and Stuart Dybek, whose portrayals of Chicago's postindustrial ethnic communities acknowledge the hope and desire that their immigrant parents and grandparents brought with them to the city.[28] Similarly, writing from Chicago's newer ethnic communities—Sandra Cisneros's poetic representation of her Mexican-American childhood home in *The House on Mango Street* (1984) is a prime example—suggests the ongoing impact of migratory dreaming on Chicago literature and culture.

Although Chicago seen through this self-consciously ethnic, multiracial, working-class perspective is not the same city portrayed by native-born provincial migrants, the similarities are worth noting. So, too, are the similarities that can be traced in literature written about other cities. Indeed, we may be better able to understand the features that distinguish one urban literature from another—whether the writing emanates from Chicago, New York, or Los Angeles—by first identifying the shared elements in these works: their common incorporation of the migrant's view of the city from the outside, their representation of how the migrant's cultural assumptions and desire for a better life shape their perception and construction of their new home, and, most important, their dramatization of the forces that make "urban" writing a kind of regional or global literature. These elements not only join the nineteenth-century city to its twenty-first-century successors, but they also cut across a wide range of national heritages, highlighting in various urban societies and assorted literary traditions the pervasive impact of migratory culture.

As for Chicago, the city itself has not moved. It still sits on the shores of Lake Michigan, facing the prairie: a beacon of opportunity on a seemingly limitless horizon.

NOTES

Introduction

1. Floyd Dell, "Chicago in Fiction: In Two Parts—Part II," *Bookman* 38 (Dec 1913): 375.
2. E. B. White, *Here is New York* (New York: Curtis Publishing Company, 1949), 121; Jonathan Raban, *Soft City* (London: Harvill Press, 1974), 50.
3. Carl Sandburg, "Chicago," in *Chicago Poems* (1916; New York: Dover, 1994), 1.
4. Steve Earle, "Telephone Road," *El Corazon*, E-Squared/Warner Bros CD, 1997; Bessie Smith, "Chicago Bound Blues," written by Lovie Austin, *Bessie Smith: The Complete Recordings, vol. 1* (disc 2), Sony/Columbia CD, 1991.
5. Here I echo the title of John R. Stilgoe's *Metropolitan Corridor: Railroads and the American Scene* (New Haven, CT: Yale University Press, 1983).
6. On the evolution of *Midwest* as a term and concept, see James R. Shortridge, *The Middle West: Its Meaning in American Culture* (Lawrence: University Press of Kansas, 1989).
7. Raymond Williams, *The Country and the City* (New York: Oxford University Press, 1973); Timothy J. Clarke, *Image of the People: Gustave Courbet and the 1848 Revolution* (London: Thames and Hudson, 1973); Eugen Weber, *Peasants into Frenchmen: The Modernization of Rural France 1870–1914* (Stanford, CA: Stanford University Press, 1976).
8. Stephan Thernstrom and Peter R. Knights, "Men in Motion: Some Data and Speculations about Urban Population Mobility in Nineteenth-Century America," *Journal of Interdisciplinary History* 2 (Autumn 1970): 7–35.

9. Richard K. Vedder and Lowell E. Gallaway, "Migration and the Old Northwest," in *Essays in Nineteenth Century Economic History: The Old Northwest,* ed. David C. Klingaman and Richard K. Vedder (Athens: Ohio University Press, 1975), 159–76; quotation is on 159. On the "Yankee West" see Susan E. Gray, *The Yankee West: Community Life on the Michigan Frontier* (Chapel Hill: University of North Carolina Press, 1996), especially 1–16.

10. Marshall Berman, *All That Solid Melts into Air: The Experience of Modernity* (New York: Simon and Schuster, 1982), 39–41; quotation is on 40.

11. Eric J. Sundquist, "Realism and Regionalism," in *Columbia Literary History of the United States,* ed. Emory Elliott (New York: Columbia University Press, 1988), 523.

12. Michel Foucault, *The History of Sexuality, Volume One: An Introduction,* trans. Robert Hurley (New York: Vintage, 1990), 19–22. Along the way, I have also profited from the work of Svetlana Boym, Henri LeFebrve, Susan Stewart, and others, whose theoretical insights have guided my exploration of the region's interior landscape.

13. Carl Smith, *Chicago and the American Literary Imagination* (Chicago: University of Chicago Press, 1984), 3.

14. Raymond Williams, *The Politics of Modernism: Against the New Conformists* (New York: Verso, 1989), 34.

Chapter 1

1. Quoted in Edward Shils, "The University, the City, and the World," in *The University and the City from Medieval Origins to the Present,* ed. Thomas Bender (New York: Oxford University Press, 1988), 219.

2. Henri Lefebvre, *The Production of Space,* trans. Donald Nicholson-Smith (Oxford: Blackwell, 1991), 97.

3. Paul Bourget, *Outre-Mer: Impressions of America* (New York: Charles Scribner's Sons, 1896), 117.

4. William T. Stead, *If Christ Came to Chicago: A Plea of All Who Love in the Service of All Who Suffer* (1894; Evanston, IL: Chicago Historical Bookworks, 1990), 123. Accounts of nineteenth-century Chicago bear comparison to descriptions of eighteenth-century London, whose furious growth prompted commentators to liken the metropolis to a huge organism that sucked in resources and people from the surrounding region. See Roy Porter, *London: A Social History* (Cambridge, MA: Harvard University Press, 1995), 131–35.

5. On this subject see Arnold Lewis, *An Early Encounter with Tomorrow: Europeans, Chicago's Loop, and the World's Columbian Exposition* (Urbana: University of Illinois Press, 1997). Lewis focuses in particular on how Chicago's architecture epitomized the city's modernity and rapid pace of life.

6. Carl Sandburg, *Chicago Poems* (1916; New York: Dover, 1994), 1.

7. Colin Loader and Jeffrey C. Alexander, "Max Weber on Churches and Sects in North America: An Alternative Path Toward Rationalization," *Sociological Theory* 3 (Spring 1985): 1.

8. John Patrick Diggins, *Max Weber: Politics and the Spirit of Tragedy* (New York: Basic Books, 1996), 60–61.

9. Henry Adams, *The Education of Henry Adams,* ed. Ernest Samuels and Jayne N. Samuels (Boston: Houghton Mifflin, 1973), 340–41.

10. See, for instance, Rosalind Rosenberg's discussion of William Rainey Harper's efforts in the 1890s to recruit eastern faculty for the newly established University of Chicago in *Beyond Separate Spheres: Intellectual Roots of Modern Feminism* (New Haven, CT: Yale University Press, 1982), 1, 28–32.

11. Bessie Louise Pierce, *A History of Chicago,* vol. 3, *The Rise of a Modern City 1871–1893* (New York: Knopf, 1957), 22.

12. William Cronon, *Nature's Metropolis: Chicago and the Great West* (New York: W. W. Norton, 1991).

13. Quoted in Lloyd Lewis and Henry Justin Smith, *Chicago: The History of Its Reputation* (New York: Blue Ribbon Books, 1929), 137.

14. Lewis and Smith, *Chicago,* 176.

15. John J. Glessner, "The Story of a House" (1923; Chicago: Chicago Architecture Foundation, 1988), page 5 in Glessner Papers, Glessner House Museum, Chicago, Illinois.

16. George Ade, "That Part of the City Which is in the Country," *The Chicago* Record's *"Stories of the Streets and of the Town,"* 4th ser., Oct. 1, 1895 (Chicago: Chicago Record, 1895), 6–8.

17. George Ade, "Clybourn Avenue and the Dandelion Crop," *The Chicago* Record's *"Stories of the Streets and of the Town,"* 2nd ser., July 1, 1894 (Chicago: Chicago Record, 1897), 30–34; James Gilbert, *Perfect Cities: Chicago's Utopias of 1893* (Chicago: University of Chicago Press, 1991), 28.

18. Raymond A. Duggan, from autobiographical paper for Soc/Anthro 264, Oct. 14, 1926; Ernest W. Burgess Papers, University of Chicago.

19. Cronon, *Nature's Metropolis,* 31–41.

20. Lloyd Lewis, *John S. Wright: Prophet of the Prairies* (Chicago: Prairie Farm Publishing, 1941), 71–72.

21. John S. Wright, *To the Owner of Chicago Property Who Desires to Sell* (Chicago, 1867), 6.

22. John S. Wright, *Wright's Proposition to a Railway Capitalist with Important Addendum* (Chicago, 1871), 94.

23. Note Ernest Poole's characterization of Bross and Wright in his *Giants Gone* (New York: Whittlsey House, 1943), 22–23: "Glad-handers like Realtor Wright, who had an exalted faith in his town, and the churchgoing editor, Deacon Bross, started in to tell the world of the amazing chances for money, life and liberty and the

pursuit of happiness hidden in Chicago's mud . . . and so fired the money-loving souls of Americans, east and west, that more hungry young men arrived to get rich and were warmly gripped by the hand and shown bargains in city lots."

24. Quoted in Lewis and Smith, *Chicago*, 137.

25. E. G. Ravenstein, "The Laws of Migration: Second Paper," *Journal of the Royal Statistical Society* 52, pt. 2 (June 1889): 241, 287.

26. Adna Weber, *The Growth of Cities in the Nineteenth Century: A Study in Statistics* (1899; Ithaca, NY: Cornell University Press, 1965), 213.

27. The term "gateway to the west" comes from Cronon, *Nature's Metropolis*, 92.

28. Carville Earle, *Geographical Inquiry and Historical Inquiry* (Stanford, CA: Stanford University Press, 1992), 318.

29. Craig Buettinger, "Economic Inequality in Early Chicago," *Journal of Social History* 11 (Spring 1978): 417. See also Buettinger's dissertation, "The Concept of Jacksonian Democracy: Chicago as a Test Case," University of Michigan, Ann Arbor, 1982; Gilbert, *Perfect Cities*, 38.

30. Joe L. Norris, "The Land Reform Movement," *Papers in Illinois History and Transactions for the Year 1837* (Springfield, IL: Illinois State Historical Society, 1938), 73–82.

31. Frederic Cople Jaher, *The Urban Establishment: Upper Strata in Boston, New York, Charleston, Chicago, and Los Angeles* (Urbana: University of Illinois Press, 1982), 496–97; quotation is on 495.

32. Olivier Zunz, *Making America Corporate: 1870–1920* (Chicago: University of Chicago Press, 1990), 104.

33. Gilbert, *Perfect Cities*, 29–30.

34. Thomas Goebel, "The Children of Athena: Chicago Professionals and the Creation of a Credentialed Social Order, 1870–1920, Vol. 1" (Ph.D. diss., University of Chicago, 1993). See especially 31–42, 125–26.

35. Edgar Lee Masters, *The Tale of Chicago* (New York: G. P. Putnam, 1933), 196, 239.

36. Howard P. Chudacoff, *The Age of the Bachelor: Creating an American Subculture* (Princeton, NJ: Princeton University Press, 1999), especially 50–58, 81.

37. Joanne J. Meyerowitz, *Women Adrift: Independent Wage Earners in Chicago, 1880–1930* (Chicago: University of Chicago Press, 1988), 9–12, 5.

38. *Biographical Sketches of the Leading Men of Chicago* (Chicago: Wilson & Clair, 1868), iv.

39. David Ward Wood, ed., *Chicago and Its Distinguished Citizens, or the Progress of Forty Years* (Chicago: Milton George and Co., 1881), 7.

40. See Carl Smith's discussion of this topic in *Urban Disorder and the Shape of Belief: The Great Chicago Fire, the Haymarket Bomb, and the Model Town of Pullman* (Chicago: University of Chicago Press, 1995).

41. Helen Lefkowitz Horowitz, *Culture & the City: Cultural Philanthropy in Chicago from the 1880s to 1917* (Chicago: University of Chicago Press, 1976), 69.

42. Gilbert, *Perfect Cities*, 41-42.

43. Paul Boyer, *Urban Masses and Moral Order in America, 1820-1920* (Cambridge, MA: Harvard University Press, 1978); William Leach, *Land of Desire: Merchants, Power, and the Rise of a New American Culture* (New York: Pantheon, 1993).

44. W. W. Smith, *That Boy "The Modern Prodigal" in Chicago. Or, From a Farm to the Snares of a Great City* (Chicago: W. W. Smith, 1903), 50.

45. Nina Mjagkij and Margaret Spratt, introduction, *Men and Women Adrift: The YMCA and the YWCA in the City*, ed. Mjagkij and Spratt (New York: New York University Press, 1997), 2-5.

46. Edwin Burritt Smith, John Cowles Grant, and Horace Mann Starkey, *Historical Sketch of the Young Men's Christian Association of Chicago, 1858-1898* (Chicago: YMCA, 1898), 73.

47. L. Wilbur Messer, *Social Forces in Action* (Chicago: Roger and Wells, 1899), 6, 7.

48. Young Men's Christian Association, *The Constitution and By-Laws of the Young Men's Christian Association of Chicago, Illinois* (Chicago: Wm. Rand, 1858).

49. "Creed Rather Than Need," undated newspaper article, L. Wilbur scrapbook, 1880s-1995, vol. 45, Collection of Young Men's Christian Association of Chicago, Chicago Historical Society.

50. The metropolitan plan is described in Edwin Burritt Smith, Horace Mann Starkey, and William Pratt Sidley, *A Chicago Need and How to Meet It* (Chicago: YMCA of Chicago, 1900). The phrase "system of supervision" comes from Messer, *Social Forces in Action*, 19.

51. Boyer, *Urban Masses and Moral Order in America*, 116.

52. Meyerowitz, *Women Adrift*, 44-49.

53. Quoted in ibid., 52.

54. Ibid., 53-54.

Chapter 2

1. Glessner Journal, Glessner Papers (GP), Chicago Historical Society (CHS), Chicago, Illinois. As the journal is arranged chronologically, the citations may be tracked sequentially in the transcribed manuscript available at CHS.

2. George B. Glessner to John J. Glessner, Oct. 12, 1870; Oct. 23, 1870, GP, CHS.

3. Mary Glessner Kimball to John J. Glessner, Nov. 6, 1870, GP, CHS.

4. George Glessner acceded to his brother's suggestion that they send money to their father in the October 12 letter cited above. Jacob Glessner asked John to "advise him [William] particularly about refreshing himself in figures. It is here only he will be deficient—if he is deficient. Instruct him as far as you can what he ought to do, in order to be proof against blunders." Days later, William wrote his brother to thank him for his "suggestions and advice." Jacob Glessner to John J.

Glessner, March 11, 1872, GP, CHS; William L. Glessner to John J. Glessner, March 15, 1872, GP, CHS.

5. Charles Macbeth to John J. Glessner, Aug. 14, 1870, GP, CHS; *Springfield Republic,* Dec. 2, 1870.

6. Illinois, 11:386, R. G. Dun and Company Collection, Harvard Business School.

7. Statistics come from *The Champion City, Springfield, Ohio,* vol. 1 (May 1876): no page; *The Champion City, Springfield in 1879* (Springfield, OH: Springfield Printing, 1879), 15. On the "Champion City" nickname, see William A. Kinnison, *Springfield and Clark County: An Illustrated History* (Springfield, OH: Windsor Publications, 1985), 42; for "Little Chicago," see Workers of the Writers' Program of the Works Projects Administration in the State of Ohio, *Springfield and Clark County Ohio* (Springfield, OH: Springfield Tribune Printing Co., 1941), 46.

8. Barbara Marsh, *A Corporate Tragedy: The Agony of International Harvester Company* (New York: Doubleday & Co., 1985), 34-42.

9. Thayer & Tobey Furniture Company to John J. Glessner, Oct. 29, 1870, GP, CHS.

10. John J. Glessner, "Mrs. John J. Glessner: An Appreciation, A Little History, A Tribute, January 1, 1848-October 19, 1932." Manuscript housed in Glessner Papers, Glessner House Museum, Chicago, Illinois.

11. John Jacob Glessner, "Migrations, Emigrations, and Transmigrations of the Glessner Family," in Percy Maxim Lee and John Glessner Lee, *Family Reunion: An Incomplete Account of the Maxim-Lee Family History* (Connecticut: privately printed, 1971), 313-14.

12. Nancy Bayard Macbeth to John J. Glessner, Dec. 20, 1870, GP, CHS.

13. Manuscript, *Census, Town of Springfield, Clark County, Ohio,* U.S. Census of Population, 1870, in National Archives Microfilm Collection, M593-1180. Interestingly, John Glessner does not appear on the census as a resident of the Macbeth household, perhaps because he was not present on June 8, 1870, when the survey was taken. He does appear in a city directory for 1868-69 as a bookkeeper for Warder, Mitchell, & Co., boarding at the northeast corner of Pleasant and Limestone (*Williams Springfield Directory for 1868-69* [Springfield, OH: J. Willis Low, 1868], 50). Helen Macbeth discusses the family's financial situation in a letter to Frances Macbeth, Nov. 18, 1866, GP, CHS. Interestingly, Helen notes that George Macbeth, the second-oldest son, owed debts totaling $140.

14. *Illustrated Historical Atlas of Clark County, Ohio* (Philadelphia: L. H. Everts and Co., 1875). By 1830, Springfield had mills for flour, lumber, woolens, cotton, powders, and paper. See Opha Moore, "Ohio as a Manufacturing State," in Emilius O. Randall and Daniel J. Ryan, *History of Ohio: The Rise and Progress of an American State* (New York: Century History Co., 1912), 5:327.

15. On middle-border towns, see Lewis Atherton, *Main Street on the Middle Border* (Bloomington: Indiana University Press, 1954), xiv-xv. For brief histories of Springfield's growth, see Workers of the Writers' Program at the Work Projects Adminis-

tration in the State of Ohio, *Springfield and Clark County Ohio,* 30-33; Eugene H. Roseboom and Francis P. Weisenburger, *A History of Ohio* (New York: Prentice-Hall, 1934), 317; Kinnison, *Springfield and Clark County,* 37-54. On Chicago infrastructure, see Bessie Louise Pierce, *A History of Chicago,* vol. 3, *The Rise of a Modern City 1871–1893* (New York: Alfred Knopf, 1957), 224-30.

16. Kinnison, *Springfield and Clark County,* 22-25, 42, 53-54.

17. Helen Macbeth to Frances Macbeth, Nov. 18, 1866; Dec. 16, 1866, GP, CHS.

18. Helen Macbeth to Frances Macbeth, Nov. 18, 1866; Dec. 16, 1866, GP, CHS.

19. Helen Macbeth to Frances Macbeth, Jan. 5, 1867, GP, CHS.

20. Helen Macbeth to Frances Macbeth, Jan. 5, 1867, GP, CHS.

21. Lizzie Fisher to Frances Macbeth, Jan. 11, 1867, GP, CHS.

22. Helen Macbeth to Fannie Macbeth, Jan. 9, 1867, GP, CHS.

23. On the importance of self-control and privacy in nineteenth-century courtship letters, see Karen Lystra, *Searching the Heart: Women, Men, and Romantic Love in Nineteenth-Century America* (New York: Oxford University Press, 1989), 17-18.

24. Timothy R. Mahoney, *Provincial Lives: Middle-Class Experience in the Antebellum Middle West* (New York: Cambridge University Press, 1999), 167.

25. Glessner Journal, GP, CHS.

26. David A. Hanks, *Isaac E. Scott Reform Furniture in Chicago: John Jacob Glessner House* (Chicago: Chicago School of Architecture Foundation, 1975), 4-6, 8-23. Francis Glessner notes that the first Scott commission took place in 1875 in the Glessner Journal Transcripts, GP, CHS.

27. On Richardson's advocacy of Morris, see Eileen Boris, *Art and Labor: Ruskin, Morris, and the Craftsman Ideal in America* (Philadelphia: Temple University Press, 1986), 35.

28. See "Morris & Co. Designs in Glessner House," partial inventory of house furnishings taken in March 1983, Glessner Papers, Glessner House Museum, Chicago.

29. Quoted in Hanks, *Isaac E. Scott Reform Furniture in Chicago,* 23-24. On the building's restoration, see *Chicago Tribune,* March 23, 1986.

30. Glessner, "Migrations, Emigrations, and Transmigrations of the Glessner Family," 314.

31. I refer here to the primary definition of *cosmopolitan* given by the online version of the *Oxford English Dictionary*: "Belonging to all parts of the world; not restricted to any one country or its inhabitants." Note that *OED* also acknowledges the urban derivations of this word in offering *metropolitan* as a parallel term.

32. William Cronon, *Nature's Metropolis: Chicago and the Great West* (New York: W. W. Norton, 1991).

33. "Shipments to June 5th 1875 incl.," Office of Warder, Mitchell, & Co. to John J. Glessner, GP, CHS.

34. "The Warder, Bushnell & Glessner Company and its Officers," *The Farm Implement News* 11 (September 1890): 19-20.

35. Benjamin H. Warder to John J. Glessner, May 18, 1872, GP, CHS.

36. "The Warder, Bushnell & Glessner Company and its Officers," 20.

37. John Glessner to Frances Glessner, Oct. 15, 1874, GP, CHS; Ohio, 25:161, R. G. Dun and Company Collection, Harvard Business School; Zanesville newspaper clipping transcribed but date not cited in Glessner Journal, November 1883, GP, CHS.

38. Glessner Journal, GP, CHS. The date of the *Tribune* article cited here is April 19, 1884.

39. "The House That Henry Built," undated article from unnamed newspaper, Glessner Papers, Glessner House Museum, Chicago.

40. Glessner Journal, 1887, GP, CHS.

41. The term *urbane* comes from James F. O'Gorman, *H. H. Richardson: Architectural Forms for an American Society* (Chicago: University of Chicago Press, 1987), 72; see also 47-49; Thomas C. Hubka, "H. H. Richardson's Glessner House: A Garden in the Machine," *Winterthur Portfolio* 24 (Winter 1989): 209-29.

42. John J. Glessner, "The Story of a House" (1923; Chicago: Chicago Architecture Foundation, 1988), 2. Glessner Papers, Glessner House Museum, Chicago.

43. John J. Glessner to George Glessner, June 16, 1924. Transcribed from photostat of original letter. Glessner Papers, Glessner House Museum, Chicago.

44. Arthur Meeker, *Prairie Avenue* (New York: Alfred A. Knopf, 1949), 89.

45. As Olivier Zunz has argued, the agricultural implement manufacturers sped the adoption of modern technology and business practices: "Corporations penetrated the farm and fostered an integrated world dependent on an unceasing stream of communication between big city headquarters and rural agencies." Zunz, *Making America Corporate 1870-1920* (Chicago: University of Chicago Press, 1990), 150-73; quotation is on 151.

46. Anna Rachel Macbeth to Frances Glessner, Jan. 15, 1871; Anna Rachel Macbeth to Frances Glessner and Nancy Bayard Macbeth, March 22, 1871, GP, CHS.

47. Glessner Journal, October 1893, GP, CHS.

48. "Her education was at Oxford, Ohio, school for girls, under auspices of Prof. David Swing, afterwards a Presbyterian minister in Chicago." Glessner, "Mrs. John J. Glessner," 2.

49. Glessner Journal, Jan. 16, 1887; Sept. 21, 1887, article, "'Tips' from the Inside—Driftwood from the Under-Current of News" cited in Glessner Journal, GP, CHS.

50. Glessner, "The Story of a House," 14.

51. Ruth Blumenberg, "Houses and Histories in the Springfield Area," independent study project, History Department, Wittenberg College, Winter 1971.

52. Hubka, "H. H. Richardson's Glessner House," 210.

53. On general New England antecedents, see ibid., 214; on the house's private and public functionality, see Elaine Harrington, *Henry Hobson Richardson, J. J. Glessner House, Chicago* (Tubingen, Germany: Wasmuth, 1993), 6.

54. Paul A Carnahan, "The Book in the Domestic Environment: The Glessner Family Library, Chicago—1886-1893" (master's thesis, University of Chicago, 1986), 24-29, 41, 120-37.

55. Eileen Boris notes that the Glessner house "exemplified the social and personal context in which House Beautiful aestheticism flourished" (Boris, *Art and Labor,* 57-58).

56. On the antimodern thrust of the Arts and Crafts movement, see T. J. Jackson Lears, *No Place of Grace: Antimodernism and the Transformation of American Culture 1880 -1920* (New York: Pantheon, 1981), 60-96.

57. Frances Glessner, "Dear Ladies of the Morning Reading Class," paper delivered Dec. 5, 1927, Chicago. Glessner Papers, Glessner House Museum, Chicago.

58. John J. Glessner, "Ghosts of Yesterday," Glessner Papers, Glessner House Museum, Chicago; "Friends of John J. and Frances Glessner," prepared by Mary Alice Molloy, July 1-9, 1982, Glessner Papers, Glessner House Museum, Chicago.

59. Glessner, "The Story of a House," 8.

60. Note, for instance, that Helen Lefkowitz Horowitz identifies the Glessners as important cultural philanthropists in *Culture & the City: Cultural Philanthropy in Chicago from the 1880s to 1917* (Chicago: University of Chicago Press, 1976); Hamlin Garland, *A Daughter of the Middle Border* (New York: Macmillan, 1921), 372.

61. Glessner Journal, Feb. 10, 1889, GP, CHS; Fuller was unable to accept this invitation, and the Glessners saved his regrets in the family journal early in 1893.

62. Glessner Journal, May 2, 1894, GP, CHS.

63. For instance, as Helen C. Callahan points out, the Glessners (especially Frances) treated their servants with the paternalistic condescension typical of their social position. See her "Upstairs-Downstairs in Chicago 1870-1907: The Glessner Household," *Chicago History* 6 (1977-78): 195-209.

Chapter 3

1. Eric J. Sundquist, "Realism and Regionalism," in *Columbia Literary History of the United States,* ed. Emory Elliott (New York: Columbia University Press, 1988), 523.

2. Richard H. Brodhead, *Cultures of Letters: Scenes of Reading and Writing in Nineteenth-Century America* (Chicago: University of Chicago Press, 1993), 107-41.

3. Joseph Kirkland, *Zury: The Meanest Man in Spring County* (Urbana: University of Illinois Press, 1956), 64, 65.

4. Clyde E. Henson, *Joseph Kirkland* (New York: Twayne, 1962), 29-33. For a discussion of *Harry Franco,* see Timothy B. Spears, *100 Years on the Road* (New Haven, CT: Yale University Press, 1995), 37-39.

5. Joseph Kirkland to Hamlin Garland, June 7, 1887, Joseph Kirkland Papers, Newberry Library, Chicago.

6. Henry Blake Fuller, quoted in Jean Holloway, *Hamlin Garland: A Biography* (Austin: University of Texas Press, 1960), 26. Though this letter (housed now in the Garland papers at the University of Southern California) lacks a year date, Holloway speculates it was written in 1893, after the publication of Fuller's *Cliff-Dwellers* and Garland's *Main-Travelled Roads*.

7. Henry Blake Fuller to George Ade, May 16, no year given, George Ade Collection, Special Collections, Purdue University Libraries, West Lafayette, Indiana. The sketch was entitled "Cousin Walter Miller" and appeared on May 16, 1895. See the listing of Ade's *Record* articles in Dorothy Ritter Russo, *A Bibliography of George Ade, 1866–1944* (Indianapolis: Indiana Historical Society, 1947).

8. Kenneth Scambray, *A Varied Harvest: The Life and Works of Henry Blake Fuller* (Pittsburgh: University of Pittsburgh Press, 1987), 155.

9. Hamlin Garland, *Crumbling Idols: Twelve Essays on Art Dealing Chiefly with Literature, Painting and the Drama*, ed. Jane Johnson (Cambridge, MA: Harvard University Press, 1960), 61.

10. Cited in Holloway, *Hamlin Garland*, 19. Garland's review appeared in the *New England Magazine*, n.s., 2 (May 1890).

11. On Garland's boyhood reading habits, see Christine Pawley, *Reading on the Middle Border: The Culture of Print in Late-Nineteenth-Century Osage, Iowa* (Amherst: University of Massachusetts Press, 2001), 12–14; quotations are from Hamlin Garland, *A Son of the Middle Border* (New York: Macmillan, 1917), 317, 320.

12. Garland, *Son of the Middle Border*, 458.

13. Hamlin Garland, *A Daughter of the Middle Border* (New York: Macmillan, 1921), 5–9. Quoted phrases appear on pages 5, 8, 9, 5.

14. Donald Pizer notes that Garland conceived of the novel in 1890, but did not begin serious work on it until 1892. By the summer of 1893, he had apparently decided that Rose's migration would take her to Chicago rather than New England. Pizer attributes this change in plan to Garland's growing interest in Chicago; I would add that Henry Blake Fuller reinforced this interest. See Pizer, *Hamlin Garland's Early Work and Career* (Berkeley and Los Angeles: University of California Press, 1960), 155–56.

15. Hamlin Garland, *The Rose of Dutcher's Coolly* (Chicago: Stone and Kimball, 1895), 403.

16. Henry Blake Fuller, "The Downfall of Abner Joyce," in *Under the Skylights* (New York: D. Appleton, 1901), 3, 4.

17. Bert Leston Taylor, *The Charlatans* (Indianapolis: Bobbs-Merrill, 1906), 5.

18. Henry Blake Fuller, "The Upward Movement in Chicago" *Atlantic Monthly* 80 (October 1897): 534–47.

19. Henry Blake Fuller, "Chicago as a Country Town," *Chicago Evening Post*, April 27, 1901, Henry Blake Fuller Papers, Newberry Library; full date cited in Scambray, *Varied Harvest*, 181.

20. For instance, see "Englewood No 'Jay' Town," *Englewood Times* (Chicago), Jan. 14, 1910.

21. Scambray, *Varied Harvest,* 30, 44, 93, 103–06, 156–7.

22. Mary P. Ryan, *Cradle of the Middle Class: The Family in Oneida County, New York, 1790–1865* (New York: Cambridge University Press, 1981).

23. According to the *Oxford English Dictionary,* 1st ed., the word *hometown* did not enter the American vocabulary until 1912.

24. Charles Hamm, *Yesterdays: Popular Song in America* (New York: W. W. Norton, 1979), 165–72.

25. *Chicago Tribune,* Dec. 10, 1889.

26. http://www.poetry — archive.com/p/home_sweet_home.html (accessed July 17, 2004).

27. See the *OED* definition of *cosmopolitan.*

28. Brand Whitlock, *The Letters and Journal of Brand Whitlock,* comp. and ed. by Allan Nevins, and intro. by Newton D. Baker (New York: D. Appleton, 1936), 1:16–17.

Chapter 4

Parts of this chapter originally appeared in *Chicago History* magazine, vol. 30, no. 1 (Summer 2001). Reprinted with permission.

1. Fatted Calf Society invitation, John T. McCutcheon Papers, Newberry Library, Chicago (NL). There were forty-seven founding members of the society, including George Ade and John McCutcheon. See "Founding Members," Indiana Society of Chicago Papers (IS), Special Collections, University Library, University of Illinois at Chicago (UIC).

2. Come on Home Society of Indianapolis, Indiana, "'Come on Home,' Being an Invitation to the Indiana Society of Chicago by the Come On Home Society of Indianapolis Society of Indianapolis, Indiana" (Indianapolis: Come on Home Publishing Co., 1911).

3. Riley's poem was reprinted in an article describing the Indiana Society's "Indiana Night" in Chicago in *The Indianapolis Journal,* Dec. 8, 1905. The newspaper clipping may be found in IS, UIC. On Hovenden at the World's Fair, see James Gilbert, *Perfect Cities: Chicago's Utopias of 1893* (Chicago: University of Chicago Press, 1991), 123–24. The best discussion of the painting's cultural significance is Sarah Burns's "The Country Boy Goes to the City: Thomas Hovenden's *Breaking Home Ties* in American Popular Culture," *American Art Journal* 20 (1988): 59–73.

4. I base this on a reading of society rosters held at the Newberry Library, the University of Illinois at Chicago's Special Collections, and Special Collections, Purdue University Libraries, West Lafayette, Indiana. While the Indiana Society began with roughly fifty members, during the 1910s and '20s it boasted several hundred members.

5. Jon Gjerde, *The Minds of the West: Ethnocultural Evolution in the Rural Middle West, 1830–1917* (Chapel Hill: University of North Carolina Press, 1997).

6. Kathleen Neils Conzen, David A. Gerber et al., "The Invention of Ethnicity: A Perspective from the U.S.A.," *Journal of American Ethnic History* 12 (Fall 1992): 4–5. See also Werner Sollors, *Beyond Ethnicity: Consent and Descent in American Culture* (New York: Oxford University Press, 1986). For a flexible, expansive definition of ethnicity, see also Abner Cohen, "The Lesson of Ethnicity," *Urban Ethnicity* (London: Tavistock Publications, 1974), ix–xxiv.

7. Here I follow Jon Gjerde's insightful discussion of the ethnicization of immigrants in the rural Midwest. Gjerede notes that immigrant allegiances to American citizenship and ethnic group identity were "in constant tension" but that their "instrumental uses of ethnic groups were at least implicitly based on membership in a larger economy and polity." He also notes that these two identities were largely "complementary." Gjerde, *Minds of the West,* 228–29.

8. Lewis Atherton, *Main Street on the Middle Border* (1954; New York: Quadrangle, 1966), xiv; Andrew R. L. Cayton and Peter S. Onuf, *The Midwest and the Nation: Rethinking the History of an American Region* (Bloomington: Indiana University Press, 1990).

9. See George Ade, "The Rising Generation Establishing New Attitude Records," George Ade Papers, NL. McCutcheon is quoted in Vincent Starrett, introduction, to John McCutcheon, *John McCutcheon's Book* (Chicago: Caxton Club, 1948), x; see also his autobiography, *Drawn From Memory* (Indianapolis: Bobbs-Merrill, 1950).

10. Although this quotation comes from a 1941 radio broadcast, the same joke is reported in the account of the 1905–6 proceedings of the Indiana Society. See George Ade excerpt from broadcast by Edwin C. Hill, CBS Radio Network, Feb. 10, 1941, George Ade Papers, NL; Indiana Society of Chicago, *An Account of the Proceedings on the Occasion of the First Annual Banquet of the Indiana Society of Chicago* (Chicago: Indiana Society of Chicago, 1905–6), 4.

11. Cayton and Onuf, *Midwest and the Nation,* 84–102, 111; Henry F. May, *The End of American Innocence* (1959; Chicago: Quadrangle, 1964), 96–99.

12. On early settlement patterns, see William E. Wilson, *Indiana: A History* (Bloomington: Indiana University Press, 1966), 10–11; Howard Peckham, *Indiana: A Bicentennial History* (New York: W. W. Norton, 1978), 46–47. The origins of *Hoosier* are discussed at the Indiana Historical Bureau Web site: http://www-statelib.lib.in.us/www/ihb/emblems/hooiser.html (accessed July 17, 2004).

13. Demographic statistics come from Peckham, *Indiana,* 126–27.

14. George Ade, "Something About the Two Important Ones," pencil-written manuscript, George Ade Papers, NL.

15. John T. McCutcheon, *Drawn From Memory* (Indianapolis: Bobbs-Merrill, 1950), 22–23, 33.

16. George Ade, "George Ade Checks Up at 70, Calls Three Score and Ten a Way Station," *Purdue Alumnus* 23 (April 1936): 9, George Ade Papers, NL. "Blur of illumination" is quoted in Fred C. Kelly, *George Ade, Warmhearted Satirist* (Indianapolis: Bobbs-Merrill, 1947), 23. On Ade's reading, see Kelly, *George Ade*, 29-32, 36-37.

17. McCutcheon, *Drawn From Memory*, 30-35; "spell" (32), "this type of reading" (30).

18. E. Anthony Rotundo, "Boy Culture," in *Meanings for Manhood: Constructions of Masculinity in Victorian America* (Chicago: University of Chicago Press, 1990).

19. Ade, "George Ade Checks Up at 70," 9.

20. Robert W. Topping, *A Century and Beyond: The History of Purdue University* (West Lafayette, IN: Purdue University Press, 1988), 122, 97-99. White is quoted on p. 99.

21. Only eight members of George Ade's original class graduated on time in 1887; some finished with other classes, while most dropped out altogether. John McCutcheon's class suffered similar losses. To compare Ade's freshman and senior year, see *The Tenth Annual Register of Purdue University* (Indianapolis: Purdue University, 1884), 8-10 and *The Annual Register of Purdue University* (Indianapolis: Indiana: Purdue University, 1887), 8. For McCutcheon's freshman and senior years, see *The Annual Register of Purdue University* (Indianapolis: Purdue University, 1886), 9-10 and *The Annual Register of Purdue University* (Indianapolis: Purdue University, 1889), 84. See also George Ade, "Our Class of '87," George Ade Collection, Purdue University Libraries, Special Collections. For clarification of graduation dates, see *The Semi-Centennial Alumni Record of Purdue University*, ed. Jack Edward Walters (Lafayette, IN: Purdue University, 1924).

22. By 1924, thirty-six years after graduating, Ade and three of his classmates were living in Indiana; not including Ade, two lived in the Lafayette area and one in Indiana. In McCutcheon's class, five were living in Indiana—two in Indianapolis, one in Lafayette, one in Muncie, and one in Hazleden. See Walters, ed., *Semi-Centennial Alumni Record of Purdue University*. For a record of the whereabouts and occupations of all Purdue graduates as of 1893, see *The Annual Register of Purdue University Lafayette, Indiana* (Indianapolis: Purdue University, 1893), 107-16.

23. Kelly, *George Ade*, 52; McCutcheon, *Drawn From Memory*, 42, 43.

24. In 1880, less than 2 percent of college-age youths were in college. By 1920, this figure had climbed to 8 percent. Helen Lefkowitz Horowitz, *Campus Life: Undergraduate Cultures from the End of the Eighteenth Century to the Present* (Chicago: University of Chicago Press, 1987), 5-6.

25. From *The Magazine of Sigma Chi* 49 (May-June 1930): 298, George Ade Papers, NL; Kelly, *George Ade*, 44-47.

26. Kelly, *George Ade*, 49.

27. Ade, "George Ade Checks Up," 10.

28. George Ade, "Purdue at Long Range," draft of article to be published in the *Purdue Alumnus,* George Ade Collection, Special Collections, Purdue University Libraries. Helen Lefkowitz Horowitz notes that extracurricular activities developed

288

sporadically in the post–Civil War years, becoming an important part of collegiate life by the turn of the century. Horowitz, *Campus Life,* 55, 41–55.

29. McCutcheon, "George Ade," in George Ade and John T. McCutcheon, *Notes and Reminiscences* (Chicago: Holiday Press, 1940), 35.

30. McCutcheon, "George Ade," 34, 33.

31. McCutcheon, *Drawn From Memory,* 45 (for quotations), 53.

32. On the prevalence and intensity of homosocial relations, see D. Michael Quinn, *Same-Sex Dynamics among Nineteenth-Century Americans: A Mormon Example* (Urbana: University of Illinois Press, 1996), especially 66–106. Quinn distinguishes homosocial from homoerotic relations, noting for instance that most "same-sex sleeping arrangements were nonerotic, yet affectionate experiences of physical closeness" (89).

33. On the development of gay identity and culture, see George Chauncy, *Gay New York: Gender, Urban Culture, and the Making of the Gay Male World 1890–1940* (New York: HarperCollins, 1994); Jonathan Ned Katz, *Love Stories: Sex between Men before Homosexuality* (Chicago: University of Chicago Press, 2001).

34. Kelly, *George Ade,* 65–72; Ade, "George Ade Checks Up at 70," 10.

35. Kelly, *George Ade,* 64; McCutcheon, *Drawn From Memory,* 60–61; McCutcheon, "George Ade," 36.

36. McCutcheon, *Drawn From Memory,* 61.

37. Ibid.

38. Ibid..

39. Ibid., 65; John McCutcheon to "Dear Folks," November 1889, John T. McCutcheon Papers, NL.

40. John McCutcheon to "Dear Folks," November 1889, John T. McCutcheon Papers, NL.

41. McCutcheon, *Drawn From Memory,* 61.

42. McCutcheon to "Dear Mother," December 1889, John T. McCutcheon Papers, NL.

43. McCutcheon, *Drawn From Memory,* 65–66; quotation is on 66.

44. McCutcheon to "Dear Mother," early 1890 (dated by library); also McCutcheon to mother, February 22, 1890. Both are in John T. McCutcheon Papers, NL.

45. For example, see James R. Grossman, *Land of Hope: Chicago, Black Southerners, and the Great Migration* (Chicago: University of Chicago Press, 1989), 89–94.

46. McCutcheon, "George Ade," 36, 39. The "glamorous" letters that McCutcheon mentions no longer exist, and Ade left very little contemporaneous explanations as to why he left Lafayette at this point. In *George Ade,* Kelly emphasizes Ade's inchoate ambitions, his job situation, and his friendship with McCutcheon on 72–75. He also stresses Ade's ties to Lafayette and possible ambivalence about leaving. Because Kelly's book lacks notes and appears based in part on his conversations with Ade, it is difficult to document.

47. Ade to Josh Hilderbrand, Aug. 24, 1890, George Ade Papers, NL.

48. Ibid.

49. McCutcheon, "George Ade," 40–45; McCutcheon, *Drawn From Memory,* 80; Harvey W. Zorbaugh, *The Gold Coast and the Slum: A Sociological Study of Chicago's Near North Side* (Chicago: University of Chicago Press, 1929), especially chap. 2, "An Area of Transition." Although Zorbaugh's study, which focuses on the 1920s, lacks a detailed historical perspective, he notes the Near North Side's transformation between the 1880s and 1920s from respectable neighborhood to slum. For Ade's account of the North Side residences in which he lived, see George Ade to Richard V. Carpenter, Oct. 27, 1923, Richard V. Carpenter Papers, Chicago Historical Society.

50. McCutcheon, "George Ade," 39.

51. Ibid., 45–46; George Ade, "Bankers I Have Met," no date, George Ade Papers, NL. While both Ade and McCutcheon agree on the regularity of these loans in the early 1890s, McCutcheon remembers paying for clothes and rent, and Ade focuses on meals.

52. McCutcheon, "George Ade," 44–45.

53. Bessie Louise Pierce, *A History of Chicago,* vol. 3, *The Rise of a Modern City 1871–1893* (New York: Alfred Knopf, 1957), 417.

54. Hugh Dalziel Duncan, *Culture and Democracy: The Struggle for Form and Architecture in Chicago and the Middle West during the Life and Times of Louis H. Sullivan* (1965; New Brunswick, NJ: Transaction Publishers, 1989), 49.

55. James DeMuth, *Small Town Chicago: The Comic Perspective of Finley Peter Dunne George Ade Ring Lardner* (Port Washington, NY: Kennikat Press, 1980), 3–5 and passim. Joining DeMuth and Hugh Duncan (cited above), Norman Howard Sims likewise notes the rural, frontier antecedents of late nineteenth-century Chicago journalism in his "The Chicago Style of Journalism" (Ph.D. diss., University of Illinois, Champaign-Urbana, 1979), 43–47 and passim. For an overview of American journalistic reporting in the 1890s, see Michael Schudson, *Discovering the News: A Social History of American Newspapers* (New York: Basic Books, 1978), 88–120.

56. The word *longing* comes from Gunther Barth's discussion of metropolitan newspapers in *City People: The Rise of Modern City Culture in Nineteenth-Century America* (New York: Oxford University Press, 1980), 58–63; quotation is on 59. As Benedict Anderson has argued, modern group identities are made possible by forms of communication — like the urban newspaper — that allow people to imagine communities over time and space. Benedict Anderson, *Imagined Communities: Reflections on the Origin and Spread of Nationalism* (New York: Verso, 1983). For a suggestive discussion of the newspaper's interpretive importance in turn-of-the-century Berlin, see also Peter Fritzsche, *Reading Berlin 1900* (Cambridge, MA: Harvard University Press, 1996).

57. Sims, "Chicago Style of Journalism," 43–44, 81–85.

58. Brand Whitlock, *The Happy Average* (Indianapolis: Bobbs-Merrill, 1904), 306; Sims, "Chicago Style of Journalism," 217–18.

59. Sims, "Chicago Style of Journalism," 216–26, 232–36. Though the Whitechapel Club is discussed in many studies of Chicago during this period, Sims's account is the most comprehensive and insightful. According to Sims, the Whitechapel Club "provided the institutional focus for the perspective that is refered (sic) to here as the Chicago style of journalism" (217). See 207–52 for the complete account.

60. John T. McCutcheon, "For the World's Fair Correspondents 1898–1933," speech given at Century of Progress Exhibition luncheon, Aug. 12, 1933, John T. McCutcheon Papers, NL.

61. Chicago *Record,* May 16, 1893.

62. "Lived Over Old Times," June 8, 1893; "Home For Hoosiers," June 6, 1893; "In State Buildings," June 3, 1893. All in the Chicago *Record.*

63. Quoted in letter Dennis wrote to Franklin J. Meine, printed in Meine's introduction to George Ade, *Chicago Stories,* ed. Franklin J. Meine (1941; Chicago: Henry Regnery, 1963), xii.

64. George Ade, "Her Visit to Chicago," *The Chicago* Record's *"Stories of the Streets and of the Town,"* 1st ser., April 1, 1894 (Chicago: Chicago *Record,* 1894), 64, 65.

65. See, for instance, James Gilbert's discussion of Ade in *Perfect Cities,* 49–51. Larzer Ziff, on the other hand, underscores Ade's attention to Chicago's small-town and rural population, calling it his "greatest strength," and argues he was a limited writer for not recognizing that "something was happening in Chicago that was not explicable in terms of it just being a metropolitan version of the rural community." Larzer Ziff, *The American 1890s: Life and Times of a Lost Generation* (New York: Viking, 1966), 159.

66. George Ade, *In Babel* (New York: McClure, 1903), 51, 53, 55, 58. The sketches contained in this volume first appeared in the Chicago *Record.*

67. Sidney H. Bremer, *Urban Intersections: Meetings of Life and Literature in United States Cities* (Urbana: University of Illinois Press, 1992), 81–112. Significantly, the writers that Bremer places in this category are all women.

68. McCutcheon, *John McCutcheon's Book,* 60–61, 60.

69. George Ade, "Several Square Miles of Transplanted Poland," *The Chicago* Record's *"Stories of the Streets and of the Town,"* 2nd ser., July 1, 1894 (Chicago: Chicago *Record,* 1897), 14–17; George Ade, "Cooped Up in Town," *The Chicago* Record's *"Stories of the Streets and of the Town,"* 5th ser., July 1, 1897 (Chicago: Chicago *Record,* 1897), 65.

70. "Cooped Up in Town," 64, 63.

71. George Ade, "Looking For a Friend," *The Chicago* Record's *"Stories of the Streets and of the Town,"* 4th ser., Oct. 1, 1895 (Chicago: Chicago *Record,* 1895), 53–54.

72. "Cooped Up in Town," 65.

73. George Ade, "That Part of the City Which is in the Country," *The Chicago* Record's *"Stories of the Streets and of the Town,"* 4th ser., Oct. 1, 1895 (Chicago: Chicago *Record,* 1895), 6–8.

74. For the story of the young man who becomes respectable in society by living an uninspiring life, see George Ade, "The Social Triumph of Sherman Miller," *The Chicago* Record's *"Stories of the Streets and of the Town,"* 2nd ser., July 1, 1894 (Chicago: Chicago *Record,* 1894), 160–63. In "The Montaye Family," Ade punctures upper-class (eastern) snobbery by having one of his characters make the point that "there are plenty of people right here in Chicago who don't want to go too far back" in their family history, since so many of them come from rural or working-class roots. *The Chicago* Record's *"Stories of the Streets and of the Town,"* 5th ser., July 1, 1897 (Chicago: Chicago *Record,* 1897), 108–10.

75. George Ade, "Clarence Was Not at the Station," *The Chicago* Record's *"Stories of the Streets and of the Town,"* 4th ser., Oct. 1, 1895 (Chicago: Chicago *Record,* 1895), 134–37; "How Jasper Swift Came and Saw and Went Home," *The Chicago* Record's *"Stories of the Streets and of the Town,"* 2nd ser., July 1, 1894 (Chicago: Chicago *Record,* 1894), 56–58.

76. For instance, see George Ade, "One of the Hannibal Boys," *The Chicago* Record's *"Stories of the Streets and of the Town,"* 3rd ser., April 1, 1895 (Chicago: Chicago *Record,* 1895), 227–30.

77. William Dean Howells to George Ade, Oct. 24, 1916, George Ade Papers, NL; William Dean Howells, in the introduction to *Great Modern American Short Stories: An Anthology* (New York: Boni and Liveright,1920), xiii.

78. McCutcheon notes Ade's influence and his shift away from realism in his autobiography, *Drawn From Memory* (Indianapolis: Bobbs-Merrill, 1950), 87.

79. George Ade, "It is an Old-fashioned and Appalling Reflection," George Ade Papers, NL.

80. George Ade, *Fables in Slang* (Chicago: Herbert S. Stone, 1899), 75–76, 82.

81. Clipping of William Dean Howells, "Editor's Easy Chair," *Harper's Monthly Magazine* 134 (n.d.), Edith Wyatt Papers, NL.

82. McCutcheon, *Drawn From Memory,* 87.

83. George Ade to John T. McCutcheon, Dec. 9, 1912, John T. McCutcheon Papers, NL.

84. McCutcheon's trip came at the invitation of his friend Frank H. Vanderlip, the assistant secretary of the Treasury. Kelly notes that Ade was also invited but that he declined because of the extensive sea travel involved. Kelly, *George Ade,* 131, 150–52, 181–86; McCutcheon, *Drawn From Memory,* 190–91.

85. McCutcheon, *Drawn From Memory,* 185; "Bird Center Argosy," undated typescript, John T. McCutcheon Papers, NL. For a discussion of the Bird Center cartoons and the play based on it, see Louis Braury, "Some Aspects of Bird Centre," *Bookman* 35 (August 1912): 645–56.

86.Brand Whitlock to John T. McCutcheon, Aug. 6, 1903, John T. McCutcheon Papers, NL. Whitlock notes his daily reading of the *Tribune* in another letter of appreciation he sent to McCutcheon on July 8, 1903 (also in the John McCutcheon Papers cited above).

87.On this tension between realism and abstraction, see Scott McCloud, *Understanding Comics* (Northampton, MA: Kitchen Sink Press, 1993), 36–41.

88.Allen Barlit Pond to "Dear Little Roomer," Dec. 17, 1903, Little Room Papers, NL.

89.Indiana Society of Chicago, *29th Annual Dinner of the Indiana Society of Chicago, Looking Back on 70 Years* (Chicago: Indiana Society of Chicago, 1940); the *Indiana Society of Chicago 56th Dinner Honoring Indiana National Bank, Saturday, December 5, 1970. Conrad Hilton Hotel* (n.p., n.d.), IS, UIC. A complete description of the twelve volumes, which were distributed as souvenirs at the society's seventh annual dinner in 1911, may be found in Indiana Society of Chicago, *Seventh Annual Dinner of the Indiana Society of Chicago* (Chicago: Indiana Society of Chicago, 1911), 3. *Who's Hoosier* (Indianapolis: Bobbs-Merrill, 1911) appeared in two volumes, and was compiled by the society's historian, Wilbur D. Nesbit. For samples of sheet music, see Indiana Society of Chicago, Sam DeVincent Collection, National Museum of American History, Smithsonian Institution.

90.Indiana Society of Chicago, *An Account of the Proceedings on the Occasion of the Second Annual Banquet of the Indiana Society of Chicago* (Chicago: Indiana Society of Chicago, 1906), 3; Indiana Society of Chicago, *An Account of the Proceedings on the Occasion of the First Annual Banquet of the Indiana Society of Chicago* (Chicago: Indiana Society of Chicago, 1905–6).

91. Indiana Society of Chicago, *An Account of the Proceedings on the Occasion of the First Annual Banquet,* 17, 21. The emphasis is mine.

92.Indiana Society of Chicago, *An Account of the Proceedings on the Occasion of the First Annual Banquet,* 10.

93.Hewitt Hanson Howland, editor of *Reader Magazine* in Indianapolis, explicitly defined the phrase: "you who have the fortune of birth and the misfortune of migration have become Hoosier-Suckers." Indiana Society of Chicago, *An Account of the Proceedings on the Occasion of the First Annual Banquet,* 25.

94.*A Dictionary of Americanisms,* ed. Mitford M. Mathews (Chicago: U. of Chicago Press, 1951), v.; *Oxford English Dictionary,* 1st ed., v.

95.McCutcheon, *Drawn From Memory,* 306–13.

Chapter 5

1. Ade sent this letter to the *Herald-Tribune* on September 8, 1926. George Ade, *The Best of George Ade,* ed. A. L. Lazarus (Bloomington: Indiana University Press, 1985), 241. For a discussion of the circumstances surrounding Dreiser's plagiarism, see Jack Salzman, "Dreiser and Ade: A Note on the Text of *Sister Carrie,*" *American Literature* 40 (January 1969): 544–48.

2. "Ade Symposium," *The Magazine of Sigma Chi,* no. 4 (October-November 1944): 241 in Sigma Chi, George Ade Collection, Special Collections, Purdue University Libraries, West Lafayette, Indiana.

3. Theodore Dreiser, *Newspaper Days* (Philadelphia: University of Pennsylvania Press, 1991), 43.

4. Ellen Moers, *Two Dreisers* (New York: Viking, 1969), 94-99; the phrase "cold-blooded analyst" is on 99. Moers writes insightfully of the sentimental attachment to home and mother in Paul Dresser's songs and notes Dreiser's similar use of these themes in *Sister Carrie.* Though Moers underscores the brothers' collaboration, she says little about their construction of an Indiana identity.

5. See Indiana Code 1-2-6-1 (accessed November 6, 2002): http://www.in.gov/legislative/ic/code/title1/ar2/ch6.html.

6. Daniel Aaron, "The Unholy City: A Sketch" in *American Letters and the Historical Consciousness: Essays in Honor of Lewis P. Simpson,* ed. J. Gerald Kennedy and Daniel Mark Fogel (Baton Rouge: LSU Press, 1987), 187-88; Thomas P. Riggio, "Carrie's Blues," in *New Essays on "Sister Carrie,"* ed. Donald Pizer (New York: Cambridge University Press, 1991), 23-41.

7. Theodore Dreiser, *Sister Carrie* (New York: Library of America, 1987), 3.

8. James C. Scott, *Domination and the Arts of Resistance: Hidden Transcripts* (New Haven, CT: Yale University Press, 1990).

9. Philip Fisher, *Hard Facts: Setting and Form in the American Novel* (New York: Oxford University Press, 1985), 154-55, 158-59.

10. Dreiser, *Sister Carrie,* 455.

11. According to Robert Crunden, Whitcock "read and admired *Sister Carrie.*" Robert A. Crunden, *A Hero in Spite of Himself: Brand Whitlock in Art, Politics, & War* (New York: Knopf, 1969), 441. Note that when the second edition of *Sister Carrie* was published in 1907, Whitlock and Garland both contributed blurbs to the back of the book. See Robert H. Elias, *Theodore Dreiser: Apostle of Nature* (Ithaca, NY: Cornell University Press, 1970), 137.

12. Willa Cather, *My Antonia* (Boston: Houghton Mifflin, 1988), 1.

13. Svetlana Boym, *The Future of Nostalgia* (New York: Basic Books, 2001), 354.

14. F. Scott Fitzgerald, *The Great Gatsby* (New York: Scribner's, 1925), 177.

15. Boym, *Future of Nostalgia,* 7-10; Raymond Williams, *The Country and the City* (New York: Oxford University Press, 1973), 12; Jean Starobinski, "The Idea of Nostalgia," *Diogenes* 54 (1966): 101-2.

16. Boym, *Future of Nostalgia,* xvi, 16, 13, quotation is on 10.

17. The phrase "provincial origin" comes from Starobinski, "The Idea of Nostalgia," 85.

18. On the erotic nature of nostalgia, see Boym, *Future of Nostalgia,* 13.

19. Williams, *Country and the City,* 12.

20. Christopher Lasch, *The True and Only Heaven: Progress and Its Critics* (New York: W. W. Norton, 1991), 84-85. For a discussion of historical studies that take nostalgia

seriously but hew to time-based definition, see Jackson Lears, "Looking Backward in Defense of Nostalgia," *Lingua Franca* (December-January 1998): 59-66.

21. T. J. Jackson Lears, *No Place of Grace: Antimodernism and the Transformation of American Culture 1880–1920* (New York: Pantheon, 1981); Michael Kammen, *Mystic Chords of Memory: The Transformation of Tradition in American Culture* (New York: Alfred Knopf, 1991), 294-96.

22. Boym, *Future of Nostalgia,* 354.

23. "How Dear To My Heart Are the Scenes of My Childhood," photograph in *The Inland Printer* 29 (July 1902): 564.

24. Bessie Louise Pierce, *A History of Chicago,* vol. 3, *The Rise of a Modern City, 1871–1893* (New York: Knopf, 1957), 22. See the handwritten constitution for the New England Society of Chicago in the Papers of the New England Society of Chicago, 1858-1859, housed at the Chicago Historical Society, Chicago (CHS); *Constitution of the Bay State Union, Chicago, May 18, 1857* (Chicago: William H. Rand Printer, 1857); Sons of Vermont, *Proceedings of the Illinois Association: Constitution, etc.* (Chicago: Beach, Barnard, and Co., 1877); and *Seventh, Eighth, Ninth, and Tenth Annual Reports of the Illinois Association of the Sons of Vermont* (Chicago: S. D. Childs & Co., 1886). According to the letterhead on a note sent to the *Tribune* columnist, Herma Clark, the Ohio Society of Chicago was founded on May 4, 1912. Letter from Lonsdale Green to Herma Clark, May 11, 1936, Herma Naomi Clark Papers, CHS.

25. The purpose of the society lay in "perpetuating the memories of the past, connected with the history of Chicago,—for social reunion, and other purposes." Anyone who arrived in Chicago before 1836 was eligible for membership, and it was "obligatory upon the members of this Society to attend the funeral of a deceased member." *Record Book of the Original Old Settlers Society Founded October 22, 1855,* Old Settlers Society of Chicago Papers, CHS.

26. Pierce, *A History of Chicago,* 3:23-47.

27. Mary Ann Hubbard, *Family Memories* (Chicago: privately printed, 1912), 92-93.

28. Caroline Kirkland, ed., *Chicago Yesterdays, A Sheaf of Reminiscences* (Chicago: Daughady and Co., 1919).

29. On images of progress in county histories, see Richard White, "Frederick Jackson Turner and Buffalo Bill," in *The Frontier in American Culture: An Exhibition at the Newberry Library, August 26, 1994 – January 7, 1995* (Berkeley and Los Angeles: University of California Press, 1994), 21-26. White links these images to similar representations of progress in Chicago histories.

30. Herma Clark, "Be a Local Historian" and "Little Home Towns of Illinois," Herma Clark Papers, CHS.

31. Arnold Lewis, *An Early Encounter with Tomorrow: Europeans, Chicago's Loop, and the World's Columbian Exposition* (Urbana: University of Illinois Press, 1997), 46-48, 58-66, 80-87.

32. *Biographical Sketches of the Leading Men of Chicago* (Chicago: Wilson & Clair, 1868), v, ix.

33. On Howells's suppression of desire, see Walter Benn Michaels, *The Gold Standard and the Logic of Naturalism: American Literature at the Turn-of-the-Century* (Berkeley and Los Angeles: University of California Press, 1987), 29–58.

34. William Dean Howells, *A Boy's Town* (New York: Harper's, 1890), 246.

35. Clipping of William Dean Howells, "Editor's Easy Chair," *Harper's Monthly Magazine*, no date, in Edith Wyatt Papers, Newberry Library, Chicago (NL). Note that Howells also wrote Ade a personal note in 1916, complimenting him on "Effie Whittlesly," which he called "the truest and humanest study of life I know." William Dean Howells to George Ade, Oct. 24, 1916, George Ade Papers, NL.

36. William Dean Howells, "Certain of the Chicago School of Fiction," *North American Review* 176 (May 1903): 734, 738.

37. Hamlin Garland, "Literary Emancipation of the West," *The Forum* 16 (October 1893): 159.

38. Will Payne, *Jerry the Dreamer* (New York: Harper, 1896), 16, 18, 13, 206.

39. Richard Lehan, *The City in Literature: An Intellectual and Cultural History* (Berkeley and Los Angeles: University of California Press, 1998), 89; Payne, *Jerry the Dreamer*, 65.

40. Payne, *Jerry the Dreamer*, 27, 48, 289.

41. Payne, *The Story of Eva* (Boston: Houghton Mifflin, 1901), 26. A description of longing is on 106–7.

42. "George Ade's First Job," *Chicago Tribune*, Oct. 3, 1931, George Ade Papers, NL.

43. George Barr McCutcheon, *The Sherrods* (New York: Dodd, Mead, 1903), 156.

44. Amy Kaplan, "Romancing the Empire: The Embodiment of American Masculinity in the Popular Historical Novel of the 1890s," *American Literary History* 2 (Winter 1990): 661 and passim.

45. Brand Whitlock, *The Happy Average* (Indianapolis: Bobbs-Merrill, 1904), 124, 126, 346.

46. Note, too, that Whitlock's physical description of Weston echoes McCutcheon's description of Ade: "He was tall, and his smooth-shaven face was refined and thoughtful; I call him good-looking; his eyes were dark and his nose straight and full of character; his lips were thin and level; his hair was not quite black and stopped just on the right side of being curly." Whitlock, *The Happy Average*, 290–91.

47. William Dean Howells, quoted in Crunden, *A Hero in Spite of Himself*, 120.

48. Brand Whitlock, *Forty Years of It* (New York: D. Appleton, 1914), 23.

49. Brand Whitlock, *The Letters and Journal of Brand Whitlock*, comp. and ed. Allan Nevins, and introduction by Newton D. Baker (New York: D. Appleton, 1936), 1:143 (quotation), 1:85 (regarding Ade).

50. Floyd Dell, "Chicago in Fiction: In Two Parts—Part II," *Bookman* 38 (December 1913): 375.

51. Dreiser, *Sister Carrie,* 267.

52. Riggio, "Carrie's Blues," especially 30–34; 38. Riggio notes Carrie's "dread" (31) of returning home, but also stresses her ongoing, psychic connection to home.

53. As Susan Stewart notes, the "nostalgic's utopia is prelapsarian"; his or her longing is "for absolute presence in the face of a gap between the signifier and the signified." Susan Stewart, *On Longing: Narratives of the Miniature, the Gigantic, the Souvenir, the Collection* (Durham, NC: Duke University Press, 1993), 23, 24.

54. Dreiser, *Sister Carrie,* 3.

55. Carl Sandburg, *Chicago Poems* (1916; New York: Dover, 1994), 15.

Chapter 6

1. Jane Addams, *Twenty Years at Hull-House* (New York: Signet, 1961), 29.

2. Lucia and Morton White, *The Intellectual Versus the City* (New York: Signet, 1961), 150–158, "spirit" on 151; Daniel Levine, *Jane Addams and the Liberal Tradition* (Madison: State Historical Society of Wisconsin, 1971), "unnatural" on 59; Robert M. Crunden, *Ministers of Reform: The Progressives' Achievement in American Civilization 1889–1920* (New York: Basic Books, 1982), 65–66. See also Jean B. Quandt, *From the Small Town to the Great Community: The Social Thought of Progressive Intellectuals* (New Brunswick, NJ: Rutgers University Press, 1970).

3. Jane Addams, "The Difference Between City Boys and Country Boys," *Dallas Daily Times Herald,* Dec. 29, 1907, Magazine Section 4 in Swarthmore College Peace Collection, Jane Addams Papers, Series 11, Swarthmore College, Philadelphia (SCPC).

4. Jane Addams, "A Function of the Social Settlement," *Annals of the American Academy of Political and Social Science,* no. 251 (May 16, 1899): 55.

5. William James, quoted in Jane Addams, "*from* A Function of the Social Settlement," in *Pragmatism: A Reader,* ed. Louis Menand (New York: Vintage, 1997), 274.

6. Charlene Haddock Siegfried, introduction to Jane Addams, *Democracy and Social Ethics* (Urbana: University of Illinois Press, 2002), xi (quotation). Note, too, that I have borrowed my characterization of multiple identities and coalition building from Siegfried, who stresses (also on p. xi) that Addams "developed a uniquely pragmatist version of feminism that recognized that women could affirm a special angle of vision, interests, and values without either falling prey to a false essentialism or closing themselves off from a multiplicity of identities and coalitions."

7. Victoria Brown, "Advocate for Democracy: Jane Addams and the Pullman Strike," in *The Pullman Strike and the Crisis of the 1890s: Essays on Labor and Politics,* ed. Richard Schneirov, Shelton Stromquist, and Nick Salvatore (Urbana: University of Illinois Press, 1999), 130.

8. Victoria Brown, introduction to Jane Addams, *Twenty Years at Hull-House, with Autobiographical Notes,* ed. Victoria Bissell Brown (New York: Bedford/St. Martin's,

1991), 4; Allen F. Davis, *American Heroine: The Life and Legend of Jane Addams* (New York: Oxford University Press, 1973), 4–5.

9. Louis Menand, *The Metaphysical Club: A Story of Ideas in America* (New York: Farrar Straus Giroux, 2001). On pragmatism's wide-ranging impact, from a contemporary and historical perspective, see Morris Dickstein, ed., *The Revival of Pragmatism: New Essays on Social Thought, Law and Culture* (Durham: Duke University Press, 1998).

10. Louis Menand, "An Introduction to Pragmatism," in Menand, *Pragmatism*, xxxiv.

11. Victoria Brown, "The Sermon of the Deed: Jane Addams' Religious Consciousness," plenary lecture given at the Twenty-ninth Annual Richard R. Baker Philosophy Colloquium, University of Dayton, Dayton, Ohio, Nov. 9, 2002.

12. Jane Addams to Ellen Gates Starr, Aug. 11, 1879, Ellen Gates Starr Papers, Sophia Smith Collection, Smith College.

13. Davis, *American Heroine*, 31; James Weber Linn, *Jane Addams: A Biography* (New York: D. Appleton-Century, 1935), 84; "The Snare of Preparation" is the title of chapter 4 in Addams's *Twenty Years at Hull-House*.

14. Victoria Brown, *The Education of Jane Addams* (Philadelphia: University of Pennsylvania Press, 2004), 148–49, 169–72.

15. Jane Addams to Alice Addams Haldeman, Jan. 10, 1887, Jane Addams Memorial Collection, Special Collections, University Library, University of Illinois at Chicago (JAMC).

16. Jane Addams to Laura Shoemaker Addams, Dec. 1, 1886, SCPC.

17. Jane Addams to Laura Shoemaker Addams, July 23, 1887, SCPC.

18. Addams, *Twenty Years at Hull-House*, 62.

19. In his biography of Addams, Allen Davis emphasizes her desire to break away from the past and all traditional gender roles. Given the competing pull of Cedarville and Addams's creative use of provincial values in later years, this conclusion seems to me overstated. See Davis, *American Heroine*, 61. On Addams's experiences with charitable institutions in Baltimore, see John C. Farrell, *Beloved Lady: A History of Jane Addams' Ideas on Reform and Peace* (Baltimore: Johns Hopkins University Press, 1965), 41–42. Farrell concludes that Addams "did not find any clear idea of duty" while she was in Baltimore (42).

20. Addams, *Twenty Years at Hull-House*, xviii.

21. Jane Addams, *The Long Road of Woman's Memory* (Urbana: University of Illinois Press, 2002), 68.

22. Addams, *Twenty Years at Hull-House*, 28–29.

23. Consider, for instance, Dreiser's account of Carrie staring through the plate-glass windows in Chicago's commercial districts, and of the implied class differences. Addams's imagined newcomer is on the inside, looking out the window of her hotel, while Carrie is stuck outside.

24. Addams, *Twenty Years at Hull-House*, 22.

25. Lois Rudnick, "A Feminist American Success Myth: Jane Addams's *Twenty Years at Hull-House*," in *Tradition and the Talents of Women*, ed. Florence Howe (Urbana: University of Illinois Press, 1991), 148–49. Addams's quotations may found in Addams, *Twenty Years at Hull-House*, 41, 87.

26. For instance, see Brown, introduction, to Addams, *Twenty Years at Hull-House*, ed. Brown, 11.

27. Addams, *Twenty Years at Hull-House*, 41.

28. Brown, introduction to Addams, *Twenty Years at Hull-House*, ed. Brown, 6; Farrell, *Beloved Lady*, 37–38; Davis, *American Heroine*, 12. I should caution that none of these studies explicitly conclude that Addams did not read Carlyle until she got to Rockford Seminary; however, the evidence suggests that she did not seriously contend with his ideas until then.

29. Farrell notes that Addams rejected Carlyle's notion of "aristocratic, elite leadership" in the 1890s in *Beloved Lady*, 52; Davis, on the other hand, finds that in 1879, Addams was still very much interested in Carlyle's advice (Davis, *American Heroine*, 16–17).

30. Jane Addams, "A Village Decoration Day," *Rockford Seminary Magazine* 11 (March 1883): 75. Rockford College Archives, Rockford, Illinois.

31. Addams, *Twenty Years at Hull-House*, 55.

32. Richard Rorty, *Achieving Our Country* (Cambridge, MA: Harvard University Press, 1998).

33. Addams, *Twenty Years at Hull-House*, 42, 43.

34. While Addams is on the 1903 membership list for the Little Room, she was not included in the cast for the play. See the Little Room membership list, dated Dec. 15, 1903, and the program for *Captain Fry's Birthday Party* in the Little Room Papers, Newberry Library, Chicago.

35. "Facts About The Joseph T. Bowen Country Club from Mrs. Joseph T. Bowen Replying to Questions of the Wieboldt Foundation," Hull-House Association Papers, JAMC; Linn, *Jane Addams*, 126–128.

36. Peter J. Schmitt, *Back to Nature: The Arcadian Myth* (New York: Oxford University Press, 1969), 78–80. Addams's support of the playground movement was in line with G. Stanley Hall's advocacy of playgrounds. Schmitt also notes that while in 1899 thirteen cities had public playgrounds, by 1917 over five hundred cities had established them.

37. Jane Addams, *The Second Twenty Years at Hull-House* (New York: Macmillan, 1930), 349–50.

38. Jane Addams, *The Spirit of Youth and the City Streets* (New York: Macmillan, 1909), 4; Addams notes the fate of country girls in *A New Conscience and an Ancient Evil* (Urbana: University of Illinois Press, 2002), 66–68.

39. Jane Addams, "The Play Instinct and the Arts," *Religious Education* 25 (November 1930): 813.

40. Addams, *A New Conscience,* 48.

41. Addams, *The Spirit of Youth,* 15.

42. G. Stanley Hall, *Adolescence: Its Psychology and Its Relation to Physiology, Anthropology, Sociology, Sex, Crime, Religion, and Education* (New York: D. Appleton, 1904), 1:203; Addams, *The Spirit of Youth,* 46, 45.

43. Thorstein Veblen, quoted in Davis, *American Heroine,* 156.

44. The book also lacks the vision of democratic mutualism that makes *Twenty Years at Hull-House* so revolutionary.

45. "Facts About The Joseph T. Bowen Country Club."

46. Ibid.

47. Hull-House Association, 1954-55 brochure, "Why Two Weeks at Summer Camp Mean More Than Just a Change of Scene for Halsted Street Boys and Girls," Hull-House Departments and Programs, Bowen Country Club (Waukegan, Illinois), Brochures c. 1935-1962, Hull-House Association Papers, JAMC.

48. Addams, "The Play Instinct and the Arts," 813.

49. Schmitt, *Back to Nature,* 96-105.

50. "Joseph T. Bowen Country Club," *Hull-House Yearbook* (Jan. 1, 1916): 55, JAMC.

51. Addams, "The Play Instinct and the Arts," 810.

52. Addams, *The Second Twenty Years at Hull-House,* 351.

53. "Joseph T. Bowen Country Club," *Hull-House Yearbook* (Jan. 1, 1913): 15, 44-45; "Joseph T. Bowen Country Club," *Hull-House Yearbook* (Jan. 1, 1916): 55; "Facts About the Joseph T. Bowen Country Club."

54. Addams, *The Second Twenty Years at Hull-House,* 351-52, quotation 353; "Facts About the Joseph T. Bowen Country Club."

Chapter 7

1. Guy Szuberla, "Henry Blake Fuller and the 'New Immigrant,'" *American Literature* 53 (May 1981): 246-65; see also Szuberla's "Babel, The Crowd, and 'The People' in Early Chicago Fiction," in *Exploring the Midwestern Literary Imagination: Essays in Honor of David D. Anderson,* ed. Marcia Noe (Troy, NY: Whitston, 1993), 151-66, especially 156.

2. There are, of course, exceptions to this generalization. For instance, Finley Peter Dunne's "Mr. Dooley" newspaper columns appeared in Irish dialect throughout the 1890s. In her study of Chicago literature, Carla Cappetti argues that the University of Chicago sociologists were "ahead" of literary critics and, she implies, writers, in conceptualizing the lives of ethnic Chicagoans. And, as she shows, ethnic writers like James Farrell and Nelson Algren depended on their theoretical insights in developing their fictional visions. See Carla Cappetti, *Writing Chicago: Modernism, Ethnography, and the Novel* (New York: Columbia University Press, 1993), 31 and passim.

3. Werner Sollors, *Beyond Ethnicity: Consent and Descent in American Literature* (New York: Oxford University Press, 1986), 30–31, 242–43.

4. Ray Stannard Baker, *American Chronicle: The Autobiography of Ray Stannard Baker* (New York: Charles Scribner's Sons, 1945), 56.

5. Ray Stannard Baker, *Native American: The Book of My Youth* (New York: Charles Scribner's Sons, 1941), 265, 272, 288.

6. *The Rights of Labor,* Jan. 24, 1891.

7. *Chicago News Record,* Nov. 30, 1892.

8. *Chicago News Record,* Nov. 30, 1892; Nov. 4, 1893; Dec. 16, 1893.

9. Baker, *Native American,* 328 ("you see"), 329 ("test"), 330.

10. Ibid.

11. Robert C. Bannister, *Ray Stannard Baker; The Mind and Thought of a Progressive* (New Haven, CT: Yale University Press, 1966), 47–49, 55, 92, 189, 232 ("apparent disloyalty").

12. Richard Hoftstadter, *The Age of Reform: From Bryan to F. D. R.* (New York: Knopf, 1956), 173–212.

13. Bessie Louise Pierce, *A History of Chicago,* vol. 3, *The Rise of a Modern City* (New York: Knopf, 1957), 22, 32–33, 516; Donald L. Miller, *City of the Century: The Epic of Chicago and the Making of America* (New York: Simon and Schuster, 1996), 468, 441.

14. Carl Smith, *Urban Disorder and the Shape of Belief: The Great Chicago Fire, the Haymarket Bomb, and the Model Town of Pullman* (Chicago: University of Chicago Press, 1995), 209 and passim.

15. Jon Gjerde, *The Minds of the West: The Ethnocultural Evolution in the Rural Middle West* (Chapel Hill: University of North Carolina Press, 1997), 251–81; Pierce, *A History of Chicago,* 3:24.

16. Orm Overland, *Immigrant Minds, American Identities: Making the United States Home, 1870–1930* (Urbana: University of Illinois Press, 2000), 27, 49.

17. The phrase "complementary identity" comes from Gjerde, *Minds of the West,* 8; Overland discusses nostalgia on 26–27 of *Immigrant Minds, American Identities.*

18. David Ward Wood, ed., *Chicago and Its Distinguished Citizens, or the Progress of Forty Years* (Chicago: Milton George and Co., 1881). Immigrants, especially Germans, are also included in *Album of Genealogy and Biography: Cook County, Illinois,* rev. ed. (Chicago: Calumet Book and Engraving Co., 1897). On German captains of industry, see Pierce, *A History of Chicago,* 3:22.

19. Chicagoans of foreign parentage were particularly well represented in journalism, publishing, music, and the hotel and leisure industries. James Gilbert, *Perfect Cities: Chicago's Utopias of 1893* (Chicago: University of Chicago Press, 1991), 10.

20. Theodore Dreiser, *Sister Carrie* (New York: Library of America, 1987), 4.

21. Dreiser, *Sister Carrie,* 8.

22. On Wyatt's life, see Babette Inglehart, introduction to Edith Wyatt, *True Love: A Comedy of the Affections* (1903; Urbana: University of Illinois Press, 1993), vii–xlix.

For an overview of Peattie's life, see Sidney Bremer and Joan Stevenson Falcone's entry in *Women Building Chicago, 1790–1990: A Biographical Dictionary*, ed. Rima Lunin Schultz and Adele Hast (Bloomington: Indiana University Press, 2001), 678–80.

23. Wyatt, *True Love*, 3, 286, 92, 125.

24. Ibid., 286–87. Robert Bray notes the fluid relation between Centreville and Chicago in "Fiction to 1915," in *A Reader's Guide to Illinois Literature* (Springfield, IL: Illinois State Library, 1985), 31–32.

25. As Sydney Bremer and Babette Inglehart have noted, Wyatt's emphasis on family connections lends her portrayal of community an "organic" quality often missing from novels written by male Chicago writers. Sydney Bremer, *Urban Intersections: Meetings of Life and Literature in United States Cities* (Urbana: University of Illinois Press, 1992), 82–93; Babette Inglehart, introduction to Wyatt, *True Love*, vii–xlix. The term *organic* is used by Bremer (87).

26. William James, letter to "My Dear Pauline," Nov. 8, 1901, Edith Wyatt Papers, Newberry Library, Chicago (NL).

27. William James, "The Social Value of the College-Bred," address given at a Meeting of the Association of American Alumnae at Radcliffe College, Cambridge, Massachusetts, Nov. 7, 1907, http://www.emory.edu/EDUCATION/mfp/jaCollegeBred.html (accessed July 17, 2004).

28. Edith Wyatt, "The Poor Old Past," paper given to the Friday Club, ca. 1935, Scrapbook, Edith Wyatt Papers, NL. The *New Yorker*'s first issue appeared in 1924.

29. Edith Wyatt, *Every One His Own Way* (New York: McClure's, 1901), 9.

30. Bremer and Falcone, entry, *Women Building Chicago, 1790–1990*, 680; Sidney H. Bremer, introduction, to Elia W. Peattie, *The Precipice* (Urbana: University of Illinois Press, 1989), ix–xiii, xii ("suffrage novel"). Peattie, *Precipice*, 106 ("great home").

31. Peattie, *Precipice*, 104–5.

32. Bremer also notes these implied criticisms in her introduction, to Peattie, *Precipice*, xiv.

33. Peattie, *Precipice*, 56, 105, 106.

34. Bremer, introduction to Peattie, *Precipice*, xii.

35. Philip R. Yanella, *The Other Carl Sandburg* (Jackson: University of Mississippi Press, 1996); Mark Van Wienen, "Taming the Socialist: Carl Sandburg's *Chicago Poems* and Its Critics," *American Literature* 63 (March 1991): 89–103.

36. The term "myth-man" comes from Yanella, *The Other Carl Sandburg*, 57.

37. Carl Sandburg, *Chicago Poems* (1916; New York: Dover, 1994), 13.

38. Ibid., 65–66.

39. Ibid., 3, 13, 7 ("with a voice"), 58 ("a million green leaves").

40. As Yanella notes, Sandburg's 1918 collection, *Cornhuskers*—which appeared just two years after *Chicago Poems*—deals at greater length with pastoral imagery and is less concerned with radical politics. Yanella, *The Other Carl Sandburg*, 102–6.

41. Sandburg, *Chicago Poems*, 29.

42. Sandburg, *Chicago Poems*, 75.

Chapter 8

1. Floyd Dell to Arthur Davison Ficke, June 2, 1913, Floyd Dell Papers, Newberry Library, Chicago (NL).

2. Floyd Dell to Arthur Davison Ficke, June 5, 1913, Floyd Dell Papers, NL.

3. William Butler Yeats, "The Lake Isle of Innisfree," in *The Collected Poems of W. B. Yeats* (New York: Macmillan, 1956), 39. For how Yeats came to write the poem, see William Butler Yeats, "The Tremble of the Veil," in *The Autobiography of William Butler Yeats* (1922; New York: Macmillan, 1953), 94.

4. Floyd Dell to Arthur Davison Ficke, May 26, 1913, Floyd Dell Papers, NL.

5. Arthur Davison Ficke to Floyd Dell, June 3, 1913, Floyd Dell Papers, NL.

6. For instance, see Bernard Duffey, *The Chicago Renaissance in American Letters: A Critical History* (Lansing: Michigan State College Press, 1954), 136–37; Douglas Clayton, *Floyd Dell: The Life and Times of an American Rebel* (Chicago: Ivan R. Dee, 1994), 88–89. Christine Stansell, *American Moderns: Bohemian New York and the Creation of a New Century* (New York: Henry Holt, 2000), 16.

7. Dale Kramer notes that in Greenwich Village, Dell became "a kind of symbol of the revolution in love and literature" in *Chicago Renaissance: The Literary Life in the Midwest, 1900–1930* (New York: Appleton-Century, 1966), 240.

8. Samuel Putnam, "Chicago: An Obituary," *American Mercury* 8 (August 1926): 417; Neil Harris, "The Chicago Setting," in *The Old Guard and the Avant-Garde: Modernism in Chicago, 1910–1940,* ed. Susan Ann Prince (Chicago: University of Chicago Press, 1990), 9 ("way station"), 14–17.

9. Putnam, "Chicago: An Obituary," 417.

10. Duffey, *The Chicago Renaissance in American Letters,* 258–59.

11. Margaret Anderson, *My Thirty Years' War* (New York: Horizon, 1969), 38. On style, see Dick Hebdige, *Subculture, the Meaning of Style* (London: Routledge, 1979). Van Doren's characterization appeared in several pieces he wrote for the *Nation* in 1921. See Carl Van Doren, *Three Worlds* (New York: Harper's, 1936).

12. Raymond Williams, *The Politics of Modernism: Against the New Conformists* (London: Verso, 1989), 35, 34, 35.

13. Ibid., 31–33, 43–47, 34 ("new imperialism").

14. For instance, Carl Smith locates the peak of Chicago's "eminence" in the mid-1890s. Carl Smith, *Urban Disorder and the Shape of Belief: The Great Chicago Fire, The Haymarket Bomb, and the Model Town of Pullman* (Chicago: University of Chicago Press, 1995), 278.

15. Vachel Lindsay, *The Letters of Vachel Lindsay*, ed. Marc Chene'tier (New York: B. Franklin, 1978), 32.

16. Susan Ann Prince notes that "early Chicago modernism," meaning the visual arts, "was defined by an attitude rather than by a style." See her introduction to Prince, *The Old Guard*, xxii.

17. Floyd Dell, *Homecoming: An Autobiography* (1933; Port Washington, NY: Kennikat Press, 1969), 148.

18. Andrew R. L. Cayton and Susan E. Gray, "The Story of the Midwest: An Introduction," in *The American Midwest: Essays on Regional History*, eds. Andrew R. L. Cayton and Susan E. Gray (Bloomington: Indiana University Press, 2001), 3.

19. Dell, *Homecoming*, 15–16.

20. Clayton, *Floyd Dell*, 21; Dell, *Homecoming*, 92–93, 120.

21. Dell, *Homecoming*, 119. Dell's initial discussion of Freeman is on 90–91.

22. On Dell's exchange with Hansen, see Clayton, *Floyd Dell*, 21; See Dell's self-portrait in *Homecoming*, 102–3.

23. Dell, *Homecoming*, 37. The cultural and political diversity of Davenport is documented in Harry E. Downer, *History of Davenport and Scott County, Iowa*, vol. 1 (Chicago: S. J. Clarke, 1910).

24. Clayton, *Floyd Dell*, 37–38.

25. Ibid., 36.

26. Dell, *Homecoming*, 169–81; Clayton, *Floyd Dell*, 41.

27. Floyd Dell to Ralph Cram, Jan. 14, 1924, Ralph Cram Papers, NL; Floyd Dell to Dale Kramer, March 24, 1963, Dale Kramer Papers, NL. Dell also thought of Chicago as a "romantic" city.

28. Floyd Dell, "Chicago in Fiction: In Two Parts—Part II," *Bookman* 38 (December 1913): 375.

29. Dell, *Homecoming*, 181, 184; Susan Glaspell to Floyd Dell, late January/early February 1909, Floyd Dell Papers, NL.

30. Anderson, *My Thirty Years' War*, 37.

31. On the adjoining rooms, see Dell, *Homecoming*, 232. Clayton refers to the couple's marital problems in *Floyd Dell*, 80, 86; the story of Dell's bohemian outfit is recounted in George Thomas Tanselle, "Faun at the Barricades: The Life and Work of Floyd Dell" (Ph.D. diss., Northwestern University, 1959), 126.

32. Claude S. Fischer, *To Dwell among Friends: Personal Networks in Town and City* (Chicago: University of Chicago Press, 1982), 65. For a discussion of how this view differs from other sociological theories of urbanism, see Claude S. Fischer, "Toward a Subcultural Theory of Urbanism," *American Journal of Sociology* 80 (May 1975): 1319–41. Here, Fischer also suggests that urban migration promotes the development of urban subcultures; see 1324–27.

33. Dell, *Homecoming*, 206; Jane Wynter Adams, "The Inkpot Revolution: The *Friday Literary Review*" (master's thesis, George Washington University, 1981).

34. Quoted in Tanselle, "Faun at the Barricades," 140. Regarding Dell's prospective move, Ficke wrote, "I should be thoroughly disgusted with you for your move to N. Y. if I were not convinced that it is the only sensible thing for you to do. But what an empty desert Chicago will be without you, its one glowing cactus plant!" Arthur Ficke to Floyd Dell, Sept. 8, 1913, Floyd Dell Papers, NL.

35. Kenny J. Williams, *A Storyteller and a City: Sherwood Anderson's Chicago* (DeKalb: Northern Illinois Press, 1988), 19.

36. Sherwood Anderson, "When I Left Business for Literature," *Century* 108 (August 1924): 489–96, 491 ("American Dream"); Harry Hansen, *Midwest Portraits: A Book of Memories and Friendships* (New York: Harcourt Brace, 1923), 130; Kim Townsend, *Sherwood Anderson* (Boston: Houghton Mifflin, 1987), 81, 82.

37. Townsend notes that "[n]o one had been more important to him than Dell" in *Sherwood Anderson*, 92.

38. Sherwood Anderson, *Sherwood Anderson's Memoirs: A Critical Edition*, ed. Ray Lewis White (Chapel Hill: University of North Carolina Press, 1942), 334; Townsend, *Sherwood Anderson*, 88.

39. Sherwood Anderson, *Sherwood Anderson's Memoirs*, 335.

40. Ibid., 338–39, 344, 336 ("literary father"); Townsend, *Sherwood Anderson*, 93.

41. Irving Howe, *Sherwood Anderson* (Stanford, CA: Stanford University Press, 1951), 56–62, 56 ("needed"), 63 ("stimulated and released").

42. Townsend, *Sherwood Anderson*, 91; Floyd Dell, "On Being Sherwood Anderson's Literary Father," *Newberry Library Bulletin* 5 (December 1961): 319–20.

43. Anderson, *My Thirty Years' War*, 38; Hansen, *Midwest Portraits*, 111–14.

44. Both letters included in the *Selected Letters of Sherwood Anderson*, comp., ed., and with intro. and notes by Howard Mumford Jones and Walter B. Rideout (Boston: Little, Brown and Co., 1953), 33, 77. On Anderson's disappointment in not being connected to Twain (and Whitman) as one of several great American writers, see William Sutton, *The Road to Winesburg: A Mosaic of the Imaginative Life of Sherwood Anderson* (Metuchen, NJ: Scarecrow Press, 1972), 302–03.

45. Townsend, *Sherwood Anderson*, 65.

46. Anderson, *Sherwood Anderson's Memoirs*, 317, 344, 347, 348.

47. For biographical information on Tennessee Mitchell Anderson, see Charles E. Modlin's entry in *Women Building Chicago, 1790–1990: A Biographical Dictionary*, ed. Rima Lunin Schultz and Adele Hast (Bloomington: Indiana University Press, 2001), 42–44.

48. Tennessee Mitchell Anderson, "Memoirs," unfinished manuscript, Sherwood Anderson Papers, NL.

49. Herbert K. Russell, *Edgar Lee Masters: A Biography* (Urbana: University of Illinois Press, 2001), 51–52.

50. Anderson, *My Thirty Years' War*, 131, 26; on Anderson's sexual persona in the pages of the *Little Review*, see Jayne E. Marek, *Women Editing Modernism: "Little"*

Magazines & Literary History (Lexington: University Press of Kentucky, 1995), 63–69.

Chapter 9

1. Sherwood Anderson, *Selected Letters of Sherwood Anderson,* comp., ed., and with intro. and notes by Howard Mumford Jones and Walter B. Rideout (Boston: Little, Brown and Co., 1953), 48.
2. Sherwood Anderson, *Winesburg, Ohio* (New York: Penguin, 1992), 247.
3. Willa Cather, *The Song of the Lark* (New York: Penguin, 1999), 71, 122.
4. Maurice Beebe, "What Modernism Was," *Journal of Modern Literature* 3 (July 1974): 1076.
5. Cather, *Song,* 43.
6. Ibid., 38, 68.
7. Joseph R. Urgo, *Willa Cather and the Myth of American Migration* (Urbana: University of Illinois Press, 1995), 5 (quotation), 130–43.
8. Cather, *Song,* 393, 307, 381.
9. Quoted in Sherill Harbison's notes to Cather, *Song,* 421.
10. Cather, *Song,* 165, 170, 171.
11. Ibid., 171–72.
12. For instance, see Hermione Lee, *Willa Cather: Double Lives* (New York: Pantheon, 1989), 124–29; Sharon O'Brien, *Willa Cather: The Emerging Voice* (New York: Oxford University Press, 1987), 170–73, 410–14.
13. Cather, *Song,* 159, 160, 269; Judith Fryer, *Felicitous Space: The Imaginative Structures of Edith Wharton and Willa Cather* (Chapel Hill: University of North Carolina Press, 1986), 293.
14. Cather, "Three American Singers," *McClure's Magazine* 42 (December 13, 1913): 44, 48, 40.
15. Anderson, *Winesburg,* 24.
16. Jean Toomer to Sherwood Anderson, Dec. 18, 1922, Sherwood Anderson Papers, Newberry Library, Chicago (NL). In a 1922 letter to Waldo Frank, Toomer explains that "CANE'S design is a circle. Aesthetically, from simple forms to complex ones, and back to simple forms. Regionally, from the South up into the North, and back into the South again. Or, From the North down into South, and then a return North." Jean Toomer to Waldo Frank, Dec. 22, 1922, included in Jean Toomer, *Cane,* ed. Darwin T. Turner (New York: W. W. Norton, 1988), 152.
17. Sherwood Anderson, "The Man of Affairs," *Agricultural Advertising* 1 (March 1904): 36, 37, 38.
18. Sherwood Anderson, *Windy McPherson's Son* (1916; Urbana: University of Illinois Press, 1993), 74, 76, 68, 22.
19. Ibid., 247, 315.

20. Anderson, *Winesburg*, 30.

21. Ibid., 119, 87, 104, 70.

22. Floyd Dell, "How Sherwood Anderson Became an Author," *New York Herald Tribune Books*, April 12, 1942; Robert Morss Lovett, "Sherwood Anderson," *New Republic* 89 (November 25, 1936): 103.

23. Dell expressed his admiration for *Windy McPherson's Son* in a letter to Stanley Pargellis, April 14, 1948, Sherwood Anderson Papers, NL. Pargellis was the curator of the Anderson papers at the Newberry. On Anderson's "revolt," see Dell, "How Sherwood Anderson Became an Author."

24. Floyd Dell, *Moon-Calf* (New York: Sagamore, 1957), 21, 95.

25. Floyd Dell, "The Portrait of Murray Swift," Floyd Dell Papers, NL.

26. Quoted in Douglas Clayton, *Floyd Dell: The Life and Times of an American Rebel* (Chicago: Ivan R. Dee, 1994), 130.

27. Dell, *Moon-Calf*, 346.

Coda

1. Edgar Lee Masters to Agnes Lee Freer, 1925, Masters-Freer Papers, Newberry Library, Chicago.

2. Carla Cappetti, *Writing Chicago: Modernism, Ethnography, and the Novel* (New York: Columbia University Press, 1993), 60–64.

3. These numbers include masters and doctoral dissertations. Robert E. L. Faris, *Chicago Sociology, 1920–1932* (Chicago: University of Chicago Press, 1967), 135–50.

4. Charles E. Lively to Bruce L. Melvin, March 12, 1925, Rural Sociology Society of America Papers, 1910–1972, Western Historical Manuscripts Collection, University of Missouri–Columbia.

5. Charles R. Hoffer, "The Development of Rural Sociology," *Rural Sociology* 26 (March 1961): 1–2.

6. John M. Gillette, "The Drift to City in Relation to the Rural Problem," *American Journal of Sociology* 16 (March 1911): 664.

7. Charles J. Galpin, U.S. Dept. of Agriculture, "Re-Planning the City as a Place Not to Live In," address given at the Agricultural College of Utah, Logan, June 20, 1923, Rural Sociology Society of America Papers, 1910–1972, Western Historical Manuscripts Collection, University of Missouri–Columbia.

8. C. Wright Mills, "The Professional Ideology of Social Pathologists," in *Power, Politics and People: The Collected Essays of C. Wright Mills*, ed. Irving Louis Horowitz (New York: Oxford University Press, 1967), 528; Fred H. Matthews, *Quest of an American Sociology: Robert E. Park and the Chicago School* (Montreal: McGill-Queen's University Press, 1977) 122–23; Henry Wu, *Thinking Orientals: Migration, Contact, and Exoticism in Modern America* (New York: Oxford University Press, 2001), 32–34; quotation is on 33.

9. Robert E. Park, "The City: Suggestions for the Investigation of Human Behavior in the City Environment," *The American Journal of Sociology* 20 (March 1915): 607, 609, 608.

10. Robert E. Park, "Human Migration and the Marginal Man," *American Journal of Sociology* 32 (May 1928): 887, 888, 892.

11. The characterization of Park as "representative citizen" comes from Matthews, *Quest of an American Sociology,* 2; Robert E. Park, "Notes on Human Migration," unfinished manuscript, no date, Robert E. Park Papers, University of Chicago.

12. Richard Wright, *Black Boy: A Record of Childhood and Youth* (New York: Harper and Row, 1966), 282.

13. On Chicago and the Great Migration, see James R. Grossman, *Land of Hope: Chicago, Black Southerners, and the Great Migration* (Chicago: University of Chicago Press, 1989); Nicholas Lemann, *The Promised Land: The Great Black Migration and How It Changed America* (New York: Vintage, 1992).

14. Fellowship application to John Simon Guggenheim Memorial Foundation, Richard Wright Papers, Bienecke Library, Yale University.

15. Richard Wright, "How Bigger Was Born," in Wright, *Early Works: Lawd Today!, Uncle Tom's Cabin, Native Son,* ed. Arnold Rampersad (New York: Library of America, 1991), 860, 866.

16. Ibid., 860.

17. Wright, *Early Works,* 472.

18. Ibid., 820.

19. Richard Wright, *12 Million Black Voices* (New York: Thunders' Mouth Press, 1988), 128, 109, 136, 86; Richard Wright, introduction to St. Clair Drake and Horace R. Cayton, *Black Metropolis: A Study of Negro Life in a Northern City* (Chicago: University of Chicago Press, 1993), xiii.

20. On migration narratives, see Farah Jasmine Griffin, *"Who Set You Flowin'?": The African-American Migration Novel* (New York: Oxford University Press, 1995).

21. Paul Gilroy, *The Black Atlantic: Modernity and Double Consciousness* (Cambridge, MA: Harvard University Press, 1993), 146-86, 150 ("homelessness").

22. Wright, *Black Boy,* 272.

23. On the setting for the film, see Arnold Rampersad's notes for Wright, *Native Son,* in *Early Works,* 923-24. On the African adventure film, see Kevin Dunn, "Lights . . . Camera . . . Africa: Images of Africa and Africans in Western Popular Films of the 1930s," *African Studies Review* 39 (April 1996): 149-97.

24. Wright, *Early Works,* 476.

25. Wright, *Early Works,* 473, 474, 477, 476.

26. Renato Rosaldo, "Imperialist Nostalgia," *Representations* 26 (Spring 1989): 107-22.

27. Wright, *Early Works,* 476.

28. On the literary representation of Chicago's postindustrial neighborhoods, see Carlo Rotella, *October Cities: The Redevelopment of Urban Literature* (Berkeley and Los Angeles: University of California Press, 1998), 40-115.

INDEX